T0387334

Unlimited Eligibility?

Inclusive Democracy and the American Lyric

RYAN CULL

Cover image: Detail of Quilt Top, crazy pattern, in the public domain, from The Metropolitan Museum of Art; gift of Tracey Blumenreich Zabar, 1989.

Published by State University of New York Press, Albany

© 2025 State University of New York

All rights reserved

Printed in the United States of America

No part of this book may be used or reproduced in any manner whatsoever without written permission. No part of this book may be stored in a retrieval system or transmitted in any form or by any means including electronic, electrostatic, magnetic tape, mechanical, photocopying, recording, or otherwise without the prior permission in writing of the publisher.

Links to third-party websites are provided as a convenience and for informational purposes only. They do not constitute an endorsement or an approval of any of the products, services, or opinions of the organization, companies, or individuals. SUNY Press bears no responsibility for the accuracy, legality, or content of a URL, the external website, or for that of subsequent websites.

EU GPSR Authorised Representative:
Logos Europe, 9 rue Nicolas Poussin, 17000, La Rochelle, France
contact@logoseurope.eu

For information, contact State University of New York Press, Albany, NY
www.sunypress.edu

Library of Congress Cataloging-in-Publication Data

Name: Cull, Ryan, author.
Title: Unlimited eligibility? : inclusive democracy and the American lyric / Ryan Cull.
Description: Albany : State University of New York Press, [2025]. | Series: SUNY series in multiethnic literatures | Includes bibliographical references and index.
Identifiers: LCCN 2024042787 | ISBN 9798855802245 (hardcover : alk. paper) | ISBN 9798855802252 (ebook)
Subjects: LCSH: American poetry—History and criticism. | Lyric poetry—History and criticism. | Politics and literature—United States. | LCGFT: Literary criticism.
Classification: LCC PS309.L8 C85 2025 | DDC 811.009/3581—dc23/eng/20250101
LC record available at https://lccn.loc.gov/2024042787

Contents

Acknowledgments		vii
Introduction	Recognizing American Lyrics	1
Chapter One	"We Fathom You Not—We Love You": Walt Whitman Resists the Emerging Politics of Recognition	31
Chapter Two	Jean Toomer's "The Blue Meridian" and the "Social Prison" of Cultural Pluralism	61
Chapter Three	Looking without Recognizing: Hart Crane's Lyric Sociality	93
Chapter Four	Burlesquing Recognition: James Merrill's Formalism	129
Chapter Five	More Rapid than Recognition: Thylias Moss's Lyric Velocity	159
Coda	"Join Me Down Here in Nowhere"	187
Notes		199
Bibliography		263
Index		283

Acknowledgments

Since this is a first book, it is hard to pinpoint its beginning, which means that it owes a good deal to many people over many years. Though it includes relatively little that I wrote during my graduate studies, I learned much from several teachers at the University of Alabama, including the late Elizabeth Meese, as well as Phil Beidler and Richard Rand. Sharon O'Dair deserves special thanks as the first person who encouraged me to try to revise toward publication (and helped me to do so). At the University of Illinois, I am grateful to my dissertation committee led by Cary Nelson and including Leon Chai, Bill Maxwell, Tim Newcomb, and Ed Brunner, who kindly participated while being a faculty member at the University of Southern Illinois. Since moving to Las Cruces, New Mexico, I am happy to thank many friends and colleagues on the faculty at New Mexico State University. Early in the drafting process, I benefitted from the insights of Sarah Hagelin, Jen Almjeld, and Peter Fine. More recently, my gratitude extends to Tyson Stolte, Kellie Sharp-Hoskins, Jean-Thomas Tremblay, Harriet Linkin, Tracey Miller-Tomlinson, and Joyce Garay. Liz Schirmer supported this project as a friend, colleague, and department head. Beyond Las Cruces, late in the drafting process, Cristanne Miller and Jackie Wang generously provided feedback. Throughout this time, I have been consistently inspired by the students I am privileged to teach at New Mexico State University. Rebecca Colesworthy shepherded this book through the publication process at SUNY Press. I am grateful for her wise counsel and for the anonymous reviewers who helped to improve this manuscript. Thanks also to Diane Ganeles and the production and design team at SUNY Press. Additionally, I wish to thank the staff of the libraries at each of the institutions listed above. I am happy to share credit for whatever this project gets right with all of these people. All oversights, of course, are my own.

viii | Acknowledgments

Two chapters began as essays and improved as a result of review processes. Thanks to *Criticism* and its editors, initially Jonathan Flatley and then renée hoogland, who published portions of Chapter 1 in the Fall 2014 issue. Thanks also to *MELUS: Multi-Ethnic Literature of the United States* and its editor Gary Totten, who published portions of Chapter 5 in the Spring 2016 issue.

Lastly, I wish to thank my family (especially my parents, Alaric and Vera Cull, brother, sister-in-law, and nephew, Evan, Christy, and Colin, and aunt and uncle, Isla Mae and Joe Mitchell) for their patience with my interminable progress reports and their encouragement to complete "the book." Here it is.

Introduction

Recognizing American Lyrics

Claudia Rankine's *Citizen: An American Lyric* begins with an anthology of aggressions, a litany placing "you" in the position of African Americans experiencing social "erasure."[1] Some accounts offer a single statement: "[W]hen the woman with the multiple degrees says, I didn't know black women could get cancer, instinctively you take two steps back."[2] In other examples, a brief narrative unfolds: a woman calls "you," her coworker, "by the name of another woman you work with." You "laugh" it off with a "friend beside you who says, oh no she didn't" but soon receive an "apology note [from the first woman] . . . referring to 'our mistake.'"[3] A few center the perspective of participant observers: "You feel your own body wince" upon seeing a child who is "knocked over" on a subway by a man who "kept walking." The mother insists that the man "look at the boy and apologize," but it is clear that he not only "did not see him, [but] has never seen him, has perhaps never seen anyone who is not a reflection of himself."[4]

After such encounters, these victims, participant observers, and implicitly "you" must calculate if and how to engage the sources of these incidents.[5] Silence tacitly tolerates the problem. Confrontation often results in denial and even outrage. Simply assessing this system, much less resisting it, is exhausting, especially if "you" are or have been the target of the racism. And this vicious circle contributes to the even more grim prospect that, for African Americans, regardless of the exertion of "energy required to present, to react, to assert, . . . no amount of visibility will alter the ways in which one is perceived."[6] "[H]ypervisib[ility]," after all, manifests itself as a vulnerability to "hurtful" language or even physical harm that "intend[s] to exploit . . . [y]our alertness, your openness, and

2 | Unlimited Eligibility?

your desire to . . . actually demand your presence."[7] Rankine observes how "[r]ecognition of this lack might break you apart. Or recognition might illuminate the erasure the attempted erasure triggers."[8] The wordplay here is as grim as it is dense. "You" recognize an absence of "recognition" or, perhaps more precisely, "you" realize how persistent misrecognition becomes recognition (the book will later say, "[T]his is how you are a citizen").[9] Either way, Rankine invites "you" to notice how acts of social erasure can be internalized and ratified by the worn-out subject.

Assessing what "you" would do under such circumstances, however, is only the start of what Rankine hopes to initiate. For readers willing to reflect on themselves as they prospectively identify with these catalogued experiences, the second-person address invites "you" to assess your position within a stratified social order, as someone unrecognized or someone largely misrecognized or someone more fully recognized or someone who has the power to (mis)recognize and whether (and how) you may fit in different positions in this hierarchy in different contexts. Rankine also challenges "you" to see how many acts of erasure fundamentally occur not only (or even at all) as a result of an individual intentionally refusing to recognize or intending to misrecognize another but as a result of this stratified system having become normalized. Whether you profit from this system or suffer from it, *Citizen* displays how entrenched it is, and, by creating space for readers to begin to identify their role in such scenes, the book raises the question of whether more mutual forms of recognition are (im)possible.

What recognition precisely means in *Citizen*, however, is left implicit, its effects encompassing yet inchoate, given how "you" are perpetually, yet not always consciously, immersed within psychosocial negotiations over degrees of (in)visibility and in/exclusion. But in a number of interviews, Rankine has linked recognition to the genre that serves as the book's subtitle, *An American Lyric*. Echoing John Stuart Mill's influential definition, Rankine explains that "the lyric is tied to the intimate . . . [and] is traditionally thought of as that which is overheard," but she also emphasizes an awareness of the broader social setting: "[T]he lyric is a place where feeling gets examined. It's traditionally grounded in the apprehensions and emotions of a subject. By coupling *lyric* with *American*, one takes the gesture into the public realm."[10] How does she conceive lyric at the intersection of subjectivity, sociality, and national identity? In another interview, Rankine identifies "the lyric as a kind of reciprocal recognition, in a sense. That, I think, is what I'm after."[11] Here, a genealogy of lyric and the concept of recognition begins to unspool. For Rankine acknowledges that she borrows the concept of "reciprocal recognition" from a passage in Frantz Fanon's *Black Skin, White Masks* that itself, as Fanon acknowledges, is in conversation with G. W. F. Hegel's understanding of subject formation, which, as this introduction later will consider, shaped Hegel's understanding of lyric poetry.[12] And Rankine additionally acknowledges poetic predecessors in the Harlem Renaissance and the Black Arts movement who developed strategies, ranging from appeals for social recognition within or demands to be liberated from America (and a variety of qualifications and interrogations of such appeals and demands), as a part of "a cultural shift towards Black people thinking away from whiteness." These legacies impelled Rankine to wonder "what if we all began to think about our racialized positioning—aggressively thinking about that," a question that set her on the path toward developing the idiom of *Citizen*, which foregrounds address, itself a topic much discussed in the late twentieth and early twenty-first centuries by yet another strand of thought attaching lyric poetry to recognition processes, insofar as theorists including Allen Grossman, Jonathan Culler, and Barbara Johnson, among others, have understood "lyric" address and apostrophe to acknowledge and even confer personhood.[13] So while Rankine draws on a variety of nineteenth and twentieth century associations with "lyric," from intimate subjective expression to political appeals for social reform and so forth, she foregrounds, as a common thread, the link between "lyric" and "recognition."

Scholars have made the same link and emphasized its importance to *Citizen*. Kamran Javadizadeh locates at the heart of *Citizen* a question: "How, in other words, can poetry continue to offer the opportunities for mutual recognition once thought of as lyric's purview after the very idea of the lyric has been exposed as theoretically naive, even politically suspect," insofar as "the idea of the transcendent [universalized, ahistorical] lyric subject . . . has been exposed as a form of white innocence"?[14] Along similar lines, Grant Farred asks: "[I]n the point of no return named 'belonging by not belonging,' is *Citizen* the text that iterates, through this lyric of recognition, the thano-political consumption of the black body into America?"[15] And Nikki Skillman further elaborates this line of thought, pointing to how "the issue of human recognition [has been] central to recent accounts of lyric," due to its perceived "tendency, through simulated utterance, to project human life and social responsiveness where it does not truly exist."[16] She adds that "[b]eyond striving to reanimate

4 | Unlimited Eligibility?

the speaker depleted by verbal and nonverbal racist assaults, Rankine's capacious 'you' also uses the symbolic, life-giving power of apostrophe to ironize the default attribution of fully human status to white citizens and exerts the mystificatory power of the vocative to animate (white) objects of address deadened by complicity, complacency, and the distortions of a racist imaginary."[17]

Like Rankine, these scholars do not explicitly define "recognition" in their articles. Instead, it is seemingly clear to them that "lyric," as a term, has become associated with an epistemological act of assessing whether and to what degree the observed should hold the privileges associated with personhood within a given society. Recognizing, thus, may be inclusionary or exclusionary, or, as it often is, an act of in/exclusion by degree, resulting from a host of measurements, albeit by no means always fully or even partially conscious ones, reflecting the recognizer's sense of where the observed should fit within facets of that social order. Scholars like Javadizadeh, Farred, and Skillman, in this way, point to how *Citizen* was written, in part, to lay bare the workings of recognition inside and outside of lyric discourse in order to make "you" more accountable for your role in this hierarchical system of unrecognized/misrecognized/recognized/recognizers.[18] But how did "recognition" become "central" (to use Skillman's word) and even the "purview" (to use Javadizadeh's word) of "the lyric" and, especially, the "American lyric"? What is the history of this merger of genre and sociopolitical function? If, as *Citizen* argues, "no amount of visibility" will yield sufficient social recognition to overcome anti-black racism, has the "lyric" (especially in its "American" iteration) been culturally calibrated to be a discursive form defined, for those lacking privileges, by appeals or even demands for recognition it never will nor even can fully deliver and, for those already privileged, a form that will continue to sustain their existing degrees of recognition? Does the conflating of lyric and recognition, in this way, figure for a larger phenomenon in American society, perhaps even indicating a limit of American democracy as it is currently practiced?

Unlimited Eligibility? Inclusive Democracy and the American Lyric examines how "lyric" and "recognition" came to be more and more closely associated in the American context since the mid-nineteenth century. During this period of time, "lyricization," Virginia Jackson's term for the gradual identification of poetry itself with the subject-centered "lyric," which had begun in the eighteenth century, continued to accelerate, obscuring from cultural memory a host of genres and subgenres.[19] The correlation between the lyricization process and the increased association of lyric with recognition is not coincidental. The narrowing of an awareness of the variety of genres parallels a narrowing of an awareness of the variety of ways poetry may intersect with politics, as the first-person speaker increasingly associated with the "lyric" increasingly becomes associated with either the expression of an allegedly universal (but, in reality, post-Enlightenment, bourgeois, white) speaker accorded (more or less) full personhood and social participation or, eventually, the expression (and, at times, interrogation) of appeals or demands for recognition by those not yet accorded this status.

This book will track the alignment of lyric and sociopolitical recognition by studying a sequence of writers who were particularly sensitized to it, not because they assented to this merger of the literary and the political but because they were developing an alternative to it. The lineage of poets outlined in this book, including Walt Whitman, Jean Toomer, Hart Crane, James Merrill, and Thylias Moss (as well as recent poetry by Mei-mei Berssenbrugge, Juan Felipe Herrera, and Claudia Rankine), investigates, at least for a time, a different strategy, which they adapt in response to their various historical moments and inflect with their own socially situated anxieties and ambitions. By calibrating metaphor, syntax, sound, and address, among other strategies that evoke and modulate a reader's relation to a speaker, their poetry stages encounters with otherness initiated by an affirmation of ontological proximity and equality, even if the latter is aspirational, sometimes collapsing and rarely sustained, rather than an epistemological evaluation of recognizability. These writers consider the possibility that prioritizing being-with over knowing-who, which Walt Whitman, a precursor, described as a commitment to unlimited "eligibility," could serve as a better foundation for democratic sociality.

Among the first generation of American writers to wrestle with Hegel, Walt Whitman developed an alternative to the German philosopher's still powerfully, even pervasively, influential understanding of social recognition. Using exceptionally nuanced modes of address as well as a nearly synesthetic receptivity to sights and sounds, Whitman calls forth in his boldest metapoem, "Crossing Brooklyn Ferry," "the rest" a (non) community without boundaries exemplifying the democracy of unlimited, ontological "eligibility" that, at his most radical, he hoped would define America. This model of sociality is evaluated and elaborated by two

6 | Unlimited Eligibility?

admirers of Whitman, Jean Toomer and Hart Crane, as a challenge to cultural pluralism, an early twentieth-century theory of democracy that asked the politically empowered to work toward incorporating minority populations into America by recognizing ethnic and racial differences. In "The Blue Meridian," Toomer apostrophizes the emergent American race that is multiethnic beyond recognition, exposing the lies undergirding biological conceptions of race and affirming an ontological proximity and equality that characterizes unlimited eligibility. Crane, on the other hand, develops in poems like "Possessions" and "Recitative" a queer poetics that models a looking without recognizing that serves as the foundation of the democratic praxis defining his initial envisioning of *The Bridge*.

Both Toomer and Crane wrote as lyricization and the politics of recognition increasingly intersected and defined each other. But because this alignment was still in-process, space remained for them to challenge it, more or less, directly. By the second half of the twentieth century, poetry and pedagogy associated "lyrics" with an abstract, allegedly universal, fully recognized speaker or a speaker appealing for or demanding or interrogating this status. Late twentieth-century identity politics movements often strategically featured lyrics as a means of contributing to the work of group self-definition, acts of attempted self-recognition pursued without cultural pluralism's tendency to defer to existing social norms. Writing at the time of (but also at a distance from) these movements, James Merrill's late lyrics use his skill at writing within poetic forms to burlesque the social forms that frame recognition processes and to evoke a comic hospitality less bound by norms. And Thylias Moss has developed a distinctive lyric idiom characterized by a velocity that rejects recognition's inclination to impose norms in the hope of more successfully reflecting the ongoing transformations that characterize the complex systems that make up the world.

While these poetic projects raise questions about whether lyric politics necessarily should be assumed to be a function of recognition processes, they also pose potential problems of their own. Is it possible—or even wise—to prioritize being-with rather than knowing-who? Thinking it is possible could come close to indulging a naive idealism about establishing a world without labels, a universalism as false as the one implied by the abstract, ahistorical, lyricized lyric. Subsequent chapters show that this risk persists even for writers who know, in various ways, the exclusionary power of such labels and how difficult they are to undermine. But questions abound even if one understands the affirmation of ontological proximity and equality as an opportunity not to avoid but, instead, to accept a responsibility to explore more democratic forms of representation. Disidentifying from existing norms can be an essential first step for evading and revising inadequate models of representation, but illegibility within a sociopolitical context often defined by recognition processes can be a source of intense pain.[20] How long should this pain be endured in the pursuit of a sociality grounded in affirming ontological proximity and equality? Might it be better to accept strategically an established minority identity and the prospect of community such an identity can foster? Why not, within such a community, make what incremental progress is possible, even if that progress implicitly may sustain a hierarchical recognition process and even certain misrecognitions? Furthermore, if the ongoing consequences of histories of enslavement or genocide have rendered certain communities virtually anontic, nowhere near full legibility as human beings, what would be the point of pursuing a lyric politics of ontological eligibility? And is poetry even a sensible means for evaluating such questions, much less attempting to imagine alternative models of social inclusion?

Subsequent chapters present writers negotiating these difficult dynamics. Indeed, the book's narrative, at times, charts the persistence of prejudice (racism and other social pathologies) in some of these writers' works as much as the development of alternatives to it. A central difficulty looms. While each of these poets offers reason to doubt whether a truly democratic social order can be predicated on the epistemological determinations central to the distribution of political recognition, their work also demands that we consider whether the prospect of a social order prioritizing being-with over knowing-who could become a fantasy fueling alleged affirmations of otherness that, in fact, may be too-easy disavowals of difference. What if "recognition," in other words, designates a practice that falls short of a democratic ideal and "eligibility" designates a democratic ideal difficult to practice?

Unlimited Eligibility argues that the history of how the "American lyric" reflects on this question illuminates both what has enabled and restricted literary interventions into the politics of representation. It claims that the recurring debate between poetic lineages seeking to affirm ontological eligibility and those seeking to confirm epistemological legibility exposes a key component of the structure of America's faltering progress toward a more truly democratic inclusivity. In doing so, it encourages a widening of theoretical and artistic horizons as a basis for developing more imaginatively democratic models of political futurity.

8 | Unlimited Eligibility?

Political Recognition and/as American Lyric Theory

Over the past several decades, influential scholars have designated socio-political recognition as the principal cultural work of lyrics in several distinct ways, each of which is worth assessing in order to appreciate how seemingly different projects have contributed to a narrowing of how we perceive the political horizon of American poetry. One group (exemplified by Allen Grossman) assumes that all discourse participates in recognition processes that structure sociality. This group's model of lyric can be linked directly to Hegel's understanding of lyric in relation to recognition processes. A second group (exemplified by Virginia Jackson) historicizes the concept of lyric to a degree that the first group does not. But advocates of this approach do not always apply the same historicist rigor to the question of whether recognition is an adequate concept for describing the social work of genre. A third group (exemplified by a number of scholars including Sarah Dowling and Urayoán Noel) seeks to historicize how recognition is distinctly conceptualized and practiced in particular contexts and, in doing so, still tends to posit recognition as definitive rather than one of a range of frameworks for understanding the intersection of poetry and the politics of representation. Important, illuminating scholarship can be found in each category, strands that, at times, have argued with each other as they variously analyze, historicize, and occasionally resist how regimes of recognition operate, but there has been little consideration yet given to poets, like those who are the focus of this book, who do not see such recognition processes as equivalent with sociality itself. And the overall result has been the establishment of a consensus, as several generations of scholars have associated various models of recognition with a wide range of poems deemed "lyrics."

How this happened begins to become clearer in light of a key, if not always acknowledged, thinker near the origin of this narrative. In his lectures on aesthetics, G. W. F. Hegel, again and again, depicts lyric poetry as a distinctly reflexive "apprehension of the mind in its own self-expression," whereby "the individual person and therefore . . . all the details of his situation and concerns . . . comes to consciousness of itself" as facilitated by the various elements of prosody.[21] Though Hegel is well aware of how poetic techniques can be overdone to the point of "artificiality, over-elegance, manufactured piquancy, and preciosity," when properly directed by a poet with a mastery of craft, they serve as an ideal artistic conduit not just for conveying subject formation but for fostering and shaping intersubjective bonds.[22] For example, rhyme, a verse technique that Hegel associates "especially" with lyric poetry, directs "the mind's and ear's memory to a recurrence of the same or associated sounds and meanings, a recurrence in which the percipient is made conscious of himself and in which he recognizes himself as the activity of creation and apprehension and is satisfied."[23] Hegel, here, writes in characteristically multivalent fashion of a "percipient" who could be both poet and reader, thus indicating how a poet's coming to self-awareness might be mirrored in the reader who also would recognize the poet.

This merger of "creation and apprehension" modeled by a lyric is not merely a potential intersection between two individuals' acts of recognition. For Hegel, the work of writing and reading a lyric in this way inherently participates in broader sociopolitical processes insofar as the "subjective reflection" at the heart of lyrics "becomes deeper in itself as it explores the depths of its own wider culture."[24] A successful lyric initiates what may seem to be a merely isolated act of mutual recognition between writer and reader that in fact is a small part of a much larger, more diffuse, by no means always conscious cascade of recognition processes. For the poem's words and idiom engage, negotiate, and extend the "wider culture" within which the poem participates. Thus, lyrics, for Hegel, serve as a mellifluous means of being more deeply drawn into and more deeply recognizable within this culture, a microcosm of a still larger process of social development wherein persons and poems participate in an increasingly expansive notion of Spirit coming to an increasingly expansive self-awareness.

Postmodernity, however, warned us to be wary of how such optimistic, albeit only gradually realized, teleologies can participate in interpellating persons within oppressive power structures. And contemporary lyric theorists often have sought to disambiguate Hegel's teleology from his association of lyrics with social recognition processes. In *The Sighted Singer*, Allen Grossman argues that a lyric, by definition, "moves from least differentiation of the self (the opening) toward most differentiation of the self (at the close)," a drama of a self not only coming to awareness of itself (a "self-recognition") but presenting itself for recognition by others from whom it is "differentiat[ed]."[25] Understood in this way, lyrics always offer, at least implicitly, a "dialectic reality," since "I use *I* only when I am speaking to someone who will be a *you* in my address. It is this condition of dialogue that is constitutive of *person*, for it implies that reciprocally *I* becomes *you* in the address of the one who in his turn

10 | Unlimited Eligibility?

designates himself as *I*" (Grossman's emphasis).[26] Realizing that the kind of reciprocity modeled here has not been socially achieved, Grossman deems "it obvious that the kinds of conflict which are most common in our world . . . are in some large part a result of representational deficit," a deficit, as he sees it, "not of wealth but of honor." Drawing a distinction that some thinkers (e.g., Nancy Fraser, Charles Mills, Iris Marion Young) have argued against, Grossman thus contends that the sociopolitical role of the lyric is to participate in "the collective task of redistributing the fundamental wealth of social visibility."[27]

Grossman remained committed to this model while becoming increasingly skeptical about the possibility of lyrics, or any human endeavor, facilitating recognition of personhood sufficiently, much less spurring truly reciprocal acts of recognition. In *The Long Schoolroom: Lessons in the Bitter Logic of the Poetic Principle*, Grossman explains that "my premise" is that "the manifest world (the only one there is) is subject to the logic of representation because it comes to mind only as representation. And representation, our only access to world, reproduces its hierarchical and exclusionary structures as social formations. The poem is the site on which originality is expressed as the attempt to discover alternative structures of intelligibility that do the work of representation in another way."[28] The social importance of such a project is incalculable: "In our time the recognition of the human other as real, and by that person's very existence a prior value to all more abstract values, is the major social crisis to which poetry speaks."[29] But Grossman is not optimistic about any poet's capacity to achieve this goal. For poetry seeks what it cannot deliver: "Discourse, like consciousness, is built—and made strong—by distinction. Such is the 'bitter logic' of poetic practice actualized as violence—the violence of religion, race, class, and gender all driven by the engine of distinction—which representation, nonetheless, requires."[30] Grossman, here, makes a consequential—and questionable—assumption often shared by other contemporary scholars of lyric (and other genres). He imagines the sociopolitical work of "representation" only in relation to a particular kind of recognition process. Drawing "distinction[s]," according to this very nearly predetermined narrative, becomes morally and politically necessary for those not-yet-recognized and for those recognizing them, without providing either side much relief. For a minority population hoping to be recognized, this distinction-making process is a never-adequate and never-ending response to a sequence of misrecognitions calculated by recognizers to keep the not-fully-recognized in submission. This is "the exchange of life for meaning" that Grossman labels "the bitter sacrificial logic of the poetic principle."[31] But this strategy of calculated misrecognition, in turn, yields unsatisfying results even for the more privileged recognizing class, who must deal with the potentially increasing anger of those not yet fully recognized. Grossman, in other words, places at the heart of lyrics the moral demands driving a dialectical model of sociality strikingly similar to Hegel's while insisting that mutual recognition is always impossibly out of reach. Whether representation might be conceptualized by a different, perhaps less "violent" model of intersubjective relation is not considered.

Nevertheless, Grossman's neo-Hegelian model powerfully influenced a number of friends, former students, and colleagues, including Susan Stewart, who is perhaps best known as a critic for *Poetry and the Fate of the Senses*, and Oren Izenberg, author of *Being Numerous: Poetry and the Ground of Social Life*.[32] The linking of lyric and recognition, however, extends beyond Grossman's associates and is present within other recent scholarship on the genre by Robert von Hallberg, Mutlu Konuk Blasing, and Jonathan Culler.[33] The latter's *Theory of the Lyric* draws from the Hegelian lyric paradigm more strictly than many of these scholars. Culler particularly admires the way that Käte Hamburger delineates a Hegelian model that refuses to read lyrics as works of fiction (even if lyrics obviously can contain fictional elements), as miniature, versified novels, while avoiding the opposite error of reading lyrics as miniature, lineated, pseudo-autobiographical psychodramas.[34] Though Culler emphasizes that "[r]eflection on lyric and society cannot but identify multiple levels at which lyric can function and make it clear that there is no one form of social efficacy for lyric," he identifies in his conclusion Hamburger's Hegelian model as an especially "promising framework."[35] "Society," he writes, "is always confronted with the problem of how matter is endowed with spirit or meaning, and poetry [here, he clearly means lyric] is one of several forces that at once makes this happen and explicates it."[36] For Culler as for Hegel, this happens through the expression of a subjectivity, amplified by distinctive modes of address and "ritualistic" features (like rhyme and rhythm), facilitating the experience of the recognition of self and other by both poet and reader.[37]

While these studies differ in various ways (e.g., historical scope and critical idiom), such divergences make the continuity linking lyric and recognition all the more worthy of scrutiny. This continuity extends to scholarship like Virginia Jackson's, which is committed to "trac[ing] the

12 | Unlimited Eligibility?

historical process by which different poetic genres began to be collapsed into an abstract idea of lyric" during the "nineteenth century" and further "consolidated in the twentieth century."[38] As a result of this trend, which became more occluded as it became more pervasive, many scholars of poetry retroproject a twentieth (and now twenty-first) century understanding of "lyric" on the nineteenth century (and still earlier periods). "What we now think of as the romantic lyric," in this way, came to obstruct an awareness of the much wider variety of poetic genres including "elegies, epitaphs, ballads, hymns, epistles, medleys, drinking songs, sea chanteys, and spirituals" that flourished at that time.[39] Jackson does not intend to recover and understand these genres in their "pre-lyricized" idioms, a goal that she deems impossible. Instead, she tries to track "the historical emergence of that [lyricized] norm" that came to dominate discussions of American poetry and poetics.[40] Indeed, Jackson agrees with Gérard Genette's description of lyric becoming an "archigenre" alongside epic and drama during the nineteenth century and locates the roots of the impulse to abstract and generalize beyond the many other historical genres and indeed beyond historical particularity itself in German thinkers like Goethe and, especially, Hegel.[41]

Jackson has become increasingly explicit about the stakes of bringing to light how the lyricization process resulted in "the thoroughly Hegelian structure of contemporary lyric theory."[42] But, at the same time, Jackson also has forwarded a quasi-Hegelian model of genre without similarly historicizing it. Jackson contends that genres—including lyric, as it became a genre (or "archigenre")—are "mode[s] of recognition instantiated in discourse" or "modes of collective recognition."[43] Though Jackson acknowledges Lisa Gitelman's role in developing this phrasing, for a number of years, she did not elaborate how she understood recognition in relation to lyricization.[44] But, in her important recent book *Before Modernism: Inventing American Lyric*, after, once again, referencing this "defin[ition]" of "genre," Jackson remarks, "As the literary was invented on the basis of genre, it was also invented on the basis of race. The lyric imaginary and the racial imaginary are both genres embedded in and formed by historical discourses that unconsciously control how easily we recognize poems and persons, and they are so intimately entwined with one another . . . [that] what we all recognize quite easily quickly becomes hard to distinguish from the genres of which we are made."[45] Jackson's emphasis on how genres function as "historical discourses that unconsciously control [our thinking]" accords with Gitelman's view of recognition as a "collective, spontaneous, and dynamic" process.[46] We "recognize poems and persons," Jackson goes on to explain, in terms of "genres (or kinds, or races, or cultures, or ethnicities)," without necessarily (or even often) knowing that we do.[47] This is how the "modern lyric . . . [became] a product of a long history of racialized social antagonism" as it became understood as an abstracted and sociohistorically decontextualized genre.[48]

Though Jackson has been thinking about "a close affiliation between lyricization and Americanization" since she wrote *Dickinson's Misery*, she makes the intersection between the history of lyricization and the history of racial animus particularly vivid in *Before Modernism*.[49] For instance, one of the defining characteristics of a lyricized understanding of lyric, one taught to generations of students since "the 1930s," is that every poem is voiced by a universal "speaker," who is without "a race or a gender or a pronoun or a proper name" and assumed to have a personhood shared by everyone.[50] But not all prospective writers or readers of poems have been equally or fully recognized as persons. In this way, the concept of a lyric speaker, rather than being truly universal, assumes membership in a recognizing (or, at least, recognized) class. Readers outside of this class cannot identify with this speaker or do so at the risk of naturalizing this model. Similar "modes of recognition" become "instantiated in the smallest details" of the lyricized lyric, including "meter" and "figures of address" like "apostrophe," inviting privileged readers to find themselves within—and thus reproduce—existing hierarchies and less privileged readers either to accept this paradigm or seek ways of resisting it.[51]

Since there is no "way out of lyric or out of lyric reading as theory or practice," according to Jackson, resistance, it seems, can only take the form of making genealogies of lyricization and practicing kinds of negative dialectics that expose the machinery of the racialized system of lyricization, or to watch for the "waning of genre," a possibility Jackson draws from Lauren Berlant's work, when "contemporary forms of recognition are up for grabs," potentially ripe for renegotiation as "the communal investments in those forms of recognition . . . might . . . change."[52] Here, echoes may start to be heard to Grossman and even to that key source of lyricization himself, Hegel. Both Jackson and Grossman depart from Hegel's positive teleology but assert that genres of discourse, including poetic genres, set parameters within which personhood is recognizable (or not) and to what degree. Both, in this way, understand lyrics (in the lyricized sense of the word), at least implicitly, as participating in subject formation and in intersubjective negotiations over social conditions.

14 | Unlimited Eligibility?

Jackson's contention that "genre is a heartbreaker," disfiguring persons by inevitably staging acts of (mis)recognition that oversimplify or obscure individual or group distinctiveness significantly parallels Grossman's rueful tone about the "bitter logic" wherein recognition, even under the best of circumstances, always does violence by misrecognizing.[53] And Jackson's focus on how literary techniques (meter, address, etc.) participate in this enfolding within misrecognitions similarly echoes Hegel's understanding of the functioning of prosody within social recognition processes.

Despite these similarities, there may appear to be a major difference in emphasis between Grossman and Jackson. When Grossman describes the sociopolitical work of lyric in terms of recognition, he seems to imagine lyrics written by (or on behalf of) a member of an un/misrecognized group being read by a class of already recognized people who are empowered to bestow greater (or lesser) recognition on the first group. While Jackson probably would acknowledge that such scenarios can occur, she (along with Gitelman and Berlant) imagines a more subtle process involving much less individual agency. Genres, in their opinion, perform recognition "collective[ly]," as a product of an often scarcely conscious affective act of group assent, wherein discursive conventions gradually accrete, resulting in a shared epistemological framework that shapes how people see and are seen (or not seen). The difference between understanding an act of recognition to be a result of an exertion of agency or a result of something more ambient like affect is a difference of opinion on the degree to which the process of distributing recognition (and the distributors themselves) can be specifically known and directly engaged. The power of the recognizers in the former instance can be directly challenged, whereas in the latter instance the power of the recognizers is more elusive and diffuse, insofar as the recognizers may be ignorant of their complicity in the process altogether.

Framing the matter in this way, however, risks overlooking the fact that in a great many, perhaps even most, instances, recognition processes play out somewhere in the middle, shaped by an irreducible mixture of social affects and a measure of individual decision-making. Hegel himself understood this, given his appreciation for the extended, inherently social, not necessarily fully conscious, always "complex process of mediation" whereby a subject achieves sense-certainty and gradual self-awareness and eventually negotiates forms of intersubjectivity—and, one senses, both Grossman and Jackson understand this too.[54] This is the crucial point: each scholar represented in these first two groups understands social-ity—and the "genres (or kinds, or races, or cultures, or ethnicities)," to use Jackson's phrase, through which it manifests itself—as fundamentally structured by an economy of recognition that distributes privilege, even if their understanding of precisely how that distribution occurs differs by degrees.[55] Their reasoning is lock-tight: if sociality is enacted through economies of recognition, then genres as products of society are defined by economies of recognition. Therefore, lyrics and, for that matter, the various genres and subgenres of poems preceding the invention of the modern lyric (or, indeed, any genre at all), must be defined by economies of recognition.[56] But there is a difference between arguing that a particular theory of genre has been powerfully influential, even to the point of occluding alternative theories, and accepting this occlusion as definitive. This book acknowledges the former and resists the latter claim and worries that Jackson, at times, loses sight of this distinction. If one, instead, did historicize the intersection of "lyric" and "recognition" in American writing, might one find not just strategies for exposing, querying, and resisting existing genres of recognition but alternative models of genre and social formation altogether?

While Jackson's *Before Modernism* argues that African American poets of the eighteenth and nineteenth centuries "influence[d] the direction of Anglophone Romanticism" and "were appropriated by White Romantic poets" as the history of lyricization and racialization developed alongside each other, becoming the "deep design of the poetry that . . . became American lyric," a third group of contemporary scholars of lyric has explored the consequences of this process on the poetry produced by disempowered communities in the twentieth and now twenty-first centuries.[57] In doing so, this third group implicitly (or explicitly) studies how the trajectory of American Hegelianism that led the American lyric to become associated with an abstract, allegedly universal speaker accorded full personhood also led it to become the site of appeals or demands for or interrogations of recognition by those who do not have that status. These scholars often realize, like the poets they study, that this system is structured against the disempowered. For the hierarchies (unrecognized, misrecognized, recognized, recognizer) inherent to this system limit the efficacy of such appeals or demands. Their poetry and scholarship, thus, reflect nuanced strategies for survival amid (negotiations with, exposing or ironizing of, rejecting altogether) various regimes of recognition.

Urayoán Noel, for example, worries in *In Visible Movement*, about forces that "mak[e] visible a marginal experience without also challenging the terms of visibility." Locating diasporic writing, and Puerto Rican

16 | Unlimited Eligibility?

diaspora poetry in particular, at the "limits of representation" due to the inherent complexity in determining boundaries of identity in relation to community, city, and nation, Noel advises that such writers "help us rethink the terms of identity and representation."[58] Acknowledging the misrecognition that occurs within or even at these limits, Ralph Rodriguez in *Latinx Literature Unbound* preserves Latinx as a necessary political category while considering the ways that, as a conceptual and aesthetic term, it can become binding, which leads him to investigate poets who opt out or foreground a "radical singularity . . . [that] frees writers from the burden of representation and cultural ambassadorship."[59] In a different way, the "post-lyric" African American poets Anthony Reed highlights query these "demands for civil recognition" that have become associated with writers from minority communities, due to this strategy having "proved palliative rather than fully emancipatory." These post-lyric poets strategically "produc[e] a kind of expression that effaces the imagined expresser," exposing the "grammatical fiction" of lyric subjecthood by making "the poems . . . documents, rather than expressions, of . . . [the] social locations" of "subjects whose race and gender position in U. S. society make them vulnerable to premature death."[60]

Sarah Dowling's *Translingual Poetics: Writing Personhood under Settler Colonialism* is particularly attentive to these dynamics, and she forwards reasons for why attempts to implement contemporary versions of "Hegel's theory" of recognition have not succeeded.[61] Drawing from "numerous critiques of the politics of recognition," including those of "Glen Coulthard (Yellowknives Dene) and Audra Simpson (Mohawk)[, who] demonstrate that recognition merely replicates the same old configurations of colonial power," Dowling suggests that, "[i]nstead of seeking to translate the other so that their personhood or humanity conforms to our own [as models of recognition, intentionally or not, often do], we need to listen for what it is that makes them distinctively different—for the sounds that we cannot understand, that do not align with our orders of meaning, but that we can, perhaps, amplify."[62] Dowling's "perhaps" is commendably candid, reflecting the difficult questions inherent within this goal: Can "we" perform this act of "amplify[ing]" without, at least to a degree, "align[ing]" or "translat[ing]" or "conform[ing] to our own" model of "personhood or humanity" these "distinctively different . . . sounds"? To what degree is this avoidable or inevitable, inexcusable or acceptable before "we" (non-Indigenous persons? non-Indigenous academics?) begin to recreate a recognition process? Or do these questions suggest, as Jackson does, that there may be no way out of the dynamics of recognition?[63]

Foregrounding paradoxes of diasporic identity, asserting radical singularity, rendering visible problematic assumptions associated with appeals made by a lyricized subject, "amplify[ing]" the "sounds we cannot understand"—these are powerful strategies. Though they do not (and are not intended to) negate the strategic pursuit of social recognition, they do complicate its identification as *the* politics of representation and *the* politics of socially engaged lyrics. Beyond hoping to expand existing norms or expressing frustration at the difficulty of expanding such norms as they may or may not wane, and even beyond exposing and undermining such a schema, this third group of scholars rejects the assumption that recognition defines the political horizons of lyric sociality, even if they are not necessarily sure what alternatives there are. *Unlimited Eligibility* extends their interrogation by mapping a group of poets who do not just want to expose and resist the history and machinery attaching lyric to recognition processes but to develop distinct alternatives to its directives.

American Lyrics beyond Recognition?

To pose this question is not to contend that poets (or anyone else) ought to avoid making strategic appeals or demands for greater sociopolitical recognition, given the pervasiveness of that discourse in American culture.[64] That pervasiveness, however, is worth inquiry. Should the pursuit of increased representation and inclusion, ongoing important goals in any number of facets of American society, so often be understood in terms of Americanized Hegelian recognition processes? This question, in turn, relates to complex, at times fraught, debates about what it means to represent an identity as a political act and even more fundamental questions about the nature of identity itself. Scholars have argued, for example, about whether an identity is something grounded in a shared cultural past or shared present experiences or shared future political goals or a combination thereof, theses dependent upon, for example, the degree to which one understands identity in realist terms or as a historical construct.[65] Some argue that strategic space for illegibility and opacity should be preserved.[66] Further debates concern whether political recognition itself can be a vehicle for achieving social justice, whether it

18 | Unlimited Eligibility?

encompasses or must be made secondary to policies that acknowledge how oppression is often located at the intersection of other vectors linked to identity including law and economics.[67] Still others ask whether conceptualizing recognition as something bestowed by established sources of power leaves intact structural inequalities that distinguish between those who recognize, those who have been recognized, and those still mis/unrecognized. Some argue that less hierarchical models of recognition are nevertheless achievable.[68] Others are not so sure that recognition models can be remedied and wonder if, in certain ways, they may be fundamentally undemocratic. This latter group of thinkers worry that pursuing recognition undermines justice by compromising with current power structures, in effect negotiating a price for a status closer to full political subjecthood or even for personhood itself.

This book will engage with elements of each of these lines of inquiry. Many poets (e.g., Langston Hughes, Adrienne Rich, Muriel Rukeyser) embed and sometimes foreground critique of economic systems in poems that also appeal for recognition, an impulse that holds true, at least to an extent, for the poets considered here who explore modes of relation and representation outside of recognition processes (even, to a small degree, James Merrill, a person of great financial privilege).[69] But the last, most challenging query, partially acknowledged in the anxieties of a poet like Rankine and a critic like Grossman (among others), concerning the possibility that recognition processes may be only superficially democratizing is especially pertinent to this project. The lyric poets discussed in subsequent chapters who seek to foreground an affirmation of ontological proximity and equality rather than an epistemological confirmation of recognizability, a prioritizing of being-with rather than knowing-who that affirms rather than assesses personhood, serve as precursors to contemporary theorists posing this difficult question.

For someone committed to democratic politics and poetics, the prospect that recognition processes may be inherently undemocratic leaves only two possible modes of recourse. Either one explores alternative, more democratizing models of representation outside of recognition, or, if one is convinced there are no such models, one makes the best of a bad situation and democratizes recognition practices to the degree that one can. Those in the first camp, like Kelly Oliver, often are more successful in critiquing recognition than in offering viable alternatives. Oliver interrogates how Hegel and a number of later thinkers he influenced imagine recognition-based sociality developing through dialectical means, an assumption that, according to Oliver, affirms and even institutionalizes a "pathology of oppression," insofar as it requires unrecognized people to "demand recognition" from their "oppressors, the very people most likely not to recognize them."[70] Oliver instead offers a different model of sociality that begins with a different metaphor for sight, "witnessing," which, unlike recognition, understands subjectivity to be "founded on the ability to respond to, and address, others . . . [a] responsibility . . . [that] has the double sense of the condition of possibility of response . . . and the ethical obligation to respond and to enable response-ability from others born out of that founding possibility."[71] Witnessing requires a carefully calibrated combination of epistemological precision and epistemological humility, a "testifying to something that you have seen with your own eyes and bearing witness to something that you cannot see."[72] However, while one might share Oliver's distaste for the way that conflict often drives and structures problematically hierarchical recognition processes, she leaves somewhat unclear how we sustain "vigilan[ce] in our attempts to continually open and reopen the possibility of response" and fulfill our "responsibility to open ourselves to the responses that constitute us as subjects."[73] Advocates for various recognition models from Hegel to Judith Butler, after all, suspect that few people are self-motivated to fulfill such lofty goals, when it threatens their empowered status.[74] As a result, they contend that successive, often awkward, generally conflict-riven recognition processes are the only way of conceptualizing how one starts to approximate what "witnessing" requires. Oliver, from this angle, offers a beautiful goal without sufficient advice for how to achieve it.

A second approach often ends up conceding a good deal to the very systems of recognition that it critiques. Like Oliver, Patchen Markell seeks to formulate a less conflictual, less hierarchical model of knowing others than recognition typically allows. Markell argues that recognition's excesses might be tempered by advocating for the "acknowledgment of others," an approach to intersubjectivity influenced by the work of Stanley Cavell that rests on a deepened awareness of "one's own finitude . . . one's practical limits . . . [a] coming to terms with, rather than vainly attempting to overcome, the risk of conflict, hostility, misunderstanding, opacity, and alienation that characterizes life among others."[75] Markell nevertheless concludes that, given the "pleasures of sovereignty [i.e., the desire for epistemic—and other forms of—mastery that acknowledgment warns against], the temptation of recognition will probably always be inelim-inable; and indeed, as long as the social salience of identity persists, we

20 | Unlimited Eligibility?

would not want the desire for recognition to be eliminated, for . . . that desire has been responsible not only for danger and injury but also for progress and justice."[76] Markell advises that we ought to find ways of managing the very real problems associated with recognition rather than overemphasizing efforts to realize alternatives to it. But this line of reasoning rests on several questionable premises: Must "the social salience of identity" only be managed through recognition processes? And must the introduction of alternative socialities necessitate the "eliminat[ion]" of strategic appeals for recognition?

Grand ambitions (like Oliver's) and candid concessions (like Markell's) point to an affective component central to contemporary studies of the politics of recognition.[77] Longing (for democratic socialities featuring an alternative model of representation), resignation (that there may be none), and everything between shape approaches for engaging established political structures.[78] Perhaps no one has navigated these difficult dynamics framing the possibility of a politics of representation outside of quasi-Hegelian models of recognition more suggestively than Fred Moten, who links such a project to a kind of thinking about the work of lyric. Moten contends that anontic and paraontic spaces of oppression, locations outside of and adjacent to recognized orders of being, can and do serve as sources of socialities beyond existing political horizons. By indicating how lyrics emerge from and evoke these sometimes still inchoate spaces, Moten offers an especially intriguing framework for engaging and evaluating the poetic projects this book studies.

Moten's conception of these anontic and paraontic spaces emerges from his "total agreement with the Afro-pessimistic understanding of blackness as exterior to civil society," an ongoing condition resulting from histories of enslavement that continue to reduce persons of African heritage to fungible objects.[79] Such a status is defined, according to Frank Wilderson, in terms of social death, an ongoing "slaveness" that "cannot enter into a structure of recognition as a being" and that demands "we [members of the African diaspora] recognize that we cannot be recognized."[80] But unlike Wilderson, Moten understands this "exhaustion as a mode or form or way of life, which is to say sociality, thereby marking a relation whose implications constitute . . . a fundamental theoretical reason not to believe, as it were, in social death."[81] Lack of social recognition, though an index of incredible oppression, has not stopped the production of extraordinary black sociality, since social recognition, according to Moten, does not designate the limits of sociality. Instead, he argues that "blackness," rather than being synonymous with social death, is "an illicit alternative capacity to desire."[82] For Moten, this implies that "blackness is prior to ontology" or "is the anorignal displacement of ontology."[83]

Moten describes the intersection of politics and poetry within this space in terms of a potential for "paralyric sociality," a concept he explains in relation to Frantz Fanon's juxtaposition of Aimé Césaire's poetics and pidgin dialects.[84] For Moten (and Fanon), there is a double danger here. To speak pidgin is to be "imprison[ed]" within an "epidemeralization," to be recognized according to racist norms associated with using dialect.[85] On the other hand, to speak standard French (though similar power dynamics, of course, inform parallel circumstances involving English and other colonizing languages) is to assimilate and concede its primacy over pidgin dialects. Either way, as Fanon notes, "the Negro has to wear the livery that the white man has sewed for him."[86] In no way does Moten downplay how this dynamic discursively sustains and extends the oppressive conditions facing persons within the African diaspora. Yet Moten also emphasizes how, even in this "impossible positionality," in "the absence and refusal of the [ontologtical] standpoint," a "sociality and sociology of the anontic" exists and, at the level of language, "the experiment [in this (non)space] is poetic; pidgin is a poetics."[87]

What are the political prospects for "impossible" cultural work? Moten, along with his friend and collaborator Stefano Harney, associate the potentialities of anontic and paraontic spaces with the term "undercommons."[88] Moten and Harney claim that "to enter this space is to inhabit the ruptural and enraptured disclosure of the commons that fugitive enlightenment enacts, the criminal, matricidal, queer, in the cistern, on the stroll of the stolen life, the life stolen by enlightenment and stolen back, where the commons give refuge, where the refuge gives commons."[89] The "undercommons" is available to all who approach it through "study," a term they intentionally leave ambiguous but that involves resisting the "call to order," refusing to reduplicate unthinkingly, at least to the degree one can, any unjust systems that organize the world, including regimes of recognition.[90] Consequently, the undercommons encompasses not only those who, for example, "problematize the university," including "maroon communities of composition teachers, mentorless graduate students, adjunct Marxist historians, out or queer management professors, state college ethnic studies departments, closed-down film programs, visa-expired Yemeni student newspaper editors, historically black college sociologists, and feminist engineers," but those who find themselves developing similar

22 | Unlimited Eligibility?

political commitments when "playing in a band . . . or . . . sitting on a porch, or . . . working together in a factory."[91] In this way, every iteration of the undercommons is capable of acting as a laboratory for discovering new, more democratic socialities, an approach that Moten and Harney root in the black radical tradition but extend to other communities made up of the unrecognized, under-recognized, and resistant to recognition who have experienced various degrees of ontological exclusion.

But the potential to open the undercommons even qualifiedly to all who "study" raises difficult questions. How would encounters between those of different ontic status, between those who, outside of these an/paraontic spaces, are in different ways and to different degrees (un/mis) recognized, reshape the undercommons itself? On the one hand, as the anontic and the ontic inevitably intersect, there is the possibility for improvising more democratic ways of seeing and being with others. On the other hand, despite the obligation to study, there remains the possibility of importing into the undercommons existing exclusionary orders of relation. And, even if the more positive potentialities are sustained, a still larger challenge emerges—how to bring the world into this sociality or to bring it into the world, when, as Moten warns, it is "seldom that even the ones who make this [paralyric] music listen to it."[92]

Though the Moten/Harney model of the undercommons does not provide a perfect parallel to all of the poetic projects addressed in this book, several of which do not relate to the black radical tradition (though several others do), all of these projects wrestle with these difficult questions. To varying degrees and in varying ways, all interrogate the "call to order" (to use Moten's phrase) that exists within regimes of recognition. All explore alternative paraontic lyric socialities, which they then struggle to imagine how to extend to and apply in the world. These struggles become central to the chapters that follow, in some instances even collapsing into forms of hierarchical (mis)recognition the poets ostensibly reject. What is the source of this unfortunate capacity for contradiction? Recognition paradigms, by definition, feature authority figures, recognizers, who evaluate one's eligibility for recognition. Insisting, as Whitman and in various ways the other poets in this book do, on an *unlimited* eligibility should remove this recognizing role. But if unlimited means welcoming all kinds of difference, a tacit impulse may remain to account for, or even tally (to use a Whitmanian word), difference in a manner that might begin to resemble an act of recognition, albeit of an ostensibly unlimited form. Each of these poets becomes aware of this risk, as well as the impossibility of a truly comprehensive tallying of difference. Yet, again and again, pivotal moments in their poems present announcements of and invitations into a social order defined by unlimited eligibility. These moments frame the speaker as a kind of welcoming host who risks slipping into this authoritative, tallying role of quasi-recognizer. So a greater challenge for these poets emerges: to understand ontological eligibility and equality not as something to be built toward or to seek to enter or to bring into the world but, instead, as an inherent, originary state of interrelation (or even enmeshment or entanglement), a kind of ontic immanence we share that has been occluded and disfigured.[93] Their argument is not that this ontic immanence itself is democratic but that affirmation of it serves as a more likely foundation upon which to build democratic sociality than extended conflicts over degrees of (mis)recognition. None of the writers considered in this book entirely avert these dangers and affirm this ontic immanence with sustained success. But learning from their ambitious attempts, even as they fall into degrees of self-contradiction, nevertheless helps to expose a more complete history of the American lyric in conversation with other movements that have sought to build better, more democratic socialities.

The Impasse of American Inclusiveness?
Recognizability, Eligibility, and Innovation

Unlimited Eligibility studies the history of these dynamics in order to determine whether they define an impasse in American poetics also characteristic of an impasse in American politics, wherein a model of sociality founded on assessments of recognizability falls short of democratic ideals and affirmations of ontological eligibility are unattainably idealistic, and whether there are, nevertheless, overlooked, potential paths forward. Since the terms and genres framing these concepts evolve considerably over the years that this book spans, from the mid nineteenth-century to the early twenty-first century, this book will defer to the writers' terminologies and the terminologies of the particular historical moments with an eye toward how these terminologies shift amid lyricization and what these shifts tell us. This book similarly defers to how these writers do not always associate lyric with brevity but feature it as a mode that may appear in much longer works. Studying these shifts in concept and in practice creates a more complete sense of the ambitions and limits of this lineage.

24 | Unlimited Eligibility?

The first chapter turns to Walt Whitman, who, early in his career, anticipates and resists a prospective amalgamation of poetry and the politics of recognition at about the same time that he first wrestles with Hegel's thought. In a characteristically cluttered drafting notebook from around 1855–1856, amid a moment when America as a concept and as a political entity was under unprecedented pressure, Whitman mourns that his nation is "without one lyric voice to seize its greatness."[94] Writing immediately after the first edition of *Leaves of Grass* failed to find popular success, he approaches this task carefully and even obliquely. In a fragment of what appears to be a speech, Whitman presents himself as someone who holds the rights and privileges of American citizenship and thus is politically empowered to recognize immigrants and enslaved persons not yet deemed fully American. But he never completes the speech and, in several subsequent passages in the notebook, he starts to develop a different means of supporting those who have been excluded. He affirms the "eligibility" of "any one" to "belong" to America without being subjected to a recognition process.[95] Adjacent to these meditations on eligibility, Whitman begins to compose his most sophisticated metapoem, "Crossing Brooklyn Ferry." Through increasingly intimate rhetorical questions and a transformative new relation to time and space that would become the hallmark of the poem, the speaker invites the reader to join him among "the rest," the name Whitman bestows on the (non)community that affirms ontological "eligibility" and equality without first demanding epistemological recognizability (78, 82).[96] But the chapter also assesses Whitman's problematic late-career attempts to align this expansive paraontic space of "eligibility" with an expansionist, imperialist American politics. Whitman's difficulty in sustaining his earlier, more radically democratic model, as much as the model itself, frames the remainder of the book.

The next two chapters consider two friends, Jean Toomer and Hart Crane, who wrote amid and against cultural pluralism, an influential movement during the late teens and twenties that responded to post–World War I debates about immigration and race relations by envisioning minority groups making successful appeals for recognition to those already recognized. Though Toomer and Crane, at various times, both qualifiedly supported a version of the cultural pluralist project promoted by a mutual friend, the critic Waldo Frank, their most ambitious work sharply differs from Frank and other cultural pluralists in favor of their shared desire to develop further Whitman's model of sociality outlined in chapter 1.

Toomer's brief alignment with cultural pluralism involved positioning himself as an African American writer in the vanguard of the emerging Harlem Renaissance. His break with that movement resulted in feelings of betrayal from those who sensed that he sought to rescind a racial identity he had embraced. Toomer, however, felt justified in identifying himself as he had prior to the Harlem Renaissance, as an "American" of many racial backgrounds. Indeed, Toomer envisions himself (and others like him) participating in what he felt was the political apotheosis of early Whitman poems like "Crossing Brooklyn Ferry": the marginalized (like "the rest") simply becoming "Americans" not by assimilating to a norm or being recognized as a multiethnic group according to cultural pluralist premises but as a result of Whitman's early social ontology of unlimited eligibility becoming definitive of democracy. Toomer's last major published work, "The Blue Meridian," is a rhetorically extravagant attempt to call into prominence this American race. After surveying an array of poetic idioms, from T. S. Eliot's modernist fragmentation to thirties-era documentary poetics to the identity-based lyrics associated with many Harlem Renaissance poets, Toomer settles on a quasi-Whitmanian prophetic mode, albeit one less subtly indirect and invitational than the one found in "Crossing Brooklyn Ferry." The affirming of the emergent, multiethnic-beyond-recognition "blue" race is, in some ways, moving. But Toomer struggles to formulate in "The Blue Meridian" a politics sufficient for the time before this hybridized American identity broadly manifests itself. In desperation to hasten these political changes, Toomer's speaker sweeps aside long legacies of racial prejudice, including the enslavement of African Americans and Native American genocide, registering those tragedies as steps toward inevitable triumphs to come. Equally unsettling, several passages present the speaker wielding the empowered position of a recognizer who coordinates the development of the American race through a kind of eugenics project that "[d]emolish[es] defectives" (63).[97] Toomer's inhabiting of a stance antithetical to what he intended his American race to exemplify serves as a warning about the difficulty of imagining viable alternatives to the incremental progress promised (if not always delivered) by models of social recognition like cultural pluralism.

Hart Crane similarly wrestled with how to actualize both poetically and politically Whitman's vision of a community defined by unlimited eligibility as he drafted *The Bridge*. The completed work is almost as riven with contradiction as Toomer's "The Blue Meridian," insofar as "The Dance," the pivotal section initiating the triumphs realized in the poem's

26 | Unlimited Eligibility?

conclusion, "Atlantis," identifies the cultural pluralist–style recognition of a Native American with the extinction of Native Americans. Unsettlingly celebratory in tone, the gesture grimly dramatizes how a measure of recognition can come at the cost of subordination. However, the earliest drafts of *The Bridge*, as well as several contemporaneous short lyrics sharing *Bridge*-like imagery, "Possessions" and "Recitative," offer a different, more consistent politics of ontological eligibility grounded in Crane's most ambitious elaborations of what he called the "logic of metaphor." Crane believed that negotiating unexpected "metaphorical interrelationships" and semantic juxtapositions enable a reader and writer to arrive at the equivalent of a "single new word" that had "never before [been] spoken and [was] impossible to actually enunciate but self-evident as an active principle."[98] In spurring such a process, he intended that his lyrics would not simply reflect or expand readers' "previous percepts or preconceptions" but, instead, "shin[e] with a sense of morality essentialized from experience directly."[99] Crane understood the risks in this strategy, as well as the fact that one inevitably constructs meaning, whether of a person or a poem, with reference to existing categories. Crane's lyrics from this period, however, seek to slow this process, not to generate confusion for the sake of confusion, nor to needlessly mix metaphors but to render meaning-making more collaborative, more beautiful, and (he hoped) more ethical. Crane tested this approach by sending "Possessions" to Jean Toomer and "Recitative" to Allen Tate, two friends who differed from him in terms of sexuality (both Tate and Toomer), racial identity (Toomer), and political tendencies (Tate). In both of these lyrics representing elements of a gay man's love life, Crane invites his reader to learn how to "[w]itness," "[r]egard," "[i]nquire," and "[l]ook" without recognizing.[100] But it is in the first drafts of *The Bridge*, written before the project became compromised by cultural pluralism, where Crane displays his highest goal for his art: that this conceptual space promised by the logic of metaphor could become a more expansive paraontic political space defined by an intimacy and equality shared by people unimpeded by disfiguring norms of recognition.

The final two chapters turn to James Merrill and Thylias Moss, who wrote in conversation with late twentieth-century movements that practiced less deferential strategies to achieve political recognition. Rather than appealing to an already empowered class of recognizers as cultural pluralist movements typically had done, many identity politics movements of the late sixties and seventies asserted the power of the mis/unrecognized to work toward group self-recognition, adopting liberationist and cultural nationalist stances in opposition to an America that tolerated and even sanctioned continued injustice. These chapters focus on how group self-recognition projects impacted later attempts to formulate alternative modes of representation within a lyric politics of unlimited eligibility.

James Merrill began his career by writing accomplished, though often "deliberate[ly] obscur[e]" formalist lyrics, at times somewhat in the style of Hart Crane, that intended to reach beyond cultural norms shaping a reader's "intelligence," a strategy that bore some resemblance to his predecessor's hopes for the "logic of metaphor."[101] By the early seventies, however, Merrill had developed in conversation with confessionalism a more breezily casual style, while deepening his confidence in his mastery of poetic form and its capacity to investigate and even intervene in other social forms. It is possible to read Merrill's immense Ouija board–inspired poem *The Changing Light at Sandover* as a remarkably reflexive anthology of lyric forms, half-ironic and half-serious about how the poet's virtuosity garners the attention of the spirit world, which has chosen JM and DJ (the personae of Merrill and his partner, David Jackson), a gay couple, as conduits for a sequence of supposedly world-saving messages spanning a quarter century. Introduced in "The Will," a sonnet sequence that serves as a prelude to *Sandover*, this campy act of divine recognition simulta-neously obscures, authorizes, and interrogates Merrill's more serious act of gay self-recognition (and vice versa). But this sly strategy is sullied by the presence of prejudices shaping the spirit world's alleged directives and revealing Merrill's (and perhaps Jackson's) desire to regulate the recogni-tion of others. For while the Ouija board messages reject hierarchies with regard to sexuality, they nevertheless assert hierarchies with regard to race and ethnicity. But Merrill's last three collections explore a different lyric politics. While early poems often invited readers into a speaker's domestic spaces, later poems like "Clearing the Title" query the speaker's (in this case, JM's) hospitality, decentering him within dramas he cannot control. This shift undermines the desire and capacity to harness a recognizer's power. But Merrill's speakers do not, as a result, simply submit to the misrecognitions of others. In these poems, Merrill develops a distinctly queer comic idiom that parodies not just particular norms that frame the recognition of others but the possibility of such framing altogether. These lyrics argue that recognition must be burlesqued, and they present the resulting comedy as an act of hospitality without a host.

While Merrill only gradually found his way toward a kind of identity politics, Thylias Moss entered university at the apex of the Black Arts

28 | Unlimited Eligibility?

movement and has continued to reimagine her relationship to its legacy. Though her early work is in conversation with the compressed, politically committed lyric idiom that became the movement's flagship literary form, Moss began to develop what she deems her mature poetic practice in *Last Chance for the Tarzan Holler*, a collection that uses the resources of line, syntax, and metaphor much more extravagantly than she had earlier in her career. If recognition finds fulfilment in a kind of epistemological rest and even capture, Moss's limited fork poetics, which she claims to have developed in light of complex systems theory, demonstrates an always mobile, always forking, subdividing, reframing attentiveness to hybridizations beyond recognition, all the while aware that its mapping can be only partial. This poetics can be placed in conversation with contemporary scholarship that sees political recognition operating most powerfully and pervasively through diffuse, often nonagential processes that circulate through networks of social affect. How does one challenge prejudicial misrecognitions when the purveyors of prejudice may not be conscious of doing so? While Moss would agree about the difficulties of combatting the potentially oppressive effects of diffusely distributed power, her conceptualization of limited fork theory attempts to trace these constantly evolving networks or, as she often calls them, "cultures" (a word present in many poem titles in *Tokyo Butter*). Though Moss, in doing so, does expose injustice, her goal is not to establish more just forms of recognition but instead to point toward the fundamental fact that we are all products of and participants within networks of irreducible interminglings. In this way, she argues that limited fork theory attests to how life is always already "mixed (up)," and she hints, as a result, that ontology itself might best be understood as fundamentally "black."[102] Whether Moss's limited fork practice of mapping "cultures" can suggest how such suppressed insights might lead toward more promising protopolitical models is debatable, but her ambitions are clear. If, at their most consistent, Crane's lyric practice sought to slow recognition until it becomes a very different form of looking and Merrill's lyricism burlesques recognition in order to affirm a more hospitable ontological proximity, Moss's mature lyrics seek to sustain a speed that denies recognition's impulse toward mastery in favor of a receptiveness toward always-shifting adjacencies that attest to a fundamental ontological entanglement.

At their best, these writers do not promote naive universalisms that aspire to transcend the histories of identity categories. Indeed, they potentially promote ways of looking at and relating to others that may

Introduction | 29

be more grounded in and responsive to history than those mediated by recognition processes. But realizing and sustaining socialities committed to affirming ontological eligibility without demanding epistemological legibility, as these chapters often show, proves difficult. The coda asks what might make it possible to break the impasse wherein "recognition," by largely working within established social hierarchies, designates a practice that falls short of a democratic ideal, and "eligibility," with its rejection of such hierarchies, designates a democratic ideal difficult to practice under present conditions. Though it would take another book to consider how a range of contemporary poets have responded to such concerns, brief considerations of Mei-mei Berssenbrugge and Juan Felipe Herrera point to how they interrogate the premises and tropes of the modern (lyricized) lyric in order to reimagine how it might expand (rather than attenuate) our ability to conceptualize democratic socialities. The coda, however, focuses on the fifth section of *Citizen*, where Claudia Rankine, in several lineated passages that may distantly echo and revise "Crossing Brooklyn Ferry," implicitly offers a sustained meditation on the future of the American lyric. In one such moment, a voice who "was creating a life study of a monumental first person, a Brahmin first person," an allusion to Boston Brahmin Robert Lowell's 1959 collection *Life Studies*, is contradicted by another voice who ambivalently says, "If you need to feel that way," before advising, "still you are in here and here is nowhere." Then, after a line break, this voice adds, "Join me down here in nowhere," a space described as "a strange beach" associated with "the Atlantic Ocean breaking on our heads," another allusion to Lowell ("Man and Wife") and, inescapably, to the Middle Passage.[103] These lines position American lyrics between the desire to participate in the social structures that promise access to, indeed recognition within, a Brahmin "I" and all of its associated cultural (and literal) capital and a more candid confrontation with a world inflected by the many afterlives of slavery. Given Rankine's direct address, readers must carefully consider how their identities shape and are shaped by the social vectors shaping this conversation, their proximities to it, and the concluding invitation to enter a kind of (para)ontic immanence in an anontic space of oppression. What would it mean to learn from and even participate in the work of such a space? Rankine offers no answers; that is each reader's responsibility. But she does make clear that the future of the American lyric, like the future of America, could be decided here.

Chapter One

"We Fathom You Not—We Love You"

Walt Whitman Resists the
Emerging Politics of Recognition

In the spring of 1874, several students from Tufts College asked Walt Whitman to write a poem for their commencement ceremonies. The result, "Song of the Universal," begins with "the Muse" bestowing upon the speaker—and by extension the speaker's audience—no small task: "Sing me a song no poet yet has chanted, / Sing me the universal" (1–3).[1] Instead of reveling in the myriad material particularities that fill everyday life as Whitman had in his early poetry, his speaker here promotes an escape from the "measureless grossness and the slag," "the bulk, the morbid and the shallow," "the mad Babel-din, the defeaning orgies," and even the "keen-eyed towering science" the graduates may have studied, in favor of a perspective that ascends above "imperfection's murkiest cloud" (5, 25, 36, 10, 32). Only from this elevation (in the "sky," "[h]igh in the purer, happier air") can one sense the "mystic evolution" at work in the world in which "[n]ot the right only [is] justified, [but] what we call evil also [is] justified," even if "[o]nly the good is universal" (15, 31, 20–21, 28). In the final section, Whitman reveals "America" as "the scheme's culmination, its thought and its reality," a claim that clinches his poem's tautological reasoning (42–43). If American history is the unfolding expression of the universal itself, then to sing in praise of the universal necessarily means singing in praise of America. With such sweeping abstractions, Whitman does not ignore his immediate occasion and audience so much as contend that their education inevitably should lead them to participate in a still

32 | Unlimited Eligibility?

higher task, to understand national ambition as eschatological necessity, a mindset aligned with a moment when America's allegedly "manifest destiny" was in fact manifesting itself through violent means across the continent. As Whitman himself likely intended, the poem served more than just its immediate purpose. Within the next week, it was republished in a number of newspapers across the Northeast.[2]

The triumphalist expansionism of "Song of the Universal" reflects Whitman's late career fascination with an Americanized form of Hegelian thinking.[3] Whitman followed the work of a group of philosophers centered in St. Louis, including William Torrey Harris, Henry Clay Brockmeyer, and Denton Snider, who, at times, argued, as Matt Erlin has noted, that the "evolution of the American republic mirrors the history of spirit *in its entirety*" (Erlin's emphasis).[4] With utter confidence in the dialectical power of Hegel's thinking, they analyzed any historical event, no matter how fraught, in terms of a thesis/antithesis/synthesis progression that rendered it comprehensible as a necessary moment in the emergence of a developing American identity.[5] Whitman corresponded with William Torrey Harris in the 1870s and 1880s, and they even met when Whitman was in St. Louis visiting one of his brothers. Harris, on the other hand, had been familiar with Whitman's work since the late 1850s, raising the possibility that before Whitman felt an affiliation with the St. Louis Hegelians, he may have influenced one of them.[6] So it is hardly surprising that Whitman's graduation poem would express sentiments that philosophically parallel Harris and his St. Louis peers.

The poem's culminating paean, however, reveals, if not explicit interest in, then perhaps momentary anxiety about the fate of the local, the individual, and the material amid these grandiose, assimilative tendencies. A single word expresses this fleeting concern: "eligible." Apostrophizing "America," Whitman states,

> Thou too surroundest all,
> Embracing carrying welcoming all, thou too by pathways
>   broad and new,
> To the ideal tendest.
>
> The measur'd faiths of other lands, the grandeurs of the past,
> Are not for thee, but grandeurs of thine own,
> Deific faiths and amplitudes, absorbing, comprehending all,
> All eligible to all.

"We Fathom You Not—We Love You" | 33

> All, all for immortality,
> Love like the light silently wrapping all (45–53)

After evoking the "surround[ing] . . . / [e]mbracing carrying welcoming" and "absorbing" that draws everything into the reiterated "all," Whitman suggests that this inevitable interpellation does not wholly render individuals mere puppets in the service of larger forces. Instead, he promises that "America" will come to designate a place in which "[a]ll [is] eligible to all," a commonwealth in which everything is shared by or at least available to everyone.

Read only in the context provided by "Song of the Universal," such an assertion of "eligib[ility]" rings hollow and undeveloped amid the "amplitudes" and intensely centripetal forces. But it is not a throwaway phrase. It explicitly echoes Whitman's assertion in the 1856 "Poem of Many in One" (later revised and retitled "By Blue Ontario's Shore") that in the still relatively new American "Nation announcing itself," the achievement of a genuinely democratic culture is measured by whether "[a]ll is eligible to all" (9, 27). The earlier poem insists that this "all" does not refer to a totalizing "universal" but instead refers to "any number of supremes," none of which "countervail another any more than one eyesight countervails another" (26). In other words, despite the shared vocabulary of eligibility, the later Whitman envisioned American democracy as the very expression of a singular, totalizing, abstract system within which the particular individual must partake, whereas the earlier Whitman envisioned the reverse, a multicentered, even decentered, materially grounded, social order.[7]

This chapter will argue that the older Whitman's nearly word for word allusion to an earlier poem is a pointed, even anxious, revision not just of his earlier understanding of democracy but of the word at the center of what may be his most radical fusion of poetics and politics. For it is not coincidental that Whitman alludes to a mid-1850s exploration of the concept of eligibility in a late poem articulating an Americanization of Hegelian philosophy. Whitman's most thorough elaboration of eligibility emerges in a notebook filled with drafts from 1855–1856, not long after he likely first grappled with and, at least for a time, turned away from Hegelian thinking. The notebook's exploration of "eligibility," which he deems *the newer better principle / through all my poems,* an affirmation that "I, you, any one [is] eligible to the condition or attributes or advantages of any being, no matter who," immediately follows initial notes for the

34 | Unlimited Eligibility?

poem that would come to be known as "Crossing Brooklyn Ferry."[8] And at the center of "Crossing Brooklyn Ferry," Whitman reveals the political implications of eligibility in a way that makes it possible to read it as an alternative to one of the most contested moments in Hegel's work, his development of the concept of recognition in *The Phenomenology of Spirit*. Affirming your ontological eligibility rather than confirming (or not) your recognizability, the speaker's eroticized address invites the reader not just to "come home" with the speaker but to join with him in a (non) community simply known as "the rest" (89, 78, 82).

What would it mean not just to join this social ontology of unlimited "eligibility" as a reader of "Crossing Brooklyn Ferry" but to understand it as the foundation of democratic praxis? For Whitman to impose answers to such a question would violate the participatory nature of the sociality the poem describes. But he does offer a few hints. In the poem's last lines, a first-person plural speaker indicates "the rest" gaining a collective voice and awakening to political consciousness and action. Whitman grants this "we" the poem's final appeal to the reader and its culminating paean to "eligibility," "We fathom you not—we love you," a phrase that might stand as the protopolitical core of Whitman's poetics at its most radically democratic (130). The chapter's conclusion evaluates the potency of this model not just by considering how Whitman later adopts an antithetical view of "eligibility" aligned with St. Louis Hegelian–style imperialism and much more easily aligned with the developing trajectory of lyricization but by looking toward how this line of thought inflects the cultural pluralism of the twenties.

Eligibility and the 1850s

Whitman developed his aesthetics of "eligibility" in response to the political chaos of the mid-1850s, a moment when a multitude of factors, many long in development, led to what Christian Samito has called a "crisis in citizenship": "Formerly marginal arguments on both sides of the debate over slavery began to take central stage, while social transformations such as industrialization, urbanization, and immigration unevenly affected different sections of the country, exacerbated strains, and generated additional questions and concerns of their own."[9] No single political dispute brought these issues together more dramatically than the Kansas/Nebraska Act of 1854, which effectively negated the Missouri Compromise by allowing "popular sovereignty" to determine whether or not a territory would permit or prohibit slavery. Approval of the act led to sweeping changes affecting both major political parties. The Whig Party splintered and eventually collapsed due to sharp disagreements between Northern and Southern members concerning the act's stance on slavery. The Democratic Party split. Most Northern Democrats who had supported the act were thrown out of office in the next election. With the party now even more dominated by Southerners than it had been, the remaining Democrats who had opposed the act began looking for a new party.[10] Adding to the turmoil, the Know Nothing party emerged as a political power as a result of the sharp rise in nativist and anti-Catholic sentiment spreading throughout the country following increased immigration especially from Ireland and Germany. The prejudice directed toward Catholics served as only the most prominent example of a widespread suspicion that many immigrants could not and would not assimilate to an Anglo-Protestant American identity and value system.[11]

A new equilibrium gradually began to appear, as Eric Foner describes: "'Fusion' movements uniting Whigs, antislavery Democrats, Free Soilers, and advocates of prohibition and nativism swept to victory in nearly every free state. But the balance of power within these coalitions varied enormously. In some states, the new Know-Nothing party, dedicated to curtailing the influence of immigrants and Roman Catholics in American politics, emerged as the primary force. In others, antislavery advocates, some calling their new organization the Republican party, dominated."[12] But much remained muddled, and less than a year later, in 1855, Abraham Lincoln, not yet a member of the new Republican Party, explained to his friend Joshua Speed, "I think I am a whig; but others say there are no whigs, and that I am an abolitionist." Lincoln scorned the nativist Know Nothings, stating that if they "get control" the phrase "all men are created equal" would mean "all mean are created equal, except negroes, and foreigners, and catholics."[13] But he also knew that Northern politicians could not afford to offend the Know Nothings, since their involvement "would be essential to any successful antislavery coalition."[14]

Though David S. Reynolds has distilled the effect of these sociopolitical upheavals on Whitman in terms of the pithy formulation "party collapse, poetic growth," this artistic growth process, along with his search for a broad, receptive audience, took time.[15] The 1855 first edition of *Leaves of Grass* drew from political oratory, musical theater, oracular transcendentalism, and various slang dialects, an array of discursive idioms that would have

36 | Unlimited Eligibility?

been familiar to many people but presented it in a verse form that, with its experiments in lineation, structure, and punctuation, had few precedents and in a volume that buried the name of its author in the middle of its longest poem while presenting him in a highly unconventional frontispiece. Commentary on the first edition frequently puzzled over Whitman's expansion of poetic discourse. Charles Henry Dana, in the first extant review, notes that the "language is too frequently reckless and indecent though this appears to arise from a naive unconsciousness rather than from an impure mind." Those who moved past content and toward formal considerations struggled to position Whitman's poem in relation to other norms with regard to diction, lineation, rhythm, and musicality. Many critics expressed varying degrees of fascination and bewilderment without offering an endorsement of the volume; a minority of critics denounced it.[16] On the one hand, this scenario reflects Cristanne Miller's observation that "antebellum American verse cherished originality" and even "wildness."[17] Whitman's work, for example, occasionally was compared to Martin Farquhar Tupper's proto–free verse volume *Proverbial Philosophy*.[18] On the other hand, Christopher Beach reminds us that "the most popular poets in America in the first half of the [nineteenth] century were . . . Byron and Scott, and the most representative anthologized poems of the 1840s and 1850s were by and large watered-down versions of various English Romantics."[19] So it is not surprising that there were limits to what even the sympathetic critics found legible and acceptable within Whitman's volume.

Critics particularly struggled with the way Whitman's refusal to be confined by poetic norms paralleled and amplified his refusal to be confined by political norms.[20] Anticipating this difficulty, Whitman's three anonymous self-reviews were acts of self-promotion, seeking to provoke those likely to condemn his poetry as much as those likely to concur, and attempts to outline how his politics and poetics coincide. Each of these reviews shamelessly promises the reader transgressive thrills. Each emphasizes the author's membership within a working class typically excluded from the arts. And each situates Whitman's literary nationalism in terms of a patriotism that unambiguously rejects Know Nothing prejudices.[21] These self-reviews, furthermore, tie Whitman's politics to the subjectivity projected in his poetry. In the September 29, 1855, self-review published in the *Brooklyn Daily-Times*, Whitman provocatively asks critics to attend to his speaker's "egotism": "There can be no two thoughts on Walt Whitman's egotism. That is what he steps out of the crowd and turns and faces them for. Mark, critics! for otherwise is not used for you the key that leads to the use of the other keys to this well enveloped yet terribly in earnest man." This feature of Whitman's poetry did not go unnoticed. George Eliot in the June 7, 1856, issue of the *Leader*, for example, puzzled over the "wild, irregular, unrhymed, almost unmetrical 'lengths'" and "all attracting egotism—an eternal presence of the individual soul of Walt Whitman in all things, yet in such wise that this one soul shall be presented as a type of all human souls whatsoever." A reviewer simply listed as "D. W." in the November 1856 issue of the *Canadian Journal* similarly attested to how the volume was "full of egotism, extravagance, and spasmodic eccentricities of all sorts."[22]

What these reviewers missed that would be central not just to the 1855 poems but to the slightly later "Crossing Brooklyn Ferry" was the way that Whitman almost paradoxically sought to use this "egotism" to promote a democratic politics. The self-review published in the September 1855 issue of the *United States Review* emphasizes how the speaker projects a "Union [that is] always calm and impregnable," stating "with [a] calm voice" amid the political upheavals of the mid-1850s that "[a]melioration is my lesson . . . and progress is my lesson and the lesson of all things." American democracy, he assures his reader, is "the only stable form of politics at present upon the earth."[23] In the October 1855 self-review published in the *American Phrenological Journal*, Whitman once again highlights his speaker's "voice," describing it as "pregnant . . . with the ideas and practice of American politics," ready to intervene in his historical moment, "[a]n age greater than the proudest of the past . . . without one lyric voice to seize its greatness."

Such statements might tempt a reader to link this "egotism" with the "lyric voice" and associate Whitman with conventions of speaker-centered lyrics as they became understood by the mid-twentieth century. This is perhaps especially the case when one considers how neither race nor ethnicity play a role in a poem like "Crossing Brooklyn Ferry," despite it having been written amid ever-intensifying debates over slavery and immigration, topics that deeply inflect Whitman's notebooks. However, it is only partly true that the desire to transcend time and space in "Crossing Brooklyn Ferry" yield an ahistorical abstraction that anticipates the lyricized lyric subject taught, for example, by the New Critics of the mid-twentieth century.

Virginia Jackson explains how "over the last three centuries, lyric has shifted its meaning from adjective to noun, from a quality in poetry to a category that can seem to include nearly all verse."[24] This process,

38 | Unlimited Eligibility?

wherein "the lyric" becomes "a vehicle of personal expression," a "transform[ation]" of what had been "an idea attached to various verse genres into an aesthetic ideal that eclipsed or embraced other verse genres," was still "uneven[ly]" adopted in the "nineteenth century."[25] Analysis of extant nineteenth-century reviews of Whitman's poetry, for example, reveal that, while "lyric" was not used as a noun to describe Whitman's work with great frequency, it was used as often as other terms (like "ode" or "ballad" or "sonnet" or "elegy") it would eclipse as lyricization progressed.[26] Jackson captures this balance with regard to Whitman, when she explains (in relation to the 1859 poem that came to be called "Out of the Cradle Endlessly Rocking") how his poetry evidences an "ongoing exchange between poets and readers and editors and printers and parodists and other writers and readers . . . that . . . was both pre-lyricized and part and parcel of lyricization," making him both "Emerson's vision of an original American genius" and "a poet who counted on his audience to recognize a derivative discourse ['Whitman's riff on the ode'] and to play along with his fashionably unoriginal uses of it."[27]

Indeed, Whitman wrote after the emergence but before the normalization of the modern, abstract, ahistorical understanding of lyric, a moment when it might have been possible for a savvy poet, if not to name this trend, then, at least tacitly, to sense a range of options and strategically seek to position one's poetry in relation to them. Yet Whitman's development in 1855–1856, a moment when his drafting notebooks reveal how his intense reflection on contemporary politics shaped his evolving poetics, cannot be fully mapped along a spectrum spanning "pre-lyriciz[ation]" to "part and parcel of lyricization." This is neither to suggest that he was uninfluenced by predecessors and contemporaries who wrote in a wide variety of established genres, nor to exempt him from the emerging impacts of lyricization. Instead, it is to suggest that, even as he was shaped by such trends and their political corollaries, he also explored, at least for a time, a distinctly different path. Even if Whitman's poetry and politics eventually began to collapse into the false universalism of the modern lyric Jackson describes, his early work's pursuit of a radically democratizing unlimited "eligibility" may still be usefully provocative.

This pivotal moment in Whitman's poetic and political development was spurred by disappointment. Despite clever self-promotion and canny attempts to balance the familiar and the unfamiliar, the first edition of *Leaves of Grass* sold poorly.[28] However, Whitman's frustration was

"We Fathom You Not—We Love You" | 39

sufficiently offset by attention from critics on both sides of the Atlantic that he quickly forged ahead with a much expanded second edition that tries to remediate this disconnection with puzzled readers in a number of ways, most obviously by giving hitherto untitled poems titles and poems simply named "Leaves of Grass" more specific titles, all of which include the word "poem." He also includes, as Mark Bauerlein observes, a series of new poems clarifying how readers ought "to dispense with their cultivated scholarly, aesthetic, and intellectual habits and to imbibe the volume's satiating, enlivening 'speech of the proud and melancholy races and of all races who aspire.'"[29] The country's unresolved political crises fueled these interests during the election year of 1856. An unpublished tract, "The Eighteenth Presidency," shows that, even if the speaker of Whitman's poems projected "calm" and confidence, Whitman himself was furious about the state of American politics and unsure of how to respond.[30] As always, he brought these political concerns into the drafting notebooks he used to compose his poems. A nearly word-for-word portion of "The Eighteenth Presidency" appears in the "George Walker" notebook, which includes various informal jottings as well as more focused drafts of poems likely written between July 1855 and September 1856, roughly the time between the publication of the first and second editions of *Leaves of Grass*.[31] The major poetic product of these ruminations is his most elusive and ambitious metapoem, "Crossing Brooklyn Ferry," a work intended to solve one of the most pressing problems unresolved by the first edition: How could he use his "calm voice" to encourage more readers and reviewers to be not just provoked by but to engage with his poetry in such a way that they have to engage with his politics?

Before Whitman begins drafting "Crossing Brooklyn Ferry," he explores two very different models of democratic polity in the "George Walker" notebook. In a series of paragraphs for what appears to be a speech, Whitman directly addresses the fears that increasingly paralyzed America during the mid-1850s.

> Gentlemen, I will be very plain with you.—I see in my country many great qualities.—I see in America not merely the home of Americans, but the home of the needy and down kept races of the whole earth.—I know just as well as you the terrible effects of ages of degradation and caste.—It is a real truth—it is a black and bloody lesson. . . . It is [also] mentioned that the Irish and German and other foreigners

40 | Unlimited Eligibility?

> mix in our politics.—Gentlemen with perfect respect I say you you [*sic*] can think what you choose about this;—It is a credit to men and no disgrace to them to take an eager interest in politics.[32]

Here Whitman rebukes Know Nothing party concerns that waves of immigrants, like those from Ireland and Germany, would undermine American culture and politics. Debates regarding slavery that had become ever more contentious in the years after the passage of the Fugitive Slave Act and the Kansas/Nebraska Act surely inform his comments about a "black and bloody lesson" learned by observing "the terrible effects of ages of degradation and caste." But Whitman's speech does not merely indicate his political opinions. Its rhetoric tests an approach for intervening in these issues. Whitman strategically slips into the passive voice, ventriloquizing what others have said ("It is mentioned . . ."). This gesture is crucial for it sets up a transformation of an act of political rejection, shaming and excluding "foreigners" on the basis of their efforts to "mix in our politics," into an act of political recognition, affirming that it is instead "a credit . . . and no disgrace" for "Irish and German and other foreigners . . . to take an eager interest [and, Whitman tacitly suggests, participate] in politics." Whitman's boldness in supporting these excluded constituencies is enabled by his subject position. He asserts himself as someone who unambiguously holds the rights and privileges of American citizenship and thus is imbued with the political authority and agency capable of correcting the nativist discourse used by some of his fellow Americans. As someone who is politically recognized, he feels politically able to recognize, to assess whether and to what degree "Irish and German and other foreigners" should hold the full privileges of citizenship and personhood, and to begin to absorb and assimilate them within a more inclusive "America [that is] not merely the home of Americans, but the home of the needy and down kept races of the whole earth."[33] But despite its hortatory swagger, Whitman never finishes the speech. He cuts it off after these sentences and goes on to comment dejectedly about how American sociopolitical discourse, as well literary discourse, has been transplanted from other sources rather than emerging from America itself, rendering it insufficient to the country's needs: "Not only American literature, but the structures of American social intercourse . . . are growing up in total severance from the roots and trunk and branches."[34]

"We Fathom You Not—We Love You" | 41

Few people responded to Whitman's first attempt to develop a more American poetic idiom, so he begins to reconsider, here, the very foundations of his art. In this same notebook, across from lines for what would become "Crossing Brooklyn Ferry," Whitman introduces his emerging, primary aesthetic goal: "*The newer better principle / through all my poems.*—(dramas? novels?, compositions of any sort.) / Present only great characters, good, loving characters.—/ Present the best phases of / character, that any one, man or woman is eligible to."[35] Whitman reiterates and clarifies this agenda a few pages later, explaining that the "Idea to pervade largely / [must be] Eligibility—I, you, any one eligible to the condition or attributes or advantages of any being, no matter who."[36] Such a statement is fascinating because of the insight it gives into the political intervention Whitman wished his poetry would make in the increasingly socially fractured mid-1850s. For Whitman, here, grounds his work on an affirmation of the ontic equality of individuals and comes close to raising questions (that become clearer in "Crossing Brooklyn Ferry" itself) about their discrete divisibility, insofar as everyone's "conditions or attributes or advantages" are "eligib[le]" to everyone. The notebook is also fascinating in how it explicitly unveils what Whitman chose to leave unclear, or at least implicit, in "Crossing Brooklyn Ferry" ("What I promis'd without mentioning it, have you not accepted?"), as it goes on to explain the strategy behind the coy guardedness of the poem's speaker (99). Simply announcing in the poem that "any one" has this "eligibility" would not be as effective as enabling people to sense it within themselves and among one another. So Whitman crafts an "indirect mode" of argument involving an intricately staged sequence of addresses intended to make a reader "wristle" (*sic*) with him since "the good comes by wristling for it."[37] But what does Whitman mean by "eligibility" and why does it become central not just to "Crossing Brooklyn Ferry" but to the politics underlying his poetics?

It is here that Whitman turns away from the process of political recognition he explored in the speech only a few pages earlier in his notebook. Rather than relying on the already recognized and empowered becoming persuaded to share this status by expanding it to others, a model that may (or may not) gradually adjust present social hierarchies while sustaining a hierarchical social system (unrecognized/misrecognized/recognized/recognizers), Whitman in "Crossing Brooklyn Ferry" begins to develop a social ontology, an understanding of being in terms

42 | Unlimited Eligibility?

of being with others, that he deems more deeply democratic. The poem begins by situating its speaker in a scenario in which they must feel their way toward these questions before explicitly involving the reader, not by directly confronting mid-1850s political issues but by raising the questions of sociality upon which those issues were being decided. In this way, the rejection of recognition-driven models, Whitman hopes, emerges out of the reader's own life experience of having felt a measure of misrecognition—and a desire to experience a more democratic way of being together.

"What Is It Then between Us?" Enacting Eligibility

"Crossing Brooklyn Ferry" begins with the speaker's "curio[sity]" about his fellow commuters on board the ferry boats shuttling between Brooklyn and Manhattan. One might expect this curiosity to be sated by an epistemologically assertive relation seeking to recognize and assimilate what he sees, but that is not what happens.

> Flood-tide below me! I see you face to face!
> Clouds of the west—sun there half an hour high—I see
> you also face to face.
>
> Crowds of men and women attired in the usual costumes,
> how curious you are to me!
> On the ferry-boats the hundreds and hundreds that cross,
> returning home, are more curious to me than you suppose,
> And you that shall cross from shore to shore years hence
> are more to me, and more in my meditations, than you
> might suppose. (1–5)

Amid the speaker's exclamatory enthusiasm, there is confusion. As he commutes home in the evening, after a day's work, he celebrates an intimacy—or at least a "face to face" relation—between himself and nature that he does not feel between himself and the other "curious" and "costume[d]" people who make up the "[c]rowds." This fascination with but also puzzlement over his fellow humans inflects his mode of address. While "Crossing Brooklyn Ferry" eventually does wish to involve the reader in a protopolitical project, the opening sections very cautiously

"We Fathom You Not—We Love You" | 43

build toward direct appeals. The speaker appears to address a "you" that first refers to the river, clouds, and sun and then comes to encompass both contemporary and future "[c]rowds" as well as the reader, but the statements actually are directed inward "to me." The speaker addresses himself, as if he realizes that he is not yet prepared to (or even knows how to) address his fellow commuters, much less the readers he already imagines.

As the second section begins, the speaker continues to keep his distance, both physically and rhetorically, but this does not prevent him from speculating in greater detail about how his fellow travelers "are more to me." He envisions a "simple, compact, well-join'd scheme" from which he draws "impalpable sustenance," a phrasing that might seem to suggest the speaker taking nourishment "from all things" in an objectifying, even vampiric manner (6–7).[38] But such a reading is undermined by how his experiencing of the scheme is not akin to mastery but a shared "disintegrat[ion]" ("myself disintegrated, every one disintegrated yet part of the scheme") (7). This is the first sign of a fundamental, yet still enigmatic, ontic immanence that somehow makes the constituent elements of our lives and even our selves available to, perhaps even eligible for, one another. After praising the "similitudes" linking "the past and . . . future" to the "glories" he sees and hears around him in the present, he locates himself on the periphery of this cosmology: "The current rushing so swiftly and swimming with me far away, / The others that are to follow me, the ties between me and them, / The certainty of others, the life, love, sight, hearing of others" (8–12). This imagery associates the shared ferry ride with the broader, metaphysical "scheme," a term that may seem to foreshadow how "Song of the Universal" pronounces "America / [as] . . . the scheme's culmination," but "Crossing Brooklyn Ferry" neither here nor anywhere advocates a triumphalist nationalism (42–43). Furthermore, the connection between the ferry ride and the "scheme" is merely suggested as a metaphor to be completed (or not) by the reader, since Whitman withholds the copula linking the tenor and vehicle (i.e., linking the current with the generations of "others"). In this way, he prepares readers not just to be recipients of his text but in a very real way coparticipants with him in its composition. Whitman's speaker finds himself in a scheme he cannot master and refuses to impose yet wants to evoke and encourage others to participate within.

This strategy for affirming ontological proximity to others without asserting epistemological mastery becomes more elaborate in the first

44 | Unlimited Eligibility?

of two great catalogs featured in the poem, extending from the end of section 2 through section 3 before being summarized in section 4. Peter Coviello has noted how the "terrific speed with which . . . [Whitman] darts and charges through this extended range of rhetorics and modes of self-presentation" in his catalogs "attests to the vastness of his perspective."[39] But though one senses this "dart[ing] and charg[ing]" in the catalogs within "Crossing Brooklyn Ferry," the grammatical, syntactical, and rhetorical strategies involved do not ultimately conceal a lurking epistemological possessiveness. The speaker begins in a predictive mode, enumerating all the sights that "[o]thers will" see that he also has seen (13–16). Then beginning with the poem's first moment of genuinely direct address ("I am with you . . ."), he shifts to a peculiarly expansive present tense that grammatically renders distances of time obsolete, encompassing not only his contemporaries but "men and women of a generation, or ever so many generations hence" (21). Whitman slyly undercuts the speaker's assertiveness in this sweeping gesture by syntactically privileging "you" as he analogizes the various "similitudes" that make the reader's life like the speaker's ("Just as you . . . I . . ."), but the speaker soon sets aside these framing devices (8, 22–26). Neither the "I" nor the "you" appear for twenty lines (28–48). One might argue that the "I" and the "you" are simply understood and reasserted in line 49: "These and all else were to me the same as they are to you." Yet Whitman's removal of the pronouns combined with the sheer length of these lines on the page as well as the breadth of what they describe (people, animals, objects, sights, sounds, etc.) diminishes the speaker. He "s[ees]" and "look[s]" for a few more lines but then even that framing device drops away after line 38. The poem becomes less and less subject-centered and the speaker happily recedes into a progressively larger world intersecting not just readers (whom he addresses as "you") but those other others a step further away, hitherto merely "look'd" upon. Once again, the poem models a movement away from an epistemological orientation and toward an ontological state of mutually being-with.

This reading of the poem's first great catalog conflicts with Tenney Nathanson who sees an initially "assimilat[ive]" tendency thwarted, leaving a "poet . . . ill at ease" and Roger Gilbert who describes the fading of the "I" as "a kind of grammatical death."[40] Wai Chee Dimock, on the other hand, argues almost the opposite, contending that the pervasive "substitutability and interchangeability" of objects in Whitman's catalogues undermines difference and performs through the speaker's "syntactic

"We Fathom You Not—We Love You" | 45

dictate . . . a kind of epistemological violence."[41] But such claims, whether finding the catalog driven by a dying or a dictatorial "I," oddly assume that Whitman can imagine only epistemologically possessive forms of subjectivity, whereas the poem begins by investigating precisely the opposite.[42] "Crossing Brooklyn Ferry" dramatizes a disarming of the speaker's epistemological drives by modeling a deepening appreciation for "the same" that does not define an abstract, universal humanness but instead evokes a plurality of shared proximities in order to imagine "near[ness]" (51). In this way, the speaker affirms an other's eligibility rather than seeking to confirm an other's recognizability, presuming only that he and you are one of the crowd that must find ways to live together. Such a sentiment surely speaks to the political unrest of the 1850s, but Whitman also makes explicit larger ambitions. He hopes that the poem can serve, across the boundaries of time ("scores or hundreds of years") and space ("place avails not"), as a shared conceptual realm, which one can return to when necessary in order to recover a sense of one's (and also others') "eligibility" to belong (55–56).

This need becomes vivid in section 5, which begins by highlighting how the speaker's caution in pursuing this basis for sociality spirals into self-doubt, as he himself starts to feel ineligible. The immense catalog that began with the speaker's confident expression of being "with you" concludes with an inquiry of "What is it then between us?" (21, 54). Still "among crowds," the speaker finds "curious abrupt questionings stir[ring] within" him (60, 59). The word "curious" echoes the first lines of the poem, a repetition that tacitly questions not just whether the speaker has achieved the longed-for being-with others but whether the speaker is at ease with himself. This pivotal moment finds the speaker repeating the word "body" three times in two lines, as if he is at the brink of being disgusted by his own desires (63–64). This sense of shame, which becomes the topic of section 6, is more than just an expression of regret over particular words or actions. It is pervasive and oddly unfocused. Though the speaker links these negative traits implicitly to the "identity" he "receiv'd" from his "body," it is not clear what he thinks this identity is (63). Could this ambiguity be due to the fact that he, like his culture, lacks a normative term for who he is or, at least, a nonpathologizing way to describe his desires? More than a century and a half after the poem was first published, it is tempting to speculate that we may see here a glimpse into the life of a man attracted to men before the development of the term "homosexual." And traces of evidence at the periphery of the poem suggest a specifically sexual dimension to the speaker's shaming.[43] Some scholars, like David Reynolds, have speculated that the absence of modern sexual taxonomies resulted in a measure of freedom for sexual minorities in antebellum America.[44] But when read in this way, "Crossing Brooklyn Ferry" emphasizes the opposite: the extreme, baffling discomfort of the speaker, who feels not only as if he does not know himself but as if even "the best . . . [he] had done" was "blank and suspicious" (67).

At this pivotal moment, the poem poses, albeit (as Whitman's note-books advise) "indirect[ly]," its central question. What the speaker seems to need most here is social recognition, an assurance not just of what and who he is but that what and who he is is acceptable and socially legible. But if such recognition is necessary, then is the later Whitman (anticipated by the brief political speech in the "George Walker" notebook conferring recognition on immigrants) correct and the earlier Whitman wrong? Does unlimited eligibility amount to a pleasant but impractical fantasy? As "Song of the Universal" shows, Whitman's post–Civil War poetry draws from Hegelian thinking, especially, according to Cody Marrs, Hegel's "conceptualization of the nation-state" and his "dialectical theory of historical development."[45] Yet what if Whitman earlier in his career, when localized concerns figured more prominently in his poetry, also evaluated how more local, intersubjective forces drive Hegel's theorizing about historical development? The remainder of "Crossing Brooklyn Ferry," especially when it is read in light of its historical context and alongside its author's notebooks, suggests that this may have been the case. This initial engagement with Hegel's thought in the 1850s may have galvanized in Whitman a sense of how he differed from the German philosopher and contributed to his development of a form of sociality affirming ontological eligibility rather than requiring epistemological recognizability (as Hegel's does) as the basis of American democracy.

The next section begins by considering the evidence for this pos-sibility before examining the very roots of Hegelian intersubjectivity as described in the *Phenomenology of Spirit* not to insist that Whitman necessarily read that specific text but to make clear how Whitman in the mid-1850s shared Hegel's interest in identifying the roots of complex political phenomena yet came to different conclusions.[46] And in clari-fying how Hegelian recognition contrasts with the politics of unlimited eligibility characteristic of "Crossing Brooklyn Ferry," the speaker's crisis in section 6 and its resolution come into focus.

"The Rest": Whitman's Democratic Sociality in Microcosm

Floyd Stovall argues that Whitman "got his first taste of Hegel's philosophy in Gostwick's *German Literature* or in Hedge's *Prose Writers of Germany* about 1854 and later developed his own ideas of it from more extensive reading, perhaps including some of Hegel's own writing," assessments that David Reynolds more recently has confirmed.[47] Stovall goes on to claim that "there seem to be more ideas akin to German philosophy in the 1856 edition [of *Leaves of Grass*] than in the 1855 edition."[48] Gostwick's anthology offers "in a concise and popular form, a general view of the Literature of the German people, from the earliest to the latest times."[49] Though the overviews of even major writers are quite brief (often only a few pages), they are pithy and point readers to primary texts for further consideration. Gostwick contextualizes Hegel within idealist philosophy as a thinker who develops a dialectical "process of reason . . . found not only in the human mind, but throughout external nature" driven by "oppositions which are at once produced and resolved" as "unity" is shown to "pervad[e] apparent opposition." This process has social dimensions shaping "individuals and communities." Even amid much "error[,] . . . all forms of government are so many finite and imperfect attempts to embody the true idea of developing in unity the greatest and best faculties of mankind."[50] In Hedge's anthology, a translation of Hegel's "Introduction to the Philosophy of History" offered prospective readers like Whitman an extensive elaboration of how this teleological trajectory should inform the study of history itself.[51] So it is not just possible but entirely plausible and even probable that Whitman in the mid-1850s built a working knowledge of the basic contours of Hegel's thought. And insofar as "Crossing Brooklyn Ferry," a poem written at that time, investigates the social consequences of intersubjective psychodynamics, it can be clarified in comparison and contrast to Hegel's understanding of such topics.

Hegel understands recognition as the culmination of a larger process of a self coming to consciousness of itself, but he argues that this process is fundamentally social from its beginning, insofar as self-consciousness is initiated by an encounter with an other and, in time, builds toward mutual recognition of self and other, a trajectory that he believes ultimately will play out on a macrocosmic scale. This development, at least initially, may seem asocial (or antisocial) as much as social, insofar as it is riven by tensions and conflicts that ostensibly build toward larger resolutions.

48 | Unlimited Eligibility?

Drawn "out of itself" by "another," nascent self-consciousness "finds itself as an other being." This multivalent act is an affirmation and cancellation of both the other and the nascent self.[52] It is an affirmation of the other insofar as the nascent self acknowledges the presence of another, parallel self. It is also a cancellation of the other since this parallel being is deemed significant only insofar as it grants the nascent self a measure of "certain[ty]" in itself. In such a moment, the nascent self "does not see the other as an essential being, but in the other sees [only] its own self." By "supersed[ing]" the other in this way, the nascent self affirms itself. But since the other had been rendered indistinguishable from itself, this "supersed[ing]" also is a self-cancelling.

Hegel is fascinated by this paradoxical moment. For it suggests, at the very first stages of social relation, a rule that Hegel finds definitive of all modes of sociality, no matter how complex: dominating an other always comes at cost to one's self. Since one does not wish to sustain this unpleasant state, there is always impetus to find an alternative way to engage others. Hegel describes this alternative in terms of a self being not just "for itself" but "being-for-self of the other." When both parties arrive in such a state, they achieve mutual recognition, or put more precisely, "they recognize themselves as mutually recognizing one another."[53] Robert R. Williams parses Hegel's reasoning here by emphasizing how "[t]he recognition that is needed cannot be coerced or controlled. Mutual-reciprocal recognition is possible only if coercion is renounced. The authentic 'cancellation' of other-being means that the other is not eliminated but allowed to go free and affirmed. But if the other is allowed to go free, this means that it is affirmed, not simply in its identity, but also in its difference."[54] Authentic recognition, thus, entails a simultaneous appreciation for an other's similarity and difference from one's self, a state of relation defined by a mutual granting of freedom.

Hegel famously goes on to apply these ideas to the relationship between a master and a slave. Following the model he had just established, he insists that the relationship between the two is inherently unstable and unsatisfactory even for the master, not in spite of the difference in power between the two but because of it. For though the master is recognized by the slave, it is an inauthentic form of recognition due to it being demanded rather than given freely. The master's self-consciousness is not fully realized due to his dependence upon (and thus vulnerability to) the slave upon whose work he relies. Thus the master, in a sense, is the slave, and the slave, in a sense, is the master. The "outcome," in other words, "is a recognition that is one-sided and unequal," an ultimately unacceptable state for both master and slave.[55] This leads Hegel to an extraordinary claim. Though the master/slave relation, a dynamic typically defined by the master's violent plunder of the slave's knowledge, life, and work, would seem to strongly favor one party over another, it ultimately *must* develop toward genuine mutual recognition resulting in greater freedom for both parties.

Hegel narrates this process in abstraction as a sequence of psychological states, but he understood that in history it could take a great deal of time to play out as a sequence of confrontations and negotiations, some explicit and some implicit, any one of which might yield a greater or lesser degree of recognition and freedom. Nevertheless, according to Hegel, the inexorable trend is toward more of both. However, for individuals enduring oppression in the present this teleological confidence offers only cold comfort. Furthermore, the doubleness Hegel emphasizes—the mutual vulnerability shared by both master and slave that ostensibly serves as the engine toward their eventual mutual recognition—also raises serious questions. For the person inhabiting the slave subject position is almost always much more vulnerable than the person inhabiting the master subject position, a fact that makes resistance more difficult. Though large-scale rebellions do occur, they are relatively rare and by no means assured of success. Challenging norms typically occurs in more subtle and less systematic ways, resulting in changes that typically render only minute degrees of additional recognition. With less to gain and more to lose, the person (or persons) inhabiting the master subject position has (or have) greater control over how recognition is distributed and how long the process of achieving anything like genuine mutual recognition takes, if indeed it is ever achieved. Thus, despite his optimistic, even triumphalistic tendencies, Hegel offers the prospect of painful gradualism. While this incrementalist approach may or may not serve as an illuminating analysis of certain historical narratives, it presents a moral problem insofar as it imagines a long road toward the freedom and mutuality that Hegel associates with justice.

Even such a brief overview of the psychosocial dynamics of recognition exposes what is at stake in section 6 of "Crossing Brooklyn Ferry," which is quoted in its entirety below due to how it serves as the pivotal moment in the poem's argument. Here we may begin to see why Whitman never completed the political speech in the George Walker notebook. For the poem furthers, with much greater sophistication than

50 | Unlimited Eligibility?

the speech, his study of the dynamics of recognition, offering an analysis that can be compared and contrasted with Hegel's.

Given how the notebook entries that led to this poem concerned how recognition of ethnic and racial identity categories determined whether one would be socially included or excluded, it seems a missed opportunity for Whitman not to engage with those topics here. But foregrounding the speaker's guilt, his pietistic sense of having violated Christian values, may be strategic. It may reflect Whitman (or his poetic proxy) candidly acknowledging his stakes in the sociality gradually staged over the course of "Crossing Brooklyn Ferry," how he himself has felt un/misrecognized.

> It is not upon you alone the dark patches fall,
> The dark threw its patches down upon me also,
> The best I had done seem'd to me blank and suspicious,
> My great thoughts as I supposed them, were they not in
>   reality meagre?
> Nor is it you alone who know what it is to be evil,
> I am he who knew what it was to be evil,
> I too knitted the old knot of contrariety,
> Blabb'd, blush'd, resented, lied, stole, grudg'd,
> Had guile, anger, lust, hot wishes I dared not speak,
> Was wayward, vain, greedy, shallow, sly, cowardly, malignant,
> The wolf, the snake, the hog, not wanting in me,
> The cheating look, the frivolous word, the adulterous wish,
>   not wanting,
> Refusals, hates, postponements, meanness, laziness, none of
>   these wanting,
> Was one with the rest, the days and haps of the rest,
> Was call'd by my nighest name by clear loud voices of
>   young men as they saw me approaching or passing,
> Felt their arms on my neck as I stood, or the negligent
>   leaning of their flesh against me as I sat,
> Saw many I loved in the street or ferry-boat or public
>   assembly, yet never told them a word,
> Lived the same life with the rest, the same old laughing,
>   gnawing, sleeping,
> Play'd the part that still looks back on the actor or actress,
> The same old role, the role that is what we make it, as
>   great as we like,
> Or as small as we like, or both great and small. (65–85)

The expansive interconnectedness evoked by the poem, wherein "time nor place—distance avails not," here, cedes to a memory when distance did prevail (20). Though the speaker continues to address "you," he recalls the experience of feeling "alone" and, in this loneliness, engulfed by the conviction that even his "best" was "blank and suspicious," even his "great thoughts" merely "meagre." At the center of this section, which itself is roughly the midpoint of the poem, the speaker descends into a litany of negative character traits, one of the darkest passages in all of Whitman's work. The list reveals how a failure to fulfill social norms stirred the "curious abrupt questionings" noted in section 5 that caused him to ask "What is it then between us?" (59, 54). It also reveals a corresponding expression of his deference and even subservience toward those who do fulfill, enforce, and, indeed, recognize according to such norms. The resulting sense of disgrace and dishonor generated an alienation from society and self so great that it seemed inconceivable that anyone would even want to be with him. This sense of alienation from society and self even shapes the poem's structure. The speaker presents this list in shorter lines of nearly uniform length, even including end (rather than initial) repetition, lending the verse an uncharacteristic sense of closure and constraint, as if the form of the poem itself is gripped by the self-doubt that had gripped the speaker.

Despite the bravado characterizing the earlier pronouncements about a social ontology beyond epistemological categorizing, the speaker's memory of his past state of mind strikingly parallels Hegel's description of a person lacking recognition. Though the speaker's experiences are not, of course, equivalent to the deprivations imposed on an enslaved person, his sense of being "fearful . . . [as if his] whole being has been seized with dread" and "quite unmanned . . . [as if] everything solid and stable has been shaken to its foundations" reinforces Hegel's claim that these psychodynamics inflect the full range of social relations. Such a disorienting sense of self results from one's "essential reality" being defined by subjection to another's authority rather than having one's identity defined by a reciprocal relation of mutual recognition.[56] And Hegel believes that the latter relation can only be achieved after passing through the former. For it is out of such deprivation that a sense of self eventually comes to be asserted, a demand for recognition that the master or authority figure must evaluate and eventually begin to fulfill. The speaker, according to Hegel, would have only two choices: to resist, to insist that the norms he has internalized be changed and that he be recognized differently, or to conform, so that he can be recognized in accordance with present norms.

52 | Unlimited Eligibility?

But since the speaker does not yet feel confident enough to demand recognition, he simply feels shame at his failure to fulfill existing social expectations.

One might even be tempted to see section 6's framing as a recollection directly addressed to "you" as an act of generosity, an attempt to embed a small scale, initial, enabling act of recognition in the poem in advance of a prospective reader's experience of social alienation. Such an interpretation would imagine the speaker implying: others see you and only offer shaming, whereas I see you in this darkest moment and offer solidarity. But there are problems with such a reading. For the speaker does not seek to impose or adjust those norms in order to create a space within which "you" might be recognized more fully. Indeed, it remains unclear what "you" (and, in the past, the speaker himself) would be recognized as—beyond "what it is to be evil" or "what it was to be evil" (69–70). The poem, in other words, pointedly raises these stakes only to turn away from them.

But another reading is available, one that much more closely corresponds to and illuminates where section 6 leads. For the speaker, rather than anticipating a need to be known, instead anticipates a need to be near, a need for ontological proximity and even immanence that affirms eligibility. It is as if someone older addresses someone younger (perhaps even a younger version of the speaker) and offers neither an empty promise that all will be well, nor a set of norms through which "you" might conditionally become socially accepted, but instead the simple, yet profound, assurance that "you" are accepted and not "alone."[57] Earlier in the poem, Whitman's speaker had used carefully calibrated modes of address and a long list of "similitudes" to overcome a less severe sense of alienation from others and affirm his participation within a larger community. Here too he uses strategies of address and recuperates the litany of negative character traits as similitudes before, once again, fading, as he returns to the present and finds himself amid a celebration of ontological eligibility, deeming himself simply one of "the rest" of these "young men," enjoying "their arms on . . . [his] neck" and "the negligent leaning of their flesh against [him]" (78–80). The very desires of the body that had been a source of fear and distress have become reintegrated into his daily life of "laughing, gnawing, [and] sleeping" (82).

Peter Coviello has argued that in moments like this Whitman's poetry evokes an anonymous intimacy involving "attachment" between strangers linked by categories like "race" and "sexuality."[58] But the kind of intimacy Whitman celebrates at the end of section 6 and throughout the remainder of "Crossing Brooklyn Ferry" is both more intimate and more anonymous than what Coviello describes. For though the speaker singles out several "young men" who "call'd" him by his "nighest name," he offers no description of the larger group that they are a part of and that also includes the speaker who, despite being addressed, "never told . . . a word" to the "many I loved" (79, 81). This relation has confused a number of readers, including Wynn Thomas and Tenney Nathanson, who have struggled with the connection between this seeming "reserve" or "reticen[ce]" and a deeply interpersonal celebration.[59] Thinking of the 1855 edition of *Leaves of Grass*, Christian Haines, instead, helpfully describes how Whitman forwards "a more general queering of social life through . . . [a] refusal of identificatory regimes and . . . [a] replacement of the poverty of heteronormativity with the plenitude of the common."[60] Though Whitman surely does, here, as much as anywhere, "refuse . . . identificatory regimes," it may be that neither the "queer" (even if one does not intend to "identify him in a strict sense" with that word) nor the "common" (nor the queerly common) nor a rejection of "heteronormativity," as terms, quite capture what Whitman, at his most radical, has in mind, as he offers his social ideal in microcosm, a community that welcomes without an epistemological need to know and to categorize others or itself or indeed make such divisions and, instead, affirms a shared ontological association.[61] Aside from this imperative, it is very nearly a *non*community with no boundaries at all, well-deserving of the sublimely understated name (perhaps the only possible name for a community defined by its evasion of normative terms by which one might define it) that Whitman three times bestows upon them, "the rest" (78, 82).[62] No wonder then that the speaker displays a kind of improvisatory ease at the end of section 6 completely at odds with his previous memory of a sense of confinement within norms. Earlier he had felt "blank and suspicious" about his body and its desires (67). But he finishes the section with an idealized image of the body recovered as an object at play and even developing political agency. "The role," he tells us, "is what we make it, as great as we like, / Or as small as we like, or both great and small" (84–85).

The remainder of "Crossing Brooklyn Ferry" takes this a step further, inviting readers to understand how they share in the democratic process of building and expanding this being-with to which all are already eligible. With this hope in view, intriguing (and difficult) questions start to emerge about "Crossing Brooklyn Ferry" regarding how such paraontic

54 | Unlimited Eligibility?

spaces relate to the world they exist alongside or within: How does one enter such a space? How do such spaces persist and develop? And how might such paraontic orders, in time, inflect the world's predominant ontic orders?

The Politics of Eligibility "Accomplish'd"?

Beginning in section 7, an increasingly overt eroticism shapes the speaker's invitation to the reader. The moment of intimacy that unfolds is as intense as the previous section's moment of isolation. Having put his crisis behind him, the speaker appears to "approach you" out of "the rest" who greet him. Yet the speaker also teasingly suggests that "you" have not been passive.

> Closer yet I approach you,
> What thought you have of me now, I had as much of
>   you—I laid in my stores in advance,
> I consider'd long and seriously of you before you were born.
>
> Who was to know what should come home to me?
> Who knows but I am enjoying this?
> Who knows, for all the distance, but I am as good as
>   looking at you now, for all you cannot see me? (86–91)

The rhetorical trajectory of these lines—from a declarative expression of the speaker's advance toward "you" (86, 88), to a pseudo-interrogatory imputation that the reader has been advancing toward him all along (87), to a flirtatious series of questions (89–91)—has led many scholars to read this scene in a sinister manner, as if it amounts to a stalker covering up his nefarious intentions by accusing his unwitting victim of leading him on.[63] But the speaker, in fact, politely pulls a step back from direct address. He asks several, oddly detached rhetorical questions neither exactly addressed to himself nor exactly addressed to "you" but instead apparently addressed to others ("who knows . . . ?"), readers not yet ready to "come home" with the speaker but who the speaker knows have been watching with interest (89–91). This welcoming of observers establishes an almost voyeuristic dynamic due to the intimacies developing between the speaker and "you." But this is an eroticized invitation to a

"We Fathom You Not—We Love You" | 55

protopolitical project, and the speaker's candor builds upon the trust he hopes to have gained earlier in the poem when he decentered himself within the larger world (spatially and rhetorically) and invited (without demanding) the reader's involvement.

Section 8 continues to chart the increasing intimacy between speaker and reader but not before unexpectedly broadening the perspective for a few lines to encompass the East River setting so vividly described in section 3 (92–94). It is as if the speaker, having recovered a sense of ontological proximity to a number of others ("the rest") and seeking it with "you," now wishes to recover the sweeping, celebratory "scheme" involving everything that he began to imagine in the poem's first lengthy catalog. After asking what could be better than the "Manhattan" vista he had started to describe, he restrains himself, refocuses more narrowly, and asks, using some of the words that appear at the end of section 6, "What gods can exceed these that clasp me by the hand, and with voices I love call me promptly and loudly by my nighest name as I approach?" (92, 95). As he describes these "hand"-holding "gods" now as the "woman or man that looks in my face," it becomes clear that the reader has joined "the rest," the community without boundaries defined by ontological eligibility (96). This merging is quite literally consummated. Turning to direct address, the speaker, after having held hands with the reader and invited him or her "home," now evokes sexual climax by asking what

> . . . fuses me into you now, and pours my meaning into you?
>
> We understand then do we not?
> What I promis'd without mentioning it, have you not
>   accepted?
> What the study could not teach—what the preaching could
>   not accomplish is accomplish'd, is it not? (97–100)

These last few questions, like those in section 7, are so filled with unclear antecedents that it begins to feel as if the speaker is responding to a conversation one had already begun with him. This is the "indirect method" Whitman mentions in his notebook at its most ambitious, for the culmination of the poem depends on a reader's willingness to engage a text that makes its huge goals explicit but leaves its conclusions implicit. This is a rhetorical risk demanded by Whitman's vision of a community not based on "study[ing]," adherence to "preaching," or any characteristic by

56 | Unlimited Eligibility?

which one must be recognized in order to qualify as a potential member. Instead, one becomes able to belong as one rests in an eligibility one already has. So rather than imposing a conclusion, the speaker invites and even needs the reader to participate in continuing to conceive the poem and the sociality it intimates.

The final section of the poem celebrates the possibility of bringing this practice of sociality into the world. The beginning of section 8 foreshadowed the almost orgasmically unleashed catalog presented here. Key moments from every step of the poem's argument are situated within the wider world, an act of conflation suitable for a poem so concerned with bringing together. We begin, again, on the ferry, crossing the East River, among "countless crowds of passengers" (104). The "young men" still "call" the speaker by his "nighest name," and he continues to revel in his ability to "play the part," whatever that might be (109–10). The sunset shining on the water reflects back a kind of secular halo ("fine spokes of light") exactly as it had in section 3, though now he finds it around not only "my head" but "any one's head" (116). The speaker also imagines a "necessary film" that "envelop[s] the soul" and recalls the "scheme" in section 2 (121). As he had learned in section 6, "my body" and "your body" are worthy of celebration and not shame (122). And he wishes for all of this to "expand" (124).

Most importantly, even as the speaker verbally recreates this vast panorama, he sustains his humility. In section 3, the first great catalog showed the speaker relinquishing epistemological control, with the "I" fading in relation to his awareness of and respect for his context. In this last list, the "I" is absent, and the objects of his attention grammatically are transformed into subjects. As James Dougherty notes, the speaker's "imperatives do not compel the river to flow or the masts to stand up, but rather recognize and applaud their autonomous being and doing."[64] Thrilled but unable to "fathom" it all, he is left with a "[t]hrob[bing], baffled and curious brain" (130, 106). The "curio[sity]" expressed at the beginning of the poem is never overcome. Instead, the speaker has learned to be comfortable with and even value his epistemological limits, enabling him to welcome ever broader opportunities to be with others.

Though trading plain-spoken political critique (as in the speech in his drafting notebook) for an "indirect mode" may seem like a turn away from, rather than toward, political practice, Whitman understood that in order for people to rethink what America means, he needed to help them reconsider the affective, discursive, and conceptual foundations of American politics.[65] "Crossing Brooklyn Ferry" attempts to do this by showing how affects that encourage us to embrace ontological intimacy (wonder, praise, humility) serve as the source of different socialities than affects that incite recognition practices (fear, alienation toward oneself and others). Whitman harnesses these affects to discursive patterns, including an extraordinary rhetorical sensitivity as well as a nearly synesthetic receptivity to sights and sounds that informs the poem's expansive lists and exuberant free verse lines, in the service of an unstated "understand[ing]" that is "accomplish'd." In the context of his notebook, we can see these larger political goals withheld in the text of the poem coming into focus and providing the conceptual foundation for his vision of a more democratic America that welcomes all, including the "needy and down-kept races of the whole earth."

The final lines of "Crossing Brooklyn Ferry" imagine this project becoming politically realized with the reader's assistance. The sudden introduction of the first person plural pronoun does not conclude the poem with a presumptuous, imperialistic, royal "we" but, instead, the "we" of "the rest" who have now gained a collective voice for themselves and are ready for political engagement. But first this collective "we" turns to the reader and says, "We fathom you not—we love you" (130). Such a statement, at this point in the poem, is no longer paradoxical but instead articulates what, for Whitman, is the protopolitical foundation of radically inclusive democracy. For "fathom[ing]," a nautical term that here connotes an overconfidence in one's ability to measure and recognize the depth of another's personhood, when taken as an epistemological imperative, works against achieving the ontological proximity necessary to give voice to a "love" that affirms "any one['s] eligib[ility] to the condition or attributes or advantages of any being, no matter who."[66]

"Ages Hence": "Crossing Brooklyn Ferry" and Beyond

But what sociopolitical "[e]xpan[sion]" of this poetic vision did Whitman imagine in his day and, insofar as the poem insists on blurring temporal bounds, might we imagine in ours (124)? The question must be approached cautiously. Though Whitman's politics certainly shifted over the course of his life, even early in his career, he supported policies that did not always reflect his more radically democratic inclinations (e.g., Whitman supported the expansionist pursuits of President Polk in the

58 | Unlimited Eligibility?

1840s).[67] The participatory rhetoric of "Crossing Brooklyn Ferry" grounds sociality on an affirmation of ontological eligibility, without dictating a particular political futurity aside from the mutuality the poem evokes and practices, an understanding of eligibility very different from the one reconciled with the neo-imperialism promoted in a late poem like "Song of the Universal." But one might wonder whether this wariness with regard to speculating about futurity is not just due to deference but as a result of "the rest" being an abstraction. Might this gesture be both tactically protoqueer and also a way in which Whitman keeps himself at a remove from more fully engaging other political particularities of his time (e.g., related to race)? In other words, this ahistorical abstraction, when considered in light of Whitman's late work, could be aligned with the long history of lyricization. But it also points to real potentialities not fully encompassed by narratives of lyricization, including the prospect that Whitman's speaker does not seek to detach from history so much as to evoke another space inside/alongside it, a paraontic poetic space not defined by a hierarchical lyric of recognition (involving a recognizer bestowing recognition on those partially recognized or unrecognized) but a "lyric voice" of eligibility that affirms anyone's ontological proximity, an invitation that Whitman associates, at least for a time, with a better model of American democracy.

Whitman's struggle to develop and maintain a celebratory but also critical vision of democracy foreshadowed heated poetic and political debates in the decades following his death. Barbara Foley notes that by the time of the Whitman centenary in 1919 discussion about "the legacy of the good gray poet serve[d] as a touchstone for the different political tendencies vying for hegemony [in American politics]," with "voices from all points along the political spectrum s[eeking] to enlist Whitman on their side."[68] William Torrey Harris, the St. Louis Hegelian who likely influenced Whitman's late-career poetry, strikingly anticipated one of the most consequential of these political movements that claimed Whitman as a precursor, the cultural pluralism of the teens and twenties that shaped the careers of Jean Toomer and Hart Crane. After becoming US Commissioner of Education during the second half of his career, Harris advocated for the education of former slaves, as well as immigrants and newly colonized peoples, so that they could be rendered more recognizable within the American sociopolitical structure.[69] He argued, for example, that "a thorough mingling of all nationalities within each school" helps "all caste distinctions [to] vanish more rapidly," including "clannishness and the odious feeling of 'nativism.'" Harris, however, also advocated for retaining "national memories and aspirations, family traditions, customs, and habits, moral and religious observances," since "these form what may be called the substance of the character of each individual."[70] Matt Erlin has explained, with reference to German immigration, how Harris envisioned these dual imperatives being achieved by applying Hegelian principles: "For Harris, the full realization of American potential is only possible to the extent that the country recognizes and incorporates what contemporaries would have termed its 'German element.' The implication of Harris's argument is that America will eventually achieve a Hegelian *Aufhebung* or sublation, in which the individual characteristics of the two races will be preserved but their one-sidedness overcome."[71] Harris's recognition strategy from the mid-1870s was partly a response to the urgent need for a post–Civil War sense of social cohesion.[72] It served as a suggestive precursor for cultural pluralist thinkers like Horace Kallen, Waldo Frank, and others, who responded to the reemergence of nativist sentiments after the arrival of millions of immigrants from southern and eastern Europe, Asia, and elsewhere at the end of the nineteenth and beginning of the twentieth centuries by offering the hope of integration through recognition of difference. A number of Harlem Renaissance thinkers cautiously adapted this political strategy as a response to racism amid the legalized injustice of Jim Crow laws and the terrorism of the Ku Klux Klan, along with the ongoing persistence of more subtle forms of prejudice.

Whitman loomed large in the minds of many such thinkers as someone who provided, perhaps especially in his late work, powerfully compelling expression of a proto–cultural pluralist politics of recognition. The next two chapters, however, show that the more radically democratic implications of Whitman's early career politics were not wholly overlooked. Jean Toomer and Hart Crane sought to further elaborate the implications of a politics of unlimited eligibility. Building on "Crossing Brooklyn Ferry," a number of their most ambitious poems reject recognition and posit an affirmation of ontological eligibility as the ground of democracy. Both camps, as we shall see, faced serious risks. Rejecting recognition can lead to the problematic assumption that the material and historical legacy of identity categories can be imaginatively transcended. Defining democratic inclusiveness in terms of recognizing people through such identity categories, however, risks establishing a hierarchical system (unrecognized/misrecognized/recognized/recognizers) that rests on essentializing norms.

60 | Unlimited Eligibility?

Both Toomer and Crane wrestled with these dynamics, sometimes even in conversation with each other. Studying their struggles amid an ascendant cultural pluralism reveals how American poetry, as it underwent the lyricization process, and the politics of recognition often developed in tandem, alongside a countertradition that included "Crossing Brooklyn Ferry," throughout the twentieth and now twenty-first centuries.

Chapter Two

Jean Toomer's "The Blue Meridian" and the "Social Prison" of Cultural Pluralism

In "On Being an American," an unpublished autobiographical sketch Jean Toomer wrote around 1934, he recalls a conversation more than a decade before with a "friend" concerning one of his earliest creative texts. According to Toomer, this now lost poem entitled "The First American" announced the emergence of "a new type of man [who] was arising in this country—not European, not African, not Asiatic—but American," resulting in "divisions mended, the differences reconciled . . . a united people existing in the United States . . . [who also are] members of a united human race."[1] His friend listened, then "looked blank" and "puzzled," before rendering a judgment as much about the poet as about the poem: "You're white."[2] Toomer replied that his friend was missing the "point. I am not talking about whites or blacks, I am talking about Americans. I am an American. You are an American. Everyone is an American. Don't you see what I mean?" But his friend "shook his head," leaving Toomer to admit that "my reality was but words to him, words quite unrelated to what was real for him."[3] Like so much of Toomer's life and art, this anecdote lays bare difficult social dynamics. Traces of colorism and perhaps class privilege lurking within Toomer (he describes his friend as "a colored fellow of more than ordinary mental grasp") likely played a role in the friend's reinscription of Toomer inside a racial binary on the side of the oppressor.[4] The friend seems to have sensed in Toomer and his poem a dangerous denialism about American racial politics being voiced by someone who, at least sometimes, was able to pass when most other Americans of African descent could not and suffered for it. Toomer, on

62 | Unlimited Eligibility?

the other hand, queries his friend's mobilizing of a racial binary and the assumption that recognition of race, whether in the service of art or politics, could yield the social justice America needs.

At the very moment when Toomer wrote "The First American," he had been voraciously reading "Whitman . . . not only all he had written, but all that had been written about him."[5] He further explains the political implications of this fascination with Whitman in a contemporaneous 1920 essay, "Americans and Mary Austin," in which he predicts that the "American race" will be "composite . . . including within itself . . . all races" yet scarcely "conscious of its composite character." Toomer, thus, is not envisioning a raceless society. Nor does he seek to submit this "composite" race for political recognition. Instead, he imagines this hybridized race existing amid (and eventually defining) a society that neither imposes an identity upon a person nor expects a person to choose between socially sanctioned identities, a sociality unconfined by a need for recognition regulated by those already recognized. Offering his multiethnic background as an example ("what is true of this writer"), the young Toomer predicts that this new race, whose "general contour and aspirations . . . [are just now becoming] visible. . . . will effectively coalesce what straggling tendencies to antagonism and disruption may still be hanging over from the former individual race consciousnesses." Toomer is confident: it is "from just such stuff will a continent of Walt Whitmans evolve."[6]

In "Crossing Brooklyn Ferry," Whitman evokes the potential appeal of a (non)community founded on the affirmation of ontological eligibility rather than epistemological confirmation of recognizability. But while the concluding section of that poem hints at this (non)community's potential for paraontic political innovation, Whitman holds back from explicitly speculating about how such a sociality might be put into broader practice. Toomer, however, felt that the implications of what he deemed "groupistic" thinking, a trend indicative of an increasingly dominant politics of recognition, necessitated an attempt to articulate and enact an alternative.[7] The differences between Toomer's and Whitman's marginalized subject positions may have played a role in generating Toomer's sense of urgency. Though there are hints that the young Whitman endured alienation as a result of being a man who preferred romantic attachments to men rather than women, the heterosexual/homosexual binary became a major sociopolitical and juridical distinction near the end of his life, long after "Crossing Brooklyn Ferry."[8] By that time, as the previous chapter shows, Whitman had moved on to a very different understanding of eligibility.

On the other hand, during the late teens and early twenties, Toomer saw racial recognition, long established as a means of facilitating prejudice, reframed as a means of fighting racism and achieving a more pluralistic democracy. However, Toomer worried that this retooled form of recognition known as cultural pluralism was only superficially democratizing, making racial difference more visible while making some sources and effects of racism less visible and, thus, even more intractable.

Toomer's disagreement with his friend, thus, might reflect, at least in part, a disagreement between a post-Whitmanian poetics and politics of unlimited eligibility and a cultural pluralism that encouraged poetic appeals for racial recognition. And something like this (along with an increasingly intense commitment to the thought and practices of Georges Gurdjieff) shapes Toomer's eventual differences from his erstwhile Harlem Renaissance peers. But the division was not between one writer (Toomer) who came to feel that cultural pluralism had failed and many others who deemed it a rousing success. Instead, the debates among writers who came to be associated with the Harlem Renaissance often concerned to what degree cultural pluralism failed and what to do in the wake of this failure. Nor did Toomer's peers necessarily disagree with his vision of a forthcoming "American race." Instead, the principal disagreement had to do with timing: When is it politically effective to invoke the new "American race" trope alongside or even instead of cultural pluralist appeals for recognition?

Criticism of Toomer does not always fully reflect this historical complexity. Many critics tie the artistic success of Toomer's most celebrated work, *Cane*, to his willingness to identify, for a short time, more closely with the African American elements of his heritage.[9] Understandably suspicious that Toomer was merely taking advantage of the publicity accorded some artists associated with what became known as the Harlem Renaissance, these critics tend to view the rest of his career as a sequence of politically and aesthetically regrettable attempts to pass as white.[10] A number of other critics have claimed that such arguments overlook how Toomer forwards an explicitly multiethnic identity.[11] Still others argue that he pursues a "raceless transcendence [that] can only be attained by people of mixed racial descent" or wishes to be "racially indeterminate."[12] Underneath these stances often is a shared presumption: that discussion about Toomer ought to focus on accurately recognizing his racial identity (even if that identity might be "indeterminate") and then discerning what political responsibilities, in light of that identity, he did or did not

64 | Unlimited Eligibility?

successfully fulfill in his life and art.[13] Insofar as such determinations deeply shaped Toomer's culture (and our own) this is unsurprising and perhaps necessary. And this chapter will attend to Toomer's inconsistency in how he represented himself, as well as his, at times, naive intent to establish social solidarity on the basis of an American race. All the same, it is important to note how scholarship often takes as its premise a practice of racial recognition that Toomer throughout almost all of his career argued against. Critiques of Toomer's inconsistency, in other words, may be warranted, even as they may obscure the substance of debates central to Toomer's work and its context.

So this chapter will resist, at least initially, the urge to draw stark distinctions between a politically reckless Toomer who loses himself in Gurdjieffan mysticism amid more reasonable peers and, instead, tarry with those moments of overlap, when Toomer has much in common with his Harlem Renaissance colleagues. The chapter begins by considering the racial politics surrounding the emergence and expansion of cultural pluralism, as well as debates over the strategic adoption of elements of the cultural pluralist program by participants in the Harlem Renaissance, debates that assessed, for example, how (and whether) various models and meanings of lyric hypothetically could facilitate greater political recognition of African American culture. During the brief time when Toomer wrote and published *Cane*, he warily accepted this strategy. But he was far from alone among these artists in suspecting success would not come easily. Toomer and many of his peers by the late twenties and early thirties largely agreed that cultural pluralism had not and likely would not bring the social justice it had promised. Toomer's 1929 essay "Race Problems and Modern Society," however, goes beyond a sharp critique of the politics of recognition by advocating for something akin to a Whitmanian politics of unlimited eligibility.

This stance would shape the later, more fully developed version of "The First American" that came to be titled "The Blue Meridian," Toomer's last major publication. With extravagantly Whitmanian apostrophes, "The Blue Meridian" attempts to call forth the "new America" of the new American race. In order to do this, Toomer evaluates the major poetic idioms of the era, from traditional to experimental. Much of his efforts focus on negotiating changes in lyric (and discourse about lyric) and, in particular, seeking an alternative to, on the one hand, a cultural pluralist compromise consisting of a "lyric expression" of what he felt was an oversimplified understanding of identity and, on the other hand, a model of

Jean Toomer's "The Blue Meridian" | 65

lyric abstracted from historical context that, as a result, implicitly shored up elements of white supremacism. Toomer sought an idiom that could move his post-Whitmanian vision forward in America at that moment. "The Blue Meridian," however, reveals the speaker's mounting frustration with this task eventually resulting in almost authoritarian assertions. Though one senses Toomer's goal of replacing an urge to recognize with an affirmation of ontological eligibility, his speaker, towards the end of the poem, attempts to orchestrate with a eugenicist's control the political and biological forces capable of creating the American race. In doing so, the poem echoes and reinforces the most problematic aspects of the politics of recognition that it ostensibly had set forth to undermine, the hierarchical division between unrecognized/misrecognized/recognized/recognizer. This paradoxical dynamic at the heart of "The Blue Meridian" illustrates the challenge of developing an alternative, inclusively democratic lyric politics at a time when the recognition model of sociality became increasingly influential.

Cultural Pluralism vs. the American Race

Toomer's memory of his friend's attachment to ethnic group identity rather than an "American" identity situates their conversation in relation to what would have been still intensifying debates during the early twenties about how ethnic and racial diversity should be represented in art and politics. Commentators responded to the migration of African Americans from the predominantly rural South to Northeastern and Midwestern cities, along with the immigration of many eastern and southern Europeans to those same cities (and occasionally also mentioned Asian immigration to the West coast), with various expressions of curiosity, nativism, ethnocentrism, and racist prejudice, as well as more speculative inquiries about what it meant to be American and, at times, a combination of all of the above. For example, in 1901, Woodrow Wilson, who had not yet begun his political career and was still an academic, envisioned a "new race" resulting from a nation that had "dominated, changed, [and] absorbed" people from "every European race" as well as people "out of Asia . . . [and] out of Africa." Wilson, however, does not mention, much less promote, interracial marriages or even multicultural communities so much as assimilation to an Anglo-Saxon norm.[14] Such a stance somewhat parallels Charles Chesnutt's virtually contemporaneous contention

66 | Unlimited Eligibility?

in 1900 that the "white, black[,] and Indian" races would amalgamate, resulting in a "future race" centered in America that, though multiethnic in origin, nevertheless "will be predominantly white." Chesnutt, however, acknowledges in a way that Wilson does not the reality of interracial relationships and insists that, though "the admixture of races in America has never taken place under conditions likely to produce the best results," there is no evidence that "people of mixed blood . . . are less virile, prolific or able than those of purer strains."[15] Only slightly earlier than Chesnutt, W. E. B. DuBois, in his 1897 essay "The Conservation of Races," does not privilege an Anglo-Saxon norm but concedes that "in our calmer moments we must acknowledge that human beings are divided into races," before cautioning that "unfortunately for scientists, . . . criteria of race are most exasperatingly intermingled," and then backtracking to propose "the final word of science, so far, is that we have at least two, perhaps three, great families of human beings—the whites and Negroes, [and] possibly the yellow race." Out of these somewhat contradictory claims, DuBois asserts that African Americans should not wish for a time when they would be "absor[bed] by the white Americans" and pursue "a servile imitation of Anglo-Saxon culture."[16] And he adds a series of probing questions: "Am I an American or am I a Negro? Can I be both? . . . Is not my only possible practical aim the subduction of all that is Negro in me to the American? Does my black blood place upon me any more obligation to assert my nationality than German, or Irish, or Italian blood would?"[17]

Such questions anticipate debates two decades later, when in an attempt to discredit World War I–era nativism, thinkers like Horace Kallen, Waldo Frank, and Randolph Bourne sought to forge a new political consensus about the role of racial and ethnic diversity in a democracy. They fashioned various forms of cultural pluralism explicitly as alternatives to those who favored either an amalgamation or a separation of races and ethnic groups, and they placed the politics of recognition at the heart of this via media. In a pivotal 1915 essay, "Democracy Versus the Melting-Pot," Horace Kallen defines a middle ground between those who feared the swiftly increasing "non-British elements of the population . . . [the] 'barbarian hordes,' if you will," and those who insist that America is a "melting-pot" capable of assimilating any "group" into the anticipated "new 'American race'—a blend of at least all the European stocks (for there seems to be some difference of opinion as to whether negroes also should constitute some element in this blend)."[18] Kallen's alternative rests on both the assimilationist and "dissimilation[ist]" impulses he finds within these various ethnic groups.[19] He describes how members of such groups conform to social norms like following fashion trends and attending movies and baseball games while sustaining their distinctive group identity. As "they grow more prosperous and 'Americanized,' as they become freed from the stigma of 'foreigner,' they develop group self-respect: the 'wop' changes into a proud Italian, the 'hunky' into an intensely nationalist Slav. They learn, or they recall, the spiritual heritage of their nationality. Their cultural abjectness gives way to cultural pride."[20] Kallen argues that this process confirms both an assimilative capability within immigrant groups and a fundamental rule that "no new ethnic types have originated."[21] Twice, he notes that, though groups can adapt to various cultural norms, "they cannot change their grandfathers."[22] So it is not terribly surprising to find him worrying about attempts to "creat[e] . . . the melting pot" or the "new 'American race'" by "law" through "enforced miscegenation." Since Kallen deems racial and ethnic identities immutable, he contends that America must "seek to provide conditions under which each [person within each "ethnic type"] may attain the perfection that is proper to its kind" in order to establish "a democracy of nationalities." With everyone accepting their proper positions, American democracy can function as "an orchestra" featuring "each ethnic group . . . [performing its] natural instrument . . . [in] the symphony of civilization."[23] When Kallen later collected this essay in his 1924 book *Culture and Democracy in the United States*, he made the political stakes even more stark: "This democracy—in character and constitution social and intellectual rather than political—for its principle is, not one man one vote, but one temperament, one point of view, one vote—is that which is to-day at stake in the United States. . . . The alternative before Americans is Kultur Klux Klan or Cultural Pluralism."[24]

Waldo Frank, another leading cultural pluralist, echoes these ideas in *The Re-discovery of America*, when he exclaims, "America needs groups. Groups to capture our chaos as consciousness captures the sense. Groups to make bowels and limbs and heart of the American body; to be our brains and our spirit." Even more explicitly than Kallen (and seemingly borrowing his metaphor of a "Symphonic Nation"), Frank understands political quietism to be a necessary consequence of this "group" focus: "revolutionary action is . . . for the present, barred; it can be effective only in a world where there is already a group integration." For those currently suffering, Frank offers a not terribly comforting vision of a future

68 | Unlimited Eligibility?

America as a vaguely neo-Hegelian "Whole" within which "there will be no time . . . to clamor for 'rights,' no breath to bewail 'injustice.'"[25]

Kallen's echoing of the taxonomizing of species depicted in the account of creation given in Genesis 1 ("proper to its kind") and Frank's narrower analogizing to bodily organs points to the essentialism (given the allusion, perhaps even divinely sanctioned essentialism) undergirding cultural pluralism at its beginning. Cultivation and preservation of groups was not enough. Groups had to be recognized, and every individual's identity within a group had to be recognized, lest your foreordained degree of "perfection" remain unclear. For it is only through the epistemological assessment involved in recognizing that it becomes possible to determine whether you are part of the group (to use Frank's phrasing) that serves as the "brain" or the "bowels" of the American body. According to Kallen, either one accepted one's recognized place in one's group and one's group's "natural" place in the American "symphony" or one, at least tacitly, aided and abetted the KKK. Of course, the irony, as Walter Benn Michaels contends, is that the opposite occasionally was true. Kallen's cultural pluralism unintentionally gave organizations like the KKK political cover.[26] For Michaels, cultural pluralism's "identity essentialism" inevitably "commit[s one] . . . to the primacy of identity; instead of who we are being constituted by what we do, what we do is justified by who we are," a convenient pretext for the KKK's program of racial hierarchies and racial separatism.[27]

However, neither Kallen's or Frank's writings from over a century ago nor Michaels' more recent account fully describe the range of pluralisms that had been proposed by the late teens and early twenties, the time when Toomer was figuring out what artistic and political contributions he could make. Some of these pluralisms were strongly anti-essentialist. Though Kallen's teacher William James wrote little about racial politics, he emphasized how all aspects of experience are always irreducibly made up of interminglings. As a result, James developed an anti-essentialist form of pluralism.[28] Randolph Bourne, writing specifically in conversation with Kallen and more generally addressing the line of thought extending back to Woodrow Wilson, argues against the Anglo-centric tendencies of the "melting-pot" model and in favor of preserving group identities. Bourne warns against "speak[ing] . . . of inferior races" and advocates for a kind of "cosmopolitanism" that would permit "dual citizenship."[29] His "transnational" model, thus, preserves Kallen's "groups" while undermining the hierarchical implications of his "cultural pluralism." Bourne's stance,

Jean Toomer's "The Blue Meridian" | 69

however, had limits, for while he explicitly undercuts American prejudice toward European immigrants, he overlooks the plight of African Americans. Indeed, Barbara Foley notes how varying degrees of "bigotry . . . [often] prevailed among putative cultural pluralists" insofar as a "quietist culturalism" featuring an ostensibly "democratic progressivism could coexist with a racist paternalism."[30] This political ambiguity perfectly positioned cultural pluralism's version of the recognition model to become not just compatible with American democracy but increasingly coidentified with it.

For a short time, Jean Toomer, like a number of other thinkers who came to be associated with the Harlem Renaissance, felt it was possible and perhaps even necessary to work out a politically productive compromise with cultural pluralism.[31] Poetry became a primary ground on which these negotiations occurred. But the status of poetry itself and its genres was undergoing a momentous shift, as lyricization, "a process in which particular poetic structures with particular modes of address and particular publics . . . were gradually abstracted into one larger genre of poetry that came to be loosely associated with the lyric," continued to accelerate.[32] According to Virginia Jackson, Paul Laurence Dunbar's "embrace" of the "twentieth century genre of the modern lyric" was pivotal—and not just for his own poetic development, insofar as his "motivated abstraction of those genres [including the incorporation of "the ballad" and other "folk (or faux-folk) sources" into the lyric, a term that became prominently featured in several titles of his collections] . . . succeeded so completely that we no longer know how to read poems any other way."[33] The word "lyric" becomes associated with a raceless abstraction, albeit one that could only ever be "partial[ly]" achieved, a universalizing impulse that may appear to offer a "utopian horizon" but that, in effacing racial identity and its histories, participates in "racial violence."[34] The "bough" in Dunbar's "The Haunted Oak," a tree upon which a lynching occurred, becomes the emblem of this dynamic central to the "long arc of post-eighteenth century American poetics." With a "bad conscience [that] changes nothing" and thus is a "stand-in for white liberal guilt," the bough "continues to witness and testify to more violence, becoming the obviously fictional 'speaker' of the poem itself" and a figure for the future filled with lyricized lyrics abstracted, albeit never fully, from the racialized history that was their source.[35]

Jackson's argument that lyricization aligns with other white supremacist social vectors is persuasive, but other scholars highlight a somewhat different Dunbar. Gavin Jones observes how the cultural "space . . . was

70 | Unlimited Eligibility?

narrow" for Dunbar and other African American artists, but they nevertheless innovated "subtle subversions" and "dynamic response[s] to the[ir] historical moment."[36] "At its finest," Dunbar's poetry presents "a playful juxtaposition of literary languages combin[ing] a variety of racial dialects" in a way that anticipated the "self-conscious use of different linguistic registers . . . by Harlem poets of the 1920s."[37] And subsequent scholars like Sonya Posmentier have shown how, even when confronted with the extremity of oppression, African American poets and critics analyzed different modalities of (and discourses of) subjecthood, participating, at times, in debates that shape, subvert, and repurpose the speaking subject amid lyricization.[38] In other words, though the network of social forces that collectively defined white supremacism may have helped to establish the abstract, (allegedly) ahistorical lyricized lyric as a predominant model, that did not mean that this process went uncontested, a point Jackson herself studies extensively throughout *Before Modernism*, as she explores a "specifically Black history of lyric reading and lyricization" and white responses to it.[39] Different degrees and kinds of both racialization and abstraction inflected the fading (and also remembering) of once-flourishing genres like, to use a list by Jackson, "elegies, epitaphs, ballads, hymns, epistles, medleys, drinking songs, sea chanteys, and spirituals" and the emergence of the "modern lyric."[40]

These cracks within lyricization (and, more broadly, a culture shaped by white supremacism) influenced many Harlem Renaissance writers' strategic, cultural pluralist appeals as they sought to exploit this "narrow" space for politically productive social recognition. And, as the next section shows, the nearly nonexistent narrowness for making still more nuanced appeals for ethnic fluidity convinced Toomer that such appeals only would support a system of recognition that was inherently hierarchical and in denial about the irreducible interminglings that defined life—and especially American life. As a person characterized by a kind of racial fluidity that enabled him to pass as a member of multiple ethnicities even as it left him often feeling outside of them all, Toomer was convinced that the time was right to craft a paraontic (and paralyric) space from which he could affirm and assert an American race. But Toomer struggled to do this and the resulting poem, "The Blue Meridian," and its poetics waver between a quite radical, multiethnic beyond recognition conception of American sociality capable of challenging white supremacism and a disappointingly vague envisioning of an American race that, at times, compromised with,

Jean Toomer's "The Blue Meridian" | 71

as much as it confronted, legacies of white supremacism associated with lyricization and beyond.

Cultural Pluralism and the Harlem Renaissance

Toomer's complex negotiation with cultural pluralism, already evident in the conversation with his friend about "The First American," intensified during the early twenties, when Waldo Frank served as a mentor and even joined him in his travels to Georgia, an experience that provided foundational materials for his multigenre masterwork *Cane*. As Toomer began to navigate the publishing industry, Frank encouraged him to "do your Negro stuff" at public readings, ostensibly in the service of building group solidarity and as a way for him to develop a profile on the literary scene. Despite anxieties about racial identification, Toomer warily agreed and briefly adopted this strategy.[41] Toomer had a similarly (and temporarily) warm relationship with Alain Locke, perhaps the foremost African American interlocutor of cultural pluralism. Locke and Toomer had known each other since late 1919, and shortly thereafter both participated in Georgia Douglas Johnson's "Saturday Nighters," weekly meetings of the black intelligentsia who lived in the Washington, DC, area.[42]

Locke's introduction to the March 1925 issue of *Survey Graphic*, "Enter the New Negro," became a key point of reference, at first positively and then negatively, for Toomer.[43] In that famous essay, Locke argues that African Americans have been essentialized in terms of an "Old Negro" category imposed by white Americans that rendered an African American into "more of a myth than a man" and "more of a formula than a human being."[44] Locke challenges such stereotypes on several fronts. He argues against "the fiction . . . that the life of the races is separate," when "the fact is that they have touched too closely at the unfavorable and too lightly at the favorable levels."[45] Racial purity, in other words, is a fantasy reflecting a deeper lie: the biological conception of race. Setting aside that fantasy demands acknowledgment that races, in fact, always have "touched," as well as a political obligation to make those encounters more "favorable." Despite understanding race as a sociohistorical reality and not a biological category (an understanding not fully shared by cultural pluralists like Kallen and Frank), Locke strategically chooses not to set aside carefully qualified essentialist discourse altogether. He commends a "deep feeling of race [that] is at present the mainspring of Negro life" and asserts that, as African Americans increasingly live outside of "the tyranny of social intimidation," they will "achiev[e] something like a spiritual emancipation" resulting in a "fuller, truer self-expression."[46] A "New Negro" will emerge that is defined—and ever redefined—by African Americans themselves in relation to a broader, changing American culture. He envisions American democracy growing as a result of this dialectical tension: "Subtly the conditions that are molding a New Negro are molding a new American attitude."[47] As African Americans gain greater, more genuinely democratic social recognition, what it means to be African American will evolve. And as African Americans consequently more fully recognize America, what it means to be American will evolve.

In exchange for this increase in social recognition, Locke cautiously disavows both a black nationalist stance like that of Marcus Garvey and economic radicalism.[48] He describes the former as a "transient, if spectacular, phenomenon" while noting that "as with the Jew, persecution is making the Negro international."[49] Locke sets aside economic radicalism with similar qualifications, stating that though "the thinking Negro has shifted a little toward the left with the world-trend, . . . fundamentally for the present the Negro is radical on race matters, conservative on others."[50] Then, Locke adds, "[Y]et under further pressure and injustice iconoclastic thought and motives will inevitably increase."[51] Such a stance reflects Locke's attempt to reach a broader public as well as a narrower audience of African American artists and intellectuals, many of whom had leftist (or, at least, left-leaning) political investments.[52] Locke accepts, for the time being, a cultural pluralist compromise that involves keeping racial and economic critique largely separate, while holding in reserve the possibility that conflating the critiques might become necessary later.

Toomer applauded Locke's approach in "The Negro Emergent," an unpublished 1925 essay written after he had published *Cane* and just before he permanently turned his back on cultural pluralism. Paraphrasing many of the major points featured in "Enter the New Negro," Toomer reiterates what drives Locke's strategic essentialism: "[I]n fruitful contact with his ancestry. . . . [and] racial heritage," each African American is "find[ing] out what lay beneath the creature that America had made of him." Like Locke, he warns against "seek[ing] a final definition of this essence" but expresses confidence that "in proportion as he discovers what is real within him, he will create, and by that act at once create himself and contribute his value to America."[53] In this spirit, Toomer works toward a strategically essentialist position with regard to the intersection of African Americans and poetry. He acknowledges that "folk-songs" and "spirituals" are sometimes used to evoke "a picture of the Negro [that] lends itself to poetic exaggeration." But he also seems to set aside such concerns when he praises a "lyricism which is so purely negro."[54] This lyricism would become one of the flashpoints of debate among Harlem Renaissance intellectuals evaluating the long-term political prospects of cultural pluralism.

In 1926, shortly after writing "Enter the New Negro," Alain Locke, for example, made it clear that "The Negro Poets of the United States," a group that included Jean Toomer, constituted the leading edge of the trends he had described. After affirming the cultural pluralist credo of American society being a "confederation of minority traditions" rather than a single "national sun concentrated in one blazing, focal position," Locke locates the African American contribution to poetry in a "folk-consciousness [that] has slowly come into being[,] . . . a folk-tradition" springing from "the ambition of a singing people."[55] Within such a frame-work, Phillis Wheatley's elevated diction and rhymed couplets, characteristic of Enlightenment-era British poetic trends, for Locke, amounted to no more than a kind of "chirping however significantly in the dawn of the American Revolution."[56] It would take another century until, in the work of Paul Laurence Dunbar, "Negro poetry came penitently back to the folk-tradition" and was rewarded with the emergence of a "lyric expression" that gave voice to "free singing from a free heart," a discursive and artistic parallel to emancipation itself.[57] Yes, there was the risk of being "shackled . . . to the limitations and handicaps of dialect," as the "Dunbar tradition . . . gradually deteriorat[ed] from minstrelsy, to buffoonery."[58] However, "lyric expression," when rooted in folk tradition but "freed from th[os]e limitations" manifests a "modernism of expression" prospectively capable of earning "cultural recognition."[59] "Discarding dialect" would enable "Negro poetry" to be "at one and the same time more universal and more racial."[60] Locke, here, evokes a delicate balance that, at least tacitly, encourages black poets to reject the abstracting impulses of lyricization while avoiding confinement within other not-at-all abstract historical legacies that associated, sometimes in racist terms, African Americans with "lyric expression." But it is no small task to avoid "persistent and oppressive race consciousness" while nevertheless achieving the "dignity of race spokesmanship" and continuing to draw on the "enviable naiveté of the slave singers."[61] Thus, at the high tide of cultural pluralism in the

74 | Unlimited Eligibility?

mid-twenties, Toomer and Locke acknowledged the stakes of this artistic balancing act. Both wondered whether attention paid to African American poetry featuring a folk-based lyricism would result in political recognition of the New Negro or reinscription within racist Old Negro stereotypes associated with the minstrelsy. Could recognition of racial difference be shifted from a tool of oppression to a tool for democratizing society?

They were far from alone in having these questions. In 1899, Paul Laurence Dunbar himself told an unnamed interviewer that "the predominating power of the African race is lyric" and went on to explain that "the black man's soul is lyric, not dramatic."[62] But, when pressed by the interviewer about a "tropic warmth" that makes "lyric expression [of the 'African race'] . . . a thing apart," Dunbar pointedly hoped that the interviewer was not "one of those who would hold the Negro down to a certain kind of poetry—dialect and concerning only scenes on plantations in the South."[63] The final phrase, like Locke's reference to being "freed," invokes imagery of slavery and social oppression to describe confinement within stereotypes projected upon the concept of "lyric." And Dunbar, like Locke and Toomer, seeks to be strategic while working amid irreducible tensions, when he forwards near paradoxes that undermine the whole enterprise of racial recognition, whether of poems or persons, as he states that "we must write like the white men" before then noting that "the white people . . . talk like us—they have imported many of our words into the language—and you know they act like us."[64]

Again and again, African American poets and critics like William Stanley Braithwaite and James Weldon Johnson, among others, would debate this intersection of poetics and politics.[65] W. E. B. DuBois offered one of the most powerful expressions of these anxieties in a 1926 essay titled the "Criteria of Negro Art," where he candidly states his "suspicio[n]s":

> With the growing recognition of Negro artists in spite of the severe handicaps, one comforting thing is occurring to both white and black. They are whispering, "Here is a way out. Here is the real solution of the color problem. The recognition accorded Cullen, Hughes, Fauset, White and others shows there is no real color line. Keep quiet! Don't complain! Work! All will be well!"
>
> I will not say that already this chorus amounts to a conspiracy. Perhaps I am naturally too suspicious. But I will say that there are today a surprising number of white people

who are getting great satisfaction out of these younger Negro writers because they think it is going to stop agitation of the Negro question. . . . And many colored people are all too eager to follow this advice[.][66]

DuBois goes on to elaborate how black artists are "hemmed in" by expectations from the white and black public alike. Furthermore, since the established power structures governing both politics and poetry (as well as other arts) went largely unchanged by cultural pluralist compromises, black artists, in effect, were "handing everything over to a white jury." So he warns African Americans to expect a forthcoming bait and switch: "[J]ust as soon as true art emerges; just as soon as the black artist appears, someone touches the race on the shoulder and says, 'He did that because he was an American, not because he was a Negro.'" Thus African Americans are left with the burdens of double consciousness, while the "white jury" is free to choose to celebrate or marginalize (or marginalize by celebrating) "lyric expression" of African American identity. DuBois, nevertheless, ends the essay by very nearly conceding that there is no alternative but to work through this system for more genuine recognition. Despite his entirely plausible "suspicio[n]s," he concludes with an affirmation of a model that Locke would have found familiar: "Until the art of the black folk compels recognition they will not be rated as human. And when through art they compel recognition then let the world discover if it will that their art is as new as it is old and as old as new."[67] DuBois's sudden concession exposes the severe tensions at work not just in his essay but within Harlem Renaissance–era poetics and politics. Recognition is both necessary and impossible, or at least implausible, due to its dependence on a hierarchical political structure (unrecognized/misrecognized/recognized/recognizers) built to delay and defer genuine recognition of African Americans.

These concerns deepened by the late twenties and early thirties, when after the onset of the Great Depression, a number of African American intellectuals, including Locke himself, had begun asking serious questions about the entire cultural pluralist program. Michael North has explained how, "despite its enthusiasm for Africa and Meso-America, despite its promises of a transnational America and a multiethnic modernism," not even the "avant garde" was "prepared to include within its conception of the new American writing any examples that actually stretched the old categories of race and ethnicity."[68] African American writers responded

76 | Unlimited Eligibility?

to this disappointment in various ways. In a 1930 article, Sterling Brown rues the fact that the burden of racial representation (the "matter of Representativeness") had both created and, he felt, impaired an audience, albeit perhaps unavoidably. Knowing the propensity for white readers to accept and expect racial stereotypes, African American readers, according to Brown, felt the need "to read in order to confute" anything other than a conventional representation of African Americans (a concept itself, of course, much disputed).[69] Claude McKay agrees in "A Negro Writer to His Critics" (1932) and, after outlining a similar, difficult dynamic, worries "that we are all floundering in a mass of race, color, national consciousness and all the correlative consciousness," and, as a result, "we are prone to put too much stress on the identity of characters, having an automatic reaction to them not just as people but rather as types representative of our separate divisions."[70] And Locke himself, in 1934, though still believing that "the main objective of Negro poetry" is "the poetic portrayal of Negro folk-life," acknowledges the "canker of theatricality and exhibitionism" imposed by white expectations placed on black artists.[71] By 1936, Locke was very nearly ready to contradict the conclusion of "Enter the New Negro," where he differentiated between racial and economic radicalism, in favor of affirming "a high compatibility between race-conscious and class-conscious thought."[72]

Even this brief overview indicates that by the mid-1930s many African American intellectuals held doubts about the efficacy of the cultural pluralist project generally and more specifically with regard to pursuing social recognition amid a tangle of discourses related to "lyric," "lyricism," and "lyric expression," which, at times, veered toward the ahistorical abstraction characteristic of lyricization, and, at other times, remained embedded within a variety of racialized sociohistorical contexts that continued to ramify, and, in still other instances, blended the latter with (or foregrounded) a left-leaning class consciousness. Along these lines, what came to separate Jean Toomer from his onetime Harlem Renaissance colleagues was not his skepticism about the politics of recognition so much as his deeper resistance to strategic compromises. Though this would lead Toomer increasingly toward various mystical and religious practices, at the heart of his 1929 essay "Race Problems and Modern Society," he advocates a merger of racial and economic radicalism based on a querying of cultural pluralism.[73]

Written at the cusp of the Great Depression, the first several pages of the essay scarcely mention race at all, not because Toomer downplays the severity of American racism but because he seeks to establish how "economic and political systems" participate in the perpetuation of racial strife. The celebration of "Henry Ford," as a "philosopher" exemplifying "the [businessman] ideal at which all people of sound sense should aim," had further privatized "the 'acquisitive urge' for land, natural resources, and cheap labor" that defined America and that "variously gave rise to the problems of the whites and the Indians, the whites and the Negroes, the whites and the Asiatics, the old stock and the immigrants."[74] Amid this trend, Toomer does not deny that a measure of progress might be made through Locke's cultural pluralist strategy. He points to the first signs of an "emergence of a fairly well-defined [black] middle class." And he emphasizes how "a deeper seated disillusion as regards the promises of the dominant white American . . . ha[d] caused an intensification of Negro race consciousness" beyond appeals for gradual inclusion within the body politic, leading to "an increased aggressiveness—more fight."[75] Though Toomer is sympathetic with this response, he notes parallel emotions emerging in other ethnic groups, with less sociohistorical justification. "Nordics," for example, demonstrated "a[n] . . . increase of separatism," and committed racists, along with their sympathizers, pursued "with greater urgency than ever" the dream of "an inviolate white aristocracy." Toomer notes with terror that "there are some whites who would like to see the darker peoples, particularly the Negroes, either deported, sterilized, or swept off by a pestilence."[76]

While most cultural pluralists would have been horrified by such goals, Toomer's concern is that cultural pluralism, after more than a decade, had not remedied American democracy in the way that it promised. "Group" identity had persisted and even deepened, but rather than producing a symphonic harmonizing of groups (as Kallen and Frank argued), "each group" had focused on its own development.[77] And, much worse, the hierarchical (even tacitly white supremacist) premises inherent to influential cultural pluralist models like those developed by Kallen and Frank had created political common ground between gradualist liberals, who might (or might not), in time, work toward policies supportive of African Americans and other minorities, and outright racists and nativists violently opposed to any such progress. That prospect made Toomer, at times, cynical. He scoffs that "liberal opinion and intelligent humanism" have had little impact in reforming "big business" and "the race question." Instead, with the blessing of cultural pluralism, the races "will undoubtedly push away from one another until they have completely occupied what

78 | Unlimited Eligibility?

small room for withdrawal is still left," a process that Toomer cryptically warns will reach a "bursting point," when "race prejudice . . . carr[ies] the entire body of America toward . . . [a] climax."[78]

"Race Problems and Modern Society" points toward an alternative democratic polity, one obscured by the cultural pluralist insistence on "drawing . . . distinctions supposedly based on skin color or blood composition" at a moment when the science behind such distinctions had begun to "appear more and more ridiculous."[79] Toomer highlights "people who cannot be classified as separatist and racial," not because they are apolitical or reactionary but because their very existence as the products of two or more ethnicities undermines the group classifications on which cultural pluralism typically rests. Quite understandably, "they may not be so defined and articulate as the separatist type," and Toomer himself struggles to find adequate language to describe them that does not fall back into identity categories or universalistic platitudes. He vaguely invokes "truly human values" antithetical to "prejudices and antagonisms."[80] However, earlier in the essay, Toomer designates these "[un]classified" people as the political progeny of "the greatest American—Walt Whitman," insofar as they favor a "conscious[ness] of being an American" that rejects the premise that placement within a socially recognized identity must serve as the gateway to democratic participation.[81]

Here, if anywhere, Toomer hopes to find an escape from the "social trap" and "social prison" created by the more problematically essentializing tendencies he came to associate with cultural pluralism.[82] Toomer's invoking of Whitman in "Race Problems and Modern Society" signals his return to the challenge that had energized his writing career at its beginning when he wrote "The First American," the pursuit of a poetic voice for those like himself, who "cannot be classified" and, as a result, are troubled by the hierarchical, undemocratic implications of a politics based on such classifying. These people became the focus of his 1932 poem "Brown River, Smile" and its expansion published in 1936, "The Blue Meridian."[83] But he continued to face the challenge posed by his friend who responded to the ambitions of the shorter version of the poem by deeming Toomer "white." How do you make an idealized, multiethnic-beyond-recognition future more than a naive, even politically irresponsible distraction in a present dominated by white supremacism? And, in terms of poetics, how do you affirm this emergent "American" identity without aligning it with the also emergent, ahistorical, abstract, modern lyric that obscures the ongoing legacies of racism?

"The Blue Meridian": Multiethnic beyond Recognition?

Toomer was not without models of lyrics expressing multiethnic identity. These poems, however, often were dramas of recognition, which made them imperfect templates for his poetic project. Claude McKay's "The Mulatto" (1925) and Langston Hughes's "Mulatto" (1927), for example, vividly depict the psychological and political burdens borne by their "self-divided, disinherited, homeless" speakers, while reinforcing, as George Hutchinson notes, "tragic mulatto" stereotypes.[84] McKay's wounded speaker threatens violence: "Because I am the white man's son . . . // I will dispute his title to his throne," and if his demands are not satisfied, "I shall not hesitate, / Into my father's heart to plunge the knife" (1, 3, 12–13).[85] Hughes's speaker repeats a refrain that goes unacknowledged by his addressee: "I am your son, white man!" (1, 43).[86] Both insist that a representative of the white supremacist patriarchy acknowledge his ethical obligation first by recognizing the multiracial child and then by fulfilling that child's needs. Georgia Douglas Johnson's contemporaneous poem "The Riddle" (1925) begins on a different note by evoking, perhaps with Toomer himself in mind, a "world man—cosmopolite—everyman's son" who "blend[s] the races in one" (4, 3). But her very brief poem ultimately reduces the man it describes to a biracial "riddle" of "white men's children in black men's skin" (7–8).[87]

A later work by Hughes, "Daybreak in Alabama" (1940), further underscores how poems seeking to query racial recognition can reinscribe it. Hughes's speaker imagines a not-yet-written "music" that would praise a multiethnic world (2).[88] Itemizing the contents of these "purtiest songs" (4), he states:

> And I'm gonna put white hands
> And black hands and brown and yellow hands
> And red clay earth hands in it
> Touching everybody with kind fingers
> And touching each other natural as dew[.] (15–19)

Hughes celebrates how this interracial intimacy involving "white . . . / . . . black . . . brown . . . yellow . . . / And red clay earth hands" is a result "[o]f black and white black white black people," a magnificent line that transgresses racial categories while also being defined, and thus constrained, by two of those very categories (14). Though it determinedly reaches

80 | Unlimited Eligibility?

toward a time beyond racial conflict and beyond even the capacity (much less need) to recognize, it performs the ongoingness of that conflict (and that need) in the present in its oscillation of words depicting a racial binary. Hughes's speaker seemingly cannot help but recognize multiracial identity in terms he knows are reductive. It is as if no amount of time and effort—not even if it is fueled by Hughes's nearly utopian level of anticipation in "Daybreak in Alabama"—triumphs over the cultural and linguistic limits of the cultural pluralist model of recognition and its lyric proxies.[89]

Toomer's awareness of these difficulties instigates the survey of poetic genres that shapes "The Blue Meridian," a work that intends to break through these limits. A small but growing body of criticism about "The Blue Meridian," however, has disagreed about how best to articulate Toomer's goals for this poem much less how to evaluate the degree to which he succeeds or fails to achieve them. Some scholars suggest that "The Blue Meridian" becomes more of a sermon than a poem, a compendium of aphorisms characteristic of Gurdjieff, the mystic Toomer followed after he broke from the literary community in the wake of the publication of *Cane*. Others make precisely the opposite claim, contending that the work is an overstuffed anthology of techniques derived from other poets.[90]

But can "The Blue Meridian" be unpoetic while also being derivative of many poetic traditions? Karen Ford, the scholar who has paid closest attention to Toomer's relation to poetic genre, explains this near-paradox in the context of how the poetic interludes in *Cane* gradually become less frequent, possibly dramatizing Toomer's increasing apprehension toward a model of poetry associated with race-based lyricism and foreshadowing his discomfort with identifying as African American. "The Blue Meridian," according to Ford, reasserts this "death of lyric" first enacted in *Cane* that "necessitated [him to write] an antilyrical poetry" not "equate[d with] . . . the African American past."[91] Though this reading is in some ways persuasive, Ford herself eventually backs away from classifying "The Blue Meridian" within a firm lyric/anti-lyric dichotomy, acknowledging that the poem ultimately becomes characterized by an "ambivalence" about "racialized lyrics" that is both "mocking and nostalgic."[92] According to Ford, these tensions yield to a kind of "supersession" wherein "the speaker must incorporate the past in himself as a means of transcending it."[93]

While the forthcoming reading will query that quasi-Hegelian interpretation of the forces driving Toomer's vision of American sociality, there is no question that Toomer struggles to conceptualize a path from

American culture as he knew it to the American culture he envisioned. The quasi-Whitmanian mode of address in "The Blue Meridian," rather than calling America out of the "social prison" of cultural pluralism and toward a shared ontic eligibility like the one characterizing "the rest" in "Crossing Brooklyn Ferry," increasingly shows Toomer's frustrations, culminating in the speaker giving voice to a violent desire to recognize, an impulse antithetical to the "blue" multiethnic-beyond-recognition race his poem proposes will soon define America.

The opening of "The Blue Meridian" gives no sign of the trouble to come. It begins with an expression of spectacular confidence not just in the forthcoming "new America" but in the role that the poem itself will have in inducing this political transformation. Capacious, Whitmanian apostrophes become refrains echoed occasionally later in the poem, never repeated in full but never left far from the reader's consciousness.[94]

> It is a new America,
> To be spiritualized by each new American.
> [. . .]
> Lift, lift, thou waking forces!
> Let us feel the energy of animals,
> The force of rumps and bull-bent heads
> Crashing the barrier to man. (50)

These lines insistently feature a present tense intended to persuade the reader that all is ready for this "new America" to be manifested. But the shifting between infinitives, imperatives, and participial forms also suggests ambiguity with regard to degrees and locations of agency. Precisely how this "new America" will be brought into being and who will be doing it is less clear than it initially seems, and these questions will become more prominent later in the poem. Toomer emphasizes the role of spirituality, but here too all is not as it first appears. For he refuses to linger in dogma and instead immediately associates, in Whitmanian fashion (albeit even more boldly), a "new America" with sexually intimate blendings. Toomer's references to "animals" and "bull-bent heads," as Stephanie Hawkins has observed, are "designed to provoke the fear of miscegenation" by raising racist stereotypes about the allegedly animalistic sexuality of African-American men.[95] Toomer knew these stereotypes well. Only a few years earlier, his 1931 marriage to Margery Latimer, a white woman, had received racist commentary in newspapers and magazines

82 | Unlimited Eligibility?

across the country.[96] Here, the remarkably blunt speaker offers a frank celebration of desire and sexuality that "crash[es] . . . barrier[s]," arguing that it is necessary ("[g]rowth is by admixture") in order to achieve not just the triumphant "new America" but to find "a new God," a new "faceless Deity" also existing beyond recognition (50–52).[97]

With continued confidence, Toomer's speaker blends into this Whitmanian idiom several allusions to T. S. Eliot's *The Waste Land*, a work associated with fragmentation and despair rather than cohesion and triumph. Toomer pays particular attention to Eliot's image systems and pointedly locates "The Blue Meridian" in relation to "[t]he Mississippi, sister of the Ganges," redescribing a river associated with slavery as a center of renewal and enlightenment amid a culturally and spiritually parched America (50). Unlike Eliot, the speaker shows no nostalgia for fading religious traditions and rejects them as a means of resolving the problems of modernity. Anticipating "revelation in our day" of a "new God," the previously noted "faceless deity," the speaker shames religious imagery associated with each of the major races considered in the poem:

> The old gods, led by an inverted Christ,
> A shaved Moses, a blanched Lemur,
> And a moulting Thunderbird,
> Withdrew into the distance and died[.] (51)

This itemizing of "old gods" leads into corresponding descriptions of the demise of each race they represent. After announcing that "[t]he great European races . . . // Sang of their swift achievement / And perished, displaced by machines," the poem depicts "[t]he great African races" in "sorrow in red fields, / Sing[ing] a swan song" and "[t]he great red race . . . / S[i]nk[ing] into the sacred earth" (52–54).

Though each race appears destined to meet its end, only two are memorialized by death songs. Both songs affect a folk lyricism but they do not aspire toward the kind of authenticity advocated by cultural pluralism. Instead, they rehearse problematic, at times racist tropes. The song of the "African races" vaguely evokes a blues rhythm while reiterating minstrel show stereotypes about watermelons.

> I'm leaving the shining ground, brothers,
> I sing because I ache,
> I go because I must,

I'm leaving the shining ground;
Don't ask me where,
I'll meet you there,
Brothers, I am leaving the shining ground.

But we must keep keep keep
  the watermelon.
He moaned, O Lord, Lord,
This bale will break me—
But we must keep keep keep
  the watermelon[.] (53)

The song of "the great red race" similarly presents a clichéd collage of images and sounds Toomer associates with indigenous cultures.

Hé-ya, hé-yo, hé-yo,
Hé-ya, hé-yo, hé-yo,
The ghosts of buffaloes,
A lone eagle feather,
An untamed Navaho,
Hé-ya, hé-yo, hé-yo
Hé-ya, hé-yo, hé-yo. (54)

The absence of a deathsong for the "great European races" underscores a still larger absence in the poem, a refusal to acknowledge that the enslavement of African Americans and the genocide of many indigenous tribes, in fact, was imposed by European colonizers."[98]

One wonders if an early version of such passages in the now lost "The First American" contributed to Toomer's friend contending that Toomer was "white." And one might be tempted, here, to merge Ford's observation concerning the death of Toomer's lyricism with Virginia Jackson's thesis about how lyricization eventually results in an abstract modern lyric that aligns with white supremacism. Is Toomer, here, really creating space for the song of a new, multiethnic-beyond-recognition American race or is he, by not presenting a parallel death song for the white race, tacitly gesturing toward its superiority, both generally and within the modern lyric? But, while such a reading seems plausible, why would a poem that initially seemed eager to provoke and challenge white readers' racial anxieties suddenly make concessions to them?

84 | Unlimited Eligibility?

There are no easy answers to this question. These death songs likely allude to "The Land of Buried Cultures," a chapter in Waldo Frank's *Our America* depicting the gradual "disappearance" of "the cultures of the German, the Latin, the Celt, the Slav, the Anglo-Saxon and the African" and especially "the Indian," who Frank, following a long-standing racist trope, flatly pronounces "dying and . . . doomed." Frank condemns the cruel consequences of European colonialism while also emphasizing that "there need be no sentimentality," since "justice is an anthropomorphic fancy."[99] Like the St. Louis Hegelians admired by Whitman late in his career, Frank's cultural pluralism simply submits to the mighty demiurge of (white) American History. Toomer, however, had broken his friendship with Frank and rejected cultural pluralism. So it is difficult to read these allusions to Frank as earnest endorsements of that ideology. Karen Ford argues that this moment in the poem is, in fact, incoherent or, at least, "divided between" Toomer's impulse to "renew and celebrate these racialized lyrics even as he disparages them in his own minstrel-style mimicry of the songs," a tension partly resolved by the plan that such "songs must [and will, by the poem itself,] be redirected toward a future vision of national spiritual enlightenment."[100] But it is also difficult to argue that the poem dialectically wishes to absorb folk lyricism from minority cultures. For that would reiterate cultural pluralism. Instead, is the attempt to absorb folk lyricism while also mocking that cultural pluralist gesture a kind of negative dialectics intended to expose and dismantle a system he distrusts? Does the potential irony involved in such a stance complicate it from being as easily aligned with the trajectory of the lyricized modern lyric described above? These questions are hard to answer beyond noting how characteristic the unresolved tensions in this gesture are to Toomer's complex, at times contradictory sense of self.

The poem, in any case, surges ahead and shifts to yet another poetic idiom, one more historically grounded and responsive to human trauma than the near-parodies of racialized lyrics. Shaming another nearly sacred image, the speaker describes America's national symbol, "[t]he eagle," as "a sublime and bloody bird" whose life is characterized by "extremes / Of affirming and denying, / Creating, destroying." This powerful, even frightful creature has "one wing . . . broken" and is "plung[ing] to earth . . . [in] panic before death" (56). Spiraling out of control, the eagle becomes "[a]n airplane, with a broken wing, / In a tail spin," resulting in a "*Crash!*" that, not surprisingly, is revealed to be a metaphor for the stock market crash that left average Americans experiencing a no less vertiginous economic descent:

Jean Toomer's "The Blue Meridian" | 85

From beings to nothings,
From human beings to grotesques,
From men and women to manikins,
From forms to chaoses—
[. . .]
Are men born to go down like this?
Violence is violence.
Our holidays leave us as we were,
Our schools do not regenerate,
Precisely the educated are the brains of war,
Our churches do not transform—
So here we are. In war, in peace[.] (58)

Here, Toomer's poem alludes to the occasionally didactic, documentary-style political lyrics of the thirties written by poets like Muriel Rukeyser or Genevieve Taggard, an idiom featuring the kind of quasi-socialist critique Toomer had advocated in his "Race Problems" essay. Traditions and institutions had died or failed, but it is most fundamentally the economic system that rendered "beings [in]to nothings," into ontological absences. Though Toomer's references to spirituality, not surprisingly, depart from a purely materialist critique, there is no question that he deems the dehumanizing effects of the Great Depression principally a result of unchecked capitalist greed. The "we" presented here is not an ahistorical abstraction but, instead, a "we" seeking to build a quasi-socialist solidarity.

Not steel, not chemicals or money
Are spirited to suffer and rejoice,
Not what we have become, this angel-dough,
But slowly die, never having birth
Above the body, above its ego and hungers,
To sit at desks, stand in lines, ask for jobs,
Fill space and pass time
Within a prison system all of wardens. (59)

Piling negatives upon negatives, Toomer emphasizes how men and women who are "spirited to suffer and rejoice" have been rendered into objects to be used like "steel[,] . . . chemicals[,] or money." Out of desperation and unaware of their unrealized potential, they "ask for" the very "jobs" that dehumanized them in the first place. Seeing no alternative, they

86 | Unlimited Eligibility?

support a system that creates the industrial equivalent of a carceral state with each serving as "wardens" over each other.

A pair of subsequent allusions to "Song of the Open Road" and "Song of Myself" return the poem to the lyricism of the young Whitman with which Toomer began, suggesting that "The Blue Meridian," despite its digressions, might yet respond to the Great Depression by melding economic critique with a Whitmanian collectivity. In the first of these passages, Toomer appears to address a professional class, people who retain, even during the Great Depression, "A fine suite . . . / A modern office" (62). He implores them to leave the labor practices, values, and accoutrements associated with the excesses that spurred the economic crisis. After each litany of professional privileges (from "a pin" and "a watch-fob" to "an ego"), he exclaims "Let go!" recalling and revising Whitman's iterations of "Allons!" (Let's go!) in "Song of the Open Road," a poem filled with similarly idealistic appeals to readers to leave the current social structure in favor of a more just, more inclusive one. The second allusion to Whitman appears a page later and offers, as Frederik Rusch has noted, a series of variations on the famous "Unscrew the locks from the doors!" sequence in section 24 of "Song of Myself."[101] Toomer's speaker exclaims: "Unlock the races . . . // Uncase the nations . . . // Uncase the regions . . . // Free the sexes . . . // Unlock the classes . . . // Expand the fields [of study] . . . // Open the religions" (64–65). With this breaking and blurring of categories with which one might be recognized, "The Blue Meridian" appears prepared to conceptualize an American race in terms of a sociality of unlimited eligibility conceived for the Depression era.

But a couple passages uncomfortably wedged between these allusions show Toomer, once again, nearly contradicting himself. Immediately after telling his reader to "let go" of the life of capitalistic excess, the speaker advises:

> Walk from it
> Wake from it,
> From the terrible mistake
> That we who have power are less than we should be.
> Join that staff whose left hand is
> Demolishing defectives,
> Whose right is setting up a mill
> And a wheel is therein, its rim of power,

Its spokes of knowledge, its hub of conscience—
And in that same heart we will hold all life.
It is the world we live in
Then let us live in it. (63)

Rather than resisting power as it has been culturally and socioeconomically constructed, Toomer's speaker, in this puzzling passage, appears to insist on more fully realizing it in a different venue ("a mill"), apparently out of a sudden sense of resignation that "[i]t is the world that we live in." Still more disturbing is the eager endorsement of "[d]emolishing defectives," an objective difficult to reconcile with a "heart" that "hold[s] all life" dear. Toomer, here, may refer to his 1935 purchase of a farm in Pennsylvania with a gristmill and (what he called) a "Mill House" that he intended to repurpose into a kind of retreat center "patterned after Gurdjieff's Fontainebleau."[102] Such a reading potentially would explain the appeal to "knowledge" and "conscience," as well as the mysterious "staff." And the aggressive rhetoric may connect to a number of similarly contemporaneous appeals Toomer made on behalf of an idiosyncratic kind of eugenics. The "Race Problems" essay, for example, momentarily argues that "the positive aspect of the race problem" is that it creates an opportunity to ask "how . . . a selective fusion of the racial and cultural factors of America" might be achieved by "exchanging [between races and cultures] on the basis of intelligence, character, and ability." Unlike more stereotypical eugenic claims made on the basis of race separation, Toomer insists that actively cultivating racial "amalgamation" will bring about "the best possible stock and culture," the New Americans for a New America predicted in "The Blue Meridian."[103]

In other words, Toomer's essay and poem pointedly entertain the possibility of "enforced miscegenation" that terrified Horace Kallen into conceptualizing cultural pluralism in the first place. But even if one contextualizes Toomer's claims as knowing provocations intended to enrage cultural pluralists as well as somewhat earnest explorations of a more widespread, pre–Third Reich discourse of eugenics, a troubling inconsistency in Toomer's thinking persists.[104] For eugenics inevitably depends upon an elite group of recognizers (the "staff" the speaker plans to "join") distributing or withholding recognition in precisely the way that Toomer elsewhere eloquently opposes and that is at odds with the politics of Whitman's early poems he references. Toomer, here, enthusiastically

88 | Unlimited Eligibility?

supports a violent act of categorization ("Demolishing defectives") in a poem otherwise committed to exposing and refuting precisely that kind of violence.

The next verse paragraph, at least initially, appears to bring us back to a tone characteristic of Toomer's typical line of argument against the politics of recognition. He worries that cultural pluralism is a ploy of the powerful, an attempt to splinter people into groups and then create friction between those groups before they can form a coalition to challenge the elite.

> Islanders, newly come upon the continents,
> If to live against annihilation,
> Must outgrow themselves and their old places,
> Disintegrate tribal integrators,
> And fix, as their center of gravity,
> As their compelling ideal
> The symbol of Universal Man—
> Must outgrow clan and class, color,
> Nationalism, creed, all the fetishes
> Of the arrested and dismembered,
> And find a larger truth in larger hearts,
> Lest the continents shrink to islands,
> Lest human destiny abort
> And man, bristling against himself, explode. (63)

This passage, in many ways, reiterates the argument of "Race Problems and Modern Society," including its warning about tensions between groups building to a destructive "climax." The speaker warns "[i]slanders" that fostering group identity will not save them from "annihilation," the process of being turned into "nothing" as a result of unbridled capitalism. These lines, however, open additional fissures in the poem's argument. After having spent pages devoted to economic critique, the speaker strangely advises his audience to "outgrow . . . class," as if some form of spiritual growth could remove the inequalities created by the Great Depression. Even his critique of cultural pluralism here disintegrates into vague affirmations of "a larger truth [found] in larger hearts," aspirations that seem suspiciously similar to the kind of lazy "liberal opinion and intelligent humanism" that his "Race Problems" essay skewers.[105]

Furthermore, the hope of uncovering a "[u]niversal[ity]" resting on a "larger truth" that dominates much of the remainder of the poem is rendered almost unintelligible insofar as he paradoxically describes this ideal both as something foundational that has been obscured by prejudice and now needs to be uncovered (a "Root Religion") and as something still unrealized and yet-to-be ("[m]ust outgrow . . . / And find a larger truth in larger hearts") (65, 63). This confusion undercuts the climactic unveiling of the poem's genuinely provocative title image, the "Blue Meridian," which Toomer intends as a replacement for prior, socially constructed lines and divisions, including the "black meridian," the "white meridian," the various "shadows," as well as "marks not made by nature," "purgatories of many names," and "self-streaks" (50, 62, 60, 61). For what is most suggestive about the "man of blue or purple, / Beyond the little tags and small marks" is not his relation to an unstated abstract truth, but instead his being hybridized-beyond-recognition in a society increasingly filled with others like himself, a status that (Toomer seems to imply) renders moot debates over ethnic categorization according to either a particular identity or a universal norm (72).

Such complexities make "The Blue Meridian" particularly difficult to assess overall. If the first half of the poem is dominated by Toomer's attempt to survey and subsume various poetics within an idiom capable of forwarding his Whitmanian poetics and politics, then the second half of the poem reveals his synthesis splitting at seams he attempts to patch by strangely invoking discourses antithetical to his project, including discourses of recognition. A sequence of violent images running throughout the poem externalizes this rhetorical instability without arriving at any resolution. Though Toomer expresses disgust at "guns" and "bombs" that shape "brutal lives, ugly deaths" in modernity, his poem also suggests that a "[c]rashing," "[d]emolishing," and "break[ing of] . . . arms" may be necessary in order to bring his Whitmanian social order to life in the world (58, 50, 63, 65). These fractures within Toomer's poem raise difficult questions. Is unlimited eligibility, as a potential premise for a democratic social order, so far from being realizable that it cannot begin to be implemented without collapsing into contradiction? And how does one compare the resulting violence with the violence inherent in how the cultural pluralist iteration of sociopolitical recognition struggles to detach itself from social hierarchies inclined to retain historical inequities?

90 | Unlimited Eligibility?

And If American "Culture [Is] Not Entirely Colorless . . ."? Jean Toomer Debates James Weldon Johnson

A sequence of letters exchanged between Jean Toomer and James Weldon Johnson in July 1930 clarifies the stakes of these questions. Johnson sought Toomer's permission to include several of his works in a second edition of *The Book of American Negro Poetry*. The 1922 first edition began with a remarkable preface linking artistic and political recognition (the fact that "the public, generally speaking, does not know that there are American Negro poets" is a significant problem if "the world does not know that a people is great until that people produces great literature and art") while also worrying a good deal (as many Harlem Renaissance writers did) about the process and result of that recognition.[106] Johnson regretted how "the colored poet in the United States labors within limitations," including the "pressure . . . to be propogandic" on behalf of his ethnicity, and conceded that "these conditions are suffocating to breadth and to real art in poetry."[107] Dialect (which Johnson deems "an instrument with but two full stops, humor and pathos"), when used in lyric appeals for recognition could contribute to racial essentialism, creating a "need for Aframerican poets in the United States to work out a new and distinctive form of expression" beyond the bounds of established stereotypes. Johnson adds that "the sooner they ["Aframerican poets"] are able to write *American* poetry spontanteously, the better" (Johnson's emphasis).[108] This difficult balance, working toward writing recognizably "American poetry" while writing as an "Aframerican," which is to say working toward achieving recognition as an American while currently being recognized all too often through stereotypes of "Aframerican[s]," became a point of contention eight years later, when Johnson wrote to Toomer.

Knowing the cultural pluralist premises framing the anthology, Toomer predictably refuses the offer, politely but firmly responding that he understood not just himself but "we all" as "Americans" and thus had chosen to "withdraw from all things which emphasize or tend to emphasize racial or cultural divisions." Toomer's energies, instead, were solely "devoted and directed towards the building of a life" of the emergent "American stock or race," given his conviction that "the time [wa]s ripe to give a definite expression of these views." And he added, "[A]s regards art I particularly hold this view."[109] Johnson's reply chides Toomer for his refusal to participate. But it is most striking for how much it concedes and where it draws the ultimate distinction between their positions. It

Jean Toomer's "The Blue Meridian" | 91

is neither Toomer's premise nor his goals that Johnson opposes. Instead, what separates the two thinkers is a matter of timing: "The elements going into the making of the new American race or stock have not yet reached a state of fusion, and until they do these group designations if only as a matter of linguistic convenience will continue to be used. In this I am merely stating what appears to me as fact."[110] Johnson does not sense a revolution in the understanding of race to be imminent in the United States. Nor does he consider, as Locke a few years later would, a possible alliance between race consciousness and class consciousness, much less a eugenics project akin to Toomer's provocation in "The Blue Meridian." Instead, he reaffirms the gradual progress resulting, in part, from "the work done by the colored creative artist" who "has begun to be so recognized" as part of "our common, national culture."[111]

Behind this debate over timing is a debate over the capacity for poetry to intervene in politics. Johnson believes poetry is capable of encouraging greater social recognition by increasing awareness of the struggles and joys shaping the lives of African Americans. As long as "the colored poet" still "labors under the handicap of finding culture not entirely colorless in the United States," he or she has a moral obligation, in this view, to identify with fellow African Americans and to appeal for a kind of recognition not yet granted.[112] Toomer, no doubt, would have agreed with Johnson's assessment of American culture remaining "not entirely colorless." Precisely for this reason, Toomer sensed a different moral obligation to seek a different lyricism from the one Johnson warily endorses. In the most striking moments of "The Blue Meridian," he crafts a poem that, by its insistent hortatory appeal, hopes to be capable of stirring awareness of a political space that defies (rather than is defined by) exigencies of recognition, a paraontic space demarcated by a democratic sociality not yet achieved in the world. Toomer believed that this possibility needed to be catalyzed now rather than restrained by the cultural pluralist focus on group identity, and he felt that his poetry could be that catalyst.

It is in this context that the failure of "The Blue Meridian" remains moving. For Toomer miscalculated not just America's readiness for a Whitmanian poetics and politics of unlimited eligibility but his own. On the one hand, Toomer's example, wherein his well-intentioned naivete sours into something almost sinister, might suggest that the cultural pluralist framework, problematic though it may be, stands as the only available option. On the other hand, Toomer's sense of moral urgency—a need for alternatives to the politics of recognition, even if those alternatives are not yet articulable—warns against complacency. Toomer's and Johnson's struggles, from this angle, indicate not just a need for new discursive space within which new socialities can be fashioned but the possibility of a new discourse itself, as well as a new poetics for stimulating this new discourse. It is this exceedingly difficult project that the subject of the next chapter, Hart Crane, pursued, particularly in a sequence of works from 1923–1924, a time when he was regularly in conversation with Toomer. How do you create "new word[s]," as Crane called them, that enable one to imagine and then begin to enact a new democratic order inspired by the aim of unlimited eligibility? The first step, Crane felt, was to fashion a poetics that enabled readers to learn how to "look" without recognizing.

Chapter Three

Looking without Recognizing

Hart Crane's Lyric Sociality

In the spring of 1923, the New York state legislature debated and then passed an "amend[ed]" version of a "disorderly conduct" law that was already well-known among African Americans and immigrants, extending its application to another group, persons "frequent[ing] or loiter[ing] about any public place soliciting men for the purpose of committing a crime against nature or other lewdness."[1] Though existing laws dating to the colonial era already prohibited "sodomy," the revised definition of "disorderly conduct" made the appearance of being a man "soliciting" another man classifiable as a criminal act. In the decades that followed, "more than fifty-thousand men were arrested . . . in New York City alone" as a result of this law, often due to police using entrapment strategies or raiding bars and nightclubs.[2] So it may be no coincidence that Hart Crane, in a March 1923 letter to Gorham Munson, expresses frustration about how even allegedly open-minded friends could irresponsibly wield knowledge of his romantic life.[3]

> I discover that I have been all-too easy all along in letting out announcements of my sexual predilections. Not that anything unpleasant has happened or is imminent. But it does put me into obligatory relations to a certain extent with "those who are in the know," and this irks me to think of sometimes. After all, when you're dead it doesn't matter, and this statement proves my immunity from any "shame" about it. But I find the

94 | Unlimited Eligibility?

> ordinary business of "earning a living" entirely too stringent
> to want to add any prejudices against me *of that nature* in the
> minds of any publicans and sinners [Crane's emphasis]. Such
> things have such a wholesale way of leaking out![4]

While poems from this period and later, in fact, suggest that Crane did continue to struggle with shame, it is moving, here, to see him expressing anger in addition to quite understandable social, legal, and economic anxiety. He wants to prevent "leak[s]," worries about how they might lead to "unpleasant[ness]" for him, and wonders if he should be more cautious in his "announcements," yet he understands that the real problem is not his own garrulousness but, instead, a social order that places him into "obligatory relations" even among those he should be able to trust. He is unnerved by the fact that being recognized as a man attracted to other men is tantamount to offering anyone in his social circle information that could be used to blackmail him. For it was not only the police who participated in this system of control. Friendship itself could come to feel like entrapment, whether it actually was or not.

Faced with this dynamic, Crane's continued cultivation of a wide circle of friends was itself an act of defiance. And he made it the bold task of his 1923–1924 poetry, perhaps the most ambitious he would write, not just to interrogate and undermine this sociopolitical system increasingly calibrated to codify, recognize, and punish but to attempt to imagine through his poetry alternative, less hierarchical, more democratic modes of social relation. In doing so, Crane did not seek to initiate in his poetry a process for understanding sexuality as an identity to be recognized. But neither did Crane stop writing about his "sexual predilections." In fact, he wrote more explicitly about it than he had before. This chapter seeks to understand the poetic and political provocation of Crane's commitment to write about sexuality and its social context, but to invite readers to "[l]ook" and "[r]egard" without recognizing or "apprehen[ding]."

Scholarship foregrounding Crane's sexuality, including some important, relatively recent work by, for example, Michael Snediker, John Vincent, and Brian Reed, frequently describes him as a "lyric" poet or a writer of "lyrics."[5] Though this risks retroprojecting onto Crane a later, post-Stonewall use of lyric to assert group self-recognition amid an identity politics that did not exist in the teens and twenties, there is historical evidence for associating Crane with the word.[6] Crane's extant letters reveal that he occasionally does describe his poems as "lyrics." Near the start of his writing career, on November 13, 1918, writing unsolicited to "Mr. Bubb," a local clergyman who also was a regional publisher, the teenage poet offers a "meagre sheaf of poems" that he deems "these lyrics" for publication as "a modest pamphlet" that, he suggests, simply could be entitled "Six Lyrics."[7] Here, and roughly seven other times in extant letters, Crane seems to use the term to designate short poems.[8] However, the frequency of "lyric" pales in comparison to his use of "poem" or "poems," which appear over three hundred times.[9] More generically precise terms like ballad/ballade and sonnet, for example, are used only six and seven times respectively, the former term sometimes with reference to piano works by Chopin. This ratio of terms, in part, reflects an already emerging tendency that Virginia Jackson and Yopie Prins find predominant by "midcentury," wherein poetry criticism, pedagogy, and practice "assumed that most poetry conform[ed] to lyric protocols" without even "think[ing] about 'the lyric'"[10] As a term, "poetry," in this way, could participate in lyricization.

Though the historical usage of such words and the politics associated with them unavoidably is oversimplified by generalizations, anthologies and critical studies of poetry published during the teens, twenties, and early thirties, the years when Crane was actively writing, can help to create a clearer picture of the cultural space within which his lyric politics developed. Still relatively recent innovations in free verse, as well as idioms like symbolism and imagism, along with Steinian verbal experiments, and the impersonal aesthetics and collage techniques of poets like Marianne Moore, Ezra Pound, and T. S. Eliot, sparked debates about what was deemed poetic at all. Some anthologies, of course, reflected either an endorsement of innovation (e.g., Ezra Pound's *Des Imagistes*) or a rejection of it that reasserts tradition in lyricized terms as subjective expression (e.g., anthologies edited by Coblentz, Squire, and Walters).[11] But many others, including some of the most frequently reprinted (e.g., Monroe and Henderson's or Untermeyer's anthologies) avoided fierce polemics out of an attempt at objectivity or ambivalence, a stance that corresponds to a similarly in-between relationship to lyricization.[12] Crane himself does not figure in many of these texts, since they predate his coming to prominence.[13] But they give a sense of how, despite quarrels between innovators and traditionalists, a broader poetic mainstream persisted, creating a fairly wide, even flexible space.[14] Crane, for example, qualifiedly admired both Eliot and Whitman, sought out Gertrude Stein when he visited Paris, and yet also insisted that "a great deal of romanticism may persist . . . [and] deserve serious consideration."[15]

96 | Unlimited Eligibility?

Of course, the degree of aesthetic flexibility available to poets in that moment related to their sociopolitical positionality. Insulated by white privilege, Crane did not need to weigh, for example, the risks of using (or not using) dialect. A broader array of idioms was more easily and uncomplicatedly available to him than was available to his black peers. At the same time, he saw the changes in the criminal code and correspondingly sensed, as the letter that began this chapter suggested, the intensified pressures of what came to be known as the "closet." This moment seems to have stirred within him a sense of political and poetic urgency, neither to hide nor to accept negotiations over his personhood mediated by recognition processes, but, instead, to try to take advantage of an increasingly but not-quite defined and regulated social-conceptual space around sexuality. Similarly, though subject-centered poetic expression was becoming increasingly inflected by lyricization, it was not yet fully defined in that way. Crane's poetry from 1923–1924, at least tacitly, is energized by a sense of these potentialities as they are on the cusp of being subsumed by a more limited set of poetic and sociopolitical norms and by the powers that enforce those norms. In this unsettling, if also generative, moment, "lyric" and "poem" were not yet fully associated with subjective expression from an abstract, allegedly universal speaker—or, alternately, an appeal or demand for social recognition by someone disempowered. It was possible for Crane (or so he hoped) to assess his culture and draw on Whitman's example in order to develop an idiom that invited readers to *look at* his sexuality *without recognizing* it in existing, increasingly oppressive terms and, in the process, to slow their acts of "apprehen[sion]," to use one of the words Crane himself wielded to convey the violence of recognition processes, and to affirm an ontological proximity and eligibility shared by writer/speaker/reader that might serve, in microcosm, as a more inclusively democratic model of American society.

This chapter begins by considering how Crane tested this thesis at an individual level, discussing his poem "Possessions" with a new friend, Jean Toomer, someone who Crane understood to be a fellow "outsider" (albeit of another sort) and someone who, as we saw in chapter two, briefly aligned with but quickly came to reject the cultural pluralist promise to recognize difference as a means of including rather than oppressing minority populations. The looking-at-without-recognizing of gay sexuality that Crane attempts to encourage in "Possessions" serves as a microcosm of what he had just begun to imagine on a much larger social scale in his early, fragmentary drafts of an ambitious (but then only single-poem) project called "The Bridge."[16] From the start, "The Bridge" was intended as an act of sociocultural affirmation counterbalancing the sociocultural disintegration evoked by T. S. Eliot's *The Waste Land*. Curiously little attention has been paid to these drafts of "The Bridge," which are the focus of the second section of this chapter, despite how they present Crane attempting to theorize his poetics with greater sophistication and ambition than ever before, especially through what he called the "logic of metaphor," a figurative correlate for personal and sociopolitical bridging itself. These drafts do not appeal for gay inclusion, a quasi-cultural pluralist political strategy that would not emerge until the fifties, nor do they assert a gay liberation from existing social norms, a strategy that would not emerge until the late sixties and early seventies. Instead, they present gay sexuality as a facet of certain persons and thus a facet of culture and, in particular, a resource for understanding the looking without recognizing that Crane finds fundamental to the democratic sociality he associates with the title image of the poem.

But while these fragmentary first drafts of "The Bridge" ecstatically evoke this sociality, Crane struggled to imagine how to span the gap between society as it is and society as he hoped it would become, a challenge that would overshadow the development of the poem and much of the remainder of his short life. After a nearly two-year break, Crane returns to the project and sets aside the model of sociality that he had been developing and instead adopts a number of very different, even contrary, cultural pluralist premises. "The Dance," in particular, celebrates recognition of and identification with an indigenous person as a violently absorptive act that makes possible the triumphant synthesis enacted in "Atlantis," the poem's triumphant conclusion. The completed, book-length version of *The Bridge*, in this way, was as much at odds with its own original poetic and political premises as Toomer's "The Blue Meridian." The remainder of the chapter, however, turns to "Recitative," a poem Crane began at the time when he wrote "Possessions" and completes perhaps not long after he set aside his first drafts of "The Bridge."[17] "Recitative" realizes the politics implied by the "logic of metaphor," including the prospect of looking without recognizing, more fully than any other work by Crane, creating a paraontic discursive space at the interface of reader, writer, and speaker, who share responsibility for meaning-making as they are invited to leave the "white buildings" associated with the corporate capitalism of the roaring twenties and approach "the bridge," "walk[ing] through time with equal pride."[18]

98 | Unlimited Eligibility?

"Witness Now This Trust": Crane and Toomer

Hart Crane and Jean Toomer shared a brief but intense friendship during 1923–1924, an intersectional encounter between an artist struggling with the ongoing legacies of American racism and an artist struggling with what would come to be called homophobia. Langdon Hammer has explained how "the two young men were brought together by [their mutual friend, the cultural pluralist thinker] Waldo Frank . . . who hailed them as the rising voices of a new national literature."[19] Crane and Toomer almost immediately liked each other, but their correspondence reflects opposite artistic trajectories. In the wake of the publication of *Cane*, Toomer was starting to turn away from not just cultural pluralism but from art as a means of investigating democratic sociality ("The Blue Meridian" being the major exception) and to focus on Gurdjieff's spiritual teachings. Crane, on the other hand, was just beginning to envision *The Bridge* as a project predicated on the power of art to intervene in American politics affirmatively, enacting a "mystical synthesis of 'America'" featuring the title image as a "symbol of our constructive future, our unique identity [as Americans]."[20] This premise, however, would lead him to a struggle with cultural pluralism as consequential as Toomer's had been.

The first extant letter from Crane to Toomer, dated August 19, 1923, indicates how quickly they shared their most intimate struggles. Crane expresses respect for Toomer's search for a spiritual "chrysalis in the mountains," while admitting that his own life toggled between "strenuous" office work by day and "complicated devastations" of secretive liaisons at night ("beckonings . . . into doorways, subways, sympathies, rapports").[21] Within weeks, Crane starts sending Toomer poems locating these personal anxieties amid the broader problematics of social recognition from the perspective of someone lacking it or suffering from oppressive forms of it, dynamics Toomer, of course, knew well. No wonder that Crane asked his new friend in a November 23, 1923, letter whether "anything in [the poems] . . . gets through at all to an outsider," a phrase that, at least in part, may acknowledge their sexual and racial differences and hint at how Crane had begun to realize that his poetics would need to support his expanding sociocultural ambitions, including the challenge of confronting forms of exclusion beyond those he had experienced.[22]

One of these poems, "Possessions," not only locates the speaker among those being legislated against but initially seems to invite or even command an act of recognition from a reader, before its argument turns toward a different poetics and politics of looking without recognizing. Instructed to "[w]itness now this trust!" we watch a tryst between two men, the kind of encounter that had become more explicitly criminalized that very year (1). We also "[w]itness" the speaker "trust[ing]" Toomer and any later readers with this knowledge.

> Witness now this trust! the rain
> That steals, softly, direction
> And the key, ready to hand, sifting
> One moment in sacrifice (the direst)
> Through a thousand nights the flesh
> Assaults outright for bolts that linger
> Hidden,—O undirected as the sky
> That through its black foam has no eyes
> For this fixed stone of lust . . .
>
> Accumulate such moments to an hour:
> Account the total of this trembling tabulation.
> I know the screen, the distant, flying taps
> And stabbing medley that sways—
> Rounding behind to press and grind,
> And the mercy, feminine, that stays
> As though prepared.
>
> And I, entering, take up the stone
> As quiet as you can make a man . . .
> In Bleecker Street, still trenchant in a void
> But dabbling sure possessions in new reach,
> I hold the stone up in a disk of light—
> I, turning, turning on smoked forking spires,
> The city's stubborn lives, dreams, desires.
>
> Tossed on these horns, who, bleeding, dies
> Lacks all but piteous admissions to be spilt
> Upon my page whose blind sum sometimes turns
> Controllable to blended voices stripped
> Of rage, catastrophy and partial appetites—
> To pure possession . . . The inclusive cloud
> Whose heart is fire shall come,—the white wind rase
> All but bright stones wherein my smiling plays.[23]

100 | Unlimited Eligibility?

The poem references the signals, the "distant, flying taps," made by a man looking to pick-up another man on "Bleecker Street," a hub of the New York City gay community (12, 19). And the speaker, with "key, ready to hand" (3), expresses relief at how the "black foam" of the night sky "has no eyes" and thus cannot witness, much less report the liaison (8). The "trust[ed]" reader learns that this is not a new experience (1). For this one night is representative of "a thousand [such] nights" (5). Additional imperatives instruct readers to "[a]ccumulate such moments" and to "[a]ccount the total of this trembling tabulation" (10, 11). But the narrative of the sexual encounters, though repeatedly implied, never quite unfolds and the idiom of the poem becomes increasingly complicated. The poem shifts back and forth between various times (anticipating and experiencing and reflecting on the encounters) and settings (inside and outside the meeting places) rather than following a linear chronology.

A number of scholars have argued that this aspect of the poem's diction, syntax, and form enacts the interplay of concealment and disclosure that define the psychosocial experience of cruising.[24] But while the speaker's desires and fears are clear, he is deeply puzzled by the "blind sum" of it all, a totality seemingly beyond his capacity to see and to assess (26). Before the defining of sexuality as an identity, what do such experiences (then deemed a criminalized activity, sin, or a kind of psychopathology), taken together as his "possessions," make him (20)? As he "sift[s]" through his past, there remain hints of his ongoing struggle with shame, a sense that he has partially assented to the social and legal stigma that renders his desire a "fixed stone of lust" and sex nothing more than the "direst" kind of "sacrifice" or even a "stabbing medley" ominously associated with "smoked forking spires" upon which the speaker "dies" (3, 9, 4, 13, 22, 24). But there is an equally powerful impulse to reject that shame and "hold the stone up" in the "light" of day or, alternately, "spil[l it] / Upon my page" of the poem for all to see (21, 25–26). Yet the speaker does not express this urge for visibility in terms of a request for social recognition. The slightly later, published version of the poem makes this especially clear. After having been "[w]ounded by apprehensions out of speech," a phrase that pointedly frames perception (and, by extension, recognition itself) in terms of seizure and arrest ("apprehen[d]"), Crane knows better, even if he has not fully conceptualized an alternative sociality (19).[25]

Anxiously awaiting Toomer's reaction to "Possessions," Crane sent a more candid, if still encoded, follow-up letter linking "the poem" to the ways "that evil accumulates, if not *in* us, at least in pockets and domains of the world without. And that the mark + gauge of our progress is quite obviously to be told in the successively more intense attacks of the dark force upon us—as we continue to defy it always more persistently. It takes flesh against our bodies, it assumes terrific marks and celebrations against our souls. The pointed finger appears through keyholes of our most sacred sanctuaries."[26] Such a gloss hints at how the work captures Crane's battle with shame over his sexuality. Crane describes an "evil" but struggles to understand what and where that evil is, whether it is associated with his very being ("if not *in* us") or with outside forces that shape how one understands ("the pointed finger" invading "our most sacred sanctuaries"), indeed how one recognizes oneself in light of the world's terms of recognition.

Having been nudged, Toomer quickly obliges with a reply only two days later, praising various facets of the poem's imagery, rhythm, and diction while avoiding comment on the most clearly sexual passages (Crane would later drop the draft's most explicit phrase: "[r]ounding behind to press and grind") or the argument of the work as a whole. But even if Toomer hesitated to address such matters, he never condemns what Crane describes and, in only slightly veiled language, praises the poem's "amazing definition" of a "torturous reality," as well as its "deep, thrusting, . . . passionate" emotions. And he signs the letter "my joy to you, and my love," leaving no doubt that his expression of support was personal as well artistic.[27] Crane expressed immediate relief and gratitude to Toomer ("You don't know how I appreciate your note on 'Possessions.'"), even as he remained somewhat coy about what his specific aims for the poem—and for Toomer's response to it—had been.[28]

If Crane sought a kind of empathy from a reader of "Possessions," what shape did he hope that empathy might take? He implores the reader to draw close ("[w]itness," "[a]ccumulate," "[a]ccount") through (and not in spite of) vivid but elusive images conveyed by idiosyncratic diction, syntactical interruptions, ellipses, and enjambments that make it difficult to draw meaning. Readers are invited to feel intensely rather than to understand, much less recognize, what they have nevertheless been told to "[w]itness." These seeming paradoxes encompass the speaker and reader and even Crane himself, who later acknowledged that "a poem like 'Possessions' really cannot be technically explained," since its puzzlements persist "to a large extent" for the author.[29] This leveling gesture, within which reader and writer share a moment of intense hermeneutic potency on equal terms, is a key part of the meaning-making mediated by what

102 | Unlimited Eligibility?

he would come to describe as the "logic of metaphor." The final lines of "Possessions" elliptically gesture toward the sociality that results from this shared, mutually constructed, space of inquiry and/as intimacy. The "fixed stone of lust" has been transformed into "bright stones" that have been "[e]rase[d]" and now only reflect "my smiling" (and in the published version "our smiling"), as he (and we) prophetically anticipate an "inclusive cloud / Whose heart is fire shall come" (9, 29–31). The sources of this image have been debated, but whatever allusive context Crane may have had in mind, it underscores a transformative power rooted in a mode of relation predicated on looking and being near but refusing to imagine "inclus[ion]" as a function of recognition.[30]

"The Bridge" in 1923: "A Living Concourse / . . . from Equal Out to Equal"

"Possessions" was a brief attempt at envisioning a mode of relation that Crane already was beginning to conceive on a national scale. While it took roughly seven years to write *The Bridge*, concentrated efforts came in two distinct phases. Crane initially drafted during early to mid-1923 and then, after a period of at least two years when he made little progress on the poem, he recommenced in late 1925 or early 1926 and brought composition to a close about four years later. Crane himself seems to have distinguished between the two phases of work, at times, as if they were nearly two separate projects, and it is not hard to understand why.[31] Relatively little material from the 1923 drafts makes it into the final poem, rendering the post-1925 work dramatically different in concept from the one he had earlier envisioned. The earlier drafts worked toward a sociality grounded on an ontological eligibility affirmed by looking without recognizing, while the later drafts reverted to the recognition-oriented model forwarded by cultural pluralism. This section seeks to understand that initial goal as well as the eventual pivot away from it.

Comparisons of the completed poem and the fragmentary, early drafts must center on what would become the final section, "Atlantis," since the limited amount of material retained from these drafts primarily was incorporated into it. As the intensely musical, densely allusive, jubilant culmination of *The Bridge*, "Atlantis" weaves together references to all of the prior sections of the poem that had collectively provided an idiosyncratic tour through American cultural history. But the early drafts initially addressed a topic almost entirely absent from the final text, a decisive shift that Thomas Yingling identifies with a "general swerve away from overt homosexual reference in his work after 1923." According to Yingling, Crane quickly learned that gay identity and poetic ambition (or, at least, ambitious poetry seeking to intervene socially) were "flatly contradictory sites," and, as a result, "subsequent drafts of 'Atlantis' replace this erotic excess with the semiotic excess of style that leads (in the language of the final version) 'Sight, sound and flesh . . . from time's realm.'"[32] Langdon Hammer also notes this desexualizing of the original drafts but then "reverse[s] the general direction of Yingling's analysis" by arguing that "Crane could never, as a homosexual poet, become a national poet. But in another sense, and precisely because he could not declare himself a homosexual poet, Crane could only become a national poet. That is, because Crane could not speak of or as 'himself,' he was able to speak to and on behalf of 'America'; because Crane could not specify his desire, he spoke of his desire in a language of universals."[33] Both Yingling and Hammer, however, rely on neatly drawn dichotomies. Stating that Crane "could only become a national poet" oversimplifies, as Brian Reed has noted, the range of writing strategies and career trajectories of a number of other near-contemporary gay poets.[34] Yingling and Hammer, furthermore, frame the earliest iteration of *The Bridge* in terms of a personal lyric and thus minimize the sociopolitical (if not explicitly national) ambitions already at work, an oversimplification that correlates to a tendency to underplay the complexity of the idiom of the earlier version. Though the final "Atlantis" certainly stands as a spectacularly intense example of "semiotic excess," it cannot be dissociated from other semiotically excessive work from 1923–1924, including the initial drafts of *The Bridge*, as well as shorter, contemporaneous poems like "Possessions" and "Recitative."

Indeed, these poems, drafts, and contemporaneous letters provide ample evidence that "The Bridge" from its beginning as a single poem was both culturally ambitious and semiotically charged, in spite of (and perhaps even initiated by) the increasingly fraught political and legal context faced by gay men, as well as other factors. Like many American poets, Crane read Eliot's *The Waste Land* not long after its publication in 1922 and soon told friends that he felt a need to respond with a work of equal scope and accomplishment.[35] These letters, furthermore, show that he found in Waldo Frank a possible, partial alternative to Eliot.[36] But Crane was ambivalent about both writers. He disliked Eliot's negativity

104 | Unlimited Eligibility?

while admiring his intellect and craft.[37] What Eliot offered was a "point of departure toward an almost complete reverse of direction," an opportunity to apply "erudition and technique . . . toward a more positive, or . . . ecstatic goal."[38] And however much Crane appreciated Frank's work and valued his mentoring, he was skeptical of his "extreme national consciousness," tendency to be "propagandistic," and the "slight touch of sentimentality attached to . . . [his] 'mysticism.' "[39] So it is perhaps not surprising that there is scant evidence of their direct influence on the early drafts of the poem beyond being points of departure from which Crane hoped to distinguish himself.[40]

Instead, these initial, fragmentary drafts of "The Bridge" reflect Crane's interest not just in the setting of Whitman's "Crossing Brooklyn Ferry" but in Whitman's hope of affirming an eroticized mutuality of unlimited eligibility on a larger scale. Crane was so committed to exploring the full extent of these cultural ambitions that he chose to begin by writing the poem's conclusion, an approach that was intended to enable him to evoke, with as little compromise as possible, the "ecstatic goal" that his poem associated with America's destiny, increasingly assuming with each increasingly sexually explicit revision the reader's tacit sympathies.[41] The trouble, however, was not simply that he wished to reverse engineer his poem but that he needed to develop an idiom through which his ambitions could be conveyed within the limitations of his cultural context. Here, we reach another version of the difficulty identified in this book's introduction, wherein a relationship must be built between, to use Moten and Harney's term, a paraontic undercommons space and the world's existing ontologies. Crane had to ask: How can the generative insights associated with the act of bridging in the many senses that it came to accrue for him (conceptual, interpersonal, sexual, political) as an emblem for an idealized America be made appealing to America as it is? How does one bring the world into this paraontic space of ontological eligibility or bring this ontological eligibility into the world? How does one build a bridge to "The Bridge"? The sense that this was an insurmountable task eventually led him in 1925–1926 to do what the project from its inception, through its development in adjacent, contemporaneous short poems like "Possessions," had avoided: compromising with a cultural pluralist politics of recognition.

Crane sends the earliest extant, albeit brief, draft of "The Bridge" in a February 20, 1923, letter to Wilbur Underwood, a gay friend who worked in the State Department and occasionally wrote and published poetry.[42] This letter is filled with the range of conflicting emotions Crane felt in relation to his sexuality, from a rapturous recollection of how "something beautiful approached me . . . as though it were the most natural thing in the world" to anger tinged with shame ("O flesh damned to hate and scorn!") to a more abstract praising of the "imagination," which he "find[s] . . . more sufficient all the time."[43] Very shortly thereafter, he introduces the "last lines" of "The Bridge." This first draft sublimates sexual energies into a more general, yet no less intense, sense of fulfillment, conveying an ecstatically achieved, wholly "consonan[t]" relation to the universe.

> And midway on that structure I would stand
> One moment, not as diver, but with arms
> That open to project a disk's resilience
> Winding the sun and planets in its face.
> Water should not stem that disk, nor weigh
> What holds its speed in vantage of all things
> That tarnish, creep, or wane; and in like laughter,
> Mobile yet posited beyond even that time
> The Pyramids shall falter, slough into sand,—
> And smooth and fierce above the claim of wings,
> And figured in that radiant field that rings
> The Universe:—I'd have us hold one consonance
> Kinetic to its poised and deathless dance.[44]

As with "Possessions," the syntax of this poem is complex but orderly, a quality amplified by the eventual arrival of rhymed couplets, whose chiming contributes to the increasingly ecstatic intensity of the imagery. The speaker's setting, "midway on that structure," appears to anticipate the "bedlamite" of "To Brooklyn Bridge," but, here, his gestures are explicitly designated as "not" those of a desperate "diver."[45] Instead, the wide-open arms evoke triumph, playfully imagining agency over the solar system itself. "Winding the sun and planets," the speaker mysteriously "project[s] a disk's resilience," a curious image, seemingly externalizing an internal mental/emotional state, that returns two lines later, when he declares that the surrounding "[w]ater should not stem [the process begun by projecting] that disk." Langdon Hammer connects this epiphany with the moment in "Crossing Brooklyn Ferry," when Whitman's speaker in the same setting looks in the water and finds his face haloed

106 | Unlimited Eligibility?

by the sun's reflected light. According to Hammer, this allusion serves as a "sacrament of poetic succession" reinforced by the "extension of the poet's [or speaker's] arms—a gesture of connection, which imitates the structure of the bridge, and signifies a priestly benediction."[46] The speaker walks in daylight, liberated, at peace, and triumphing in Whitmanian fashion over time ("beyond even that time / the Pyramids shall falter") and space ("[w]inding the sun and planets," "above the claim of wings").

This brief draft's central, hieratic gesture closely parallels the moment in "Possessions" (which was written a few months later) when the speaker's burdensome "fixed stone of lust" becomes transformed as he "hold[s] the stone up in a disk of light" available to be seen. Might the "arms / . . . project[ing] a disk's resilience" in the earlier draft of "The Bridge" anticipate the risky effort to invite a reader's looking but not recognizing present in the slightly later poem? Might Crane have hoped that the mysterious conclusion of "Possessions," when the speaker imagines many other "bright stones wherein my smiling plays," would find its larger fulfillment in the conclusion of "The Bridge"? The shared imagery suggests thematic resonances. And the triumph the speaker celebrates in this early draft is not just his own. With joyful bravado, he invites "us" all to realize, sustain, and expand this "one consonance" that is not the poem itself so much as a shared immanence, a "radiant field that rings" not just a community or America but "[t]he Universe" itself.

A second brief set of lines written only weeks later, likely sometime in the spring of 1923, shows Crane returning to the same moment, tentatively attending to the issue that he ignored in the first fragment and that would shadow the project for the next seven years: How do we reach such rapture from present sociopolitical realities? These lines begin to confront this challenge by briefly contrasting the experience of being seen by a lover and being recognized by someone who may be antagonistic. On the one hand, he describes a "steady . . . gaze incorporate," an affectionate stare shared by a couple who have experienced other intimacies "of [the] flesh" (1–2).[47] On the other hand, even as this couple, with seeming confidence, "surmount[s] all" as they approach the "[e]xpansive center" of the bridge ("midway on that structure" described in the first brief draft), a fear momentarily intrudes, requiring "eyes" that "must look always down" (2, 4, 5). The literal and figural space of the bridge, however, offers "reconcilement of . . . [their] chains," not a momentary release from "chains" that must be taken up again after departing the bridge but a grand resolution to all such fears (6). With an "ecstasy" paralleling or even emanating from the lovers, the bridge itself becomes a great mechanized loom (6). The "chains" that had suggested the literal (or internalized) gaze of an oppressive social system producing shame and isolation become transformed into a device capable of creating "concord" (8). The fragment ends with the lovers'/looms' feet and, no doubt, Crane's poetic feet merged, confidently "shuttl[ing] silvery with speed" as they "tread and weave our answering world," a phrasing that offers a fleeting hint of grim determination redeemed, once again, by a deep confidence in a "recreant" power shaping poetry that also shapes people who can reshape the world (12–14).

While the persons connoted by the plural pronouns in these first drafts are wholly aligned with the speaker ("us" and "our"), the references to "divers" and eyes that "must look always down" remind us that Crane always knew that he had to consider the impact of those who were less sympathetic. Crane tellingly makes little additional progress toward this goal in the two other extant, early drafts of "The Bridge." But in other ways Crane pushes his project boldly forward, making explicit the physical intimacy shared by the lovers. These conflicting impulses—postponing full consideration of the antagonistic world while deepening a depiction of what the world antagonized—show Crane bringing his project to an unavoidable moment of decision. He had to begin to describe the path toward his poem's daring, increasingly unambiguous climax: a moment of sex between men serving as the metaphor of a "mystical synthesis of 'America.'"[48] But precisely what mechanisms—aesthetic or sociopolitical—could facilitate the transition from the 1923 status quo, in which mere socializing could be deemed illegal, to this idealized apotheosis?

Crane sent the first of the final pair of extant draft-fragments to a new friend, the famed photographer Alfred Steiglitz on July 4, 1923. The letter is of particular interest because it contextualizes this draft in relation to Crane's earliest elaboration of the "logic of metaphor," a concept he developed in order to clarify the intersection between his poetics and intersubjective and even sociopolitical ambitions. Heaping praise upon Steiglitz ("you are the first, or rather the purest living indice of a new order of consciousness"), who was the older, more well-connected of the two, Crane asserts a shared artistic, political, and even "spiritual" mission. While they both acknowledge that "the city" can be, in almost Eliotic terms, "a place of 'broken-ness,'" Crane believes that Steiglitz is "setting the keynote" for the next generation to appreciate the city as the locus of

108 | Unlimited Eligibility?

social renewal, a place where "a new stage is created . . . a higher tranquility . . . an even wider intensity." But Crane contends that the two share a common impediment, "those really sincere people, but limited, who deny the superior logic of metaphor in favor of their perfect sums, divisions and subtractions." These "really sincere people," a not altogether clear category that seems intended to be expansive given its lack of a particular referent, congratulate each other when "they do nothing but walk ably over an old track bedecked with all kinds of signposts and 'championship records,'" ignoring the fact that they merely "catch up with some predetermined and set boundaries." Whatever one's field, the challenge, Crane seems to say, is to resist the urge to allow one's ambitions, by default, to be set in terms of inhabiting and extending existing frameworks rather than interrogating and exceeding them. The "logic of metaphor," along these lines, alleviates the "cramping" caused by unrelenting adherence to such norms by creating conceptual and discursive space beyond these "boundaries" in the hope of imagining a "higher quality of life."[49]

Crane's understanding of metaphor's power and purpose is out of alignment with some peers who deemphasized the trope on account of its association with nineteenth-century tendencies in figurative language or even on quasi-moral grounds (or both).[50] Harriet Monroe, founder and editor of *Poetry*, for example, felt justified in "wondering," a few years later in 1926, "by what process of reasoning you [i.e., Crane] would justify this poem's ["At Melville's Tomb"] succession of champion mixed metaphors" like the "dice of drowned men's bones" and "[f]rosted eyes . . . that lifted altars" that had "confounded" her.[51] In his reply to Monroe, Crane maintained that his metaphorical practice, in particular, and his poetics generally were not exercises in cultivating difficulty for its own sake ("juggling words or images until I found something novel, or esoteric").[52] Crane argued, in other words, that he was not driven by the values Leonard Diepeveen identifies with experimental modernism: "elitism ["one's membership in high culture"], originality, professionalism, and the strenuous nature of good art."[53] Or, at least, these were not his primary motivators. Furthermore, unlike the most extravagant assertions of artistic ruptures made by futurists, dada devotées, and other avant garde trends, Crane understood that making meaning whether of a poem or a person unavoidably occurs with some measure of reference to existing norms, not all of which are negative influences. And he acknowledged that a "reader's sensibility simply responds [to a poem] by identifying

Looking without Recognizing | 109

this inflection of experience with some event in his or her own history of perceptions—or rejects it altogether."[54]

This deference, however, is counterbalanced by a sense of responsibility to challenge Monroe's impulse to "preserv[e] . . . logically rigid significations"—the "predetermined and set boundaries" he mentions in his letter to Steiglitz.[55] Crane argues that such a concession would "limit the scope of the medium so considerably as to outlaw some of the richest genius of the past."[56] More precisely, Crane contends that there is no way for a poet "to ever get beyond the simplest conceptions of emotion and thought, of sensation and lyrical sequence" if one is "to be held completely to the already evolved and exploited." Instead, "trusting" that metaphors, even unusual ones, can serve as a "connective agent" with at least some readers, he defends their power to provoke "fresh concepts, [and] more inclusive evaluations."[57] While Crane offered no guarantees that the logic of metaphor would yield insights superior to those it challenged, it was this challenging, as a thought experiment, a pathway to the paraontic innovation that "The Bridge" emblematized, that Crane felt worthwhile and that critics like Monroe found threatening.[58]

In "General Aims and Theories," a 1925 text overviewing his poetics, Crane presents his most striking elaboration of what the "logic of metaphor" might offer an openminded reader: "it is as though a poem gave the reader as he left it a single, new *word*, never before spoken and impossible to actually enunciate, but self-evident as an active principle," a "new *word*" that would "shin[e] with a morality essentialized from experience directly, and not from previous percepts or preconceptions."[59] John Irwin parses these ambitions by explaining that "language in Crane's poetry attempts to break a purely mimetic relationship to the external world and to establish in its place a creative relationship wherein the conjunction or juxtaposition of words on the basis of wholly linguistic features enables us to build new relations between the things they name."[60] Crane's distinction between a word that has been "spoken" and "enunciate[d]" and a "new" one that, strangely, cannot be but nevertheless is "self-evident" as an "active principle" is key. He does not only seek to further elaborate an existing vocabulary or taxonomy or exchange it for another one but to nudge a reader toward a different, more "creative" (to use Irwin's word) or "active" (to return to Crane) way to use language. As in a poem like "Possessions," Crane is willing, even eager, to trade immediate legibility in favor of inviting readers to feel and "[w]itness" before they understand,

110 | Unlimited Eligibility?

in the hope of unsettling unquestioned reliance on existing frames of reference (the "old track bedecked with all kinds of signposts"). In this way, if Whitman's "indirect mode" of querying invites the reader into the social space within which "the rest" may find each other, Crane's logic of metaphor might be understood as an attempt to create the discursive idiom in which they can do their work, stirring within them a practice of looking-without-recognizing at the world and others, that they might mutually acknowledge ontological proximity and ontological eligibility and slow the epistemological need to determine recognizability.[61]

Crane more or less acknowledged to Steiglitz that the "fragmentary and not . . . entirely finished" draft he enclosed in his letter did not achieve these high goals, and he requested the recipient to "please don't show them [the pages of his draft] around."[62] This draft brings us back to the familiar scene, a bridge emanating out of the speaker's relationship with his lover, while intensifying both its intimacy and grandiosity.

> The baited rock precipitate with sound
> Of waters bending and astride the sky,
> Until, as though an organ pressing doom
> Should set this nave of time atremble, we feel
> Through brimming clay and signaling upright,
> Beneath us lift a porch, a living concourse
> Whose alignment rears from equal out to equal,
> Yielding mutual assumption on its arches
> Fused and veering to the measure of our arms. (1–9)[63]

Though the imagery recalls the biblical account of the division of the waters and subsequent emergence of land (Genesis 1:6–9), Crane's depiction of a sacred act of creation (in "this nave of time") is not enacted by an external Divinity, so much as an ongoing, inevitable outgrowth of something revolutionary, a deeply shared, if not yet fully defined, sense of mutuality. The two people walking hand in hand are more than just a personification of the bridge with its two towers; they literally become the source of the structure itself.[64] And this structure—"a porch, a living concourse"—literally and figuratively evokes the "new stage" Crane mentions to Steiglitz whereby the city of "broken-ness" becomes something radically connective. Here, once again, Whitman's influence is felt. Crane describes this "equal out to equal" relationship as a "mutual assumption," recalling the opening lines of "Song of Myself" ("what I assume you shall

Looking without Recognizing | 111

assume / For every atom belonging to me as good belongs to you") but without the flicker of imperiousness ("shall") present in Whitman's lines. Of course, "assumption" also bears a religious connotation associated with Mary being delivered to heaven rather than suffering death. But the designation of divine favor, here, is transformed into a privilege "mutual[ly]" shared from person to person and enacted by the work of bridging.

The next stanza recalls Crane's complaint to Steiglitz about those "who deny the superior logic of metaphor in favor of their perfect sums," while offering a contrasting evocation of "sum[s]":

> O whitest instruments, in pain addressed
> And so applied in beams of driven fire,
> In ordered sheaves remission gathered up
> And multiplied with steps to such a sum,—
> That, scathless, we assume and guide
> The tempered axis of the world in moving
> Sidereal phalanx to that tolling star
> That fills us and renews us as a sun . . . (10–17; Crane's ellipsis)

Summing, here, serves a distinctly different purpose than to designate "predetermined and set boundaries," Crane's correlates for strict conceptual or poetic limits. Instead, summing, like the "trembling tabulation" that is "[ac]count[ed]" for in the slightly later "Possessions," references a tallying of "pain[s]" that are not accentuated as they are "gathered up" like "sheaves" of grain but relieved, granted a "remission" that itself is transformed beyond any sense of a debt that needed forgiving into a "scathless" license to "assume and guide / The tempered axis of the world." The dazzling figurative invention shows us the "renew[al]" these lines assert as the speaker and his companion are illuminated by the joyful, life-affirming light of trope itself. After another paean, wherein the speaker expresses his desire "[t]o be, Great Bridge, in vision bound of thee," the draft received by Steiglitz concludes with slightly edited versions of the previous two draft-fragments described above.

A few weeks later, on July 21, 1923, Crane sent the last extant early draft to Charlotte Rychtarik, who along with her husband Richard were friends of his in Cleveland, where Crane grew up and his family still lived. With new lines, once again, preceding those composed for prior drafts, Crane sets the scene by becoming dramatically more explicit about the kind mutuality from which "The Bridge" emerges.

112 | Unlimited Eligibility?

> The hand you carry to the rock knows lime
> And all the mineral wariness of earth . . .
> Yet, touch its cloudy buried throat where light
> Is branched like prayers unspoken that await
> Your deepest thrusting agony for answer: strike
> Its breast precipitate, its lust-forbidden flanks,
> Sleek with your sweat's erosion,—til we hear
> The sound of waters bending and astride the sky:
> Until, as though an organ pressing doom
> Should set this nave of time atremble . . . (1–10)[65]

These lines retain the primal setting of creation ("the rock") established in the previous draft, while indicating that the formation of the bridge is a direct result not just of this couple but of their coupling. The speaker appears to be metaphorically dead ("knows lime") and voiceless ("cloudy buried throat") but becomes, through sex with "you," the conduit for the extraordinary renewal promised by the bridge. With reference to "deepest thrusting agony" and "lust-forbidden flanks, / Sleek with your sweat's erosion," Crane leaves little to the imagination. Indeed, paralleling "Crossing Brooklyn Ferry," "you" are not a voyeur or a source of social recognition but a coparticipant (and, it seems, the more active party) in the sexual act and a co-contributor to a revitalization that ultimately extends over everything.

Given Crane's enthusiasm, why did progress on "The Bridge" so quickly stall? In an August 25, 1923, follow-up letter to Steiglitz, Crane summed up his crisis by describing himself in "such despair about . . . not seeing my way to introduce it ["The Bridge"] in the way I want (the end and climax, what you have seen, is all that's done so far) and not getting the needful hours to ripen anything in myself."[66] His professional life, often spent working at advertising agencies, made it nearly impossible for him to find the time necessary to develop the poem.[67] But here and in other correspondence, there are hints that more than a lack of time and money stalled the project. From the start, Crane worried about the project's potential length and ambition.[68] By the late summer of 1923, it seems that real doubt had crept in. If the provocative potential for his project rested in its refusal to accept the premise that incrementally expanding present norms of value provided the best pathway toward a different, not yet fully elaborated, democratic order, and if the logic of metaphor offered a discursive idiom for beginning to think beyond those normative frames, the fact remained that catalyzing even a few fascinated readers would take time. And time is precisely what Crane may have felt he did not have. It was not just the New York state legislature's actions that would have reminded him of this. A number of hitherto willing readers and friends, like Gorham Munson, Allen Tate, and Yvor Winters, would come to accuse Crane, sometimes publicly, with homophobic undertones and a measure of condescension toward his limited formal education, of having developed an "irrational" and borderline immoral poetics. Though Crane vigorously defended himself, doing so was a source of stress.[69]

So it is perhaps not surprising that Crane, amid work responsibilities, lack of time to think, self-doubt, and implicit prejudice, was unable to move forward. When he finally did gain a more extended period of time to work in 1926, these pressures appear to have led him to concede that his project might need to be more legible to his audience, more directly related to existing norms and models of relationality and political inclusion, a concession that radically changed the poem in both size and concept. The epicenter of these changes was a willingness to embrace, in spite of his earlier concerns about Waldo Frank and in spite of the impetus driving "The Bridge," a cultural pluralist politics of recognition.

Cultural Pluralism and *The Bridge* (1926–1930)

As late as April 5, 1926, Crane felt deep self-doubt about the future of "The Bridge," when he told Gorham Munson that "I know what I WANT to do" but "the actual fleshing of a concept is so complex and difficult" (Crane's emphasis).[70] However, a number of events in 1925–1926 enabled Crane to gain momentum on his foundering project. He was encouraged by the fact that his first book, *White Buildings*, finally would be published. And Otto Kahn, a wealthy supporter of the arts, in late 1925 donated two thousand dollars to Crane, affording him the long-desired luxury of focusing his energies entirely on completing the poem in a setting he felt would be conducive to his efforts, the property owned by his mother's side of the family on the Isle of Pines, a territory of Cuba, during the late spring and summer of 1926. Furthermore, during the first several weeks of his time in the Caribbean, he was joined by Waldo Frank, who was by now, regardless of Crane's early cautiousness, a trusted mentor and friend.[71] Under these conditions, Crane soon was writing with an

114 | Unlimited Eligibility?

unprecedented intensity akin to "dancing on dynamite," as "all sections [of the poem were seemingly] moving forward now at once!"[72]

The previous chapter showed how Waldo Frank, like his fellow cultural pluralists Horace Kallen and, at least for a time, Alain Locke, believed that commitment to recognizing difference (and especially ethnic and racial difference) could initiate a grand act of synthesis in American culture. For Kallen, the great synthesis promised by cultural pluralist acts of recognition would not remove difference per se but would "provide conditions under which each might attain the cultural perfection that is *proper to its kind*," allowing each of these "kind[s]" to sound forth their differences contrapuntally, like various musical lines in a "symphony" (Kallen's emphasis).[73] Frank was more triumphalistic than Kallen in his envisioning of a symphonic America and, as a result, Frank's work makes explicit a thinly veiled condescension and even authoritarianism more often left implicit in Kallen's writing. In 1926, Frank was beginning to develop ideas that would appear in *The Re-discovery of America*, wherein he expresses his ultimate desire that America might become "the symphonic nation." He saw a country brimming with "groups" defined by class, religion, and especially race and ethnicity and proposed in quasi-Hegelian fashion reminiscent of late Whitman and William Torrey Harris that each "group" not view itself as "a noun, . . . [or] a substance bent on fattening itself or its members . . . [but as] a potential verb of the American subject."[74] Whether the group happens to be "Jews" or "Negroes" or "labourers," according Frank, they must reject "egoistic falsehood" and, instead,

> accept their limitations whatever they are, knowing that the particular conditions of their life make it one with all lives which also have their particular conditions; and that these limitations are the condition for work, the stuff for creating. They will know that life's oppressions are due to the oppression of a "self" clamoring to be absolute and eternal; that the way to be free is not to envy their brother who has the identical problem—whatever his place in the sun. Itself a microcosm of the Whole, the group will accept its chaos to transfigure it.[75]

Frank's contention that this theory does not condemn the less fortunate to lives of political "quietism" is somewhat undercut by his subsequent insistence that if your "group" happens to be currently downtrodden "revolutionary action is . . . barred."[76] In return for accepting the status quo, Frank insists that "these groups will harmonise one with another," eventually producing "a symphony" in which "all the innumerable notes lift their instant voices, and pass, and only the symphony remains. Such would be our nation; save that its creator would not be 'outside' the music. He would be the individual note, itself—the group of notes, building the structure of the Whole by knowing the Whole and by living it, personally, in its several parts."[77] As a paraphrase of Crane's ambitions for *The Bridge* after 1925, one could scarcely do better. Given the friendship shared by Frank and Crane, it is even within the realm of possibility that *The Bridge*, consciously or not, became a remarkable poetic gloss of these ideas.[78] Or perhaps the reverse occurred. Or a more complicated act of cross-pollination. In any case, in his *Memoirs*, Waldo Frank called the relationship between *The Re-discovery of America* and *The Bridge* "self-evident."[79]

Here we reach a key conceptual transition that distinguishes the 1923 drafts of "The Bridge" (as a single poem) from what *The Bridge* (as a book-length, multipart poem) eventually became. Though Crane's letters show that he occasionally used cultural pluralist watchwords earlier in his career, including the term "symphonic," to describe both "For the Marriage of Faustus and Helen" and, on at least one occasion, the 1923 envisioning of *The Bridge*, his ambivalence about cultural pluralism's sociocultural ambitions—and certainly Waldo Frank's ambitions—seems to have prevented him from seeking a parallel, "symphonic" synthesis of American otherness.[80] Indeed, as we have seen, Crane seems to have stopped his 1923 drafts precisely at the point when he had to link his ecstatic rendering of all that the bridge emblematized to the outside world, at the moment, in other words, when he had to make a difficult decision about how to link the paraontic poetic space he hoped the logic of metaphor might open, affirm, and even expand with the world as it is. He could either utterly trust in the social hopes of the logic of metaphor, which may have come to feel far-fetched even to him, or attempt to blend elements of that poetics with an existing model of sociality like cultural pluralism. Approximately three years after his previous extant draft, with Waldo Frank at his side, Crane makes this latter concession. Though one can find evidence of this decision in echoes of cultural pluralist thought appearing in subsequently drafted poems, a subtle yet significant shift in perspective is equally consequential. For the 1923 poem that had increasingly foregrounded the perspective of a mis/unrecognized person and, in its poetics, queried the politics of recognition became after mid-1926 a

116 | Unlimited Eligibility?

poem that significantly (though not exclusively) gave voice to someone empowered to enact recognition and ultimately to narrate its culmination in a way that echoed Waldo Frank's "harmoni[zing]" of the "Whole."

By August of 1926, only a couple months after Frank's extended visit on the Isle of Pines, Crane felt comfortable arguing that the "basic center and antecedent of all motion" undergirding the cultural pluralism-informed reenvisioning of *The Bridge* was the newly developed section entitled "Powhatan's Daughter."[81] Given the fact that Crane was writing amidst the Harlem Renaissance, a movement with considerable, if wary, affiliations to cultural pluralism, and was a friend of Jean Toomer, who was briefly a major figure in that movement, it may seem somewhat counterintuitive for him to focus on an indigenous person as an exemplar of racial otherness needing to be assimilated. However, in the late teens and early twenties, the moment when American cultural and literary history was first becoming understood as a potential field unto itself in works like Waldo Frank's *Our America* (1919), D. H. Lawrence's *Studies in Classic American Literature* (1923), and William Carlos Williams's *In the American Grain* (1925), "the Indian" became typecast as the primal racial other whose legacy—and repeated drama of demise at the hand of European settlers—overshadows the country and its literature.[82] *The Path on the Rainbow: An Anthology of Songs and Chants from the Indians of North America* (1918), edited by George Cronyn with an introduction by Mary Austin, similarly begins with a dedication noting that "the Art Forms of a Vanishing Race . . . are genuine American classics" without "the slightest traces of European Influence."[83] Crane follows their lead, establishing Pocahontas as his "mythological nature-symbol chosen to represent the physical body of the continent, or the soil." And "Powhatan's Daughter," as a group of poems, from its beginning in "Harbor Dawn" to its climax in "The Dance" becomes (as Crane put it) "a gradual exploration of this 'body' whose first possessor was the Indian."[84] Understanding the origins of American culture, in other words, can only be achieved by recognizing "the Indian" in the way that Frank imagines an act of cultural recognition, an act that hypothetically incorporates into American history its land's original inhabitants and opens up the triumphant synthesizing emblema-tized by the poem's title image. And insofar as Crane additionally makes Pocohontas and her suitor in "The Dance," Maquokeeta, representative of nature/fertility gods, he forwards this act of recognition as a rebuttal of T. S. Eliot's *The Waste Land*.[85] For if the embers of cultural regeneration can be found in the indigenous cultures (allegedly) pushed to the brink of extinction, then (according to Crane's logic and the racist trope of the dying Indian it was based on) Eliot's pessimistic outlook on the future of Western civilization might not be earned.

In a February 1927 letter to Allen Tate, Crane would unequivocally identify "The Dance" as "the best thing I've done."[86] The poem's task is to find the seeds of triumph within tragedy, or as the poem would have it, a wedding in the midst of a war. He fashions the opening stanzas around a symbolically multivalent chase scene that is both erotic (a lover chasing a bride) and militaristic (chasing/fleeing an enemy), while also evoking the passage of time. Sustaining each of these threads simultaneously is a test for Crane's poetic resourcefulness and offers evidence that he did not leave behind the frequent bridging of disparate concepts by daring metaphors so much as place it in the service of a different politics. His 1923 stance encouraged a looking without recognizing, a tarrying with the illegible that potentially makes it more possible to avoid repeating, without examination, forms of relation rooted in one's previous "experience[s]" and "percepts" by creating space and allowing time for meaning to be made more slowly and collaboratively. But when Crane resumes concerted work on the poem in 1926, he begins to feature speakers who inhabit the role of a recognizer rather than inhabiting the role of someone subjected to a recognizer's gaze. This leads Crane to appeal to the cultural pluralist tendency to recognize within established and, here, deeply problematic, indeed racist, terms.

An image of Maquokeeta pursuing Pochahontas's hair ("[y]our hair's keen crescent running") suggests his erotic intent while also merging her identity with the river and underlining her status as an emblem of nature (19). When, a few lines later, the "fleet young crescent die[s]," the image serves multiple purposes again (24). At a literal level, Maquokeeta has reached the end of the river, as he approaches the location of the mythical battlefield storm that is to come. But "crescent" also refers to a fading moon replaced at daybreak by "one star" (25), images that refer to Pocahontas and Maquokeeta (the former as the moon, the latter as the star) while foreshadowing the transcendental dawning that will come, at the conclusion of the book, in "Atlantis." As Crane nimbly moves between these various literal/symbolic/archetypal registers, his speaker becomes increasingly intertwined and ultimately coidentified with Maquokeeta. Jared Gardner has read this merging as the poet's veiled attempt to define a founding American myth in homosexual terms, a hint that Crane did not entirely eliminate what he had foregrounded in the 1923 drafts, even

118 | Unlimited Eligibility?

if he frames the poem's drama in heterosexual terms.[87] Crane's rhetoric, however, suggests a more troubling relationship between the poet and the Native American, one that is less an expression of an unsuccessfully repressed sexual identity than a miniature depiction of the triumphalistic cultural pluralism he now is working within.

Crane's own commentary on this section, featured in several letters, shows how this act of recognition follows Waldo Frank's lead in *Our America*, wherein the "rich and fertile" indigenous peoples are "savage only by the materialistic measure of the Caucasian" and were "buried by the Caucasian floods," comments that almost gesture toward interrogating racist stereotypes, while, on the other hand, simply "dying and doomed," a reiteration of racist tropes.[88] Writing to his benefactor Otto Kahn, Crane parallels Frank, claiming that "not only do I describe the conflict between the two races in this dance—I also become identified with the Indian and his world before it is over, which is the only method possible of ever really possessing the Indian and his world as a cultural factor. I think I really succeed in getting under the skin of this glorious and dying animal." [89] That Crane could slide from "identif[ying] with the Indian" to "possessing the Indian and his world as a cultural factor" to "getting under the skin of this glorious and dying animal" is revealing. Identification, here, rests on more than just the possibility of empathy but on a belief that there is a stable, essentialized "Indian" race-identity available for him to recognize and possess. This was a "very complicated" section, he explained in a July 4, 1927, letter to "Aunt" Sally Simpson, the caretaker of the Isle of Pines property, because he had to find a way to "unlatch the door to the pure Indian world . . . to the pure savage world."[90] Desire to find an authenticity to recognize, here, does not lead to deference but to further dominance.

"The Dance," thus, becomes a lyric of a recognizer empowered to interpellate those he describes (and even addresses) into the narrative of American history. Through a kind of rhetorical dance, the speaker stands both inside and outside the drama, as evidenced by a freely floating point of view that shifts between (and in-between) first and third person, enabling both measured empathy (through which the other is recognized) and undisputed mastery (through which the other is assimilated). The following lines, which merge sounds of "distant . . . thunder" with "the padded foot" of assembling men preparing for battle and the "rhythm[ic]" feet of the poem itself, give a sense of how Crane's speaker is both within ("I heard it") the scene, identifying with Maquokeeta, and outside, an entity not just describing but controlling Maquokeeta's destiny and demise ("Know, Maquokeeta . . . /—Fall, Sachem"):

> A distant cloud, a thunder-bud—it grew,
> That blanket of the skies: the padded foot
> Within,—I heard it; 'til its rhythm drew,
> —Siphoned the black pool from the heart's hot root!
>
> A cyclone threshes in the turbine crest,
> Swooping in eagle feathers down your back;
> Know, Maquokeeta, greeting; know death's best;
> —Fall, Sachem, strictly as the tamarack! (41–48)

The speaker's "greeting," here, becomes a metonym for both the recognition and the extinction of indigenous peoples—or even recognition as extinction. If Crane is intending to show sympathy for this suffering, then why does he shift to a third-person point of view, making what is described something the speaker seems to have himself ordained? Nor can one easily read the increasingly intense imperatives of the third-person speaker as an intended exposure of moral culpability for the historical tragedy of genocidal violence.[91] After completing his death-dance, Maquokeeta is transformed into various celestial imagery foreshadowing "Atlantis," rendering him unimportant as an individual and significant as a representative of a group only insofar as he serves as a cog within metaphysical machinery (e.g., 77–80, 101–4). But the speaker also continues to identify with him. "We danced, O Brave," the speaker declares at the poem's end, encompassing himself, as well as any reader, within what constitutes a "strong prayer" conveyed by an image developed over the course of *The Bridge* that would return at the end of "Atlantis": "[t]he serpent with the eagle in the boughs," an evocation of the conquering of time (the serpent) and space (the eagle), Crane's figure for a triumphant, unifying consummation.[92]

What is Pocohontas's role in all this? She is the silent land awaiting its manifest destiny in crude terms as a "virgin to the last of men" (92), a climax predicted in "Harbor Dawn" where Pocahontas is first figured as slumbering in the speaker's bed, a passive receptacle of the speaker's "seed" and soon to be subjected to those "myriad snowy hands . . . [already] clustering at the panes," a deeply unsettling and tellingly Caucasian description of a frost-covered window (25).[93] The forced sexual submission of an

120 | Unlimited Eligibility?

indigenous woman, thus, becomes a figure for the inescapable absorption of racial others into America. And, throughout it all, Hart Crane places his considerable poetic resources—of address, of temporal compression through trope, of florid diction, and uncannily agile syntax—at the service of this program grounded in cultural pluralism.

Very near the conclusion of writing *The Bridge* (if not at the conclusion of the poem itself), Crane returns to a primary source of inspiration, Whitman. Though "Cape Hatteras" is ultimately driven by a prophetic neo-imperialism derived in no small part from late Whitman, including an epigram and allusions to "A Passage to India," the poem also deems Whitman "[n]ot greatest, thou,—not first, nor last,—but near," an affirmation of "Crossing Brooklyn Ferry"-esque ontological proximity that leads to a final image featuring the speaker (clearly here a surrogate of Crane) with his "hand / in yours, / Walt Whitman" (200, 232–34). And Edward Brunner and Brian Reed both note that, as late as 1928, Crane seems to have intended to develop additional, never-to-be-realized sections of *The Bridge*, including one entitled "Calgary Express" that would have focused on the "the racial history of the negro" through the eyes of a black railroad porter. Though that poem might have been as problematic as "The Dance," it also, according to Reed, could "have given a welcome revolutionary edge and precedent to the book's inchoate presentation of a community of men and women marked as queer or circulating in queer-marked interstitial spaces." Instead, "Crane's fervent transcendentalism and occasional naïve nativism"—rooted, it is worth noting again, in cultural pluralism—"vitiated" the prospect of "incisive social commentary" appearing in the final version of *The Bridge*.[94]

Like Toomer's speaker in "The Blue Meridian," Crane's speaker in "The Dance" adopts the position of an empowered recognizer, despite the fact that this is the position "The Bridge," like "The Blue Meridian," initially had been designed to oppose. But while Crane's completion of *The Bridge*, again like Toomer's "The Blue Meridian," fails as it falls into self-contradiction, it is worth considering an often-overlooked addendum to the 1923 fragments of "The Bridge." Edward Brunner has noted how Crane's preliminary organization of his first collection, *White Buildings*, placed "Recitative," another poem conceived in 1923–1924, first, with "The Bridge," as it was originally envisioned as a single lengthy poem, placed last, a model suggesting that "'Recitative' . . . might, in fact, have served as a proem to the 1923 *Bridge*."[95] While Crane eventually decided to position "Recitative" later in the book and make *The Bridge* into a book

Looking without Recognizing | 121

of its own, its initial status as a title poem (given its reference to "white buildings") bookended with "The Bridge" remains suggestive. If this plan had been realized, "Recitative" would have stood implicitly as a poetic and political exemplar, drawing readers into his whole project, confidently asking them to engage the logic of metaphor's hope of social transformation through looking without recognizing in order to draw ontologically near. "Recitative," thus, offers a glimpse of what may have been Crane's last major attempt to develop his 1923 vision. Unlike the early drafts of *The Bridge*, "Recitative," especially in the expanded version published in *White Buildings*, connects semi-autobiographical content, direct address appeals to the reader, and the wider world, dramatically opening outward, assessing the relationship between the culture of American capitalism in the roaring twenties and the couple approaching "the bridge."

"Recitative"—a Final Attempt to Realize the 1923 Model of "The Bridge"

In a December 10, 1923, letter to Gorham Munson, Crane candidly describes an initial, now lost version of "Recitative" that had been a "confession" derived from a recent, "somewhat flamboyant period in NY." Then, after noting how his writing was becoming more "tight and particular," he cites the revision of "Recitative" that would appear in the *Little Review* a few months later in early 1924.[96] By that point, Crane characteristically had circulated the poem among other friends. A March 1, 1924, letter to Allen Tate explains "Recitative" metapoetically, as a study of a writer's relationship with an audience: "Imagine the poet, say, on a platform speaking it. The audience is one half of Humanity, Man (in the sense of Blake) and the poet the other. ALSO, the poet sees himself in the audience as in a mirror. ALSO, the audience sees itself, in part, in the poet. Against this paradoxical DUALITY is posed the UNITY, or the conception of it (as you got it) in the last verse. In another sense, the poet is *talking to himself* all the way through the poem." Crane then appends a further hint: "[T]here are, as too often in my poems, other reflexes and symbolisms in the poem, also, which it would be silly to write here—at least for the present."[97] Thomas Yingling reads this comment as evidence of Crane's unwillingness to "divulge" the poem's sexual content.[98] But Crane, here, cues Tate, exactly as he did Jean Toomer (about "Possessions") and Gorham Munson (as noted above), to look

122 | Unlimited Eligibility?

beyond a Blakean reading, a far from subtle suggestion of more than just abstract, metapoetic intentions. After all, the *Little Review* version and the expanded version published in *White Buildings* are the antithesis of reticence.

The latter version adds the fourth, fifth, and sixth stanzas and makes even more explicit the poem's Whitmanian series of eroticized invitations to "[r]egard . . . [i]nquire . . . [l]ook . . . watch," a strategy that parallels the invitation in "Possessions" to "[w]itness" without "apprehen[ding]."[99] Both poems invite readers near while cautioning them against using this proximity as an excuse to impose "rigid significations" the logic of metaphor seeks to unsettle. But in addition to underscoring the imperative to look but not recognize, Crane expands the scope of the poem to include a strikingly sharp economic critique of days spent "suspend[ed] . . . from atrocious sums" while working in the "white buildings" of New York. In doing so, he positions "the bridge" itself as an alternative to the social forces undermining both his nights and his days.

> Regard the capture here, O Janus-faced,
> As double as the hands that twist this glass.
> Such eyes at search or rest you cannot see;
> Reciting pain or glee, how can you bear!
>
> Twin shadowed halves: the breaking second holds
> In each the skin alone, and so it is
> I crust a plate of vibrant mercury
> Borne cleft to you, and brother in the half.
>
> Inquire this much-exacting fragment smile,
> Its drums and darkest blowing leaves ignore,—
> Defer though, revocation of the tears
> That yield attendance to one crucial sign.
>
> Look steadily—how the wind feasts and spins
> The brain's disk shivered against lust. Then watch
> While darkness, like an ape's face, falls away,
> And gradually white buildings answer day.
>
> Let the same nameless gulf beleaguer us—
> Alike suspend us from atrocious sums

Built floor by floor on shafts of steel that grant
The plummet heart, like Absalom, no stream.

The highest tower,—let her ribs palisade
Wrenched gold of Nineveh;—yet leave the tower.
The bridge swings over salvage, beyond wharves;
A wind abides the ensign of your will . . .

In alternating bells have you not heard
All hours clapped dense into a single stride?
Forgive me for an echo of these things,
And let us walk through time with equal pride.

The first imperative ("[r]egard") leads into a depiction of a tense encounter described as a "capture" (which is akin to the "apprehend[ding]" that "Possessions" wishes to evade). More than in the 1923 drafts of "The Bridge" or even "Possessions," the audience is actively implicated here in one of Crane's most ambitious attempts to place the "logic of metaphor" to artistic and even moral and political use in order to create a poem that not only enacts but reflects in its imagery this process as it develops. For the probing, desperate "eyes" are not just those of the speaker surreptitiously glancing at a possible pick-up but of the reader searching and similarly evaluating and categorizing the writer. And the pairs of "hands that twist this glass," an act of mutual distortion masquerading as simple reflection, evoke a socially constructed sense of self as a result of a violently dialectical process. But it is not just the construction of the speaker's sense of self that is forged here. This image also serves as a figure for how words are wrought into a poem and then submitted to interpretation. Crane launches a critique of the potential violence within each of these relations, suggesting how the existing social order serves as the common denominator linking his struggles with both poetry and sexual politics. For the distortion depicted in each of these relationships is defined by an act of recognition, wherein each party struggles not just against the other but against the norms they live amid. The vulnerable space inhabited by gay persons in New York in 1923, a space in which they are defined inherently as law breakers, is here made symptomatic of a larger system of recognition poised to damage anyone insofar as it inevitably constructs agonistic relationships that yield acts of, at best, mutual misrecognition. The prospective lovers, in effect, "cannot see" one

124 | Unlimited Eligibility?

another. Nor can the reader/writer as they face each other in the poem's "glass."[100] Both "capture[s]" dictate a difficult to "bear" recitation hamstrung between "pain or glee." Crane's hope is that by openly "[r]egard[ing]" this dynamic we may not only begin to understand it but begin to see each other differently. The poem, in this way, becomes a gradual unfolding of the larger implications of looking without recognizing.

Stanza two further underlines the nature of the relationships between the lovers and the reader/writer as "[t]win shadowed halves." The brevity of the encounter ("the breaking second") sunders the possibility of sustained unity, leaving them with only the most superficial ("the skin alone") aspects of a relationship. The speaker then makes a series of propositions in an effort to remedy this dynamic. Since the people described in the opening stanza "cannot see" what they do to each other, he first offers a "plate of vibrant mercury," an image of an early twentieth-century photographic plate that points, once again, to the poem itself. In these mirroring devices, he shows the implicit violence described in the first lines of the poem.

The third and fourth stanzas encourage the reader to continue this "[i]nquir[y]," depicting the place of desire in the recognition drama the poem describes and critiques. Stormy images of "blowing leaves" and wind that "feasts and spins" likely follow Dante's depictions of "lust" in canto 5 of the *Inferno*. Crane's use of similar phrasing in a February 20, 1923, letter to Wilbur Underwood addressing his romantic struggles ("Those who have wept in the darkness sometimes are rewarded with stray leaves blown inadvertently") may indicate a specifically gay overtone to the image.[101] And his description of "[t]he brain's disk shivered against lust" parallels similar "disk" imagery in "Possessions" (the "fixed stone of lust" that he ultimately "hold[s] . . . up against a disk of light," a gesture indicating the bravery involved in bringing aspects of Crane's private life to public view) and the 1923 drafts of "The Bridge" (a more triumphant depiction of "arms / That open to project a disk's resilience"). The poem walks a fine line here. We are told, on the one hand, to "[l]ook steadily" and to see how the speaker is seeking, at considerable risk, what self-expression is available, however chaotic it may be. But knowing what he describes and how some might react, he asks readers to "ignore" the more lurid "drums and darkest blowing leaves" in favor of finding room for a sense of solidarity and even "tears" of sympathy.

These "tears," emblems of the new "morality" Crane encourages, are signs of regret from the reader for ever having withheld the newfound solidarity in favor of the needlessly painful and seemingly doomed pursuit

Looking without Recognizing | 125

of mutual recognition. He wants to achieve what the speaker of "The Wine Menagerie" knew for only a moment: "This competence—to travel in a tear" and bring people together beyond "their separate wills" (31, 25). But there is more irony than triumph here. For as darkness and its secrets "falls away," the "white buildings" of Manhattan, the epicenter of another kind of "capture" and another kind of "lust," come into view and "answer day." Crane would later explain to Yvor Winters that this phrase, which provided his first book's title, in part, was intended to have "Woolworthian" overtones (the Woolworth Building was the tallest in the world at that time and built to serve as corporate headquarters for the F. W. Woolworth Company).[102] He now turns his critique toward the unchecked corporate capitalism of the roaring twenties, a moment when economic vulnerabilities compounded the vulnerabilities related to his sexuality.

By the time Crane wrote "Recitative," he had endured various unfulfilling business office jobs, which revealed to him how corporate greed ("atrocious sums," "[w]renched gold of Nineveh") could produce a host of uniformly unfulfilled people.[103] The speaker's desperation is analogized to Absalom, who hung helplessly by his hair until being killed (2 Samuel 18).[104] Crane's request remains the same as it has throughout the poem: see how "the same nameless gulf" separating us from each other "beleaguer[s] us" in each of these situations—at day in those skyscrapers driven by economic possessiveness, at night when his loneliness may find partial fulfillment in an encounter deemed criminal by the law, and also, perhaps less dramatically, as the poet and reader each compete for control of the other. Crane's point seems to be twofold: that we all know of what he speaks, to one degree or another, and that, for people like him, there is no refuge (at day or night, in work or leisure) from this dynamic.

Crane's poetics, thus, becomes a search for an escape from a world shaped by misrecognition and exploitation, a search that would lead him to "[t]he bridge." This transition, which forms the core of what Crane added to the poem between the time he completed the 1924 version and before publication of *White Buildings* in 1926, becomes especially dense and difficult to interpret. Crane's rhetoric shifts as his object of critique shifts. The first stanzas reflecting his sexual experiences had insistently invited the reader to observe without recognizing. Now, Crane takes what sounds like a very different stance: "Let the same nameless gulf beleaguer us—// . . . let her ribs palisade." If undermining recognition required active commitment, then why does Crane's associated critique

126 | Unlimited Eligibility?

of capitalism involve what appears to be passivity? Julie Taylor suggests that this moment, which leads into "one of Crane's unequivocal utopian visions of reciprocal brotherhood," evokes a "glorious simplicity . . . [that] belies the difficult negotiations [preceding it in the poem] that are the necessary conditions of its production"[105] Such a claim implies that "[t]he bridge" isn't emblematic of an alternative to what is previously described in the poem so much as a supersession of it. "Recitative," however, does not link "[t]he highest tower" and "[t]he bridge." It argues the opposite: that a reader ought to reject the sociality associated with the "tower" by "let[ting]" it be what it is and then "leav[ing]" it in favor of "the bridge." There is no development process linking the two locations and their associated socialities.

The final stanza makes the distance between the tower and the bridge even clearer. A Whitmanian emblem of overcoming separations and limitations of time ("All hours clapped dense into a single stride") and space, the bridge provides a place where he and a beloved may openly walk together, outside the miserable white buildings, away from the storms of lust, surrounded by a more inspirational breeze ("A wind abides the ensign of your will"). And the poem's language (ideally) enacts and envisions the speaker's escape from miserable nights and days, extending its freedom to readers, whom he invites to join with him on the bridge, "walk[ing] through time with equal pride." Amid the lofty hopes and ambitions, there is modesty, even an appeal for "forgive[ness]" that he can only offer "an echo of these things." What things? Perhaps Crane is merely conceding that the poem can only "echo" the ecstatic intensities of the relationship he shared with the person he was dating at the time, Emil Opffer. But Crane is addressing his reader and surely he is also pointing to the limits of his poetics, which, even at its most rhetorically intense and metaphorically dense, can only invite and provoke readers to collaborate in realizing its possibilities.

The 1923–1924 poems, perhaps exemplified by "Recitative," arrive at this mutual model of lyric politics, foregrounding an eligibility to participate in a relation based on affirming ontological proximity, as a result of Crane thinking through his place as a marginalized, mis/unrecognized person who was unnerved by an increasingly oppressive, legalized system of recognition. There is no guarantee, of course, that a fully realized version of *The Bridge* expanding on such premises would have been free from the impulses that mar "The Dance." But there is little doubt that the post-1925 version of *The Bridge*, especially the "Powhatan's Daughter" section, results from Crane identifying with his position of racial privilege. Conforming to cultural pluralist politics enabled the poem to be completed within the norms of its time. However, it is the 1923–1924 poems, with their call to a different sight, inviting and enacting a looking without recognizing, and different voice ("new word[s]") that offers an imaginative resource perhaps still worthy of consideration.

Chapter Four

Burlesquing Recognition

James Merrill's Formalism

It was not just the length ("a 7-column spread") or generosity (being identified as "one of our indispensable poets") that made James Merrill grateful to Helen Vendler for her appraisal of *Braving the Elements* (1972) in the *New York Times Book Review*.[1] Vendler's "easy + sensible" way with the collection's "erotic themes" that Merrill had been gradually introducing into his poetry during the previous decade turned a potentially awkward moment into "far + away my finest hour vis a vis the media."[2] Neither scandalized nor proud for making a connection Merrill no longer attempted to hide, Vendler simply accepts Merrill's sexual identity as a premise of his love poetry. Vendler additionally attempted to understand this intersection of the poetic, personal, and unavoidably political in relation to Merrill's commitment to writing in forms. In the fifties, Merrill had received harsh reviews by poet-critics like Louise Bogan, who found his poems "impeccabl[e]" but "frigid and dry as diagrams," and James Dickey, who impugned a "needless artificiality, prim finickiness, and determined inconsequence" accentuated by an "almost disdainful ease . . . [with] whatever verse-form he wishes."[3] By 1972, many advocates of beat, confessionalist, or cultural nationalist poetics had popularized intensely personal free verse idioms that tacitly associated formalist poetry with a passé, even reactionary, sensibility.[4] Vendler made no such judgment. Neither did she praise Merrill for developing an increasingly conversational diction and syntax or for speaking more clearly from the standpoint of his own sexuality. Instead, Vendler praises his mastery of matching "contour," the forms and tropes

130 | Unlimited Eligibility?

of poetry, with "content," in poems that are "autobiographical without being 'confessional.'"[5] Merrill admitted that he "ke[pt] repairing to [the review] . . . again + again" weeks later "as if the two intervening Book Sections hadn't made of it ancient history."[6]

The euphoria did not last. Shortly thereafter, Richard Pevear's assessment of the same collection appeared in the *Hudson Review*, a journal that semiregularly had featured Merrill's work since the late forties. Pevear credits Merrill's writing with "brillian[ce]," describing "[h]is language [a]s a singular achievement[,] . . . at once lyrical and sarcastic, conversational and quaintly formal," a warmly positive evaluation until the last modifier pointedly introduces echoes of Bogan and Dickey.[7] Pevear senses an "upper middle class" (rather than what was, in fact, a decidedly upper class) background now left "in fragments," having "exploded or fallen to pieces" along with the "break-up of the American idea." While crediting Merrill with acknowledging and even interrogating his own social status, Pevear sees this as only a half measure. Instead of promoting a "new world taking shape on the ruins of the old," Merrill merely offers mildly remorseful "acceptance of that [increasingly broken] condition" of bourgeois life. Lacking "radicalism," Merrill's poetry does not seek to intervene amid the world's "social forces." Merrill identifies no Ginsbergian Moloch, no racist or patriarchal social order, no antigay legal system.[8]

Faced with two starkly contradictory reviews, one coronating him as "indispensable" and another declaring the opposite, Merrill soon fixated on the latter and, stirred to self-reflection on his social obligations, entered a period of depression and writer's block.[9] He had long understood that his status, as a child of the founder of the Merrill-Lynch brokerage firm, obliged him to be generous. Aside from the occasional teaching job, usually lasting only a semester or two at a university, Merrill lived primarily on the income provided by trusts with a total value of "about $20 million." Langdon Hammer's biography notes that Merrill "traveled when and where he wanted" and had "good seats at the opera" but otherwise "lived quite modestly," never buying "expensive cars" or "extravagant real estate" (as his father had) and generally "g[i]v[ing] away more money than he spent on himself."[10] In 1955, he established the Ingram-Merrill foundation as a vehicle for helping financially struggling artists and supporting humanitarian causes.[11] Hammer notes other gifts, often discreetly distributed so the recipient would not know where the money originated and feel a sense of obligation.[12] Yet Merrill's private generosity, an understated attempt to reckon with a scion's privilege, inadvertently may have reinforced it, making it easier for him to resist more public commitments against systemic injustices. Pevear's review pushed Merrill to reflect on the sources of his own reserve. As he did so, he began to consider with greater seriousness than he had before the premises structuring the socially engaged poetry of his moment and to start what would be a fraught process of further developing his own lyric politics.

There remains a tendency to consider Merrill apart from rather than in conversation with his time.[13] A few recent scholars like Piotr Gwiazda have resisted this trend, noting how some of Merrill's poems like *The Changing Light at Sandover* can be related to acts of "homosexual self-definition" increasingly characteristic of the post-Stonewall "liberationist atmosphere of the 1970s." But Gwiazda focuses more on Merrill's relation to W. H. Auden than his relation to the politics and poetics practiced in those liberation movements.[14] The poetry Merrill wrote in the seventies, however, indicates that he came to understand that the work being done by his contemporaries' socially committed lyrics reflected a significant shift in the practice of the politics of recognition. This chapter begins by considering this sociocultural context. The early gay rights movement adopted cultural pluralist strategies, including what was, at the time, a bold reframing of sexuality as an identity category and thus a source of a culture that could be socially recognized and assimilated into mainstream America. But after the Stonewall uprisings, younger, more radical participants within the gay rights movement, influenced by (and indeed including) younger, more radical participants in other identity-related social movements, began to doubt the efficacy of cultural pluralist–style appeals for recognition and assimilation. More assertive claims of group self-recognition emerged that focused on liberation from rather than gradual incorporation into American social norms.

Though these liberationist poets, like most poets writing in English from the second-half of the twentieth century, expressed themselves in relatively short, subject-centered free verse poems, Merrill continued to write in established forms (albeit with occasional excursions into free verse) as he began to respond more explicitly to the political trends around him. Much of the poetry from the second half of his career tacitly argues that these forms, rather than being necessarily indicative of nostalgic naivete, illustrate how our lives are shaped by existing discursive structures, a fact sometimes obscured by free verse's tendency to affect individual voice,

132 | Unlimited Eligibility?

agency, and authenticity. The second section of the chapter focuses on one such poem, "The Will," which embeds JM and David, personae of the poet and his partner David Jackson, in a sonnet sequence that introduces JM signing his last will and testament just before he leaves on a trip to attend a friend's wedding. Juxtaposing a relationship gaining social recognition (his friend's) with a relationship excluded from such social recognition (his own) inside a verse genre principally associated with the former, "The Will" assesses impulses aligned with both assimilative and liberatory models of social recognition, with a desire to be incorporated within existing social structures and with a very different desire to be freed from existing social structures and the prejudices that can define them. But a sudden turn introduces a spiritualist narrative featuring the poem's other "will," Ephraim, a familiar spirit summoned by JM and David at the Ouija board. This second narrative recontextualizes and burlesques the poem's earlier considerations of sociopolitical recognition, insofar as the mediums conjure an entity who conveniently confers upon them, as romantically linked gay men, a form of recognition withheld by the society in which they live.

The turn toward spiritualism described in "The Will" proved consequential for Merrill, who would go on to write, with the aid of David Jackson and a metaphysical menagerie extending far beyond Ephraim, a nearly 600-page poem, *The Changing Light at Sandover*. A brief consideration of *Sandover* shows how Merrill's burlesquing of debates about sociopolitical recognition barely conceals his own desire to wield the power to recognize at times in grotesque ways, as evidenced by a racist thread running through the *Sandover* narrative. Section 3 concludes the chapter by examining how lyrics in Merrill's last collections begin to acknowledge this problematic contradiction in his lyric politics. In poems like "Clearing the Title," Merrill's domestic spaces become theaters, a location that positions his speakers within larger dramas in which they no longer hold a host's or a medium's (or, indeed, a recognizer's) power. These post-*Sandover* poems argue that not just existing frames of recognition but the act of framing itself must be burlesqued. They present the resulting comedy as a democratizing act that affirms ontological eligibility and opens space for improvising more mutual modes of relation. But the potential limits of this burlesquing also raise questions about its efficacy as a response to the injustice that spurred so much of the lyric poetry of Merrill's generation.

The Emergence of Gay Culture and "Gay Culture-Hero[es]"

Buoyed by Vendler's review and not yet dejected by Pevear's, Merrill wryly wrote to Elizabeth Bishop in 1972 about fan mail he had started to receive, explaining with mostly faux exasperation that he "hope[d he was] . . . not turning into a Gay culture-hero." The comment reflects Merrill's political reticence, a quality he shared with Bishop, along with a hint of understated pride. While Langdon Hammer argues that Merrill "was no more involved in . . . [the gay rights] movement than he had been in any other political struggle," Merrill found the fan mail "flattering," began to assess the political prospects of such movements, and eventually, in his own way, made a poetic contribution to the cause.[15]

Merrill's comment to Bishop also may have reflected a measure of surprise that the role of "Gay culture-hero" even could be conceived. Yes, by 1972, the more radical post-Stonewall gay rights groups like the Gay Liberation Front affirmed the existence of gay culture and insisted that it bore a responsibility not to assimilate within so much as to be liberated from a homophobic American culture.[16] But the boldness of such a stance belied how only a few decades before, early gay rights activists in America wrestled with how to categorize themselves. In the twenties, Henry Gerber invoked a universal humanity when he proposed a Society for Human Rights as a prospective affiliate of the British Society for the Study of Sex Psychology, an organization that sought to educate the public toward greater toleration of "inverts." While participants in the British group like Edward Carpenter certainly took an interest in artists who they perceived to be members of the "intermediate sex" (like Walt Whitman), neither they nor Gerber publicly posited that nonheterosexual persons had created a distinct culture.[17] By the forties, Robert Duncan, referencing—and critiquing—the legacy of cultural pluralism, praises those "Negroes" and "Jews" who sought social recognition not by foregrounding group identity but by appealing for "human freedom[,] . . . *human* recognition and rights" and scolds closeted gays and lesbians (especially artists) who do not commit to a parallel "struggle toward recognition." Duncan disavows a cultural pluralist-style "Zionis[m] of homosexuality," featuring gay men "asserting in their miseries their nationality," as a means of seeking tolerance within the American body politic. "Disown[ing] *all* the special groups (nations, religions, sexes, races) that would claim

134 | Unlimited Eligibility?

allegiance," Duncan presents homosexuality not as a distinct identity or culture but simply as a morally neutral form of human behavior, a part of the "universal human experience" that ought to be acknowledged and accepted.[18]

The question of positing a politically legible gay culture began to be debated in the late forties and early fifties in terms that, at times, seem shadowed by shame. While the Mattachine Society would become one of America's first gay rights organizations, its founder, Harry Hay, in 1950 initially conceded that "regulat[ing] the social conduct of our minority in such matters as, for example, exhibitionism, indiscriminate profligacy, [and] violations of public decency" might be achieved "clinically" via "clinical personnel" or even "churchmen" who might "adjust and alleviate where possible the emotional and psychological development of Androgynous tendencies in minors."[19] Hay, thus, first envisioned not a "minority" identity to be socially recognized as a culture but a set of desires and behaviors that, especially when practiced "indiscriminate[ly]," required diminution or even elimination via therapeutic treatment (his initial name for what became the Mattachine Society was Bachelor's Anonymous, which, of course, echoes Alcoholics Anonymous) or theological intervention, rather than scorn and incarceration.[20]

What spurred an awareness among an increasing number of non-heterosexuals that they collectively constituted a minority identity with its own culture(s) deserving social recognition? Hay and the early members of the Mattachine Society gradually came to believe that if the legal and cultural prejudices they endured significantly paralleled the injustice endured by other "recognized minorities" like "Jews or Negroes," then perhaps a parallel solution should be pursued. Implicitly if not explicitly echoing cultural pluralist ideology, Hay began to suggest in 1950, initially alongside and in tension with the psychiatric and religious concessions noted above, that the path toward social acceptance begins with a group knowing itself. With some awkwardness, he explains that "people are bad not because they are Jews or Negroes but because of the external nature of their political and economic environments. We must endeavor to understand ourselves and then demonstrate this knowledge to the community." Only then will "myth[s,] . . . fears[,] and antagonisms" be dispelled.[21] And one year later, in 1951, Hay, who had insisted from the start that the Mattachine Society would be open to people of any "race, color, creed, or political affiliation" and promised to "mak[e] common cause . . . contributing to the reform of judicial, police, and penal practices" impacting all minorities, affirmed that it was "possible and desirable that a highly ethical homosexual culture emerge . . . paralleling the emerging cultures of our fellow-minorities—the Negro, Mexican, and Jewish Peoples."[22] Furthermore, Hay promised to work toward "better social integration of the membership Minority into the community-at-large," echoing the cultural pluralist goal of recognizing distinct groups for their contributions to the "common good of the community" or "general morale of the community."[23] A few years later, in 1955, a small group of women, some of whom had been affiliated with Hay's original (and quite male-dominated) chapter of the Mattachine Society, founded the Daughters of Bilitis, shining light on hitherto overlooked lesbian issues. These women continued to emphasize, in conciliatory language paralleling Hay's, the "education of the [sexual] variant . . . to enable her to understand herself and make her adjustment to society" alongside "education of the public[,] . . . leading to an eventual breakdown of erroneous conceptions, taboos and prejudices" against "this minority group."[24] And, on the east coast, Frank Kameny, a cofounder of Washington, DC's branch of the Mattachine Society, directly petitioned President John F. Kennedy on similar grounds in 1961 ("homosexuals—a minority group in no way different . . . from the Negroes, the Jews, the Catholics, and other minority groups").[25]

However, by the mid-sixties, some of the ethnic groups that Duncan and Hay and their peers had looked toward as models for assimilating into American culture had grown impatient with a cultural pluralist strategy that had failed to create the truly multicultural democracy it had promised. As chapter 2 showed, African American advocates of cultural pluralism often had seen it for what it was, a political strategy with limits and flaws. Calculated concessions to a system structured to continue to empower those already recognized over those mis/unrecognized were made in pursuit of incremental improvements to black lives. These concessions, however, came with qualifications that proved prescient. Even in "Enter the New Negro," an essay often linked to the conceptualization of the Harlem Renaissance, Alain Locke warned that, though "the Negro" was not presently a "genuine radical[,] . . . under further pressure and injustice iconoclastic thought and motives will inevitably increase." Locke knew that black nationalisms with no interest in assimilating into an America shaped by white supremacism had powerful advocates, including Marcus Garvey.[26] In the thirties, W. E. B. DuBois, though he still hoped for assimilation, began to think it might take the building, at least temporarily, of "a Negro nation within the nation" characterized

136 | Unlimited Eligibility?

by a "careful autonomy and planned economic organization" that was "so strong . . . that 12,000,000 men can no longer be refused fellowship and equality in the United States."[27] And all of these thinkers knew that, since the beginning of slavery, African Americans often had been forced to survive by establishing their own institutions rather than trusting the institutions of the state.

Building on these precursors, as well as the example of postcolonial movements emerging in Africa and Cuba, an explosion of more assertive forms of ethnic nationalism developed first in the black community and soon thereafter in other minority communities during the late sixties. Manifestoes redirected the Declaration of Independence against the United States on behalf of a black nation (Huey Newton and Bobby Seale's 1966 Black Panther platform), reclaimed much of the American southwest on behalf of Chicano, Mexican, and Indigenous peoples from whom it had been taken (*El Plan Espiritual de Aztlán*), asserted the need for Asian Americans to "determine our own destiny" and reject "white washed" models of inclusion (Larry Kubota's "Yellow Power!"), and defined "the Black Artist's role in America" as "aid[ing] in the destruction of America as he knows it" (Amiri Baraka's "State/meant").[28] These assertions of self-determination within ethnic nationalisms—assertions of self-determination as groups of embodied persons—find a kind of analogue in the movements pursuing women's liberation and gay liberation. Significant differences, of course, existed between and within these movements, each of which had distinct histories, internal debates, and splinter cells.[29] But despite (and perhaps because of) such debates, these movements point to a significant shift. Working toward liberation from—rather than assimilation within—mainstream American culture, for a time, became the center of activist energies, a trend that manifested itself as a tendency to deemphasize (substantially, though not necessarily entirely) appealing for recognition from established authorities in favor of rejecting (substantially, though not necessarily entirely) those authorities and declaring group self-recognition.

Melissa Williams describes this major political shift as a consequence of how "state recognition practices," despite movements like cultural pluralism, "have as often been a vehicle for sustaining structures of domination . . . as an instrument by which justice is served." Rather than building more democratic political practices and institutions, "states' strategic interests—in maintaining sovereign authority within their territories, rendering populations legible for the purposes of administration, fostering economic growth, and containing and managing social conflict—actively shape and significantly constrain the policies of recognition that they embrace."[30] The rhetoric of recognition, in this way, has been wielded as a political ploy, a gesture toward a democratization that never fully occurs. As a result, "subjugated peoples' practices of self-organization and self-affirmation" increasingly began to emphasize what some political scientists have called "bottom up" or "from below" strategies of recognition rather than "top down" or "from above" strategies.[31] Neither strategy is wholly separable from the other (indeed, they collectively echo Hegel's dialectical path toward mutual recognition) and they reflect a spectrum of political possibilities rather than merely two polarities. Furthermore, with regard to the LGBT+ movement, Christopher Nealon rightly has warned that an oversimplified "'pathology to politics' story" obscures how in "each new stage of queer integration into urban, national, or international systems new problems of representation, cultural integrity, and political danger emerge to replace or reshape old ones."[32] Nevertheless, distinguishing between broad trends can be clarifying, if held in tension with the fact that each context inevitably also is characterized by its own distinct dynamics. Approaches that seek "from above"–style recognition tend to resemble cultural pluralism, wherein minority populations appeal to and, in doing so, acknowledge that they depend upon, the willingness of those persons and social structures that are already empowered to distribute recognition more broadly. Given this "from above" power structure, such appeals typically request accommodation within present political, juridical, and economic structures. Activists adopting a "from below" approach, on the other hand, tend to emphasize a group's capacity for self-determination that often corresponds to a greater intent to challenge existing political, juridical, and economic structures. "From below" forms of recognition typically defer not only to intragroup formation of group identity but to the group's preference for a measure of inclusion in—or separation from—the state.

Social movements during the late sixties and seventies appropriated the lyricized lyric's projection of personhood in order to voice liberatory, "from below"–style politics of recognition. James Smethurst has noted, for example, that the "importance of poetry as a Black Arts [movement] genre is not merely because it is more easily and dramatically performed than prose, particularly the novel, but also that the relative brevity of the lyric poem lends itself to the space and economic constraints of journal and small press publishing far better than the novel."[33] This kind of lyric,

138 | Unlimited Eligibility?

typically written in free verse featuring a first-person speaker merging if not the poet's voice then a personae of the poet with group concerns, however, should not be oversimplified. Keith Leonard has argued with regard to Audre Lorde's "lyric practice" but with implications extending to many other poets writing amid these movements, that this kind of lyric often includes "self-contradictory wrinkles in the logic of identity politics by juxtaposing the claim to assert identity transparently on one hand with . . . [a] self-conscious critique of that language of transparency as hegemonic and exclusionary on the other."[34] Leonard's observation also reflects what occurred earlier in the twentieth century, when poets associated with the Harlem Renaissance negotiated in a variety of ways and to varying degrees with cultural pluralist models. Though the Black Arts movement, like a number of other cultural movements in the late twentieth century, emphasized intragroup recognition of group identity rather than appealing for recognition by presiding, external power structures, different writers mobilized identity differently in their lyrics (compare Lorde to, for example, Gwendolyn Brooks or Nikki Giovanni or Carolyn Rodgers), and this mobilizing remained strategic in its awareness of the powers and limits of what identity means in various contexts. Nevertheless, amid this diversity of expression, certain poets and even certain lyrics gained a nearly metonymic status. Amiri Baraka's "Black Art" shared its name with the movement it energized with its call for a "Black World" that itself would "be a Black Poem."[35] Somewhat similarly, Rodolfo "Corky" Gonzales's "Yo soy Joaquin/I am Joaquin," a work that was first printed by the Crusade for Justice, Gonzales's Denver-based wing of the emergent Chicano Movement, became, according to Gloria Anzaldúa, central to the "recognition" that "we were a people[,] . . . a distinct people."[36]

Even if no single poem became so closely associated with gay liberation (and, of course, individuals within every movement would have favorites of their own), poets and poetry often were foregrounded. The Gay Liberation Front's *Come Out!* newspaper (1969–1972) featured poems in every issue, often written by GLF activists themselves (e.g., Ron Ballard and Martha Shelley) and occasionally printed articles directly addressing lyric poetry as an important political vehicle.[37] Winston Leyland, founder of the journal *Gay Sunshine*, in 1978 pointed to how an "ongoing Gay Cultural Renaissance" initiated by "the current gay liberation movement, . . . [especially after the] rise and spread of post-Stonewall gay consciousness . . . deep[ly] [a]ffect[ed] . . . many writers, freeing them from societal or self-imposed restraints."[38] Leyland had in mind many of the authors included in his anthology *Angels of the Lyre* (1975), one of the first featuring gay poets who consented to be identified as such. The collection brought together many poems that had been published in movement-based periodicals (like *Gay Liberator*, *Fag Rag*, or Leyland's own *Gay Sunshine*), alongside those published in more mainstream venues.[39] Reclaiming cultural territory in a way that mirrored their ethnic nationalist peers who, at times, also sought to reclaim geographic territory, this anthology identifies homoerotic roots of the Western lyric tradition.

> The lyre, of course, is the harp-like stringed instrument that was used by the ancient Greeks for accompanying song and recitative. The word is also used in a figurative sense as the symbol of lyric poetry. And in Greek mythology the sun-god Apollo, patron of music and poetry, was adept on the lyre, no doubt using it to charm his lover, Hypnos. The musician Orpheus, son of Apollo, was said to be able to move rocks and trees by the power of his lyre. According to one of the Orphic myths, Orpheus went to Thrace and started a cult of boy-love there.[40]

A somewhat similar argument spurs Judy Grahn's *The Highest Apple: Sappho and the Lesbian Poetic Tradition*, as she opposes a "female/lyric/Sapphic" to a "male/epic/narrative/Homeric" lineage. Grahn observes that the destruction of the vast majority of Sappho's lyrics meant that "women in the West" and lesbians in particular "fell out of our own story."[41] Like Leyland's anthology, this is not an appeal for assimilation but a liberationist attempt to repossess what prejudice had taken away, an imperative that created the conditions within which a number of poets, including Robert Duncan, Allen Ginsberg, Gloria Anzaldúa, Adrienne Rich, Pat Parker, Audre Lorde, and Judy Grahn herself, along with earlier writers like Walt Whitman, Oscar Wilde, Hart Crane, and Gertrude Stein, eventually did become "Gay culture-hero[es]" as they were grafted, despite their differences, into post-Stonewall narratives of group recognition of group identity.

Merrill had watched these trends from their beginning, initially with great wariness. After a 1956 poetry reading in San Francisco, Merrill briefly met Robert Duncan and Allen Ginsberg. Though Merrill "liked" Duncan, Ginsberg, along with fellow Beat poet Gregory Corso, made a scene, insisting that Merrill should be more assertive, more outrageous:

140 | Unlimited Eligibility?

"What's the matter? . . . Why don't you scream? That's what people out here want! Embarrass yourself! Talk about cock!" It is hard to know whether or not such comments reveal that Ginsberg (who was gay) and Corso (who was not) had deduced (then, if not before) Merrill's sexuality and placed expectations on his expression of it, or whether they merely wished him to embrace the aesthetics of excess that they currently cultivated. Merrill, however, was never going to "scream" like a Beat poet, and after the encounter he "gave away his copy of *Howl*" to a friend when he left San Francisco "the next day."[42] A decade later, Merrill continued to express caution about combining politics and poetry. In a 1968 interview, when asked about the "social poetry" related to the "war in Vietnam" and "the Negro revolution," he dryly acknowledged these "immensely real concerns," advised writers not to get in competition with the "editorial page," and dismissed "overtly political" poetry in a way calculated to provoke his critics by comparing "a word-cluster like *napalm-baby-burn*" to the "high C of a Donizetti mad scene." Analogizing audiences of protest poetry and opera, he stated that both "have been prepared for what they get and are strongly moved" but "when the tide of feeling goes out, the language begins to stink."[43]

However, such snark, at times, scarcely conceals Merrill's jealousy of the attention paid to socially-engaged confessionalist and identity-focused idioms. And that envy, from the start, included a measure of grudging admiration. Langdon Hammer reports that Merrill "resented [Robert] Lowell's dominance of the poetic landscape in the 1960s" after the intensely wrought merger of the personal and political in *Life Studies* (1959). Even so, that volume and W. D. Snodgrass's *Heart's Needle* made an almost "immediate impact" on Merrill's work.[44] Elizabeth Bishop provided an example of a quieter candor, sometimes projected through poetic forms, that may have seemed to Merrill more credible than confessionalist performances of exhibitionism. Hammer argues that "An Urban Convalescence" shows Merrill beginning to combine poetic form with more socially contextualized personal reflection. Written between late 1959 and early 1960, the poem pivots, "in a bolder modulation than anything in Bishop or in his own work previously," from free verse into pentameter quatrains at the phrase "With self-knowledge," inverting Lowell's shift from formal to free verse in *Life Studies*.[45] Merrill's suspicion that the trend to use free verse to signify personal and political liberation was a bit naive would inflect the course of the rest of his career.

Indeed, as Merrill became more forthcoming about his sexual identity throughout the late sixties and seventies, his formalist ambition increases.

This might seem to make Merrill's lyric politics as old fashioned as the forms he favored, insofar as seeking mastery of those forms could appear to constitute an artistic appeal for recognition within established norms rather than liberation from them. But Merrill knew these dangers and circumspectly warned that "both the formal and the experimental poet too often use their gifts as an easy way out." Passively resting in forms or blithely casting them aside for free verse or experimental idioms were equally unreliable strategies, according to Merrill, for escaping from the discursive norms those forms typically channeled.[46] Instead, he believed that mastering "the forms, the meters and rhyme-sounds," rather than making one inevitably into a "stolid 'formalist,'" could "liberat[e]" a poet "from one's own smudged images and anxiety about 'having something to say'" and "*into* the dynamics of . . . craft itself."[47] Though Merrill, to be sure, never became a protest poet or an activist of the left, such a statement is not necessarily reactionary. Merrill is not arguing against saying "something" in one's poetry. He is warning about how "anxiety" associated with that task might result, even against one's best intentions, in confinement within normative discourse. To delve more deeply into "craft itself" in a way that "liberat[es]" involves more than a default adoption of free verse or redeploying forms as vehicles for expressing, for example, group recognition of group identity. It requires one to develop something more difficult and more unsettling, an awareness that the concept of recognition itself is a discursive form, framing and even limiting our social imaginations with its history and tropes. In the second half of Merrill's career, he develops a formalism that does just this, as he chooses to participate in but ultimately burlesque the process of asserting group recognition of an identity within established forms. However, amid this difficult task, which might be understood as a queering of gay identity politics, Merrill falls into contradiction, longing for recognition and indeed desiring to be a recognizer in deeply problematic terms. It would take Merrill nearly a decade before he began to develop a less hierarchical, more democratic politics and poetics of representation.

Queering Recognition

"The Will," a poem first published in 1974 in *Poetry* magazine and then collected in *Divine Comedies* (1976), initiates this turn toward foregrounding (while simultaneously burlesquing this foregrounding of) the recognition of identity.[48] It features a self-critical speaker whose initials (JM) and spouse's

142 | Unlimited Eligibility?

name (David) assert that he is, more explicitly than any of Merrill's previous speakers, a personae of the poet as a member of a sexual minority. This facet of the poem reflects a work very much in conversation with post-confessional, identity-focused lyrics. But rather than being written without apparent artifice in free verse, "The Will" is a poised, intricately crafted sonnet sequence that describes its own coming into existence in parallel with the speaker's struggle to come into a kind of political consciousness. Two wills mediate these processes, reflecting the speaker's status as a person possessing great privilege of one sort and lacking another. The first sonnet presents a team of lawyers visiting JM to collect his signature on the latest iteration of his last will and testament, while the eighth sonnet abruptly introduces the other "will," a voice named Ephraim emanating from a Ouija board. Insofar as Ephraim extends an idiosyncratic form of cosmic recognition (from above) to his gay mediums (JM and David) within a poem that had hitherto been an idiosyncratic assertion of gay identity (from below), Merrill positions "The Will" as a peculiarly complex contribution to early seventies lyrical investigations of political recognition.

According to Langdon Hammer, the earliest drafts of the poem emerged as Merrill, in fact, was revising his will and processing the guilt induced by Richard Pevear's critique of *Braving the Elements*. In a 1972 drafting notebook, Merrill candidly acknowledges that "what I had scorned + avoided in the world—politics, money—or, more exactly, profited by with eyes averted, turned out to have shaped me to its own quite scrutable ends."[49] But this confession becomes more rhetorically complicated when placed in verse.

> I have set down these lines
> With the utmost diffidence
> With eyes averted
>
> It is as if, with untold means
> At my disposal I had cut myself
> Out of my own will.[50]

Are the "eyes averted" here out of embarrassment at having overlooked political obligation? Or are the "eyes averted" out of continued reticence at accepting this accountability and its material consequences? Or both? And there is something extravagantly melodramatic about Merrill feeling "as if" the mere act of "set[ting] down these lines" is akin to giving up the entirety of his wealth. This particular acknowledgment would appear, with slight rewording, midway through the completed poem. And all of this ambivalence, the speaker's difficulty in parsing his own competing motives and how those motives connect to his multiple identities, becomes central to "The Will."

Despite the title, the speaker in the published poem initially lacks willpower. He is scarcely able to act and thinks only through barely conscious dreams and fantasies. This torpor distorts what had become a characteristically Merrillean opening gesture, a welcoming into the domestic space of the speaker and the formal space of the poem. David Kalstone argued that in Merrill's work "houses . . . become charged conductors of meaning—shelters explored, destroyed, mended, invoked; reflectors for glimpsing the larger patterns of his life," settings of family fractures but also "shelter[s] improvised against a larger exposure" and, with some frequency in his mature work, locations characterized by a winsome hospitality extended to his reader.[51] But in this poem, the inert speaker is unable to muster any kind of welcome for the lawyers seeking his signature.[52]

> I am standing among the coal black
> Walls of a living room that is
> Somehow both David the Wise's and not his.
> Outside, the dead of winter, wailing, bleak.
>
> Two men and a woman, dressed in black,
> Enter with a will. A will of mine?
> They nod encouragement. I sign,
> Give each my hand in parting. Now to pack
>
> This canvas tote-bag. I have wrapped in jeans
> With manuscript on either side for wadding
> Something I'm carrying to a . . . to a wedding . . .
>
> Then, wondering as always what it means
> And what else I'm forgetting,
> On my cold way. A car is waiting. (392)[53]

All of the "ing" words implying potential or ongoing motion turn out to be gerrunds or verbs describing stasis or puzzlement, underscoring a

144 | Unlimited Eligibility?

baffled speaker who wonders "as always what it means," a strange reaction to signing a document ostensibly reflecting his most explicit personal intentions. But "it" is expansive, ominously stretching over all that JM is "forgetting," including the "wedding" he will soon attend. And having haphazardly packed his bags by using his current manuscript as "wadding" protecting his wedding gift, JM leaves "[o]n my cold way," a reference to the winter weather and perhaps even a nod to early detractors like Bogan and Dickey, as if to suggest this poem might help to explain his allegedly cold formalism.

Merrill's choice of form, a sonnet cycle that becomes a kind of epithalamium, offers a window into how the speaker's listlessness does not reflect apathy so much as an unresolved tension between competing social obligations that he finds difficult to describe. Aside from a few important exceptions that prove the rule (including Shakespeare's sonnets to a young man), sonnet cycles typically have projected and reinforced heteronormative social structures. "The Will," instead, prominently features a sequence of neo-medieval paeans to the male speaker's male partner, "David the Wise," "David the Fair," and "David the True," evidence of a union that was not socially sanctioned, while focusing on JM's journey to participate in the socially recognized union of his heterosexual friends. Signing a will further highlights this distinction. For JM's home is "both David the Wise's and not his." As a result, readers are brought into the mind of a man both privileged (by wealth) and lacking privilege (in terms of sexuality), dissociated from the domestic space he shares with his (legally unrecognized) spouse, and dissociated from a journey he is about to take to celebrate two soon-to-be spouses, within a poetic form that underscores this dissociation. Internally conflicted about his identities, the speaker is not yet ready to consider whether persons like himself should seek recognition within normative structures like sonnets and marriage laws or liberation from them and whether his wealth demands taking additional responsibility in such tasks.

Instead, as signaled by the parentheses, gentle surrealism, and different location (near the "Seine"), we enter into a "dream" displaying JM still struggling toward self-consciousness, much less sociopolitical consciousness (393). Approaching a seemingly familiar, "dark hotel" labeled "I," JM finds a doorbell that does not work, leaving him unable to enter and emblematically closed to himself. Alongside, he sees a smaller building labeled in barely "legibl[e]" scrawl, "I*bis*" (392). As Timothy Materer notes, Merrill has in mind the way that French street numbers ending in "bis" can designate buildings added after addresses already were established or spaces created when a building is subdivided.[54] The dream, thus, leads from a grandiose, seemingly inaccessible "I" to a "humbler way into the edifice" designated "I*bis*." But later in the poem another meaning emerges as his wedding gift is revealed be an Egyptian-made stone sculpture of an ibis. So Merrill plants a hint here. The way into self-knowledge—into perhaps even a better sense of "what it means"—may be linked to his feelings about the wedding (392). This reverie placing social obligation (associated with the ibis wedding present) in tension with yet inextricable from partial self-consciousness (I *bis*) ends with a sudden, bawdy pun (a "[s]team[ing] . . . manhole" that "bore / Wetness to the dream" and left him "heartsore"), demonstrating the desires present within the allegedly "cold" JM (393).

After the dream, the poem returns to the wedding trip. JM is still "waiting" as he was in the first stanza, but now is in an airport, where he continues to worry about his frequent mental "[l]apses" (393). A "growing puzzlement" about "things losing / Their grip on me" extends to a faltering sense of embodiment ("I nearly removed my thumb") as well as an equally ominous, if ambiguous, "numbing inward leak" that he is unable to stanch (393). Nikki Skillman has observed that, "throughout his oeuvre," Merrill "is most confident that he is advancing toward the truth of the mind when he is exaggerating failures of memory."[55] On the occasions when Merrill uses multiple personae in a poem (here, the speaker and JM, and later, in a different way, perhaps also Ephraim), this strategy becomes something related if also slightly different: an intricate performance of prior and present degrees of self-awareness. This process moves forward in a five-sonnet sequence following the numbed speaker's narrative as he visits his mother somewhere in the "South" before moving on to the location of the wedding (393). Amid this exposition, JM describes how he leaves in the taxi the bag containing his wedding gift (the "wall-eyed, stone-blond / Ibis") and the manuscript he had been drafting (394).[56] This culminating memory lapse stirs Merrill to a moment of "Self-inflicted / Desolation" (395). Speculating about the effect of all this on his unconscious (and vice versa), he wonders about whether

> . . . tonight's pint-size amphibian
> Wriggler from murky impulse to ethereal act
> Must hazard the dimensions of a man
>
> Of means. Of meanings. Codicil
> And heir alike. White-lipped survivor hacked
> Out of his own will. (395)

146 | Unlimited Eligibility?

This dream ("tonight's . . . / Wriggler from murky impulse . . .") depicts JM's ongoing, inchoate attempt to reckon with his financial and cultural status. The poem began with JM scarcely sure of what he was signing, an indication of his ambivalence about his inheritance. Now he becomes the mechanism and recipient of the legal judgment, both the "[c]odicil," the superseding amendment to the last will and testament itself, and the "heir" impacted by that amendment. And he is left "[w]hite-lipped" with terror at what will result for him as a person and a poet.

Here we reach the moment when the completed poem quotes the early draft, as the speaker worries about "set[ting] down these lines" with "eyes averted" that involuntarily "cut . . . / [him] [o]ut of . . . [his] own will." However, a strange reinterpretation of these worries begins to occur in the next stanza as an abrupt flash-forward introduces another, very different will that also might be described as a "[w]riggler from murky impulse to ethereal act," the imposing voice of the familiar spirit JM and David contact through a Ouija board, Ephraim.[57] This is not their first encounter with Ephraim, whose history with JM and David turns out to have been the topic of the manuscript lost in the taxi. Indeed, Ephraim himself has much to say about JM's continuing anxieties about losing his wedding gift and manuscript. "DISINHERIT[ANCE]" of "THAT STONE BIRD" was necessary to avoid the "DISASTER" it "BROUGHT" its new bearers "COMME TOUJOURS" (395). Ephraim similarly dismisses JM's anxieties about the vanished manuscript: "SINCE U DID NOT CONSULT / THEIR SUBJECT YR GLUM PAGES LACKED HIS GLORY" (396). Then Ephraim commands JM to start again, working collaboratively with the spirit in order to "SET MY TEACHINGS DOWN" and warning that "IF U DO NOT YR WORLD WILL BE UNDONE" (396). While Ephraim had been hoping to "POSSESS REPEAT POSSESS" JM, whom he deems his "L OBJET AIME" as well as his prospective compositor, he found it impossible due to "SO MANY DAVIDS TO COMBAT" for primacy in JM's priorities (a reference to the poem's praise for "David the Wise," "David the Fair," and "David the True") (396). A Goliath thwarted, Ephraim must acquiesce to the Ouija board as the vehicle of communication, with his "will" reduced to possessing a "WILLOWARE" cup serving as a planchette for "WALTZING WITH THE [Ouija board's] ALPHABET" (396).

What does this radical redescription of the speaker's experience of being "hacked / Out of his own will" mean? By transferring focus from a legal will with financial implications to an allegedly metaphysical will with allegedly "WORLD"-wide implications, is JM conveniently dodging more concrete, more material forms of sociopolitical responsibility? It's hard not to view JM's turn to Ephraim, after having seemingly deepened his sociopolitical awareness of both his experience of prejudice and the insulation of privilege, as perversely frivolous, as if difficult self-reflection has been replaced by flattering fantasy. What seemed to be a potential opening for candid consideration of the relationship between social recognition and financial redistribution, an intersection much debated in subsequent decades, regrettably seems to close.[58] Does this indicate that Merrill had greater capacity and determination to reflect on the politics of his sexual identity than on his class identity (much less potential intersections between the two)? In any case, the economic subtext is largely lost, as the camp spirituality opens other, queerer political valences. As Piotr Gwiazda notes, it is perhaps still too "conventional" to understand campiness as indication of being "politically disengaged," rather than as a means of powerfully "problematiz[ing] the norm."[59] Ephraim's advent, after all, does introduce a remarkable analysis of the mechanics of social recognition. For Ephraim is an emblem of a curiously closed system. JM and David are both the recognizers (as creators of Ephraim) and the recognized (by Ephraim). Contacting Ephraim, thus, is an attempt on the part of the mediums to master both "from below" and (quite literally) "from above" styles of recognition, while also, given the sheer strangeness of all that flows from the Ouija board, rendering the whole project scarcely distinguishable from farce. But what does Merrill mean by evoking a desire to control recognition processes alongside a desire to burlesque them?

Though Ephraim's appearance does not alleviate JM's "[p]aralysis," which extends to the composition of this very poem ("No headway . . . / . . . writing (or not writing) this"), several months later, a curious breakthrough begins that is paralleled in the poem's form, climaxing with the twelfth sonnet interrupting the eleventh sonnet between its octave and sestet (397).[60] Here, JM, once again, takes us into one of his dreams—or, more precisely, into a dream responding to an earlier dream. In the first of a series of archaeological images, "a lucky stroke [that] unearths the weird / Basalt passage of last winter," JM recalls the moment when he was unable to enter either the dream-hotel that he identified as "I" or the neighboring "I*bis*" (397). Now he successfully excavates a different space, an "underground / Chamber made ready," filled with all that had been lost earlier in the poem (397). Alongside various funerary

148 | Unlimited Eligibility?

items, "goblets, fans and fruits," there is the stone ibis, previously a symbol of the tension between social obligation (wedding gift) and sexual identity ("Ibis"), and the missing "manuscript" about Ephraim (397). Amid all this, it is surely not coincidental that Thoth, ancient Egypt's ibis-headed deity, was the scribe of the gods, a position Ephraim hopes JM will assume. These recoveries explain why entry into this sonnet/sarcophagus amounts to an unprecedented entry into "My word!" (397). As the author and subject of the manuscript (and indirectly, via Ephraim, its critic), JM is both the entombed pharaoh and the "slave" who created the tomb, as well as archaeologist or looter and the tomb being looted, as well as the source of the Divine and its scribe (397). Victimizer, victimized, and observer combine, a complex merger reflecting how the contradictory features of JM's personality and positionality (e.g., a gay man who is also a scion of the Merrill estate) have contributed to his personal crisis.

Assessing it all, JM admits that what he found in his dream is "not / Quite the profoundest or the most ornate" monument but, with newfound optimism, he advises, "Give it time" (397). What appeared to be merely "bric a brac / Slumbered in bonds that of themselves would break / . . . at any chance unsealing, / To shining leaf and woken shades of feeling" (397). Given what the ibis and manuscript represent, JM predicts future conditions within which his identity, experiences, and the artistic representations of them become more admired. Earlier interpellation within and negotiation with various heteronormative cultural vectors had resulted in a numbed sense of nonexistence (remarkable, though that may seem, for someone of his financial privilege). Now, within this sonnet/ sarcophagus, which is, from one angle, still emblematic of absorption within a normative structure, JM appears willing to wait, to inhabit a more composed, confident version of the speaker's inertia. But a less passive reading is equally available, with JM responsible for the cleaving of the eleventh sonnet. Such a gesture indicates a "subver[sion of] . . . canonical authority" exemplary of how Merrill's "rhetoric of formalism," according to Mutlu Konuk Blasing, "questions the historical and metaphysical authority of conventions as much as it challenges free forms that appeal to 'experience'—whether personal or sociopolitical—for their legitimation and authority."[61] And from still another angle, this subversion of authoritative discourse becomes hard to distinguish from a claiming of that authority. As Stephen Yenser notes, Merrill "establishes," with the interior twelfth sonnet made of seven couplets interrupting the split octave and sestet of the eleventh sonnet, "an 8-7-6 progression that mends even as the interpolation scissors."[62] The development of this slyly balanced strategy, figured in Ephraim (an entity JM and David create who recognizes them) and the broken/mended sonnet (as an emblem of its author's interpellation within and breaking of existing discourse), poised between culturally assimilative and liberatory impulses, shows Merrill's refusal to align his sexuality with any single model of sociopolitical recognition.

One can debate whether this constitutes a problematic evasion of existing lyric politics or a welcome complication of them. What is clear is that the development of this stance readies JM finally to confront the poem's destination, an assessment of his experience at his friends' wedding. Unlike the dark winter scene that began "The Will," the sun is shining, trees are "in bloom," and "doves and finches" are singing as "rings [are] exchanged for life" between JM's friends (397–98). However, the marriage (and even epithalamium) clichés are soon complicated. Merrill associates the daylight with "[l]emon[s]" described as "thickskinned little suns," a metaphor that may reflect the speaker's emotional defenses (397). More of the speaker's feelings are projected upon an approaching "helicopter," which he tellingly associates with a "bad fairy" briefly "[d]rowning out the vows" (398). In a poem filled with puns, is there a hint that JM was tempted to play the part of the bad fairy, interrupting the wedding as he had interrupted a sonnet? But having sensed this capability, he does not, at least in person. That the poem hints at the possibility, however, complicates the seemingly gracious conclusion that "[l]eav[es] to lovers' lips / All further argument" (398).

"The Will," thus, stands as a complex response to Merrill's more explicitly politicized poetic peers and the guilt induced by Richard Pevear's review of *Braving the Elements*. After all of the dreams and digressions, the speaker's forgetful, enervated, tortured state becomes, by the end of the sonnet cycle, remarkably poised and strategically arch, balanced between assimilation and assertion, burlesquing not just the heteronormative discursive and legal systems he confronts but the related architecture of sociopolitical recognition that he finds confining. Having developed this stance, Merrill goes on to elaborate it—and the occult narrative begun in "The Will"—at great length over the next decade in what would become *The Changing Light at Sandover*. Though space does not permit an extensive analysis of the over 500-page *Sandover*, the unsettling (indeed offensive) apotheosis of Merrill's blurring of whether he longs to control (mockery as mastery of) or seek alternatives to (mockery as escape from) the alignment of lyric and the politics of recognition deserves brief consideration.

150 | Unlimited Eligibility?

In "The Will," the speaker's slowly developing ability to navigate a host of heteronormative social vectors is focalized through a sonnet sequence. Operating on an entirely different scale, *Sandover* features a veritable anthology of forms, including ballad-esque rhymed quatrains, villanelles, (more) sonnet sequences, several passages in terza rima, a canzone, among others, as well as a coda ("The Ballroom at Sandover") that is a kind of ode to form itself. This remarkable display wields the history of English (and even European) prosody and its associated cultural authority to frame what Thom Gunn deemed "not a minor triumph and . . . not an incidental one": "the most convincing description I know of a gay marriage."[63] Paralleling this display of discursive authority is a vastly enlarged menagerie of metaphysical authorities, including Ephraim but extending to a heavenly bureaucracy who now designate both "BLEST DJ [as David is now called, and] BLEST JM" as chosen vehicles for disseminating allegedly world-saving doctrines (114). Merrill himself later offered an overview:

> Our familiar spirit [Ephraim] is no longer a human shade but one of a host who describe themselves now as fallen angels, now as volatile subatomic particles; the scale accordingly wobbles throughout, from vast to microscopic. They have numbers for names, they are in aspect—to those who "see" them—huge red-hot bats. Our particular favorite, however, is soon transformed into a peacock and named by us Mirabell. His main fields are History and Science, often much mythologized. Thus we are told of an Arcadian Atlantis whose immortal denizens resembled centaurs and themselves created the bat-angels to serve them. It didn't work. Two rival worlds—one electrically, one atomically powered—ended in mutual destruction. It would be for Man to reconcile those opposites. We learn of one attempt that misfired when Akhnaton used solar power to explode a pyramid of quartz.[64]

And so on. Merrill never seeks (nor wants) to resolve the tensions between high culture (poetic forms) and low (pulpy sci-fi; New Age doctrines informed by self-help bestsellers), seriousness of purpose (making visible in the seventies a long-term gay relationship; foregrounding threats to the environment) and silliness (decades of consulting a Ouija board), asserting and being subjected to authority.

These ambiguities rest on another, the lack of clarity about the degree to which JM and DJ are self-aware about their participation in composing the messages received through the Ouija board. In the second book of *Sandover*, "Mirabell's Books of Number," JM states that "one benefit of doubt, / As of credulity, is its tiresomeness. / Let ours [his and DJ's], then, be the first thing I suppress, / Or try to" (115). On the other hand, JM also insists that even if "Fear and doubt [had been] put by," they were "still kept handy" (166).[65] Thus, rather than simply submitting to what may have felt like an external, mystical process, JM and DJ established guardrails guiding it and suggesting a deeper, albeit less than conscious, involvement. And from the beginning, JM and DJ wonder if Ephraim was "a projection / Of what already burned, at some obscure / Level or another, in our skulls" (31).[66]

All of this matters a great deal to Merrill's project because burlesquing recognition (whether from above or from below or both) ostensibly must rest upon a refusal to participate in it seriously. But *Sandover*, ultimately, reveals that what "burned . . . / . . . in [their] skulls," in fact, was an intense, if not wholly conscious, desire to be empowered to recognize (or not) others. For the spiritual realm Ephraim and his compatriots describe operates as a vast, eugenic scheme. JM and DJ learn that humans are made up of various "densities," resulting in elaborate taxonomies that divide the population into "run-of-the-mill souls" and "an elite" (139). One such "density" draws repeated attention.

> *Jew.* Density in man par excellence.
> Human uranium. A tiny pinch
> Sweetens and fortifies the happenstance
> Soul in question. (138; Merrill's emphasis)

JM knows that this kind of commentary, however ridiculous, cannot be explained away in terms of camp excess, so he awkwardly advises that this is "[n]ot to be confused / With 'Jew' in any easy ethnic sense." But the compressed, historically specific imagery betrays such simplistic disavowals: the bizarre phrase "[h]uman uranium" conflates the victims of one Holocaust with the element that can cause another (138). And the crudeness continues in a ranked list of ethnicities, featuring "GREEKS" prominently placed "NEXT IN LINE OF DENSITY TO THE JEW" and extending, in succession, to "[t]he chief subdensities /—African, Arab, Teuton, Slav, Chinese / Down to a murky aboriginal" (141, 139).[67] Though

152 | Unlimited Eligibility?

especially glaring throughout "Mirabell's Books of Number," this ethnic stereotyping is anticipated in the first section, "The Book of Ephraim," and never contradicted in the final volume, "Scripts for the Pageant," making it an unavoidably central feature of Merrill's midcareer lyric politics.[68]

Though Merrill acknowledged in interviews that "there's a vast amount of questionable dogma in *Sandover*" and David Jackson flatly condemned the "elitist shit," neither quite accepted responsibility for such passages.[69] But why did so calculating a writer as Merrill not leave out sentiments that he and Jackson opposed, when he was winnowing down the vast verbiage filling the Ouija transcripts?[70] Timothy Materer argues that "elitism and contempt for the non-elite are a feature not only of ancient apocalypses like [the biblical book of] Revelation but also modern works" like Merrill's volume.[71] *Sandover*, however, is no typical apocalypse, given its decidedly camp tone and its focus on a gay couple, so it is hard to accept that adherence to generic convention necessitated Merrill to preserve the racism in the published text. Langdon Hammer points to Merrill's sexuality and argues that the odious hierarchies reflect "the snobbery of a gay man trying to convert a style of life commonly seen as sinful, self-centered, or simply alien, into a sign of his spiritual superiority."[72] But why should the upending of sexual hierarchies have anything whatsoever to do with asserting racial and ethnic ones? Here, a comparison to Toomer and Crane may be clarifying. All three poets betray a need for control, a desire to be the recognizer, that their work had ostensibly rejected or mocked. Toomer's turn toward authoritarian, eugenic rhetoric after becoming frustrated in his attempt to summon the American race, Crane's concession to a cultural pluralism aligned with settler colonialism, and Merrill's attempt to master what is meant to feel like the whole history of Western prosody, each underscore this need for control. Does JM's campy, New Age mythology, thus, merely serve as a disingenuous distraction from something sinister? Does Merrill's publishing of it all reflect growing self-awareness and a willingness to acknowledge and even confess these hitherto sublimated desires for a position of mastery? Parsing such questions, as well as the degree of distance between the alleged spirit realm, JM and DJ as mediums, and Merrill the poet, may become a less suggestive, increasingly tiresome prospect the longer *Sandover* lasts, even as the display of prosodic skill reaches its climax.

A number of the most interesting poems from Merrill's last decade and a half side with the skeptical reader of *Sandover* and acknowledge

JM's problematic desire for mastery. They expose JM's tendency to be a charming but subtly controlling host and reveal him struggling to accept the fact that he is a mere participant, rather than a chosen one, inside a theater filled with human performances as intriguing as his own.[73] This dynamic inflects the poems' forms, which do not frame someone or something to be recognized but, instead, continue to reimagine form as a space for improvisation outside the limiting, hierarchical structure of recognition narratives, a space for affirming unlimited ontic eligibility.[74] Cultivating this space by burlesquing not just existing frames of recognition (and JM's desire to mock/master such forms) but the possibility of framing/recognizing altogether becomes a central, if never fully realized, ambition of late Merrillean lyricism.

Burlesquing Recognition and All Forms of Ontological Framing?

The first major poem Merrill wrote after *Sandover*, "Clearing the Title," serves as a bookend to the spiritualist narrative and lyric politics set in motion by "The Will," while opening up the new directions Merrill would follow in the last phase of his career.[75] Readers are invited into a characteristically Merrillean kind of domestic drama: a change of address offers an opportunity for personal and poetic growth, conditions that also offer ample opportunity for the speaker to address the privileges of his mobility. The beginning of the poem, however, raises the question of how much its speaker is capable of growing at this stage in his life and art. We meet a nearly scornful JM scrambling to understand why an unnamed but unambiguously implied DJ, who is no longer the idealized lover depicted in "The Will," has brought him to Key West, Florida.

> Because the wind has changed, because I guess
> My poem (what to call it though?) is finished,
> Because the golden genie chafes within
> His smudged-glass bottle and, god help us, you
> Have chosen, sight unseen, this tropic rendezvous
> Where tourist, outcast and in-groupie gather
> Island by island, linked together,
> Causeways bridging the vast shallowness (406)

154 | Unlimited Eligibility?

The fact that the "wind has changed" reflects how JM finds an ill-considered whimsy within DJ's plans, but it also foreshadows a not fully realized change within his poetry. Reference to "the golden genie" similarly might be read as self-congratulation on JM's part concerning his increasingly acclaimed poethood, or, alternately, near-ridicule of DJ merely "chaf[ing]" to visit a different place. But JM saves his real derision for the people with whom they are "linked together" on the island, people whom he dismisses with a metaphor merging the region's shallow waters and its residents' (and visitors') allegedly shallow minds. The characteristic elegance with which JM delivers this slur makes one wonder whether he has learned anything about the elitism undermining aspects of *Sandover*, the "poem" noted in the second line.

Merrill's annoyance deepens considerably as the cloudiness both overhead and inward parts to reveal an "appalling truth [that] now bores / Into my brain," the fact that DJ surreptitiously has "*bought* a house" (407). But the "title" indicated in the name of the poem refers to more than just a legal document confirming the real estate purchase. The word describes his attempt to find an overall title for the recently completed *Sandover*. Underlying these two storylines, however, is a third: a deepening awareness of his own sense of entitlement. As he looks with disdain at the "floors" of his new house, something begins to happen, both to his perception of his new home, his spouse, as well as the poetics through which he sees the local community. Gazing

> Between the muddy varnish of whose lines
> (But can you picture *living* here? Expect
> *Me* to swelter, year by sunset year,
> Beneath these ceilings?—which at least aren't low.
> What about houses elsewhere, rooms already packed
> With memories? That chiffonier
> Would have to go, or else be painted white . . .)
> More brightly with each word the daylight shines. (407)

The opening and closing rhymes, here, poetically parallel the problematic conceptual frames, the "muddy varnish" through which he sees the world. But rather than working through a more rigid form like ottava rima, Merrill's stanzas reveal a flexibility inflected by interruptions (parentheses, sentence fragments, dashes) that unsettle the already loose formal structure. These fits and starts signal not an emerging denial of the reality of framing (cultural, poetic, etc.), nor merely the aspiration to develop a more accommodating frame through which one might recognize the world, but a reenvisioning of framing altogether, an awareness of its unavoidability, its powers and limits, as well as a concern for its consequences on what exists both inside and outside of it.

For now, however, the clouds begin to break inside and outside the speaker and his stanzas. Hammer notes that the poem offers "aspects of a new style" that "gives up any residual concern about lyric purity[,] . . . mixing high and low diction, intricate, impressionist word painting and pop culture slang in an amalgam alternately jaunty and plangent."[76] For JM (as a speaker) begins to perceive what Merrill (as a writer) has already made clear to his readers, the parallel between JM's resentment about not being consulted before DJ signed a title and DJ's implied (though politely left unstated) resentment about seeing what Merrill admits was "[o]ur poem" only, in the end, "signed JM" (408). Both must face the difficult realization that "what [things] at first appall precisely are the changes / That everybody is entitled to" (409).

In Merrill's earlier works, as he made mastery of poetics and politics analogous to learning the role of a host, the speaker oversees the space within which he welcomes others. Merrill, in his post-*Sandover* work, senses that if he is to be serious about engaging otherness, he needs a more complex image around which to envision lyric sociality. Though he positions JM, his poetic proxy, in a doorway ("[t]urning the loose knob onto better-late- / [t]han-never light"), the door opens not into a house or room he owns but into a theater where he must share the stage (408). As they walk down the pier at the water's edge, Merrill observes,

> Here at the end's a landing stage swept clean
> Of surplus "properties" and "characters."
> Gone the thick banyan, the opaque old queen.
> Only some flimsiest human veil
> Woven of trickster and revivalist,
> Musician and snake-charmer (and, yes, us as well)
> Pot- and patchouli-scented floats between
> The immense warm pink spotlight and the scene. (409)

At land's end, nearer life's end, and perhaps at the end of one way of doing lyric politics, he finds himself without "surplus 'properties' and 'characters,'" without the metaphysical menagerie. And he hints at a comparison

156 | Unlimited Eligibility?

of the *Sandover* experience to the "banyan" tree, which starts as a seed suspended in another tree and then grows vines downward, ultimately choking its host (409).[77] If the Ouija-board mediated process of writing his poem did not wholly consume him and DJ (and there are indications in *Sandover* that it nearly did), it reproduced a racially hierarchical social order, a distressing mirror image of other hierarchies Merrill, as a gay man, had sought to undermine. Here, instead, on stage at the beach-front dock, rather than seeing himself as a distinguished recipient of a divine message, he sets aside his earlier condescension toward his fellow Key West residents and finds himself fitting in ("and, yes, us as well").[78] For he knows that he too has played the roles of "trickster and revivalist," an awareness that lets him see "the Iguana Man," a Salvation Army band, and others gathered nearby as fellow artists doing their "act[s]," just as he is (409). Merrill does not go on to make a reductive generalization about a shared humanity. Instead, everything on "stage" is collectively allowed to be performance, and pleasure is found in preserving it as such (409).[79]

As the poem ends, JM implies that their spiritualist endeavors had "let the life cloud over" (408). Right on cue, as he is learning how to "break through those clouds," Merrill happens upon his trilogy's title, as they witness the suddenly resplendent "changing light" of the setting sun (408, 410). The concluding link to *Sandover*, like those that came before in the poem, does not remove his ambivalence about that text so much as position it as a step in an ongoing process rather than as a definitive literary triumph. Indeed, the final stanza, as a whole, is beautiful but bittersweet.

> Whereupon on high, where all is bright
> Day still, blue turning to key lime, to steel
> A clear flame-dusted crimson bars,
> Sky puts on the face of the young clown
> As the balloons, mere hueless dots now, stars
> Or periods—although tonight we trust no real
> Conclusions will be reached—float higher yet,
> Juggled slowly by the changing light. (410)

The clown's face that the sky with balloons resembles bears a tear, an acknowledgment of regrets amid a growing awareness of mortality, even if "no real / Conclusions will be reached." More life and art are still to come in this theater.

Burlesquing Recognition | 157

But what conclusions can be reached about Merrill's burlesquing of not just particular frames of recognition but such framing altogether? A figure at the edge of the poem's frame suggests one answer to this question. Just before sunset, JM reports that a clown on a unicycle rode around "brandishing a hammer fit for Thor" while "[y]ell[ing]," as a parody of the Salvation Army members, "Give or Ah'll clobber yew!" Then JM adds,

> Though no one does, no thunder strikes. Because—
> Say, because a black girl with shaved skull
> Sways on the brink: flexed knee and ankle-bell
> And eyes that burn back at the fiery ball
> Till it relenting tests with one big toe
> Its bath, and Archimedean splendors overflow.
> As the sun sets, "Let's hear it for the sun!"
> Cry voices. Laughter. Bells. Applause (409)

The repeated conjunction, interrupted by dash, line break, and verbal pause, creates a hesitation, perhaps because the poem broaches the metaphysical (as "Thor" and "thunder" suggest) after Merrill had seemingly set it aside, or perhaps because of who he grafts into the scene at this moment. The "black girl" is described more extensively than the others in the scene (including JM and DJ) and wryly attributed a power that prevents the thunder and makes the sun set. Though this hyperbole aligns with the droll depictions of other performances on the pier, her appearance does not. Her "eyes that burn back" as she "[s]ways on the brink," though descriptive of her gaze and location, contain overtones that veer close to white clichés about black women. If this trace of earnestness falls back into racial framing, it is not because a campier approach to the young African American woman would have been an improvement. And this suggests a limit to Merrill's lyric politics. Burlesquing the possibility of ontological framing itself is indeed an important, queer tactic, particularly when used to confute a more empowered world imposing confining frames of recognition. It also can be a useful way to defuse one's internalization of the world's desire to recognize. But Merrill hesitates to apply such a tactic here and struggles to find another way to affirm someone less privileged than himself. Is everyone in this beautiful (if also wistful) scene equally empowered to improvise? To burlesque each other's improvisations? Just how unlimited is the eligibility Merrill imagines here? Though "Clearing the Title" is a self-reflective poem, it is not clear how far this self-reflection extends to these questions that lie near the root of the hesitation acknowledged by this stanza. Instead, we are left to wonder whether the concluding, celebratory "[b]ells" include the young black woman's "ankle-bell," whether she chooses to contribute to the "voices" and "[l]aughter" and "[a]pplause," whether she feels a part of the emergent community greeting the Key West sunset's changing light.

Chapter 5

More Rapid than Recognition

Thylias Moss's Lyric Velocity

In the early 2000s, Thylias Moss offered the following provocative paragraph for a projected but never published manuscript, "Quotes Community: Notes for Black Poets."[1]

> The presumed accuracy of metaphors isn't well disputed; proof is seldom required. There's no testing to determine how long the figurative deception lasts, to say that one thing is another may not really cure the entity undergoing total figurative metamorphosis. Metaphor: another form of identity theft. While perhaps not meant to be taken literally, metaphor is a form of figurative equation that can be, though often isn't, tested with figurative algebra. Perhaps poets could be a little more accountable for the mergers that they sponsor. A little less casual about their privilege to breed and manufacture hypothetical hybrids.[2]

Moss's worry that metaphor is too often akin to appropriation, "identity theft," or even eugenics suggests a racial dimension that scarcely needs to be made explicit. By emphasizing how metaphor may reflect models of relationality defined by epistemological, social, and reproductive control, Moss illustrates how the trope can perpetuate (consciously or not) rhetorics of mastery and enslavement.

160 | Unlimited Eligibility?

But Moss's mini-polemic is against a thoughtless, "[un]accountable," "casual" practice of metaphor and not against metaphor per se. While she may have partly inherited from mid-twentieth-century precursors what Gillian White describes as a concern with regard to how "forms of mimesis and metaphor-making . . . produce problematic, even shamefully self-centered poetic subjects and forms of subjective experience," Moss, unlike an older (and white) poet like Elizabeth Bishop, does not so self-consciously tarry with (absorb and also interrogate) a sense of shame about metaphor and, instead, pivots toward a profuse metaphorical practice.[3] Here, as much as anywhere, Moss proudly inherits the legacy of the Black Arts movement's insistence on claiming cultural territory taken by the white supremacism concurrent with lyricization. As a result, Moss's candid assessment of metaphor misused and her extravagant use of it are not contradictory. The resulting stance is a politically strategic act, albeit one that would follow a political trajectory not entirely in alignment with other Black Arts movement legacies.

Driven by a deepening sense that nature and society act as "dynamic systems," Moss advocates "metaphor" as a means of "catalog[ing]" these "processes of interactions" and as "a tool of navigation that can enable instantaneous access to other event locations on any scale."[4] In doing so, she hopes to make poetry better reflect that which is "already there, but needing to be named in order to be perceived," the predecessors, participants, and consequences that constitute these dynamic systems.[5] But is this "nam[ing]," this ability to "recogni[ze] . . . the galactic within the microscopic, the sombrero within the galactic," the very power she warns about in the paragraph for "Quotes Community"?[6] Does Moss, in fact, seek the kind of control she warns against, a kind of unacknowledged desire for mastery akin to what undermined the prior poets examined in this study? Not exactly. For the metaphorical practice she advocates, which plays an important role in what she came to call "limited fork poetics" (and later "limited fork theory") "delights in the unavailability of . . . certainty" and in the acknowledgment of "lapses," "gaps," and "contradiction[s]" rather than seeking to repress such potential limits.[7]

This stance may suggest an artistic path somewhat mirroring Hart Crane's. Hoping to expose and undermine metaphor's propensity to perpetuate hierarchical social structures and disseminate their (mis) recognitions, Crane, in his most rigorous applications of the "logic of metaphor," invites a reader to look carefully but not to recognize in an effort to construct more mutual relations built on affirming ontological eligibility rather than establishing epistemological mastery. Like Crane, Moss is conscious of the need to undermine mastery's allure. However, Moss's poetry since the late nineties, rather than encouraging modes of watching that resist recognition by slowing epistemological closure, instead, seeks to display and exceed recognition's inertia. She intends the velocity of her figuration in her more recent work to evoke the speed with which a variety of complex systems (biological, cultural, etc.) constantly evolve around us, exposing how irreducible interminglings make up the stuff of life itself, an awareness that she hopes can serve as a basis for more democratic socialities.

The first section of the chapter shows how Moss reaches this poetic practice after careful study of (and, to a degree, participation within) cultural nationalist models of recognition-from-below prominent in the late sixties and early seventies, models that sought to assert group self-determination and, in doing so, aspired for liberation from the often racist power structures shaping American society rather than continuing to appeal to those power structures to distribute sociopolitical recognition more broadly. For Moss, this meant wrestling with the legacy of the Black Arts movement. Recent scholars have shown how, on the whole, the Black Arts movement allowed greater space for internal critiques of sexism and heterosexism than were present in American culture at large.[8] Ajuan Maria Mance, for example, argues against the way that "the label of 'sexist' has been applied to male poets of the Black Arts movement as a justification for dismissing the entire possibility of an emancipatory Black nationalist politics," while also noting that "African American women poets . . . [did have] to establish a role for Black womanhood within the patriarchal landscape of nationalism."[9] This social space defined Moss's formative, initial years in college. More than a decade later, in the late eighties and early nineties, she built her first collections on the social analysis offered by the Black Arts movement, including the intersectional feminisms that followed from it. In a poem like "Lessons from a Mirror," she addresses racial as well as gender prejudice, bearing witness to the ways that those who inhabit multiple minority identities suffer multiple layers of misrecognition and erasure.

While Moss never rejects this assessment, she does begin to reenvision how her poetics might challenge such confinements. Increasingly ambivalent about elements of the cultural nationalist legacy and frustrated by publishers and critics imposing what she felt were "definitions of *Blackness* that deprived . . . [her] of the complex structure of identity"

162 | Unlimited Eligibility?

(Moss's emphasis), Moss announces a new lyric practice and lyric politics in three pivotal texts published in 1998, an essay, "The Extraordinary Hoof," a memoir, *Tale of a Sky Blue Dress*, and a poetry collection, *Last Chance for the Tarzan Holler*.[10] This last text features an idiom open to a wider variety of cultural vectors, sometimes via dramatic monologues, sometimes via digressive reflections initiated by literary, mythical, or religious texts, but always locating the reader at complicated points of intersection, moments when discourses (with regard to race, religion, criminality, etc.) determine who is granted full personhood, to what degree, and with what consequences. In order to reflect the mind's not always conscious engagement with these forces, the way that they circulate through diffusely distributed networks of social affects, Moss's poetry becomes more digressive and faster in its figuration than it had been earlier in her career. But instead of finding a sure path to greater inclusion via recognition processes, she begins to doubt the pursuit of recognition as a political and lyric practice altogether.

As the primary trope of relation, metaphor becomes central to this development. A poem like "Advice," a dramatic dialogue between a Black woman poet and a Jewish male professor concerning the former's plan to write a poem commemorating Jewish resilience after the Holocaust, presents a member of one community that has suffered ontic erasure offering a member of another such community a kind of mutual recognition from below on which intersectional solidarity hypothetically could be built. But the politics of metaphor immediately inflects the project as the poet's implicit comparison of suffering is understood by the professor as misrecognition, cultural appropriation, and even an aestheticizing of violence. The professor's condescending tone, however, makes his critique difficult for the poet to hear, and her frustration leads her toward unspoken but not entirely unthought anti-Semitic tropes. "Advice," thus, presents an undoing of the impetus to build intersectional solidarity on a mutual recognition from below.

Nevertheless, Moss's most recent work aims for an even more expansively inclusive sociality, albeit through a further reconceptualized lyric practice, which she calls limited fork poetics or, more generally, limited fork theory. Convinced that the "interactions . . . processes, . . . [and] entanglement[s]" shaping life might best be understood through complex systems theory, Moss seeks to develop a parallel poetic idiom.[11] Though this necessitated further opening her work to considerations of a wider range of vectors (biological, economic, technological, etc.), this did not entail a minimizing of sociohistorical contexts. She continues to emphasize that "Black [identity] remains something so powerful that whatever I do invites an opportunity to consider race," which for her entails seeking to "define *Blackness*, redefine it, reconfigure it, as it must be able to embrace anything I do, anything I think, anything I imagine."[12] Moss insists that "Limited Fork Theory is a black concept," partly because it is the product of a writer socially legible as "black" but also fundamentally because it is a "mixed (up) concept" reflecting how life (indeed, Being itself) is always irreducibly entangled, at times beyond legibility, an acknowledgment antithetical to white supremacism.[13] The productive tension between these associated claims suggests how disrupting epistemological recognizability can be an extension and not an evasion of racial identity. In fact, the central characteristic of her limited fork poetry is its use of metaphor less as a trope intended to define who or what may be brought together and how each is recognized and more as a trope attesting to (and adding to) existing and expanding entanglements. An inclusively democratic society, she suggests, might be built on an acknowledgment of this fundamental ontological proximity and even immanent relation to each other. A poem like "The Subculture of the Wrongfully Accused," which describes how an African American man named Ronald Cotton was falsely convicted of sexually assaulting a white woman named Jennifer Thompson, shows the way that metaphorical profusion is central to Moss's limited fork theory as it confronts expansive, seemingly intransigent systems of social prejudice. Such a poem wonders what it would take for a society grounded on exclusionary, hierarchical systems of (mis)recognition to be reorganized around affirming an originally "mixed (up)" social ontology.

Moss and the Legacy of the Black Arts Movement

In the early seventies, during Moss's first year in college, her white English composition teacher responded to her analysis of a poem by Robert Frost by giving her a C, inviting her to "repeat the assignment" and "explain[ing]" that "he appreciated how intimidated . . . [she] must feel as the only minority student," before finally advising her to "be intellectually honest" and not "suppress . . . [her] natural hatred for whites."[14] Academic success now rested upon her willingness to perform black identity in a manner recognizable to a politically self-congratulatory white person. Moss resented the proposed arrangement and, faced with no good option, chose to transform the command performance into a parody.

164 | Unlimited Eligibility?

> For the occasion, I wrote "Harlem Rap," a poem in which
> Black Panthers forced all white people to march into hell. I
> said it was written by Akira Nkwome and published in some
> nonexisting black journal whose name I don't recall. For the
> occasion, I installed Cleopatra eyes on my face and sported a
> burgeoning Afro wig just purchased from Woolworth's and got
> the A I already deserved. It was one of my best performances.
> How they raved about the authenticity; it was as if I brought
> the six o'clock news right into the classroom. *Are you related
> to Angela Davis? Yes*, I said; a sister of circumstance.[15]

At the center of this episode, poetry's place should not be overlooked. Chapter 2 showed how Harlem Renaissance writers often felt hemmed-in, rightly proud of their distinctly African American forms of "lyrical expression" but also aware that white readers and critics, the primary, empowered distributors of social recognition, would associate these poems, at times, with grotesquely exaggerated minstrel show stereotypes. Recognition in such circumstances risks becoming blended with the prejudice it supposedly repairs. Moss's white instructor similarly wielded the promise of allyship and recognition within the context of his classroom, all the while attempting to minstrelize black anger.

When Malin Pereira, in an extensive 2010 interview, used this anecdote to initiate a broader consideration of how Moss as a young woman "navigate[d] . . . expectations that you should align yourself with [the] Black Arts Movement," Moss added several other contemporaneous anecdotes concerning (mis)recognition and the performance of identity. She found that collegiate theatrical productions cast roles "according to assumptions about . . . appearance and cultural authenticity."[16] The theater department did not grant her a speaking part in *A Midsummer Night's Dream*, so she was excited when a "production offered by the Black Studies Department" featured her as the "lead" in a new work by a "black male playwright whose name I've forgotten." The latter role, however, forced Moss to inhabit what she felt were gender stereotypes that "deni[ed] . . . Francine's [her character's] sacred womanhood."[17] As Moss internalized her discomfort with that production, as well as its burden of being the singular alternative to what effectively was a white-only production of Shakespeare, she came to feel that "the Black Arts Movement as practiced in my local learning sphere" effectively "offer[ed] me nothing better, just something louder and much more crude, than

More Rapid than Recognition | 165

American canonical exclusions offered."[18] Soon thereafter, Moss left the university and would not return to higher education for another five years.[19]

Moss, however, warns Pereira that these anecdotes should not be understood as a blanket judgment, and she goes on to affirm the cultural work accomplished by a "larger and presumably more reasonable and healthy Black Arts Movement."[20] This qualified endorsement reflects Moss's awareness of the movement as a decentralized array of voices and institutions from across the country that developed distinct regional and local identities. Moss also knew that her own early work built on African American women poets who participated in the movement. Carolyn Rodgers and Sonia Sanchez, for example, re-taxonomized poetry itself and African American lyrics, in particular, outside of Eurocentric norms.[21] But Moss's early work also built on a number of internal critiques of the movement forwarded by black women who felt that the movement was not always fully committed to purging the patriarchal norms dominating America that rendered black women vulnerable to prejudice from whites of both genders as well as some African American men.[22] Demanding greater social recognition or working toward group self-recognition, though crucial and, at times, effective strategies, did not necessarily remedy this dynamic. Though recognition processes may be less fraught when they take place within and between subgroups of a minority community, hierarchical dynamics can persist. Smaller, more disempowered subgroups may find it necessary to make appeals to the more dominant faction of the group. Kay Lindsey, for example, understood that "classifications and categorizations of groups of people by other groups have always been for the benefit of the group who is doing the classifying and to the detriment of the classified group."[23] Facing this predicament, Toni Cade (Bambara) affirms a multiplicity of models of black womanhood ("What Black woman did you have in mind?") and even wonders whether "we need to let go of all notions of manhood and femininity" in favor of "creating a new identity, a self, perhaps an androgynous self" more capable of contributing to revolutionary "struggle[s]."[24]

These debates continue to inform Moss's books published throughout the eighties and early nineties.[25] Her 1989 collection *Pyramid of Bone* depicts these tensions on a single page, with a grimly cynical lyric about an irreparable quantity of misrecognitions facing another with a more optimistic sentiment. Neither tonality assists her in finding an escape. As a tool for analyzing these dynamics, Moss here and with some frequency (and increasing daring and sophistication) in her career draws

166 | Unlimited Eligibility?

from an African American "persona poem" tradition, including works by Dunbar, Hughes, Brooks, Hayden, and many others. Howard Rambsy II has explained how foregrounding "first-person perspectives of characters other than the poet-authors" enables a poet to lean either toward "sampling" another voice entirely or toward a "rewir[ing]" of their voice or to facilitate "embodying multiple characters" in a way that extends "beyond conventional Eurocentric traditions and definitions" of dramatic monologues and, instead, presents "the acts of masking, passing, catching holy ghosts, speaking in tongues" from a distinctly black perspective.[26] In doing so, persona poems also challenge lyricized readings that downplay the rhetorical intricacy of poetry by marginalized writers, assuming it to be the voice of the author or a decontextualized speaker and often also assuming that voice to participate in an uncomplicated appeal for social recognition from above or group self-recognition from below. Moss is but one example of why such assumptions almost always oversimplify both poetics and politics.[27]

"Lessons from a Mirror" presents an African American speaker who compares herself to Snow White. The poem begins by subjecting Snow White to some good-humored mockery ("she's so white / the gown seemed to disappear when she put it on") before exposing the broader social system that such a mythic figure perpetuates (1–2).[28] The speaker initially notes Snow White's invulnerability. Power and prestige require no effort, since they inhere to her whiteness. Her name's near redundancy reinforces how this closed circuit of privilege rests on an endlessly assumed accrual of recognition. The speaker participates without her consent. She must complete this "study of chiaroscuro," even if it demands of her "a shadow's constant worship," the relation established by those who "[p]ut me beside her" while elevating Snow White (4, 8, 3). However, the speaker admits that, satisfying though it might be, "[t]urning the tables" would not resolve the problem so much as extend it, establishing a kind of endlessly revolving cycle or, worse, initiating a kind of "Russian roulette" for the less privileged of the pair (11, 12). After all, the speaker has a disadvantage: recognition of Snow White's preeminence has been thoroughly naturalized, as indicated by her name, whereas "nothing falls from the sky / to name me" (13–14). Instead, she bears the burden of seeming not only naturally inferior but nearly invisible, an unnamable—and unrecognizable—"empty space" or "gap" diminished by comparison to whiteness or "fill[ed]" by the phallus (15, 17–18). Thus she warns the reader, "When you look at me, / know that more than white is missing" (19–20). Such a conclusion, though it refuses to compromise with the fairy tale, is nevertheless confined by it, hinting at an array of oppressions, each exacting a cost on the speaker so great as to make her feel as if she is little more than a paradoxical totality of absences, a lack of recognition or a near-totality of misrecognition that she doubts will ever be remedied.

On the facing page of the same collection, Moss continues to investigate how children's stories often illustrate and perpetuate unequal distributions of power and opportunity by interpellating young people within established regimes of recognition. "The Wreckage on the Wall of Eggs," however, uses a somewhat more positive tone in an effort to derive consolation and even affirmation, at least momentarily, from tales that seem to exclude.[29] The poem's young, African American speaker interprets her life through the nursery rhyme "Humpty Dumpty" and the children's book about a young Swiss girl, *Heidi*. Adopting the role of Humpty Dumpty, she imagines "[t]otal unobstructed vision" as she sits precariously on "the wall," a perspective offering a view of "both sides" that she "loathed" (9–10). Extending outward, as far as she could see "east and west," were "hundreds of girls / perfect for the part of Heidi," girls "eas[y]" to "hat[e]," even if they "couldn't control [their] ancestry" (15, 10–11, 15–16). In the foreground, all she can see are "Egg shells . . . on the path . . . / . . . like so many babies mercy-killed / out of slavery" (18–20). After facing the stark contrast between the countless white children unaware of their privilege and the countless eggshells serving as grisly emblems of her people's oppression, she draws an unsettling conclusion.

> My life on the wall is anything but easy.
> I want to but can't hate Heidi well.
> I can't maintain tragic responses to breaking eggs.
> When I look down at the wreckage on the wall of eggs that
> came out of me, I see that what's inside is as white and
> gold as Heidi. (21–26)

The speaker seeks a stance that is critical yet generous. But setting aside "tragic responses to breaking eggs" troublingly leaves the speaker identifying with the oppressor even as the oppression continues. While "Lessons from a Mirror" yields an impassioned despair, a determined optimism, here, fosters little more than the dangerous self-deception that life might be livable in a world that recognizes personhood in terms of whiteness. As the speaker

168 | Unlimited Eligibility?

signals a willingness to tolerate the status quo, we see her risk her own destruction ("the wreckage on the wall of eggs . . . / came out of me"), aligning her life with the legacies of slavery she had sought to evade.

Attempting to "Transcend Identity" amid a "Crisis of Affective Recognition"?

Poems like "Lessons from a Mirror" and "The Wreckage on the Wall of Eggs" eventually led Moss to wonder whether she had reached a dead end. While early models like Sylvia Plath and Ai were women writers who unapologetically projected "force" and "authority," Moss came to suspect that they found "authenticity nowhere but in the brutal," and she worried that this might reinforce as much as challenge poetic and political limits.[30] Though Moss always has understood the social salience of "the facts of my identity," she began to reconsider its role in the (at times, seemingly hopeless) pursuit of social recognition in her poetry. Thinking back on this moment, Moss recalls her decision: "I abandoned the protocols of poetry that I had, blindly, I concluded, accepted; why wasn't I questioning more of the rules? I was as capable of making rules as anyone else, so I made my own that were more consistent with my emerging beliefs about experience and existence."[31] In 1998, Moss unveiled some of these beliefs in a polemical essay entitled "The Extraordinary Hoof."

> I am simply not astonished anymore by my racial heritage(s) alone, my sex alone. Only when something occurs to restore astonishment through fresh rankling of my awareness. . . . There is more in the universe than the components of my identity and more, much more than anything I have ever noticed or considered—and it is sometimes an unassuming hoof [of a horse or an ox] that leads me to a glimpse of the more. . . . I don't think that I ignore the facts of my identity. . . . But a hoof is something I find, at least right now, more interesting and compelling than obligation to identity and identity's trappings. . . . I prefer that what is written transcend identity and intentions. That is best.[32]

One might worry that such an argument concedes too much to the text to which it responds, a condescending dismissal of identity-focused poetries by Harold Bloom, "They Have the Numbers; We the Heights."[33] Moss, however, carefully qualifies her claims, refusing to repeat the blanket condemnations made by Bloom. Even so, the essay is puzzling in how it does not elucidate how she intends to "transcend identity" so much as repeatedly assert her entitled topic, the "gift of hoof."

Moss's intentions become clearer in light of a difficult balance she sought to achieve. On the one hand, her poetry continued to reflect deep awareness of how categories like race and gender remain powerful cultural constructs requiring analysis. On the other hand, by the late nineties, not unlike some of her Harlem Renaissance predecessors, she had tired of reviewers who made assumptions about her artistry based on assumptions about her identity.[34] Anthony Reed has described the early twenty-first century iteration of these trends as a "prevailing tendency [among critics] to approach black literature exclusively through thematics of race or the social narrowly conceived," a tendency "that has persistently led to the exclusion of . . . black experimental writers."[35] As important as "testimony . . . about so-called race relations" through first person lyrics has been and continues to be, Reed argues that attention also must be paid to writers who "disrupt th[at] genre's hermeneutic enclosure, which figures the expressions and experiences of a singular intending consciousness that is in turn metonymic for race."[36] These "disrupt[ive]" writers see how "contemporary discourses of multiculturalism and cultural nationalism alike render blackness textual—existing in advance of any example" and available for commodification or discrimination rather than full sociopolitical recognition much less reparation.[37] Reed highlights Douglas Kearney and Claudia Rankine when he describes a "postlyric" genre that displays what expressive first-person, lyricized poems often conceal, "the poetic production of an 'I' situated within vectors of power and history," and in doing so, "confront[s] readers with a subject that does not easily reduce to an appropriable object of knowledge."[38]

Much of Moss's poetry since the late nineties also fits this description. Her desire to "transcend identity" is not an embrace of an empty, ahistorical abstraction or universalism but a rejection of the tendency to "render blackness textual" (in Reed's phrase), all too easily recognizable within confining norms, and a commitment to attend to the intricate sociohistorical details that fueled this tendency in an effort to challenge and move beyond it. "Transcend[ing] identity," in this sense, is additive and not reductive. It rejects focusing on a single facet of a person "alone" in favor of considering the "more, much more" adjacent to "the

170 | Unlimited Eligibility?

facts of . . . identity." Moss, in other words, promotes an expansion of what an identity might be brought to bear on, situated in relation to, and, ultimately, what it might mean. She realizes that "if I am capable of an endeavor, then that endeavor evidently falls within what is possible within a definition of *Blackness*, or I couldn't execute that endeavor."[39] In this way, Moss, despite her experiences as a student, hopes to fulfill some of the Black Arts movement's highest purposes by knowing the world through a black lens but refusing to submit to socially imposed definitions of blackness.

As a result, Moss's next collection, *Last Chance for the Tarzan Holler*, which was published in 1998, the same year as the "Hoof" essay, becomes "a breakthrough; in some ways, my first book," designating "the first time, the complexity of my identity was indulged" while also being a more generalized "investigation" not just of the boundaries of "Blackness" but "the boundaries of humanity" and in particular "the ways in which humanity seeks to extend itself, to be more."[40] Here, once again, Moss is not working toward an all-too-easy, ahistorical, universalized definition of "humanness." Instead, she imagines personhood amid (and as a product of) a shifting mesh of adjacencies, a model ultimately suspicious of, rather than driven by, a desire to recognize and be recognized, which she knows can become a kind of epistemological capture. Consequently, *Last Chance for the Tarzan Holler* introduces a more intense and digressive idiom, one that reflected with greater clarity the many cultural vectors shaping the world. While earlier lyrics like "Lessons from a Mirror" and "The Wreckage on the Wall of Eggs" center on a single associational framework like children's literature, the poems in *Last Chance for the Tarzan Holler* feature much longer lines, filled with a greater range of diction, discourses, and allusions, suggesting a breathless enthusiasm to account for how individuals connect with each other and their sociohistorical context. Presenting passionate speakers who weave their way through and are woven by this cultural nexus, these poems investigate the possibility of building or resisting or revising coalitions across the categories wielded in social recognition processes, as well as an increasingly restless interest in finding alternative paradigms for social inclusion.

"Advice," for example, presents a dramatic dialogue featuring an African American woman poet who has been told by a male Jewish professor not to write "about the Holocaust" since her efforts would be at best "forgeries" (99).[41] Rather than evoking what the professor calls "a universal cloud" casting all the "shadows" falling across various ethnic groups, the poet is advised to "stay out of . . . [the Jewish] region of abjection; / [since African Americans] . . . have misery a-plenty in . . . [their] zone" (99).[42] And the poem goes on to show the poet's response, including anti-Semitic sentiments antithetical to the generosity she initially projects. The persona adopted, here, tempts a reader to attribute these experiences and even sentiments to Moss herself. Why does she take this risk? The poem can be read as an inquiry into (in some ways perhaps even a parody of) the politically engaged, subject-centered lyric itself, along with the historical and rhetorical intensities shaping it and its reader's response. Above all, Moss is interested in investigating whether such a genre can help establish and sustain a kind of mutual recognition from below or, at least, a generative solidarity between two groups who have faced extreme vulnerability.

The drama "Advice" depicts might be understood as a failed attempt at what Michael Rothberg has termed "multidirectional memory." Rothberg distinguishes his paradigm of collective remembering from "competitive memory," which views the "public sphere as a pregiven, limited space in which already-established groups . . . struggle to achieve recognition . . . [in a way that] necessarily exclude[s] the memories and identities of others."[43] Negotiating "claims of [group] memory or identity," to be sure, is "necessary and inevitable," especially when group history has been obscured or falsified.[44] But recovery and presentation of a "pure and authentic" group narrative is impossible since "displacements and contingencies . . . mark all remembrance," making it difficult even to establish the grounds of a consistent, intragroup form of self-recognition.[45] Multidirectional memory, instead, challenges the premise that "the boundaries of memory parallel the boundaries of group identity" and argues that

> memories are not owned by groups—nor are groups "owned" by memories. Rather, the borders of memory and identity are jagged; what looks at first like my own property often turns out to be a borrowing or adaptation from a history that initially might seem foreign or distant. Memory's anachronistic quality—its bringing together of now and then, here and there—is actually the source of its powerful creativity, its ability to build new worlds out of the materials of older ones.[46]

Within these complex spaces, Rothberg argues that high stakes "comparative thinking," which at times must "traverse sacrosanct borders of ethnicity and era," might enable a reconsideration of "cultural recognition beyond [the] zero-sum logic" of "identitarian competition"[47] However,

172 | Unlimited Eligibility?

any resulting "new forms of solidarity and new visions of justice" must balance a sociohistorical circumspection and "a certain bracketing of [the demands of an ostensibly] empirical history" in order to sustain nuanced, creative acts of "comparison" while rejecting reductive acts of "equation."[48]

Here, in this difficult, if potentially transformative, space, Rothberg, like Moss, finds that confronting the politics of comparison requires managing the poetics of metaphor. And, like Rothberg, Moss envisions metaphor less as the replacement or appropriation of meaning, along the lines of A is B, but instead as adaptation and revision, a more etymologically accurate understanding of the trope as a process of transference and even transformation and extension. For Moss, this transference process need not be only in one direction. She prefers that neither tenor nor vehicle dominate the other and rejects resolution or synthesis in favor of proliferating alternatives, not just the possibility of "a" becoming "b" but, if subsequently reversed, the possibility "b" could lead back to "a . . . [or] a different form of a . . . [or] c or even some [other] form of b, etc."[49]

This approach to comparison, at least hypothetically (it is worth keeping in mind that Moss describes this model in an essay about her poetics rather than in "Advice"), appears democratizing in its capacity to diffuse the powers of meaning-making in ways that acknowledge the complexity of memory and identity. But Rothberg and Moss know that historically this capacity to transfer and transform memories and the identities they help constitute has not been equally distributed.[50] The "enormous horror" of the Holocaust and subsequent debates over how to remember it, of course, serve as a vivid example of this dynamic (99). So it is not hard to understand why the professor in "Advice" feels morally bound to exert a measure of control over narratives of Jewishness and Jewish suffering when confronted by someone who asserts her "rights to witness" while nevertheless being removed by several degrees from being a witness (she claims "descen[t]" through the "memories" of a Jewish couple who cared for her as her parents worked) (101). The more immediate context also raises the professor's suspicions, as the poet makes her inquiry about writing a Holocaust-related poem at a fancy, rather insular academic conference, where she serves as a "key-note / speaker enticing an audience to laughter that does not resound / beyond the auditorium and the four-star accommodations" (99). The poet has not "earned" her topic in the professor's eyes (99). She has not yet come to terms with the challenges inherent in doing the cultural work of multidirectional memory and thus has not yet created the conditions necessary for establishing solidarity.

More Rapid than Recognition | 173

After presenting the professor's complaint as a prosaic flashback with lines justified to the right margin of the page, Moss reorients the poem to the left margin and offers the poet's far more lyrical response to his concerns. Though the shifting between right and left margins may or may not be a political judgment, the discursive distinctions between the two speakers illustrate how different experiences of collective memory yield different models of relationality. The professor's complaint is structured by straightforward imperatives ("Do not write about," "stay out of," "don't think this / the only sadness; don't respond so quickly," "there is no need") that underscore his desire to maintain clearly demarcated identity boundaries (99). The poet, while no less confident, speaks in a very different discursive register intended to challenge these boundaries. She begins by noting her "offen[se]" at

> his assumptions that I could not be justified
> in becoming another echo of lamentation, surrounding
>   myself
> with vespers as impossible as silk
> that falls from my body without feeling it . . .
> [. . .]
> I had wanted
> to take silk with me into the shower; I had believed it
> to be my skin; I have to take with me everything anytime I
>   travel (100)

What is striking, even in this brief excerpt, is how she not only challenges the professor's more sharply drawn identity politics ("stay out of . . . [the Jewish] region of abjection") but uses an associative lyric practice that cannot help but address identity in a different way. Her "vespers," a word historically designating evening prayers in the Christian church but here further evoking her "lamentation" for the suffering of Jewish people, reach across identity boundaries almost involuntarily, like a garment that she has put on and taken off without even realizing it, as if it was as natural as her "skin." The imagery of chrysalis, as she describes herself encircled by "fiber[s]," is unsettling. It asserts her ability to transform herself poetically, if not into someone Jewish, then into someone who understands Jewish suffering. But she does not pause to consider that weighty claim and responsibility. Her image rushes forward, troublingly conflating her attempt to grasp the Shoah with a personal sense of rebirth, before then

174 | Unlimited Eligibility?

describing it as another piece of baggage that she "take[s] with" her "anytime" she "travel[s]."

The poem began with the poet casting (what she perceives to be) a condescending professor's identity politics in a critical light. Here, we begin to see how the poem interrogates the lyric politics of the poet, who does not fully appreciate the complexities of achieving mutual recognition through multidirectional memory. She notes in italics, not without condescension of her own, *"Professor, this poem is not revenge, / it is forgiveness / for that is what everyone needs"* (100). The poet does not simply lecture him in the way that he had addressed her. She pointedly calls him "Herr Doktor," appropriating Sylvia Plath's appropriation of Holocaust imagery in "Lady Lazarus" (101).[51] Then she elaborately fantasizes with Plath-like excess about the professor sexually taking advantage of her, a fantasy that concludes with her "burn[ing] up" in a Holocaust of her own imagining (103).[52] The poet's line of thought is both absurd and lucid. After feeling insulted, she casts herself in the Jewish role being victimized by the Jewish professor, who she places in the role of the Nazi.

How did this offensive sentiment emerge from the impulse to express solidarity with Jewish people by praising their resilience? One hint may be found in the introduction of the poet as a "young sable lady" (99). The modifier indicating the speaker's race echoes the most famous poem by the first published African American woman poet, Phillis Wheatley, who in her poem from 1773, "On Being Brought from Africa to America," notes that "[s]ome view our sable race with scornful eye" (5).[53] That single word ("sable") suggests how the passions of the poet, here, may be driven less by outrage at the professor than at the possibility that he may be ventriloquizing one of the persistent, historical legacies of anti-black racism, a refusal to credit the intellectual and artistic talents of African Americans and especially African American women.[54] At this intersection of not entirely (or, at least, initially) intended acts of mutual disrespect, the contrasting idioms of the "sable lady" and the professor display how both fall into stereotyping that short-circuits even tenuous attempts to reach out. In the brief concluding section, the "sable lady," now as defensive as the professor, reasserts her "poem" and its "attempts to touch much of what keeps touching me / shaping me into a woman who hopes to finish knowing herself / in time to begin to know something else" (103). But the poem leaves it very unclear whether she is capable of achieving either kind of knowledge.

The conclusion of a single poem, of course, does not prove impossible the worthy goal of achieving intersectional solidarity based on mutual recognition from below. But it does vividly show the challenges involved in that task and the constraints of certain predominant lyric discourses, including the limits inherent to their practices of recognition. And throughout *Last Chance for the Tarzan Holler*, Moss continues to use her lyric practice to depict the struggle to conceptualize solidarities across identities that may still each be vying for more sufficient social recognition. Frustrated with such dynamics, the speaker of "Glory" detests how "identity" categories confine a person's existence and make "[t]he body, always a problem" (38). Desperate for freedom from such limits, the speaker initially advocates a kind of neo-gnosticism, railing against the divinity who created the world as it is before inciting the literal burning of bodies. But this gesture, though initially driven, it seems, by the experience of being a victim of prejudice like the speaker of "Lessons from a Mirror," becomes difficult to differentiate from the opposite, from a victimizer's murderous prejudice represented in the poem by hostility against ethnic and racial minorities (the Holocaust, lynching of African Americans, etc.). With increasingly exuberant, intensely lyrical language, the speaker of "Glory" unleashes the violence that the "sable lady" of "Advice" kept inside. Both poems are deeply frustrated with the limits of incrementalist recognition processes, but both poems also worry that the impulse to pursue more expansive adjustments may collapse into something worse than incrementalism—even, in the case of "Glory," nihilistic destructiveness. Alternative socialities seem out of reach.

Though Moss is no conventional adherent to Christianity, "A Man" locates a prospective counterexample in the life of Christ, praising the Incarnation as the only way for God, who the poem identifies as male, to have "learned maternal heartbeat // and . . . learned that some radiance is not his, [but] hers [i.e., Mary's]" (61). Christ accepts that embodiment inevitably is experienced amid social vectors without assuming that this unavoidably makes bodies into boundaries wholly constrained by norms. Instead, he models charity and seeks justice across identity categories: "erasing the lines between / Gentile, Jew, . . . [he] invited any who wanted to come to his father's house for bottomless milk, / honey, ripe fruit, baskets of warm bread and eggs, wine, live angels singing" (61). Christ, however, sets an unattainable ideal, and other poems in *Last Chance for the Tarzan Holler* show how later believers struggle to follow his example

176 | Unlimited Eligibility?

(e.g., Saint Anthony in "Saint Anthony's Ecstasy" and "Ode to the Cat-Headed Consort in a Painting by Bosch," as well as Saint Bernard in "The Saint and the Modern Equivalent of the Miracle of Lactation"). And the apotheosis of Christ's generosity is martyrdom, an example that might make even more vulnerable those already disempowered.

With the identity-based conflicts depicted in poems like "Advice" and "Glory," *Last Chance for the Tarzan Holler* reaches an impasse as Moss struggles to imagine a lyric politics through which to channel a desire for connection without it turning toxic. The shocking inflection points of these poems, rendered with special attention to their speakers' mix of competing desires situated amid complex psychosocial vectors, reflect how Moss's poetic idiom increasingly encompassed the circulation of social affects. The personae her poems study bring the entirety of themselves—culturally, geographically, linguistically, temporally situated—when they participate (albeit not always consciously) in the social experience of emotion as they are shaped by and continue to contribute to the establishment of a system of diffusely distributed political, economic, and legal norms. Though this embodied experience of social affects may be prerational, it is never ahistorical. As Moss's poems make clear, these processes make those disadvantaged by these norms, those bearing the burdens of multiple, compounding misrecognitions (as described in "Lessons from a Mirror"), increasingly vulnerable insofar as the norms become the de facto distributors of social recognition. In these moments, Moss, despite her assertions of agency in the "Hoof" essay, almost aligns with Tyrone Palmer's warning that even acute assessments of the work of social affect, far from providing "freedom from the trappings of (racial, sexual, gender) difference," instead reveal the persistence of prejudice and privilege.[55] Palmer describes a "crisis of affective recognition" intransigently rooted in a psychosocial environment defined by anti-blackness that makes "[t]he Black . . . endlessly affectable but unable to 'affect' or have agentive power within an affective economy."[56] And adjusting the ontological frames applied to African diasporic peoples in order to facilitate greater social recognition, according to Palmer and others writing from the Afro-pessimistic standpoint, is a hopeless strategy, insofar as they have been placed outside of ontology and are recognizable only as an object or a commodity and never as a subject or agent. The impact of such crises in affective recognition continue to be felt in Moss's poetry, even as she continues her search for a lyric politics unbound by the logics and limits of recognition.

Limited Fork Theory:
Affirming a "Mixed (Up)," "Black" Ontology

In Moss's more recent work, especially her 2006 collection *Tokyo Butter*, this search becomes still more bold. She reframes her approach to exploring the social circulation of affects in terms of what she calls "limited fork poetics" (and later simply "limited fork theory"), which she designates as a "platform for understanding poetry as a complex adaptive or dynamic system."[57] Moss describes how "clouds[,] . . . trees[,] . . . the human body[,]" and also products of the brain, including "poetry" itself, might best be understood as "locations of interactions that tend to occur on all scales simultaneously, with feedback from those interactions shaping and reshaping the temporary forms that structures occupy within the system and subsystems on all scales (including time scales) simultaneously."[58] Occasionally, a branch will reach an end that might later become a point of intersection, while "memor[ies] of prior activity" serve as "limiting factor[s]" shaping decisions.[59] Throughout, the trope most foregrounded in limited fork poetics, metaphor, opens up new terrain by bringing together boundaries that ordinarily might not touch.

Moss's exuberance in describing this approach, including its promise of "instant gratification of instantaneous access" to these "locations of interactions," may seem to be nearly at odds with her own warnings, noted at the start of this chapter, about poets being presumptuous, committing "identity theft," or even participating in a kind of figurative eugenicism.[60] But her warnings concern a practice associated with the lyricized, subject-centered lyric whose powers have become naturalized, whereas "limited fork" poetics seems intended to be a self-conscious practice that brings to light a poet's capacity to construct relation. She emphasizes how the wielding of tropes like metaphor can be life-giving or death-dealing: "[S]hift the frames and there's latitude and longitude, shift the scale of the grids and framing systems themselves become the substance. . . . No frames, no existence."[61] Thus, she emphasizes that in a system (or network of such systems and subsystems) involving many such makers, one must write with an appreciation of how one's "usual state" is "to be both host and hosted," a center or node of interactions and also a subsidiary participant in other interactions directed by other makers.[62]

Moss is well aware of how limited fork theory imagines and encourages an exertion of agency that does not necessarily reflect the lived experience of many people who, like herself, grew up enduring

178 | Unlimited Eligibility?

forms of social exclusion, and then, as a writer, endured a literary context also shaped by those exclusionary forces. But since her young adulthood coincided with the Black Arts movement, she inherited more than just the abstract, ahistorical, lyricized lyric. She observed a very different lyric idiom declare group self-recognition. Moss brings into the present some of the assertiveness of the latter and redirects it through yet another adopted poet persona, one she enacts in-person, her alter-ego, "Forkergirl," an advocate of limited fork theory who has appeared in poetry performances and YouTube videos and with hip-hop DJs.[63] Forkergirl embodies "the spirit and energy field form of the theory" as if she is "almost some kind of superhero" while being "presently my [Moss's] most authentic identity."[64] Using Forkergirl, Moss intends to model a kind of boldness that is "not afraid to make those connections that might be impossible for those not granted a healthy dose of audacity; I am not afraid to make those connections where the outcomes might be mutations or total transformations of structures in place before those wild (and sometimes discouraged) fusions (such as, as was once thought, mixed-race people)."[65]

Worrying about how "U. S. educational institutions" still do not sufficiently support "black women," Moss intends to "deliver to them the objects of access, which include strategies of converting information . . . into forms that can exist."[66] This does not necessarily involve wielding subjective expression to appeal for or demand social recognition. Instead, she intends to give those who have been historically excluded "access" to "Limited Fork Theory . . . [as] a black concept . . . [and thus also] a mixed (up) concept . . . [that] reconfigure[es] boundaries[,] . . . mak[es] connections, build[s] symmetries . . . without the (dis)pleasure of building something heading for permanence."[67] Limited fork theory, of course, does not contend that all such connections are positive. But it does find deep importance in attesting to the fact that life is always already "mixed (up)," which, Moss hints, implies that ontology is always already "black." Rather than entering seemingly hopeless contests over (mis)recognitions, Moss wonders whether acknowledging this fundamentally "mixed (up)" ontology might serve as a better ground on which to build more democratic socialities.

Some readers, while being largely sympathetic with Moss's intentions, have critiqued her emerging limited fork methodology for engaging complex systems theory only impressionistically. One review of *Tokyo Butter* contended that Moss ultimately betrays the "responsib[ility] for upholding the integrity of those ideas [associated with complex systems theory] and really coming to understand them" rather than merely "appropriating them." The reviewer, for example, notes that complex systems, rather than growing like a sequence of spokes extending out of a central wheel, instead, are characterized by the emergence of "connection[s] between sub-nodes." The secondary (and tertiary, etc.) components, in other words, interact with each other and become "subsystems." Moss's limited fork poems, according to the reviewer, offer merely a series of "linear" extensions off "one hierarchical node."[68] The reading of "The Subculture of the Wrongfully Accused" that follows, however, indicates that something like subsystems, in fact, can be seen developing in Moss's limited fork work. But fundamental questions remain. Despite Moss's distinctive speed of invention and occasional idiosyncrasy, just how different are such subsystems from secondary topics or image systems found in much poetry? Just how different is a limited fork poem from a poem in *Last Chance for the Tarzan Holler*, aside from a perhaps still greater attentiveness to the place of the poet amid psychosocial forces shaping the stream of consciousness? Can limited fork theory generate, to use Fred Moten's term, a "paralyric" space defined by, to use Moss's term, a "mixed (up)" ontology?

The poems in *Tokyo Butter* tend to approach these formidable ambitions (and lingering questions) implicitly rather than explicitly. The collection begins as a response to the memory of a beloved but now deceased cousin (the collection's subtitle is "A Search for Forms of Deirdre"). This search, however, soon takes many digressions, involving a Japanese company selling spoiled milk, the disappearance of a young Korean woman, diagrams of balloon warfare, references to Boolean algebra, allusions to the Chernobyl nuclear disaster, and much else. But Moss also points to how order emerges out of these many digressions by her frequent use of "Culture" in poem titles ("The Culture of Glass," "Accidental Culture," "The Culture of Funnel Cake," etc.), a term that encompasses far more than the discursive cultures of humans (e.g., bacterial cultures) and comes to serve as an analogy for complex adaptive systems. "Cultures," according to Moss, "are populations whose numbers and interactions have given rise to protocols that seek to maintain the circumstances that supported the initial bursts of proliferation"[69] But what happens when such "protocols" oppress some within that culture? This, in part, is the topic of "The Subculture of the Wrongfully Accused," which attempts to apply limited fork theory to questions of justice and, in doing so, may be the most metapoetic and the most overtly socially engaged poem in the collection.

180 | Unlimited Eligibility?

Here, once again, the study of metaphor, the principal "tool of navigation" in limited fork theory, serves as a guide, permitting us to watch Moss test the limits of her evolving lyric sociality.[70] If metaphor too often facilitates the distribution of misrecognitions (as governing "protocols"), can Moss conceptualize how to bring into the world a different practice of metaphor that conveys an unlimited eligibility—and even ontological entangling or enmeshing—by attesting to a "black," "mixed (up)" ontology?

The poem centers on the true story of two individuals brought together amid this "subculture," Ronald Cotton, an African American man imprisoned for nearly eleven years for crimes (rape and burglary) he did not commit, and Jennifer Thompson, the victim who picked Cotton out of a line-up of photographs, mistaking him for another man who, in fact, had committed the crimes. Thompson's error soon becomes linked with the work of metaphor:[71]

. . . interrelatedness   spreads
and the understandable error of   metaphor
becomes less erroneous over time:
eleven years in prison, innocence   locked up, protected

although in prison, it resembled   something else. (40)[72]

Read in isolation, the tone of this passage, even with the qualification offered in the last line, unsettles in how it coolly acknowledges the injustice—and metaphor's role in it—with a puzzling magnanimity. That Cotton and Thompson later worked together promoting important criminal justice reforms (as the poem goes on to note) would scarcely seem to justify describing Cotton's time in prison in such accepting terms ("understandable"? "protected"?). But the poem gains in subtlety as it continues. Even as it eventually asks whether it is possible to ground the making of metaphors in the "mixed (up)" ontology Moss sees as fundamental to the democratizing implications of limited fork poetics, the poem does not blithely ignore divisions that perpetuate. The gap running through the poem creating two columns only rarely is bridged—and, in the end, persists.

The opening lines introduce the first of several moments of interpretive instability. We meet Cotton in his cell illumined by the "slant light" he will be "[u]ltimately improved by" (39). Perhaps an allusion to Emily Dickinson's "Tell all the truth but tell it slant," a poem warning about the inevitability of perspectivism and the necessity of multiple angles ("Success in Circuit lies") in order to approximate anything resembling "Truth," Moss's

More Rapid than Recognition | 181

line might be read as an expression of either dry, bitter irony or earnest affirmation. Cotton was exonerated (albeit much later) by another "slant" (DNA evidence) on the crime he did not commit, but it seems odd to hint that he himself was "improved."[73] A sequence of images (that one might even call a subsystem) associates Cotton in his cell with the iconography of the state responsible for his imprisonment. He hears a cardinal, North Carolina's state bird, that happens to be eating "snails / which seemed like polished fossils / of trophy hog tails (after prize   butchery)," associations that could simply seem quirky were it not for the ominous last word (39). Then Moss extends the analogy a step further, adding that "his hair [was] a mess of replicas [of the previously listed animals and objects]," similar in shape due to its curls. The police-related association with pig, alongside the words "trophy" and "prize," might reflect how law enforcement saw him—and how he may have experienced all this as a kind of "butchery." Here, too, Moss assembles her poem with such care that it is possible to build an almost precious reading or a sinister one.

The next passage, which places Cotton in a broader context beyond his cell, offers a first glimpse of why what one hears in and associates with a particular description matters. Moss lists agricultural products displaying North Carolina's "industrious[ness]" before turning to another product:

. . . poultry & eggs   tobacco & soybeans

as well as convictions:

None as tightly knit as Jennifer's   (not even the state flag)
that she could identify Cotton

that cotton's taking on appearances   other than burst white
of a dense localized haze from which to weave memory, following
pink-petaled start, rather a satellite   dish of a flower, pollen/sensor-
studded antenna protruding from   the center

undeniably; the jury couldn't acquit   Cotton
of its role in documenting and altering   Jennifer's history,

many lives changed   (39)

The swiftly moving system of associations displayed here evokes how Cotton was caught inside the discursive web within which he lived. That a pun ties

182 | Unlimited Eligibility?

legal "conviction[s]" to Jennifer's sense of certainty may seem all too easy, both juridically and as a poetic gesture. But that is Moss's point. Thompson's identification of Cotton was too easy. The similarly obvious pun on Cotton's name is equally necessary, an unavoidable metonym, pointing to how histories of slave labor blur into contemporary acts of racial injustice as a "dense localized haze from which to weave memory," including "Jennifer's history" (which involved "altering," willfully or not, the events that occurred) and extending to the jury's refusal to "acquit" Cotton.

In this context, understanding Jennifer Thompson's misidentification of Cotton as an "understandable error of metaphor" is less an attempt to make an excuse for Thompson than a coolly analytical condemnation of an entire system that Cotton, Thompson, the jury, and law enforcement were caught within (40). Inside that system, metaphor was inherently inclined to transmit all-too-available, historically engrained racist associations: "The eye witnesses all the time, / even the unseeing eye is turned toward a focus / on black, saturation dense as conviction" (40). The poem notes that the perpetrator was another African American man who "bore a just resemblance to Cotton," but this fact makes Ronald Cotton no less innocent nor the society around him less structurally racist. Instead, insofar as "the composite sketch / . . . displayed a metaphor for men / like Cotton, the seeds of capability   in the structure of the face," the "sketch" (as "metaphor") merely serves as a subset of a social system that makes a claim of "innocence" from an African American man almost inconceivable (42).

Having established a context within which to understand how racist tropes can permeate social affects and render men like Ronald Cotton unduly (mis)recognizable as criminals, Moss could have worked toward a conventional conclusion celebrating how Cotton and Thompson eventually achieved a too-easy kind of mutual recognition, becoming friends and activists making joint appearances advocating on behalf of reforms to how victims identify potential perpetrators. And Moss does present Cotton sustaining his "quiet manner," "rationality," and "contemplativeness," qualities that had once been deemed evidence of a "lack of emotion" toward a crime committed, as he generously "accept[s]" Thompson's "regret and apologies" and begins working alongside her (41, 42). But Moss disturbs what could have become a moment of congratulation (and by extension, for the reader, potential self-congratulation) by supplementing conventional sentiments, once again, with unsettling associations. Cotton is freed on the basis of

More Rapid than Recognition | 183

> . . . DNA [evidence] whose precision   detects human exactitude,
> and could build as many Ronalds as   time would permit
>
> something Jennifer now desperately   wants to do, restoring
> what was lost because it was like   something else (41)

While one can commend Jennifer Thompson's effort to make some kind of amends for Ronald Cotton's incarceration by looking for other parallel instances of unjust imprisonment, Moss presents her fervor here with an almost eugenic ("build as many") overtone. Is she trading one form of mastery for another—or at least stirred by such a possibility? The question becomes even more complex a little later in the poem, when her intensity becomes almost erotic in how "[s]he felt better in her cotton-touched skin" (42). The fleeting pun might be set aside were it not for Jennifer's "face" being described as "also in Emmett Till's way," inscribing Thompson and Cotton's partnership as activists in relation to one of the most notorious acts of lynching. Even though "this generation of Jennifer has another side / . . . in which she and Cotton team up," their work exists in and is almost subsumed by history's shadow (42).

The poem's concluding paean to the power of metaphor evokes images of entanglement intersecting with histories that almost render such a paean impertinent.

> Metaphor is a form of forgiveness; a short rope of it knots-up
> those that can't come together any other way into being defined
> by the other. Strange
>
> and estranged pairings give rise to mutable truth
> that can yield to both dawn and twilight
> demands that things be seen differently. (42)

Metaphor, as a trope, does indeed perform a "knot[ting]-up," a bringing "together" wherein both components may become "defined / by the other," here emblematized by the poem's two columns of text momentarily merging. But using a "short rope" with a knot as a meta-metaphor also invokes the iconography of the noose. Can one ensure that metaphor's potentially democratic impulses triumph over the deadly? Moss offers no easy answers in her pairings of opposites (strange/estranged; dawn/

184 | Unlimited Eligibility?

twilight) and warns that "[m]emory is as accurate as metaphor," ready "to submit / to any vessel into which it's poured.   Just to be guzzled" (43).

In "The Subculture of the Wrongfully Accused," Moss's limited fork idiom itself tests each reader as just such a "vessel." Does one guzzle the connotations suggesting a sentimentalized reading that finds resolution to Cotton's tragedy in his forgiveness of and friendship with Thompson? It is only fair to Cotton to take that profound act of forgiveness with the utmost seriousness. But it would also be unfair to ignore the more troubling associations that imply social structures enabling an exploitative relationship still persist and are even amplified by an unacknowledged eroticism, even as Thompson seeks, along with Cotton, to make important changes to the criminal justice system. Moss's poem asks us to trace each of these threads carefully, even as they overlap, and to consider which cluster of associations we want to hear and which system of cultural connotations we find ourselves participating in.

Though one, of course, cannot comprehensively trace every association, the effort to become more aware of how these social vectors work on us and develop—and how we may intervene in this process, in fact, may be the "figurative algebra" Moss advocates in her contribution to "Quotes Community," when she encouraged writers and readers to "be a little more accountable for the mergers that they sponsor."[74] But poems like those studied in this chapter can make this seem, at times, an almost impossible task. Acts of recognition are always negotiated within existing (and thus normalized and sometimes scarcely traceable) systems of meaning sustained by networks of social affects. Insofar as this structure is shaped by unjust hierarchies, it may feel nearly pointless, for example, to attest to a foundational, "mixed (up)" ontological association upon which solidarities might be built. And Moss directly addresses the risk of cynicism—even as her own figurative trajectory becomes grim:

> . . . the fact of similarity   is compelling, convincing;
> if connections could not be made,   there'd be no havens, no fugitive
> status lost to fusion, no links   to God, no human
>
> murmurings whose   constant echoes
> are also the gentle silvery hum   of fans praying
> over computer motors to cool them   and also mimic
> motion of small wings amplified   to make sound
>
> in the distance much like   the electric razor
> preparing a head on death row   clean as a light bulb. (41)

The speaker's assessment here quickly sours from reaching toward "havens" to acknowledging the reality of "deathrow." And the poem ends with the page, once again, conclusively divided into columns, with a final metaphor poised (or hamstrung) between a despair (the "brink") and a hope ("infancy") that are disturbingly indistinguishable: "North Carolina is shaped   like an embryo: / Humanity still on the brink   of infancy" (43).

One might argue that Moss's mature poetics, with insistence and nuance, inhabits this uncomfortable space, as the exuberant energy and optimism characteristic of her metapoetic writing (like "The Extraordinary Hoof" and her various elaborations of limited fork theory) becomes unsettled by application to the world. But the result is not the same misery demonstrated in her early work concerning the limits of recognition. Part of the struggle her later work conveys may be due to the fact that finding a poetics that is both a product of and a mirror to the complex systems of the world is extraordinarily difficult. Her poetics, in this way, is perhaps not (yet) quite so distinctive as it promises to be. But this gap between her theory and practice also reflects forces she cannot control, a world still wary of acknowledging its ground state to be always already "mixed (up)" (or "black"). To cross that "brink," Moss suggests, would be to begin to build more than just poetry on more democratic forms of being-with.

Coda

"Join Me Down Here in Nowhere"

The lineage outlined in this book is hardly alone, especially among contemporary poets, in exploring a range of politics beyond the post-Hegelian, recognition-oriented models that overshadow much scholarship on and theorizing of lyric. Though these poets deserve a book of their own, this coda briefly highlights Mei-mei Berssenbrugge and Juan Felipe Herrera, before returning to Claudia Rankine. Like those featured in previous chapters, their poems affirm ontological equality and explore unlimited eligibility with an awareness of how difficult these practices are to develop and to sustain, along with an appreciation that the pursuit of increased representation and even strategic appeals for recognition continue to be necessary. These tensions may appear to demarcate a narrow conceptual space within which to work, especially considering how some of the most basic functions of language—like using address to engage another and initiate a relationship or using abstraction to generalize a concept so it is broadly communicable—have become appropriated by lyricized lyrics that occlude the impacts of sociohistorical forces. But these poets argue that this need not be so. The various tropes that assist in the essential tasks of language may be rethought and lyric practice may be renewed, potentially enabling poets to participate in a necessary widening of the theoretical horizons of democratic politics.

In 2019, looking back on her 1989 collection *Empathy*, which was being republished, Mei-mei Berssenbrugge described the poems as a study of "abstraction as lyric" that intended to "diffuse polarities between emotion and thought, between image and discourse, representation and abstraction, material and immaterial" and, in doing so, to "explor[e] how much one

188 | Unlimited Eligibility?

person can communicate with another, can know another."[1] Despite this interest in abstraction, or perhaps, as she goes on to show, because of it, Berssenbrugge is conscious of social context. Certain poems like "Tan Tien" and "Chinese Space" address her matrilineal cultural background.[2] And the same 2019 note mentions that another goal of *Empathy* was "to feminize scientific language and philosophic language."[3] Even when Berssenbrugge's work seemingly becomes more decontextualized, "abstraction" is enacted as a means of creating sufficient distance to bring into relief (and, at times, to relieve) the social vectors that have shaped the terms and frames of being. So while her poems are not ahistorical, they do evoke "a consciousness that is formless and floats in an area more vast / and open than the historical."[4] "Abstraction as lyric" functions here in the way that direct address, the logic of metaphor, burlesquing, and speed of invention ideally functioned in earlier chapters, as a kind of practice used for opening a paraontic discursive workspace less bound by the demand for recognition within existing orders of being.

Berssenbrugge acknowledges that the title of the final poem of the collection, "Honeymoon," references its roots in a collaboration with the sculptor Richard Tuttle that led to them beginning a relationship and eventually marrying.[5] But she originally entitled the poem "Hiddenness."[6] So is it a celebration of union or separation? The poem only gradually answers this question by framing the matter, as one might expect of this collection and this poet, abstractly: "Though relations with oneself and with other people seem negotiated in terms secretly confirmed / by representation, her idea of the person's visibility was not susceptible to representation."[7] The first phrase, which might serve as a brief summary of the kinds of recognition processes assessed and ultimately critiqued by poets throughout this book, is complicated by the second, an anxiety that also afflicts a number of these same writers. "[R]epresentation," as a socially "negotiated" form of abstraction, is inherently unstable, inflected by evolving power dynamics. The terms that frame how we represent ourselves to the world and how the world reads this act amid other, parallel acts around us are consistently challenged. The speaker of this poem resists this process. We soon learn why. Rather than being freeing, an awkward muddle results from these negotiations: "the other person and I keep getting in the way of" each other realizing as individuals or together "the volume or capacity of [possible] relations." Or, put slightly differently, "[t]here are dimensions of an assessment of human relations, which go before and after our relation to the picture."[8] Representation, as a negotiated act of abstraction, often generalizes in ways that do not do justice to the person represented. This, of course, impacts one's sense of self, potentially generating a desire to retain or recover the lost particularity. The poem, for example, emphasizes "my fixation on *my* body's opacity" (Berssenbrugge's emphasis).[9]

If various forms of representation, nevertheless, are useful and necessary (e.g., for all sorts of thinking and decision-making, for political action, etc.), then how does Berssenbrugge's poem suggest that we mitigate the way that it also limits "the volume or capacity of relations"? Subsequent sections offer a number of approaches to this inescapable problem. The poem proposes, for example, a kind of "distanc[ing]" that enables better forms of relation, a privacy described as akin to "hiding behind something that is transparent."[10] The "particular distance" created here is not the same as absence or being near but out of sight. Nor does it imply an invitation (in an erotic sense or in an aesthetic sense of the sublime) to attempt to traverse or master this space. Furthermore, this "distance" is not simply measured between the speaker and someone else. It is also the "distance" between "you" and "the person in your memory," your self-representation. This self-objectification is not presented as a painful act of dissociation but as a potentially reparative impulse that "dar[es] yourself to imagine the person as even more beautiful."[11]

"Honeymoon," in this way, works toward an understanding of how sustaining a measure of epistemological distance makes it more possible to affirm ontological eligibility in both oneself and others. This "distanc[ing]," the poem suggests, paradoxically creates the conditions for an idealized intimacy wherein "[s]he would wish his wish was to illuminate her behavior by means of referring to what she is feeling, / in order to reach the same place her reference to herself occupies, that is, before / she would express the feeling."[12] Commenting on this passage, Charles Altieri praises how "intimacy is beautifully defined as being able to refer to what someone is feeling at the site where the person enters the expressive process rather than at the site produced by the representation."[13] That the delicate balance between "distance" and intimacy is never fully or permanently achievable does not wholly undercut the worthiness of the lessons it may offer for lyric practice. Berssenbrugge's experiment in "abstraction as lyric" is a reminder that, as she states in another poem in this collection, "abstraction occurs in all forms of communication" and thus is an inevitable facet of language use that can be abused but also cannot be avoided and, thus, must be used well.[14] With its intense focus

190 | Unlimited Eligibility?

on address and the powers of figurative language to blend or to break, the lyric is a discursive medium well-suited for learning this (amid and even as a corrective to the kind of abstraction associated with lyricization) and, in the process, for learning how epistemological demands to recognize may impede more mutual ways of being-with.

While Mei-mei Berssenbrugge's poem highlights how the discursive tools associated with lyrics can be used to calibrate "a particular distance" that might help to repair old or open new intersubjective potentialities, Juan Felipe Herrera has shown interest in lyric's capacity to intervene in larger sociopolitical contexts. The longest of the new poems concluding Herrera's 2008 volume *Half of the World in Light: New and Selected Poems*, "The Glue Under," refers to the fundamental premises of social cohesion and argues that "lyric" need not serve as a potent discursive "glue" within "the Nomenclature" of the powerful but an idiom for evoking an ontological proximity and equality that may aid in building a "buried city without borders."[15]

Herrera's speaker begins by identifying with those on both sides of an unnamed conflict: "The glue under / and in between the camps and the settlements / attracts me, shames me and leaves me in whimpers."[16] It is not hard to understand why the prospect of affirming interconnectedness invigorates and also unsettles him. For emphasizing "[t]he glue under" potentially ignores history in favor of forwarding an empty notion of universality, a problem Whitman, Toomer, and Crane also struggled with, that can perpetuate rather than challenge an unjust status quo. And, as Herrera's poem develops, it becomes an "answer" to the "the Glue-Smearers, the Glue-Squeezers, / the Glue Smoothers," those who deploy the rhetoric of ontological equality as a means of sustaining rather than redressing inequality.[17] In the poem's culminating moment, the speaker declares: "This is not a *lyric* as they say in the Nomenclature," not a lyric in discourse approved by reactionary power structures and their corporate and political and military-industrial bureaucracies.[18] But the thought haunts Herrera. Another poem in this section, with near hopelessness, exclaims, "if only I could write without the Nomenclature / in between my teeth, the ideology lapel stuck / to my chromosome lines."[19] The "ideology" of the "Nomenclature" is inherited, whether it has literally begun to shape our genetics or whether we wear it like clothes. What can be done under such circumstances? In "The Glue Under," Herrera turns to a Polish poet, Tadeusz Różewicz, who responded to a form of "Nomenclature" (Nazism) so horrific that he felt he needed to begin anew simply by naming, with no figurative language or metaphorical blending of concepts or even poetic argument beyond the imperative to re-taxonomize a world ruined by oppressive discourse. Initially, Herrera is unsure of whether he can go that far, given how deeply the "Nomenclature" has shaped us: "I want to say, / 'This is a table . . .' like Różewicz says." And then he does ("This is a table, this / is not a napkin"), and it leads to a bittersweet memory of having "shed many tears / entertaining my musician friends at small wedge tables." This memory hints at a kind of resistance to the "Nomenclature" and maybe even a kind of paraontic sociality of the undercommons as he and his friends "howl[ed] drunk equations / only we could decipher."[20]

But that, it seems, is in the past. Ending modestly, with a single, Różewicz-esque declarative statement defining what this alternative to the Nomenclature's model of "lyric" can do in the present, the poem concludes simply, asserting "this is an elementary school drawing / of apples," equivalent to the work of a child beginning to learn how to represent basic pieces of the world. One might be tempted to detect a Biblical overtone in this image and, given the association of apples with Eden, a suggestion of a prelapsarian state, albeit one already containing temptation. But reality returns after an em-dash: "in a buried city without borders."[21] No theory of sociality is offered here and no optimism. But there is an affirmation of connection and ontological eligibility. Not through the "glue" offered by recognition within the "Nomenclature" but beyond its discursive reach, there is a form of "writing on the rubble of the dead" that happens in the "buried" places. And this different kind of lyric still reaches toward others confronted by anontic existence, the "[h]alf of the [w]orld" that Herrera's book title warns is not "in [l]ight," mapping a space, even a "city." This is, as another poem at the volume's conclusion explains, "what a poem brings," a poem that is "no poem / to speak of" yet, "a way to attain a life without boundaries."[22]

The great challenge of rebuilding lyric and, Herrera implies, democratic practice in a "buried city without borders" can be further brought into focus by the fifth (and most explicitly metalyrical) section of Claudia Rankine's *Citizen*, which offers a stark invitation to participate in building a sociality surviving a similar, nearly anontic space: "Join me down here in nowhere."[23] Rankine does not promise a celebration among "the rest," or an exuberant announcement of a "new America" defined by a multiethnic "blue" race, or the more understated joys of "walk[ing] through time with equal pride" toward "the bridge," or simply opening a door to "better-late /

192 | Unlimited Eligibility?

-than-never light" illumining a shared community in Key West. Though the context of Rankine's invitation invokes a "black . . . mixed (up)" social ontology somewhat akin to Moss's, it conveys none of her effusive enthusiasm. The introduction suggested that Rankine's flatness in tone corresponds to a wariness about overinvesting emotionally or politically in the pursuit of recognition with which socially committed American lyrics have tended to be linked. So what form of sociality is implied by this invitation near the center of Rankine's American lyric? What does it tell us about the more than century-long debate between poets who have sought to envision a more democratic United States by seeking to expand the epistemological frames through which a person is legible and others who affirm a fundamental ontological eligibility, between those trying to work within a system that demands to know-who and those trying to affirm a being-with among equals? And will this poetic debate continue to reflect and even inflect larger debates about social inclusion in American democracy?

Like many other moments of address in *Citizen*, Rankine leaves unclear who her speaker hopes will "[s]it here alongside," prompting readers to probe these ambiguities in order to come to terms with the stakes of the gesture.[24] This task, in turn, is complicated by the fact that the invitation is embedded within several passages that recontextualize the identities of both speaker and addressee. Initially, section five encourages "you" to "just cry out" after suffering micro- (and macro-) aggressions, not because the "cry" will stop the aggressions but in order to "know what you'll sound like." Then, immediately thereafter, the speaker cautions that doing so may draw the attention of a police-like "blue light" and the implied threat of state-sanctioned violence.[25] Though grammatically and semantically any reader may be encompassed within the second-person pronoun, the events experienced by "you," especially when considered alongside many other anecdotes featured in the book, parallel life experiences shared by African Americans. Eligibility within Rankine's address, an eligibility that she implies is often denied elsewhere, is truly unlimited but no more emptied of context than the lives of any of its prospective readers.

Rankine underscores this by positioning the invitation to "[s]it . . . alongside" after a passage that complicates the identity of both addressor and addressee. The speaker explains, "Sometimes 'I' is supposed to hold what is not there until it is. Then *what is* comes apart the closer you are to it" (Rankine's emphasis).[26] The next lines then divide into a dialogue between two voices, a debate (within the speaker's "I"? or between discrete individuals?) concerning the efficacy of first person, post-Romantic lyric appeals for social recognition. One voice flatly states that "the first person can't pull you together" and has limited social impact ("Tried rhyme, tried truth, tried epistolary untruth, tried and tried"). The other voice initially queries ("did you try?"), then sympathizes ("You really did"), then suggests that failure might nevertheless be useful ("Your ill-spirited, cooked, hell on Main Street, nobody's here, broken-down, first person could be one of many definitions of being to pass on"), before finally reasserting, after all, that successful lyric appeals are possible: "Drag that first person out of the social death of history, then we're kin."[27] The logic of the final line of this sequence appears to be: if those who are empowered to recognize you will not, then you should work hard enough so you can somehow do it on your own. That this is spoken without much concern for "history"—and the difficulties involved in the task—displays a startling naivete. This blithe optimism, along with the reference to a current lack of "kin[ship]," suggesting a difference in background and even ontic status, seem most attributable to a white interlocutor. If that is the case, then the two voices, at this stage, reflect two different persons. Or perhaps we are confronted here with a white voice that has been internalized within a black speaker?

But this abstract tangle of external and internal forces and voices framing the invitation to "sit . . . alongside" raises yet another possibility—that the invitation is not intended to diminish distance between discrete individuals or to (re)establish a kind of internal psychological coherence within the speaker, but instead is an invitation to acknowledge an existing, irreducible interrelation. These voices and even selves inherently interpenetrate in ways that discourses of interiority and exteriority, individuality and sociality, subjectivity and intersubjectivity oversimplify. This possibility may align Rankine with poets who reject recognition in favor of affirming an ontic immanence. But Rankine also poses a challenge to such writers, including those this book has considered. For the only way to begin to move from attesting to this fundamental ontic interrelation toward developing more democratic socialities is by studying the history, even if it is never fully recoverable and is subject to retroprojection, of the forces that have obscured and disfigured this interrelation in the service of establishing and sustaining hierarchies.

Rankine leaves no doubt that the dominant lyric idiom, like the dominant culture that created it, has resisted facing the ongoing presence of the past. She singles out one such example as representative of many others.

194 | Unlimited Eligibility?

Why are you standing?

Listen, you, I was creating a life study of a monumental
first person, a Brahmin first person.

If you need to feel that way—still you are in here and here
is nowhere.

Join me down here in nowhere.

Don't lean against the wallpaper; sit down and pull together.

Yours is a strange dream, a strange reverie.

No, it's a strange beach; each body is a strange beach,
and if you let in the excess emotion you will recall the
Atlantic Ocean breaking on our heads.[28]

References to Robert Lowell's *Life Studies* frame this passage, another
one of Rankine's elliptical dialogues, with one voice fantasizing about
access to, indeed recognition within, a "Brahmin" lyrical subject with all
of its associated cultural capital and the other voice interrogating such
ambitions, implying that they are naive, and advocating, instead, a candid
acceptance of where "you" actually are: "here and here is nowhere." The
initial question ("Why are you standing?") may allude to the abjected
speaker of "Skunk Hour," who still "stand[s] on top" (or thinks he does)
even after accumulated humiliations.[29] The other voice in this passage
does not shrink from this unflattering comparison and acknowledges
Lowell-esque ambitions. The succeeding lines continue invitations into
a different lyric ambition linked with a different, less hierarchical mode
of association, "sit[ting] down and pull[ing] together," in a different lyric
space, "nowhere."

The voice offering critique of Lowell-esque ambitions then, in a
gesture that initially seems counterintuitive, uses an allusion to Lowell to
describe this "nowhere." "[T]he Atlantic Ocean breaking on our heads,"
as Kamran Javadizadeh notes, echoes the final lines of "Man and Wife,"
where it is a metaphor for the wife's "old-fashioned tirade," a moment of
scolding as a result of a marital betrayal that "renders" the husband "mute,
unknowing, even as it reaffirms the power of his identity . . . [,] produc[ing]

in other words, the condition of white innocence."[30] However, read in the context of Rankine's book, with its intensive display of the afterlives of slavery, this phrase surely also evokes a very different Atlantic intended to undermine the "white innocence" manifested by Lowell's speaker and to expose the ideology underlying the ambition of "creating a life study of a monumental / first person, a Brahmin first person."

But if Rankine aligns lyricized lyrics with the legacies of white supremacism, then what does it mean, instead, to "Join me down here in nowhere"? The word "our" in the last line of this passage introduces, again, questions of address, in this case, given the plural pronoun, collective address, and by extension the high stakes of evoking a sense of ontological immanence potentially among readers whose positionalities relate them to history in radically different ways. White readers of Rankine (including the writer of this book) could approach this invitation by briefly identifying with black trauma while avoiding, for example, consideration of networks of complicity in systemic racism. Using a potentially self-congratulatory moment of empathy, such a reader might rush to answer rather than remain within the question of who Rankine addresses and what that address might mean and call a reader toward. Indeed, reaching after certainty of inclusion within this "our" might betray a desire to define and dominate even "nowhere," the anontic space of historical trauma. In this desire, there might exist the ironic apotheosis of the colonizing impulse: a drive to master the space of victimhood created by the drive for mastery. This may be one reason why *Citizen* continues to catalogue, after the invitation to "[s]it . . . alongside" (and to "Join me down here in nowhere"), micro- (and macro-) aggressions, culminating on the final pages with a reproduction (and close-up) of J. M. W. Turner's "Slave Ship."[31] Rankine, in the end, is not necessarily any more optimistic about the success of her invitation in drawing readers toward a socially transformative awareness of ontological immanence than the success of appeals for recognition.

Yet Fred Moten, commenting on this passage in *Citizen*, cannot help but linger on the "trace of a *we* that comes before" the "address" from "*nowhere*." Even in a dire, anontic space of "dislocation . . . lies . . . a chance for interpellative failure, for misrecognition[,] . . . where we might begin to think the radical informality of we, the nothing, the blackness that is before, and deep."[32] Moten frames black sociality as the referent of Rankine's first-person plural pronoun, while also making clear that "blackness" is not merely a product of recognition processes. Instead,

196 | Unlimited Eligibility?

it exists "before" and beyond them, constituting a shared (Moss might say "mixed (up)"), original ontic state, perhaps even the very source of ontology itself. This is not an attempt to recover some mythical, uncomplicated, ahistorical ontic immanence. Rankine does not minimize the miseries produced by processes wherein people identified as black are entirely unrecognized or less fully recognized than other persons. For understanding social ontology in terms of blackness demands attending to this history, which is the history of how ontological thought itself has become associated with white supremacy (among other hierarchies). When Rankine's American lyric invites "you" to a gathering at this "strange beach," in other words, she points to the location of horrific acts and of evidence that even those acts do not countermand the fact of a fundamental being-with that, against all odds, continues to resonate and ramify even from the "nowhere" of social death.

What might it mean to read and write poetry from this standpoint (or from those suggested by Berssenbrugge or Herrera)? Some might find motivation to build a new lyric politics more democratic than those yet imagined or to extend socialities of ontic immanence into our (inter) relations with the natural world or to explore whether attesting to such immanence also may help spur class solidarity in a time of grotesque income inequality. Others might look to the past and elaborate unrealized lyric politics, revising them in light of their limits or failures. The persistent direct address throughout *Citizen* might even point to this possibility, insofar as it may distantly echo "Crossing Brooklyn Ferry." In this spirit, one might revisit Crane's curtailed attempt to infuse a sense of ontic immanence with a sustained mutuality by building a lyricism that looks without recognizing, Merrill's burlesquing of forms (and form itself) that define legibility, and Moss's attempt to craft a poetics of complex systems beyond the logics and limits of recognition. Each of these projects, at their best, seek to envision versions of unlimited eligibility, while working toward alternative models of minority representation without falling into ahistorical universalisms. On the other hand, their limits cast a pall over these ambitions. And some might find that the failures of projects like those of Whitman, Toomer, Crane, and Merrill, which contain white supremacist elements, place them beyond repair and invite only additional assessment of the workings of the social pathologies they contain.[33]

Citizen does not ultimately elaborate an alternative paradigm or even encourage planning toward such a goal. Instead, it insistently seeks to bring readers closer to an impasse defined by injustice and insufficient responses to that injustice, in effect suggesting that horizons (theoretical, political, affective) first need widening.[34] Taking a very small facet of that vast task, this book has argued that the tendency to theorize socially engaged lyrics according to (or, at least, in conversation with) Americanized, post-Hegelian recognition paradigms is one such attenuated conceptual horizon. The point, once again, has not been to impugn brave appeals for recognition and increased representation, which often remain strategically necessary. Many of the writers considered in this book, even as one accounts for their flaws and limits, develop poetics that, in their own way, advocate for increased minority representation outside regimes of recognition. Instead, the point is to avoid undue constraints on how we theorize and enact concepts like genre and representation, given the powerfully important work such concepts do within existing aesthetic and sociopolitical discourse.

Does such a claim, when made in a study of lyric poetry, risk exaggerating the importance of a little-read genre (or network of genres)?[35] After all, as Anahid Nersessian has recently reminded us to ask, "What's the point of reading a poem as a record of verifiable social and historical processes? What will that tell you that you don't already know?"[36] Perhaps the beginning of an answer to these searching questions is to consider how tropes like address and metaphor, which recur in the poets considered in this study, function as experiments in protosociality insofar as they instigate encounter and then negotiate relation. Similarly, form functions as the frame within which these protosocial enactments are tested, requiring one to accept, adapt, or escape the structure one would be included within. To be sure, neither the writing nor the reading of poetry (much less writing readings of poetry) often constitute the most effective means of social critique—or the most effective means for evaluating models of social inclusion. But these boundaries can become blurry in the production of culture. Debates over legibility and eligibility, topics with vast social impact, are in fundamental ways debates over the histories of who gets to determine how tropes function and where. So it cannot hurt to read writers who, at times, illuminatingly and, at times, falteringly tried to learn the language of democracy, a task we must continue today.

Notes

Introduction

1. Claudia Rankine, *Citizen: An American Lyric* (Minneapolis: Graywolf, 2014), 11.

2. Rankine, *Citizen*, 45.

3. Rankine, *Citizen*, 43.

4. Rankine, *Citizen*, 17.

5. Commentators considering the complexities of reader engagement with Rankine's direct address include Evie Shockley, "Race, Reception, and Claudia Rankine's 'American Lyric,'" *Los Angeles Review of Books*, January 6, 2016; Maria Windell, "Citizenship in Citizen," *Los Angeles Review of Books*, January 6, 2016; Fernanda Lai, "Publication without the Publicity of the Self: The Lyric 'I' in Emily Dickinson and Claudia Rankine," *Oxford Research in English*, no. 8 (2019): 83; Andrew Gorin, "Lyric Noise: Lisa Robertson, Claudia Rankine, and the Phatic Subject of Poetry in the Mass Public Sphere," *Criticism* 61, no. 1 (2019): 117; Kamran Javadizadeh, "The Atlantic Ocean Breaking on Our Heads: Claudia Rankine, Robert Lowell, and the Whiteness of the Lyric Subject," *PMLA* 134, no. 3 (2019): 482; and Kyle Frisina, "From Performativity to Performance: Claudia Rankine's *Citizen* and Autotheory," *Arizona Quarterly* 76, no. 1 (2020): 151–52.

6. Rankine, *Citizen*, 24.

7. Rankine, *Citizen*, 49.

8. Rankine, *Citizen*, 24.

9. Rankine, *Citizen*, 151.

10. The first quote in this sentence is from an interview concerning Rankine's first American lyric, *Don't Let Me Be Lonely*: Claudia Rankine, "Interview: Claudia Rankine," interview by Jenny Buschner, Braulio Fonseca, Kristen Paz, and Josalyn Knapic, *South Loop Review* 14 (2012): 63, https://www.yumpu.com/en/document/read/35429709/an-interview-with-claudia-rankine. The second quote in this sentence is from a 2016 interview after the publication of *Citizen*:

200 | Notes to Introduction

Claudia Rankine, "An Interview with Claudia Rankine," interview by Claire Schwartz, *TriQuarterly*, no. 150 (2016), https://www.triquarterly.org/issues/issue-150/interview-claudia-rankine. Elsewhere, in an interview with Spencer Bailey, Rankine points to a traditional lyricism in *Citizen* and its predecessor, *Don't Let Me Be Lonely*: "Even though the sentence appears in *Lonely* and *Citizen*, the impulse is a lyrical impulse. The organizational principles of those two books were framed and pushed forward by a kind of poetics that had to do with the regular mechanisms of poetry, sound, all of that" (Claudia Rankine, "Claudia Rankine on Confronting Whiteness Head-On through Language," interview by Spencer Bailey, *Time Sensitive* [podcast], episode 60 [2022], https://timesensitive.fm/episode/claudia-rankine-on-confronting-whiteness-head-on-through-language/). In "Thoughts on Poetry and Its Varieties," John Stuart Mill explains that "[p]oetry and eloquence are both alike the expression or utterance of feeling. But if we may be excused the antithesis, we should say that eloquence is *heard*, poetry is *over*heard. Eloquence supposes an audience; the peculiarity of poetry appears to us to lie in the poet's utter unconsciousness of a listener. Poetry is feeling confessing itself to itself, in moments of solitude, and embodying itself in symbols which are the nearest possible representations of the feeling in the exact shape in which it exists in the poet's mind" (*The Crayon* 7, no. 4 [1860]: 95).

11. "Visionaries Series: Claudia Rankine in Conversation with Judith Butler," New Museum, October 29, 2020, https://vimeo.com/473984783. The comment from Rankine can be found about 17 minutes and 40 seconds into the conversation, immediately after she references Frantz Fanon in relation to "reciprocal recognitions."

12. Frantz Fanon's *Black Skin, White Masks* describes "reciprocal recognitions" as the defining characteristic of a "human world" Fanon "do[es] battle for. . . . in a savage struggle" against "[h]e who is reluctant to recognize me" (trans. Charles Lam Markmann [London: Pluto, 1986], 218). The most overtly theoretical reference in *Citizen* describes Judith Butler, in a question and answer session, explaining how "our very being exposes us to the address of another. . . . We suffer from the condition of being addressable" (49). Butler explores this thesis in *Giving an Account of Oneself* (New York: Fordham University Press, 2005) with reference to Hegel's understanding of social recognition processes (26–35).

13. Claudia Rankine, "Claudia Rankine on Confronting Whiteness Head-On through Language," interview by Spencer Bailey, *Time Sensitive*, episode 60, https://timesensitive.fm/episode/claudia-rankine-on-confronting-whiteness-head-on-through-language/. See, for example, Jonathan Culler, "Apostrophe," *Diacritics* 7, no. 4 (1977): 59–69; Barbara Johnson, "Apostrophe, Animation, and Abortion," *Diacritics* 16, no. 1 (1986): 29–47; William Waters, *Poetry's Touch: On Lyric Address* (Ithaca: Cornell University Press, 2003); Ann Keniston, *Overheard Voices: Address and Subjectivity in Postmodern American Poetry* (New York: Routledge, 2006). Nikki Skillman notes that "most" of the features that appear to make *Citizen*

non-lyrical "have been theorized as essential to the [lyric] genre at one point or another" ("Lyric Reading Revisited: Passion, Address, and Form in *Citizen*," *American Literary History* 31, no. 3 [2019]: 422).

14. Kamran Javadizadeh, "The Atlantic Ocean Breaking on Our Heads," 477.

15. Grant Farred, "*Citizen*, a Lyric Event," *Diacritics* 45, no. 4 (2017): 109.

16. Nikki Skillman, "Lyric Reading," 436, 435.

17. Skillman, "Lyric Reading," 438.

18. For a study of how recognition processes presume social hierarchies, see Kelly Oliver, *Witnessing: Beyond Recognition* (Minneapolis: University of Minnesota Press, 2001), 8–12 and passim.

19. One of Jackson's most expansive descriptions of this process can be found in the entry on "Lyric" in the *Princeton Encyclopedia of Poetry and Poetics*, 4th ed., ed. Roland Greene, Stephen Cushman, et al. (Princeton, NJ: Princeton University Press, 2012), 826–34.

20. José Esteban Muñoz defines "disidentification" as a term "descriptive of the survival strategies the minority subject practices in order to negotiate a phobic majoritarian public sphere that continuously elides or punishes the existence of subjects who do not conform to the phantasm of normative citizenship" (*Disidentifications: Queers of Color and the Performance of Politics* [Minneapolis: University of Minnesota Press, 1999], 4).

21. G. W. F. Hegel, *Aesthetics: Lectures on Fine Art*, vol. 2, trans. T. M. Knox (Oxford: Clarendon Press, 1975), 1113. See also pages 1118–20, 1133. For a useful overview of Hegel's model of lyric, see Jonathan Culler, *Theory of the Lyric* (Cambridge: Harvard University Press, 2015), 92–109.

22. Hegel, *Aesthetics*, 2:1006.

23. Hegel, *Aesthetics*, 2:1031, 1028–29.

24. Hegel, *Aesthetics*, 2:1153.

25. Allen Grossman with Mark Halliday, *The Sighted Singer: Two Works on Poetry for Readers and Writers* (Baltimore: Johns Hopkins University Press, 1992), 261.

26. Grossman with Halliday, *The Sighted Singer*, 264, 263. The final sentence of the section "'I' in Lyric" makes it clear that Grossman is well aware that he is following a Hegelian model: "Remembering and forgetting participate at the festival where Lordship and Bondage cease to be" (265).

27. Grossman with Halliday, *The Sighted Singer*, 193. Iris Marion Young, for example, argued that "misrecognition" is not "usually a political problem independent of other forms of inequality or oppression" (*Inclusion and Democracy* [Oxford: Oxford University Press, 2000], 105). For an influential debate about whether or not recognition should encompass redistribution of cultural and material resources, see Nancy Fraser and Axel Honneth, *Redistribution or Recognition? A Political-Philosophical Exchange* (New York: Verso, 2003). Charles Mills, for example, warns that "a multicultural politics that confines itself to

202 | Notes to Introduction

'recognition' without seeking to address these other dimensions [including 'the interrelation of economic subordination, juridical color-coding, racialized state policy, and white moral psychology'] will necessarily be a politics that changes very little" ("Multiculturalism as/and/or Anti-racism?," in *Multiculturalism and Political Theory*, ed. Anthony S. Laden and David Owen [New York: Cambridge University Press, 2007], 109). A recent study considering whether the left should foreground class or identity is Asad Haider, *Mistaken Identity: Race and Class in the Age of Trump* (New York: Verso, 2018).

28. Allen Grossman, *The Long Schoolroom: Lessons in the Bitter Logic of the Poetic Principle* (Ann Arbor: University of Michigan Press, 1997), 11. Precisely why Grossman locates such a social project as the special domain of poetry is not altogether clear even if he does profess an unusually broad definition of poet: *"The poet is the person who, by reason of the calling, is committed to do his or her human work within the logic of the calling, that is, the logic of representation of the poetic kind.* And everyone is a poet" (9; Grossman's emphasis).

29. Grossman, *Long Schoolroom*, 57.

30. Grossman, *Long Schoolroom*, 9.

31. Grossman, *Long Schoolroom*, 67.

32. Susan Stewart's *Poetry and the Fate of the Senses* (Chicago: University of Chicago Press, 2002) can be read as an eloquent elaboration of Grossman's compressed argument. Beginning, as Grossman does, "in the darkness," Stewart similarly contends that "the poet undertakes the task of recognition in time, the unending tragic Orphic task of drawing the figure of the other—the figure of the beloved who reciprocally can recognize one's own figure—out of the darkness." Stewart knows that such a process aligns closely with "Hegel's position on the ontology of self-consciousness," but she shares Grossman's wariness about Hegel's teleology and invokes Emmanuel Levinas to try to counterbalance Hegel (2–3). And, much more than Grossman, Stewart opens the door to a materially grounded understanding of recognition by conceptualizing the work of the lyric in relation to how Marx understood the "objectification of sense experiences" as the "accomplishment" that ostensibly sets humans apart from the rest of nature (16). Nevertheless, in most ways, she echoes Grossman's quasi-Hegelian model: "Lyric brings forward, as the necessary precondition of its creation of a world of 'I's' and 'you's' in mutual recognition, this place of language as the foundation of intersubjectivity and intersubjectivity as the foundation for the recognition of persons" (47). And, like Grossman, Stewart's narrative of recognition inevitably ends in disappointment (329). Oren Izenberg also takes up his mentor's challenge in *Being Numerous: Poetry and the Ground of Social Life* (Princeton, NJ: Princeton University Press, 2011), but, perhaps in an attempt to mitigate the hierarchies structuring recognition processes (un/misrecognized/recognized/recognizer), does not seek a poetics capable of full recognition. Instead, he hopes to discover a poetics capable of identifying a lowest common denominator, a shared "personhood"

that is both "minimal" and "universal" (4). Izenberg's book looks to writers from historical moments with very different poetic idioms, including Yeats, O'Hara, Oppen, and Ammons, in order to evaluate the prospect of a poetics of "minimal personhood." Most intriguingly, Izenberg argues that language poetry, which thwarts the lyric speaker's role at the center of poetic meaning-making ("Imagine," Izenberg invites, "language . . . without a speaker"), nevertheless fulfills the task of recognition he associates especially with lyricism (142). But, ultimately, Izenberg does not find in either lyric or language poets one "who could show what it might mean to undertake the work of disclosing the real of personhood as the starting point of an affirmative poetic project" (169). Thus Izenberg, much like Grossman, concludes "that poetry is the genre that knows only by knowing worse[,] . . . but in the experience of . . . its failure . . . it is producing occasions for . . . exercis[ing] . . . such powers as we have" to recognize personhood (187).

33. In *Lyric Powers* (Chicago: University of Chicago Press, 2008), Robert von Hallberg, like Hegel in his lectures on aesthetics, argues that lyric poetry has been associated with social recognition at least as early as Pindar (46–47). But like Grossman, von Hallberg cautiously argues that recognition inevitably occurs as "particular instances of a general phenomenon" that might be sufficient "in the case of grass and birds" but offer "little solace to a man sinking into generic folds of skin" (206). Mutlu Konuk Blasing's *Lyric Poetry: The Pain and the Pleasure of Words* (Princeton, NJ: Princeton University Press, 2007) explains that lyric is distinct in how it is not only "not mime[tic]" but "keeps . . . the linguistic code and the otherness of the material medium of language" before the reader, insofar as it "foregrounds a linguistic nonrational that is not a byproduct of reason; rather, it is the ground on which rational language and disciplinary discourses carve their territories" (2–3). A lyric, in this way, "makes audible a virtual subjectivity in the shape of a given language" (4). Thus, lyrics create and are created by lyric subjects. Skillful poets like Whitman can craft a poem like "Crossing Brooklyn Ferry" wherein we "recognize" the "I," but by "reading and repeating his words, 'I' too becomes a text, a typeface looking back at 'me'" resulting in an "uncanny recognition of ourselves in an object as one among other 'objects than which none else is more lasting.'" Whitman's poem, in her reading, enacts in an especially reflexive, indeed nearly Hegelian, manner "the lyric objectification of subjectivity in the material medium of language: we as readers experience what a lyric 'I' is" (66). Blasing, however, insists that this does not indicate a triumph of lyric, since "experienc[ing] what a lyric 'I' is" amounts to learning that "one is born—as words," a realization that one can "never know oneself [much less others] but in a second language" that is never adequate to its task of recognition (85). Several other recent studies have foregrounded a "shame" with regard to the lyricized lyric that has been internalized and interrogated by poets since the mid-twentieth century (Gillian White, *Lyric Shame: The "Lyric" Subject of Contemporary American Poetry* [Cambridge, MA: Harvard University Press, 2014]), examined "the mind

204 | Notes to Introduction

sciences' conceptual diffusions within American poetics" (Nikki Skillman, *The Lyric in the Age of the Brain* [Cambridge, MA: Harvard University Press, 2016], 5); and explored how American poets have engaged modern information technologies (Seth Perlow, *The Poem Electric: Technology and the American Lyric* [Minneapolis: University of Minnesota Press, 2018]).

34. Culler, *Theory of the Lyric*, 108–9.

35. Culler, *Theory of the Lyric*, 347, 350.

36. Culler, *Theory of the Lyric*, 351.

37. Culler explains that "the formal dimensions of lyrics—the patterning of rhythm and rhyme, the repetition of stanza forms, and generally everything that recalls song or lacks a mimetic or representational function—contribute to their ritualistic as opposed to fictional aspect." *Theory of Lyric*, 37.

38. Virginia Jackson and Yopie Prins, eds., *The Lyric Theory Reader: A Critical Anthology* (Baltimore: Johns Hopkins University Press, 2014), 14.

39. Virginia Jackson, "American Romanticism, Again," *Studies in Romanticism* 55, no. 3 (2016): 322, 323.

40. Jackson, "American Romanticism, Again," 323.

41. Jackson and Prins, *Lyric Theory Reader*, 12.

42. Virginia Jackson, *Before Modernism: Inventing American Lyric* (Princeton, NJ: Princeton University Press, 2023), 230.

43. Jackson, *Before Modernism*, 45, and Jackson, "American Romanticism, Again," 330.

44. Similarly, in "Poe's Common Meter," Jackson describes "generic term[s]" as "term[s] of mutual collective recognition" (in *The Oxford Handbook of Edgar Allan Poe*, ed. J. Gerald Kennedy and Scott Peeples [New York: Oxford University Press, 2019], 132). Also see "Specters of the Ballad," *Nineteenth-Century Literature* 71, no. 2 (2016): 180n5.

45. Jackson, *Before Modernism*, 45.

46. Lisa Gitelman, *Paper Knowledge: Toward a Media History of Documents* (Durham, NC: Duke University Press, 2014), 2. Gitelman explains that "genre is a mode of recognition instantiated in discourse . . . that is collective, spontaneous, and dynamic." She goes on to say that genres "are ongoing and changeable practices of expression and reception that are recognizable in myriad and variable constituent instances at once and also across time. They are specific and dynamic, socially realized sites and segments of coherence within the discursive field" (2).

47. Jackson, *Before Modernism*, 45, 17.

48. Jackson, *Before Modernism*, 49.

49. In *Dickinson's Misery* (Princeton, NJ: Princeton University Press, 2005), Virginia Jackson notes that "[s]uch a close affiliation between lyricization and Americanization will come to seem familiar in these chapters, though there is much to be said about the relation between national and generic identity that will fall outside the chapters themselves" (11). Jackson additionally speculates in

this book about a number of potential sources of lyricization, noting how an "imaginary version of the lyric in print" as well as the emergence in the nineteenth century of an "increasingly professionalized [field of] literary interpretation" contributed to "an idea of the lyric as a poetic norm" (44). Between the publication of *Dickinson's Misery* and *Before Modernism*, see, for example, Jackson's essay on Paul Laurence Dunbar, "Specters of the Ballad." As this chapter and its notes make clear, quite a number of other scholars also have studied, in various ways, the intersection between race and lyricization.

50. Jackson, *Before Modernism*, 7.

51. Jackson, *Before Modernism*, 7.

52. Jackson, *Dickinson's Misery*, 235. Virginia Jackson, "The Function of Criticism at the Present Time," *Los Angeles Review of Books*, April 12, 2015. In the latter, Jackson explains that "we are organized by *genre* in ways that are already intelligible to others because genres are sites of mutual collective recognition," which is to say that, according to Jackson (and, she would also say, Lauren Berlant, as well, who is the subject of this essay), we perform facets of our identity through the genres we inherit and exist amid. In doing this, we occasionally find those genres to be "more fictitious and less attainable" as they "wan[e]," a moment filled with confusion but also rife with potentiality. Jackson notes that "Berlant wants . . . recognition to mean that genres can become the vehicles of social change, or at least of degrees of adjustment," a process facilitated by "criticism," which takes as its purpose "to create better worlds, worlds in which genres are not settled states of common disappointment . . . but are instead signs and figures for shared world-making." Jackson, in yet another essay, commends "thinking" amid "varying degrees of recognition of various poetic genres" rather than in relation to "a singular abstraction of form." Virginia Jackson, "Thinking Dickinson Thinking Poetry," in *A Companion to Emily Dickinson*, ed. Martha Nell Smith and Mary Loeffelholz (Malden, MA: Wiley, 2014), 214.

53. Jackson, "The Function of Criticism at the Present Time."

54. G. W. F. Hegel, *The Phenomenology of Spirit*, trans. A. V. Miller (Oxford: Oxford University Press, 1977), 58. Judith Butler rightly warns against oversimplifying Hegel's model of recognition, especially with regard to its subtle consideration of social contexts: "Although Hegel is sometimes faulted for understanding recognition as a dyadic structure[,] . . . it is important to see that the struggle for recognition as it is staged in the *Phenomenology* reveals the inadequacy of the dyad as a frame of reference for understanding social life. After all, what eventually follows from this scene is a system of customs (*Sittlichkeit*) and hence a social account of the norms by which reciprocal recognition might be sustained in ways that are more stable than either the life and death struggle or the system of bondage would imply" (*Giving an Account of Oneself*, 28–29). Of course, Hegel does imply that passing through such scenes of struggle is necessary in order to reach this reciprocal recognition.

206 | Notes to Introduction

55. Jackson, *Before Modernism*, 17.

56. Studying eighteenth- and nineteenth-century African American poets, Jackson is conscious of the availability of Hegelian readings. Phillis Wheatley's poetry, thus, offers an example of a "negative dialectics" that "is not, like Adorno's theory of poetics, Hegelian, so does not share the commitment to historical progress that Hegel and Marx envisioned" (Jackson, *Before Modernism*, 6). According to Jackson, Wheatley wields couplets and other features of verse "recognizable as a [facet of a] genre" of her time while showing how that genre "also makes the person who wrote it unrecognizable" (7). Similarly, Frances Ellen Watkins "offers us an alternative to the thoroughly Hegelian structure of contemporary lyric theory" (230). While Jackson rejects the positive Hegelian teleology, genre and the work of recognition remain bound together in otherwise Hegelian ways as "poetic reading publics generated by spontaneous collective generic recognition began to turn into poetic reading publics generalized by individual vicarious identification. Over the next two centuries, genres of verse that everyone could recognize were replaced by genres of persons that everyone and no one could recognize" (232).

At one level, Jackson, in passages like this, makes trenchant observations about the historical intersections between the work of genre with regard to categorizing poetry and the work of genre with regard to categorizing people. But one might wish for Jackson's description of this to be less confined by a post-Hegelian framework of recognition processes. Historicizing, which Jackson in other ways models so well, might lead one to acknowledge the scope of Hegel's influence without adopting a version of his framework as if by default. As Jackson notes, one should not retroproject Hegelian assumptions about lyric and genre and sociality on pre-Hegelian poets like Wheatley and Watkins. Neither should one project Hegelian assumptions about lyric and genre and sociality on a post-Hegelian era that also includes lineages of poets and other thinkers who reject those assumptions (even if they became, in certain ways, increasingly predominant).

57. Jackson, *Before Modernism*, 6.

58. Urayoán Noel, *In Visible Movement: Nuyorican Poetry from the Sixties to Slam* (Iowa City: University of Iowa Press, 2014), xxii, xxxvi, 176.

59. Ralph Rodriguez, *Latinx Literature Unbound: Undoing Ethnic Expectation* (New York: Fordham University Press, 2018), 100.

60. Anthony Reed, *Freedom Time: The Poetics and Politics of Black Experimental Writing* (Baltimore: Johns Hopkins University Press, 2016), 2, 101–2.

61. Sarah Dowling, *Translingual Poetics: Writing Personhood under Settler Colonialism* (Iowa City: University of Iowa Press, 2018), 126.

62. Dowling, *Translingual Poetics*, 122–23, 148.

63. There are parallel examples by feminist and queer scholars. Linda Kinnahan, for example, notes how some feminist poets like Adrienne Rich

believed that the "political labor" of poetry rests upon the recognizability of a "feminist lyric 'I' . . . radically altered [from its post-Romantic, male correlate] through its regendering." But Kinnahan, on the other hand, acknowledges how "the lyric subject popularly supported by the poets of the women's movement," a lyric subject used to appeal for greater sociopolitical recognition of women, "nonetheless retains primary conventions inherited from a patriarchal tradition" that has long restricted women (*Lyric Interventions: Feminism, Experimental Poetry, and Contemporary Discourse* [Iowa City: University of Iowa Press, 2004], 4). Eric Keenaghan, facing a similar near-paradox, rejects the "biopolitical mandate" demanding that subjects "[b]e confident in your own identity, so as to insure the stability and security of the collective with which you identify" (*Queering Cold War Poetry: Ethics of Vulnerability in Cuba and the United States* [Columbus: Ohio State University Press, 2009], 3).

64. Dorothy Wang, for example, rightly critiques a tendency among some white critics to praise "good minority poetry" that effaces identity and to dismiss "bad minority poetry, which focuses on 'identity' " or a related tendency to argue that to be an "experimental [poet] . . . is, implicitly, not to discuss race or ethnic identity" (*Thinking Its Presence: Form, Race, and Subjectivity in Asian American Poetry* [Stanford, CA: Stanford University Press, 2014], 31).

65. The literature on this topic, of course, is extensive. See, for example, Satya P. Mohanty, *Literary Theory and the Claims of History: Postmodernism, Objectivity, Multicultural Politics* (Ithaca, NY: Cornell University Press, 1997); Linda Martín Alcoff, Michael Hames-García, Satya P. Mohanty, and Paula M. L. Moya, eds., *Identity Politics Reconsidered* (New York: Palgrave MacMillan, 2006); Gurminder K. Bhambra and Victoria Margree, "Identity Politics and the Need for a 'Tomorrow,' " *Economic and Political Weekly* 45, no. 15 (2010): 59–66. A crucial, pioneering statement about strategic essentialism appears in Gayatri Spivak, "Can the Subaltern Speak?," in *Marxism and the Interpretation of Culture*, ed. Cary Nelson and Lawrence Grossberg (Urbana: University of Illinois Press, 1988), 271–313. Iris Marion Young argues that "identity" is an irresolvably problematic category that cannot capture the political salience of "group difference" as well as the analysis of the "differentiated relations" that a group's members have toward social "institutions" and "structures" that establish "configuration[s] of power, resource allocation, [and] status norms" compared to members of other, more privileged groups (*Inclusion and Democracy*, 99). And Charles Taylor's "The Politics of Recognition" explores the potential tensions between recognition as an affirmation of "difference" as understood by a particular identity group and recognition as a universalizing confirmation of "equal citizenship" across various such groups (in *Multiculturalism: Examining the Politics of Recognition*, ed. Amy Gutmann [Princeton, NJ: Princeton University Press, 1994], 38–39 and passim).

66. See, for example, Édouard Glissant, *Poetics of Relation*, trans. Betsy Wing (Ann Arbor: University of Michigan Press, 1997). See also Ralph Rodriguez,

208 | Notes to Introduction

Latinx Literature Unbound: Undoing Ethnic Expectation and José Esteban Muñoz, *Disidentifications: Queers of Color and the Performance of Politics.*

67. See note 27.

68. This is a topic addressed by the contributors to a volume edited by Avigail Eisenberg, Jeremy Webber, Glen Coulthard, and Andrée Boisselle, *Recognition versus Self-Determination: Dilemmas of Emancipatory Politics* (Vancouver: University of British Columbia Press, 2014).

69. Though the surge of interest in lyric theory and the historicizing of "lyric" over the past two decades has not engaged Marxist frameworks a great deal, Cary Nelson's scholarship on American poetry offers a fruitful point of entry into such a project. See, for example, *Repression and Recovery: Modern American Poetry and the Politics of Cultural Memory, 1910–1945* (Madison: University of Wisconsin Press, 1989) and also *Revolutionary Memory: Recovering the Poetry of the American Left* (New York: Routledge, 2001).

70. Oliver, *Witnessing*, 9. Yen Le Espiritu, for example, warns about how such dynamics create scenarios wherein the disempowered are offered "differential inclusion . . . as subordinate subjects" (*Home Bound: Filipino American Lives across Cultures, Communities and Countries* [Berkeley: University of California Press, 2003], 212).

71. Oliver, *Witnessing*, 15.

72. Oliver, *Witnessing*, 18.

73. Oliver, *Witnessing*, 19.

74. Space does not permit an assessment of Butler's rich engagement with Hegel's thought throughout their career. For an early example, see *Subjects of Desire: Hegelian Reflections in Twentieth-Century France* (New York: Columbia University, 1987). A couple more recent examples illustrating how Butler's thinking about recognition draws from Hegel's include *Giving an Account of Oneself* (26–35) and *Frames of War: When Is Life Grievable* (New York: Verso, 2010), 2–6.

75. Patchen Markell, *Bound by Recognition* (Princeton, NJ: Princeton University Press, 2003), 38.

76. Markell, *Bound by Recognition*, 188.

77. For a trenchant, recent examination of affect in relation to lyric, see Gillian White's *Lyric Shame: The "Lyric" Subject of Contemporary American Poetry.*

78. Judith Butler grapples with these issues when they note that "to be radically deprived of recognition . . . can be, depending on the circumstance, both terrible and exhilarating." To have "the very viability of one's life . . . called into question . . . also means that we can be at the threshold of developing the terms that allow us to live" (*Notes toward a Performative Theory of Assembly* [Cambridge, MA: Harvard University Press, 2015], 40). A number of other thinkers emphasize that such spaces of "social death," a term that originated in Orlando Patterson's attempt to describe the experience of being rendered a slave, enervate in ways that do not permit "exhilarati[on]" (*Slavery and Social Death* [Cambridge, MA:

Harvard University Press, 1982]). Lisa Cacho, for example, worries about the impulse to "reintegrat[e] the socially dead into a capitalist society" or aspire to "'breathe life' into the spaces of social death (gentrification, privatization, and democratization)." Butler, to be sure, does not have these options in mind when they describe the process of "developing the terms that allow us to live." But Cacho emphasizes the extreme constraints placed on the forms of life permitted to those who are disempowered. Cacho suggests that "we might conscientiously work against the logic of survivability" so often developed according to established racist, "neoliberal" norms (*Social Death: Racialized Rightlessness and the Criminalization of the Unprotected* [New York: New York University Press, 2012], 33).

79. Fred Moten, *The Universal Machine* (Durham, NC: Duke University Press, 2018), 195.

80. Frank Wilderson, *"We're Trying to Destroy the World": Anti-Blackness and Police Violence after Ferguson* (Ill Will Editions, 2014), 8–9, https://illwill. com/print/were-trying-to-destroy-the-world. Wilderson explains that for people of African heritage to "enter into a structure of recognition as a being" would necessitate "recognition and incorporation being completely destroyed" (9). This is the "destr[uction]" of "the world" that his title implies, even as he is not optimistic about achieving it.

81. Moten, *The Universal Machine*, 193.

82. Moten, *The Universal Machine*, 234.

83. Moten, *The Universal Machine*, 194 (and for more on anontic and paranotic spaces, see 221, 224–25, 234).

84. Moten, *The Universal Machine*, 216.

85. Moten, *The Universal Machine*, 219.

86. Fanon, *Black Skin, White Masks*, 34.

87. Moten, *The Universal Machine*, 223, 225.

88. Stefano Harney and Fred Moten, *The Undercommons: Fugitive Planning and Black Study* (New York: Minor Compositions, 2013).

89. Harney and Moten, *The Undercommons*, 28.

90. Harney and Moten, *The Undercommons*, 111–12, 126.

91. Harney and Moten, *The Undercommons*, 30, 110.

92. Moten, *The Universal Machine*, 226.

93. For a highly original account of enmeshment/entanglement derived from how these concepts have been used in modern physics, see Karen Barad, *Meeting the Universe Halfway: Quantum Physics and the Entanglement of Matter and Meaning* (Durham, NC: Duke University Press, 2007).

94. This quote is from a self-review of *Leaves of Grass* that Whitman published in the October 1855 issue of the *American Phrenological Journal*. See Matt Cohen, Ed Folsom, and Kenneth M. Price, eds., "Reviews: *Leaves of Grass* (1855)," Walt Whitman Archive, accessed July 1, 2024, https://whitmanarchive. org/commentary/reviews/leaves-of-grass-1855. This portion of the Whitman

210 | Notes to Chapter One

Archive includes all of the extant, contemporaneous reviews of the 1855 first edition of *Leaves of Grass*.

95. Walt Whitman, *Notebooks and Unpublished Prose Manuscripts*, vol. 1, *Family Notes and Autobiography, Brooklyn and New York*, ed. Edward F. Grier (New York: New York University Press, 1984), 234.

96. The line numbers listed correspond to the text of the poem presented in Walt Whitman, *Leaves of Grass: A Textual Variorum of the Printed Poems*, vols. 1–3, ed. Sculley Bradley, Harold W. Blodgett, Arthur Golden, and William White (New York: New York University Press, 1980). The phrase "the rest" is repeated three times across two lines.

97. The page number listed corresponds to the text of the poem presented in Jean Toomer, *The Collected Poems of Jean Toomer*, ed. Robert B. Jones and Margery Toomer Latimer (Chapel Hill: University of North Carolina Press, 1988).

98. Hart Crane, *Complete Poems and Selected Letters*, ed. Langdon Hammer (New York: Literary Classics of the United States, 2006), 163.

99. Crane, *Complete Poems and Selected Letters*, 163.

100. Crane, *Complete Poems and Selected Letters*, 13, 18.

101. James Merrill, *Collected Prose*, ed. J. D. McClatchy and Stephen Yenser (New York: Alfred Knopf, 2004), 93.

102. Malin Pereira, ed., *Into a Light Both Brilliant and Unseen: Conversations with Contemporary Black Poets* (Athens: University of Georgia Press, 2010), 149–50.

103. Rankine, *Citizen*, 73.

Chapter One

1. Unless stated otherwise, quotations from Whitman's poetry follow the texts presented in Walt Whitman, *Leaves of Grass: A Textual Variorum of the Printed Poems*, vols. 1–3, ed. Sculley Bradley, Harold W. Blodgett, Arthur Golden, and William White (New York: New York University Press, 1980). For convenience, line numbers are cited at the ends of sentences in the main text. The information concerning the origins of "Song of the Universal" appears in the footnote to the poem in Walt Whitman, *Leaves of Grass and Other Writings*, ed. Michael Moon (New York: Norton, 2002), 189.

2. Michael Moon notes that "the poem ['Song of the Universal'] received nearly simultaneous publication in several newspapers—the *New York Daily Graphic* and *Evening Post* on June 17 [the day of the commencement ceremony], the *Springfield Republican* on June 18, the *New York World* on June 19, and the *Camden New Republic* on June 20" (Whitman, *Leaves of Grass and Other Writings*, 189).

3. See also Whitman's "Sunday Evening Lectures" (in *Notebooks and Unpublished Prose Manuscripts*, vol. 6, ed. Edward F. Grier [New York: New York University Press, 1984], 2009–18) and "Carlyle from American Points of View"

(in *Prose Works, 1892*, ed. Floyd Stovall [New York: New York University Press, 1963], 1:254–62).

4. Matt Erlin, "Absolute Speculation: The St. Louis Hegelians and the Question of American National Identity," in *German Culture in Nineteenth-Century America: Reception, Adaptation, Transformation*, ed. Lynne Tatlock and Matt Erlin (Rochester, NY: Camden House, 2005), 93.

5. For examples of their rationalizing, see Erlin, "Absolute Speculation," 91–92; Henry Pochmann, *German Culture in America: Philosophical and Literary Influences 1600–1900* (Madison: University of Wisconsin Press, 1957), 268.

6. For Whitman's letters to William Torrey Harris in 1879 and 1880, see Walt Whitman, *The Correspondence*, vol. 3, *1876–1885*, ed. Edwin Haviland Miller (New York: New York University Press, 1964), 166–67, 187–88. For evidence of Whitman meeting Harris in St. Louis, see Walt Whitman, *Daybooks and Notebooks*, vol. 1, *Daybooks 1876–November 1881*, ed. William White (New York: New York University Press, 1978), 168. When Whitman visited Niagara Falls, he sent Harris a postcard (Whitman, *Daybooks and Notebooks*, 200). Kurt F. Leidecker, Harris's biographer, notes that, though Harris came to prefer John Greenleaf Whittier among American poets, "*Leaves of Grass* was among his first collection of books" as an adult (*Yankee Teacher: The Life of William Torrey Harris* [New York: The Philosophical Library, 1946], 66, 353, 637).

7. "Says," a poem first published in 1860, then revised 1867, before finally being removed from *Leaves of Grass* altogether after the 1876 edition, also addresses eligibility in a way that shows Whitman's political evolution (see Michael Moon's note in his critical edition of Whitman, *Leaves of Grass and Other Writings*, 522–24). Though such a revision and removal process is not unique in Whitman's oeuvre, here, it indicates the poet's increasing anxieties about a political model he eventually deems too radical. Structured largely as a sequence of statements beginning with the phrase "I say," the poem serves as a manifesto that builds toward a sweeping conclusion affirming "even . . . the lowest" who "illustrate the whole law" (24–25). Invoking a category like "the lowest" might appear to violate the "whole law" of eligibility that affirms "that every right, in politics or what-not, shall be eligible to that one man or woman, on the same terms as any" (26). But the trajectory of the original 1860 version of the poem, which begins by mentioning the "most perfect person," applies pressure to such categorizations by framing a commitment to eligibility in terms of a denunciation of slavery: "I say man shall not hold property in man; / I say the least developed person on earth is just as important and sacred to himself or herself, as the most developed person is to himself or herself" (1, 4–5). And the speaker goes on to proclaim: "I say where liberty draws not the blood out of slavery, there slavery draws the blood out of liberty / I say the word of the good old cause in These States, and resound it hence over the world" (6–7). Whitman expunged such sentiments from the 1867 version of the poem and gave it a more subdued title "Suggestions."

212 | Notes to Chapter One

Though the revised poem maintains its concluding commitment to eligibility, it does so in a less materially grounded way that anticipates the abstract Hegelian amplitudes of "Song of the Universal." Yet Whitman does not yet fully indulge in the absorptive logic of the later poem. This leaves "Suggestions" hamstrung between divergent poetics and politics, a status that, one suspects, eventually led Whitman to excise the poem from his canon.

8. Walt Whitman, *Notebooks and Unpublished Prose Manuscripts*, vol. 1, *Family Notes and Autobiography, Brooklyn and New York*, ed. Edward F. Grier (New York: New York University Press, 1984), 232–34. Though the notebook primarily features drafts of material used in "Crossing Brooklyn Ferry," it also includes references to material related to (or literally incorporated in) several other poems, including "Poem of Many in One"/"By Blue Ontario's Shore."

9. Christian Samito, *Becoming American under Fire: Irish Americans, African Americans, and the Politics of Citizenship during the Civil War Era* (Ithaca, NY: Cornell University Press, 2009), 13.

10. William W. Freehling, *The Road to Disunion*, vol. 2, *Secessionists Triumphant, 1854–1861* (Oxford: Oxford University Press, 2007), 62.

11. Samito, *Becoming American under Fire*, 17–19.

12. Eric Foner, *The Fiery Trial: Abraham Lincoln and American Slavery* (New York: Norton, 2010), 73.

13. Abraham Lincoln, *The Collected Works of Abraham Lincoln*, ed. Roy Basler (New Brunswick, NJ: Rutgers University Press, 1953), 2: 322–23.

14. Foner, *The Fiery Trial*, 77.

15. David S. Reynolds, *Walt Whitman's America: A Cultural Biography* (New York: Knopf, 1995), 127.

16. Matt Cohen, Ed Folsom, and Kenneth M. Price, ed., "Commentary: Contemporary Reviews of *Leaves of Grass* (1855)," Walt Whitman Archive, accessed July 1, 2024, https://whitmanarchive.org/commentary/reviews/leaves-of-grass-1855. This website includes all of the extant, contemporaneous reviews of Whitman's 1855 first edition. For examples of reviewers puzzled by Whitman's form and genre, see Charles Eliot Norton's September 1855 review in *Putnam's Monthly* and an anonymous review published in the *Brooklyn Daily Eagle* on September 15, 1855. Examples of critics denouncing the first edition include Rufus Griswold's November 10, 1855, review in the *Criterion*, the anonymous review in the March 15, 1856, issue of *Saturday Review*, and the anonymous review in the April 1, 1856, issue of the *Critic*.

17. Cristanne Miller, *Reading in Time: Emily Dickinson in the Nineteenth Century* (Amherst: University of Massachusetts Press, 2012), 20.

18. See, for example, the anonymous review in the March 22, 1856, issue of the *Literary Examiner* or the review written by George Eliot and published in June 7, 1856, issue of the *Leader*. Both reviews are available on the Walt Whitman Archive (see note 16).

19. Christopher Beach, *The Politics of Distinction: Whitman and The Discourses of Nineteenth-Century America* (Athens: University of Georgia, 1996), 42.

20. Though several early reviewers noted Whitman's debt to Emersonian literary nationalism, only a couple connected the poet's adventurousness at the level of form and content to an attempt to intervene in the politics of the mid-1850s, including a largely critical, anonymous reviewer, writing in the January 1856 issue of the *Crayon* and a more complimentary May 1856 review by Fanny Fern in the *New York Ledger* (both reviews are available on the Whitman Archive; see note 16).

21. These anonymous self-reviews appeared in the September 1855 issue of the *United States Review*, the September 29, 1855, edition of the *Brooklyn Daily Times*, and the October 1855 issue of the *American Phrenological Journal* (all are available on the Whitman Archive; see note 16).

22. The word "spasmodic" references a group of British poets (including Alexander Smith, Sydney Thompson Dobell, and others) from the late 1840s and early 1850s who explored extreme subjective states that they reflected in metrical experimentation.

23. Whitman likely had in mind the aftereffects of the 1848 rebellions in Europe, a topic he had addressed in an 1850 poem, "Resurgemus."

24. Virginia Jackson, "Lyric," in *The Princeton Encyclopedia of Poetry and Poetics*, ed. Roland Greene and Stephen Cushman (Princeton, NJ: Princeton University Press, 2012), 826.

25. Jackson, "Lyric," 830. It is worth noting that resistance to lyricization began quite early. Consider, for example, John Keats's critique of an increasing number of "Contemporaries" including "Wordsworth &c" for being "Egotist[s]" who cultivated a "wordsworthian or egotistical sublime" (*The Letters of John Keats 1814–1821*, vol. 1, ed. Hyder Edward Rollins [Cambridge, MA: Harvard University Press, 1958], 223, 387).

26. Of the more than two hundred extant reviews spanning Whitman's lifetime, fourteen use lyric as an adjective and twelve use it as a noun (no review uses the term as both an adjective and a noun). These are spread across approximately four decades of reviews. For example, two 1855 reviews (out of four total that use variations of the word lyric) use "lyric" as a noun. The *Brooklyn Daily Eagle* states that "[i]t [*Leaves of Grass*] is a poem; but it conforms to none of the rules by which poetry has ever been judged. It is not an epic nor an ode, nor a lyric." The *Christian Spiritualist* associates Whitman with an anticipated flowering of poets with "mediatorial" (i.e., having the qualities of mediums) natures writing "Epics and Lyrics, of individual Spirits and societies of Spirits." The fact that only 11.4 percent of reviews (twenty six out of 228) use any form of the word lyric may seem to suggest its relative lack of importance as a category. But it is useful to compare the frequency of lyric-related words to other terms. "Hymn" appears in only twenty-one reviews. "Ode" and "ballad" occur in only

214 | Notes to Chapter One

a dozen reviews each, the same number of times as "lyric" is used as a noun. "Sonnet" appears eleven times and "elegy" only six times. More general terms like "song" (appearing in one hundred reviews) and "poem" (appearing in 180 reviews) occur much more frequently, in part due to Whitman's frequent use of such terms in titles of poems and in part due to some puzzlement among some reviewers over whether existing genre categories could be applied. The online Walt Whitman Archive allows for the use of keyword searches across all extant nineteenth-century reviews of Whitman's work (https://whitmanarchive.org/commentary/reviews/search).

27. Virginia Jackson, "American Romanticism, Again," *Studies in Romanticism* 55, no. 3 (2016): 341–42.

28. Whether one believes the elderly Whitman's estimation that hardly any copies of the first edition sold at all or David Reynold's estimation that perhaps as many as "several hundred copies" sold, there is no question that (as Reynolds puts it), the sales were "not what . . . [Whitman] had had in mind" when he hoped to be "absorbed by his country" (*Walt Whitman's America*, 340).

29. Mark Bauerlein, *Whitman and the American Idiom* (Baton Rouge: Louisiana State University Press, 1991), 15.

30. In perhaps the climactic section of the tract, the portion with the subtitle "MUST RUNAWAY SLAVES BE DELIVERED BACK?," Whitman immediately answers, "they must" and gives a bland, somewhat regret-laden, legalistic rationale based on the fourth article of the Constitution. But immediately thereafter, he seems to switch sides and argue against "what is called the Fugitive Slave Law," since it had been "insolently put over the people by their Congress and President" and "contravenes the whole of the organic compacts, and is at all times to be defied in all parts of These States," even by "the bullet and the sword" ("The Eighteenth Presidency!," in *Walt Whitman: Poetry and Prose*, ed. Justin Kaplan [New York: Library of America, 1996], 1344–45). In light of such tensions, Ivy Wilson has argued that in "The Eighteenth Presidency" Whitman "employs abolitionist rhetoric but not actually in the service of abolitionism itself" (*Specters of Democracy: Blackness and the Aesthetics of Politics in the Antebellum U. S.* [Oxford: Oxford University Press, 2011], 89). The tract's competing positions and affective registers represent competing political approaches within Whitman—and among white people in the North, generally—toward slavery.

31. The almost word for word portion of "The Eighteenth Presidency" that appears in the "George Walker" notebook addresses Whitman's frustration that the small minority of the American public that held slaves continued to make demands on the majority of Americans: "There is more hullabaloo made for the hourly whims of these 350,000 slaveholders, than, has ever been made, or ever will be made, about the lives on earth and the eternal lives afterwards of the whole main body of the inhabitants of these states, the good thirty millions of men, women, and children" (*Notebooks and Unpublished Prose Manuscripts*, 1:237).

Notes to Chapter One | 215

32. Whitman, *Notebooks and Unpublished Prose Manuscripts*, 1:227.

33. Do "the needy and down kept races of the whole earth" also include African Americans? It may be telling that the place of African Americans is left less clear (despite the reference to the "black and bloody lesson") than that of Irish and German immigrants. Elsewhere in the "George Walker" notebook, Whitman does express regret that "the land that has a place for slaves and the owners of slaves has no place for freeman," and he advises himself to "say to Slavery / Go, and return no more" (*Notebooks and Unpublished Prose Manuscripts*, 1:235, 237). Of course, it is entirely possible for Whitman, like many White northerners, to denounce slavery and express empathy for slaves and former slaves without recognizing them politically to the degree he did Irish and German immigrants.

34. Whitman, *Notebooks and Unpublished Prose Manuscripts*, 1:227. Whitman echoes these ideas later in the notebook: "American society literature [*sic*] is settling itself, in utter defiance of American principles. It is settling itself in accordance with European principles, and on a far larger scale than the European scale—as much larger as the American proportions are larger than the European proportions.—The modes on which it arranges itself involve the idea of caste—involve servants, masters, superiors inferiors" (241).

35. Whitman, *Notebooks and Unpublished Prose Manuscripts*, 1:232–33.

36. Whitman, *Notebooks and Unpublished Prose Manuscripts*, 1:234.

37. Whitman, *Notebooks and Unpublished Prose Manuscripts*, 1:232–34. A curious footnote argues that these lines about "eligibility" do "not seem to be related to the facing draft of 'Crossing Brooklyn Ferry,'" since the former was written on the "versos," whereas the draft of the poem was continued "on successive rectos" (232). But this seems a dubious conclusion. Why would one presume writing on facing pages to be unrelated? It seems more likely that Whitman used one side of the page to draft the poem and the other side of the page to make notes about the poetics and politics he wished to practice in the poem. After all, the comments about using an "indirect mode" requiring a reader to "wristle" with the poet, which surely must refer to the rhetorical strategies Whitman uses in "Crossing Brooklyn Ferry," also are found on the versos, just like the "eligibility" comments.

38. The "scheme" may also indicate Whitman's interest in Swedenborgian mysticism. See Reynolds, *Walt Whitman's America*, 266, 272.

39. Peter Coviello, "Intimate Nationality: Anonymity and Attachment in Whitman," *American Literature* 73, no. 1 (2001): 89.

40. See Tenney Nathanson, *Whitman's Presence: Body, Voice, and Writing in Leaves of Grass* (New York: New York University Press, 1992), 31, 33; Roger Gilbert, "From Anxiety to Power: Grammar and Crisis in 'Crossing Brooklyn Ferry,'" *Nineteenth-Century Literature* 42, no. 3 (1987): 350.

41. Wai Chee Dimock, *Residues of Justice: Literature, Law, and Philosophy* (Berkeley: University of California Press, 1996), 118–19. In response to Dimock's

216 | Notes to Chapter One

concerns, Charles Altieri has defended Whitman by noting that his "constantly shifting" gaze is crucial "because the basis for overall identifications as citizens of a democracy is precisely one's awareness of sharing such fluidity." And he adds, "[P]erhaps rather than worrying only about the facts of contingency we also need to imagine what these various subjects might have in common as they pursue those contingencies[,] . . . [otherwise] there is little possibility that we can have any emotional bonds at all to those whose contingencies do not match our own." But Altieri's defense of Whitman, like Dimock's critique, presumes that Whitman's goals are principally "epistemic" rather than ontological ("Spectacular Antispectacle: Ecstasy and Nationality in Whitman and His Heirs," *American Literary History* 11, no. 1 [1999]: 51, 46, 53).

42. This debate over Whitman's cataloguing serves as a microcosm of a broader, longstanding critique of the political implications of Whitman's poetics. As early as the 1920s, D. H. Lawrence challenged a prevailing reading of Whitman as a heroic champion of liberal individualism by arguing that there was something troubling about his tendency to "forc[e] his soul . . . into other people's circumstances" in a manner resembling "Myself monomania" more than "Sympathy" (*Studies in Classic American Literature* [New York: Penguin, 1977], 183, 182). Several decades later Pablo Neruda deemed Whitman not just a "lyric moralist" and a poet of democracy but "the first totalitarian poet" ("We Live in a Whitmanesque Age," in *Walt Whitman: The Measure of His Song*, ed. Jim Perlman, Ed Folsom, and Dan Campion [Minneapolis: Holy Cow! Press, 1981], 140). This formulation was further elaborated by many other scholars during the past several decades, who find evidence in "Crossing Brooklyn Ferry" of Whitman's preference for synthesis rather than difference, a poetics of presence rather than absence, and above all, a mastering gaze, tendencies that they believe compromise his democratic social vision before he finishes articulating it. See, for example, Quentin Anderson (*The Imperial Self: An Essay in American Literary and Cultural History* [New York: Vintage Books, 1971], 121, 164), Barton Levi St. Armand ("Transcendence through Technique: Whitman's 'Crossing Brooklyn Ferry' and Impressionist Painting," *Bucknell Review* 24, no. 2 [1978]: 63), C. Carroll Hollis (*Language and Style in Leaves of Grass* [Baton Rouge: Louisiana State University Press, 1983], 100), Kerry Larson (*Whitman's Drama of Consensus* [Chicago: University of Chicago Press, 1988], 12), and Tenney Nathanson (*Whitman's Presence*, 10). Tom Cohen offers perhaps the most hyperbolic of such arguments, contending that an "'evil' Whitman" positions the poem's reader as "subordinate" through a rhetorical strategy of "entrapment and seduction" that culminates in "rape or buggery" ("Only the Dead Know Brooklyn Ferry: The Inscription of the Reader in Whitman," *Arizona Quarterly* 49, no. 2 [1993]: 23, 34, 39, 43). More recently, both liberalizing and imperialistic readings of Whitman have been scrutinized by criticism influenced by deconstruction and queer theory. See for example, Stephen Railton, "'As If I Were with You'—The Performance

of Whitman's Poetry," in *The Cambridge Companion to Walt Whitman*, ed. Ezra Greenspan (Cambridge: Cambridge University Press, 1995), 21; Michael Warner, *Publics and Counterpublics* (New York: Zone Books, 2002), 284–85.

43. After the 1856 edition in which the poem first appeared, Whitman removed the phrase "solitary committer" (i.e., masturbator) from the list. This removal of what would have been considered a sexually deviant practice (the "adulterous wish" that remained invokes a more conventional kind of lust) may point to a more telling omission. For this climactic passage may echo a similar list of negative character traits in the sixth of Whitman's "Sun-Down Papers," one of a sequence of articles with a title that strikingly anticipates the original title of "Crossing Brooklyn Ferry," the "Sun-Down Poem" (*The Uncollected Poetry and Prose of Walt Whitman*, vol. 1, ed. Emory Holloway [Garden City, NY: Doubleday, Page, 1921], 35–37). Whitman wrote these "Sun-Down Papers" during his early adulthood precisely when, evidence suggests, he experienced social shaming due to his emergent sexual attractions to men (see Gay Wilson Allen, *The Solitary Singer: A Critical Biography of Walt Whitman* [New York: Macmillan, 1955], 35–37; Justin Kaplan, *Walt Whitman: A Life* [New York: Simon and Schuster, 1980], 84–87).

44. Reynolds argues that prior to the emergence of the heterosexual/homosexual binary "same-sex passion . . . was seen everywhere in antebellum America." "Adhesiveness" is the phrenological term Whitman uses to describe "friendship between people of the same sex" (Reynolds, *Whitman's America*, 198, 249). The term appears in "Not Heaving from My Ribb'd Breast Only" and "Song of the Open Road," and it is implied throughout the "Calamus" poems, where it seems to include but also potentially extend beyond merely platonic affections for those of the same gender.

45. See Cody Marrs, "Whitman's Latencies: Hegel and the Politics of Time in *Leaves of Grass*," *Arizona Quarterly* 67, no. 1 (2011): 53.

46. That text was not translated into English until the beginning of the twentieth century. See G. W. F. Hegel, *The Phenomenology of Mind*, trans. J. B. Baillie (New York: Macmillan, 1910). It is unlikely Whitman attempted to read it in German.

47. Floyd Stovall, *The Foreground of "Leaves of Grass"* (Charlottesville: University Press of Virginia, 1974), 197. Also see Frederick Henry Hedge, *Prose Writers of Germany*, 2nd ed. (Philadelphia: A. Hart, 1852); Joseph Gostwick, *German Literature* (Edinburgh: William and Robert Chambers, 1849). David Reynolds explains that Whitman considered "Frederick Henry Hedge's *Prose Writers of Germany* . . . 'a big valuable book.' He owned a copy that was given him by a friend, F. S. Gray, inscribed August 29, 1862. But he had been aware of the volume long before that, perhaps as early as 1847, when it was first published, and almost certainly by 1852, when another edition appeared. Whitman did not have much firsthand exposure to European Romantic philosophy but received it through edited collections like Hedge's and through magazine articles he clipped.

218 | Notes to Chapter One

Although it was not until the 1860s that German philosophers, particularly Hegel, had a profound effect on him, their impact was visible in the early poems as well." Later, Reynolds adds that "Whitman's interest in Hegel, dat[ed] at least from the fifties" (*Walt Whitman's America*, 253, 480).

48. Stovall, *The Foreground of "Leaves of Grass,"* 197.

49. Gostwick, *German Literature*, v.

50. Gostwick, *German Literature*, 269–70.

51. Hedge, *Prose Writers of Germany*, 446–56.

52. All of the quotes in this paragraph are from G. W. F. Hegel, *Phenomenology of Spirit*, trans. A. V. Miller (Oxford: Oxford University Press, 1977), 111. Robert R. Williams helpfully elucidates "the double significations in the concept of recognition" (*Hegel's Ethics of Recognition* [Berkeley: University of California Press, 1997], 52ff).

53. Hegel, *Phenomenology*, 112.

54. Williams, *Hegel's Ethics of Recognition*, 56.

55. Hegel, *Phenomenology*, 116.

56. Hegel, *Phenomenology*, 117.

57. By focusing the entire litany on "you," Whitman's speaker does not just assert, as Wynn Thomas notes, "solidarity in weakness" (*The Lunar Light of Whitman's Poetry* [Cambridge, MA: Harvard University Press, 1987], 113). His refusal to condemn the impulse to confess confirms Michael Warner's observation that Whitman aspires to "imagin[e] . . . a commonality not predicated on the erasure of shame" and "not [predicated on] being ashamed of the shame that the shame of the Other provokes in me" ("The Pleasures and Dangers of Shame," in *Gay Shame*, ed. David Halperin and Valerie Traub [Chicago: University of Chicago Press, 2009], 294).

58. Coviello acknowledges that "in some respects [Whitman] resists" identity categories like race and sexuality ("Intimate Nationality," 88). "Crossing Brooklyn Ferry" certainly foregrounds this resistance.

59. See Thomas, *Lunar Light*, 112; Nathanson, *Whitman's Presence*, 91.

60. Christian Haines, *A Desire Called America: Biopolitics, Utopia, and the Literary Commons* (New York: Fordham University Press, 2019), 92.

61. Christian Haines, *A Desire Called America*, 93.

62. Elsewhere in the poem, Whitman characteristically notes "crowds of men and women" or "men and women of a generation" or "the woman or man that looks in my face" or uses gender-neutral language ("others"). Only when he mentions the members of "the rest" who call out to him does he offer a specific identity category (i.e., "young men"). It is not clear that "the rest" is constituted only by men, but a skeptical reader perhaps could make the argument that this gesture (repeated in l.109) is the single instance when Whitman comes close to undercutting his own argument and offering a less than capacious social ontology in this poem.

63. See note 42 for several such readings.

Notes to Chapter Two | 219

64. James Dougherty, "Crossing Brooklyn Ferry," in *A Companion to Walt Whitman*, ed. Donald Kummings (Malden, MA: Blackwell, 2006), 486. Here, Dougherty does not use "recognize" in the post-Hegelian sense that I have been using the word in this essay.

65. Whitman, *Notebooks and Unpublished Prose Manuscripts*, 1:233.

66. Whitman, *Notebooks and Unpublished Prose Manuscripts*, 1:234.

67. David Reynolds points to Whitman's early "admiration for [President James] Polk" and his "expansionist" goals, which were in the "spirit" of "manifest destiny." Unlike Polk, Whitman also supported the proposed Wilmot Proviso, which would have banned slavery from newly acquired territories (*Walt Whitman's America*, 116). For instances of a colonizing impulse in Whitman's later poetry, see "Song of the Exposition" and "Passage to India."

68. Barbara Foley, *Spectres of 1919: Class and Nation in the Making of the New Negro* (Urbana: University of Illinois Press, 2003), 194–95.

69. See, for example, Harris's Spanish-American War era essay, "An Educational Policy for Our New Possessions" in which he argues that "expansion [of the country's territory overseas] is unavoidable in some form" and rejects "the party of opposition which declaims against imperialism" (*National Educational Association: Journal of Proceedings and Addresses of the Thirty Eighth Annual Meeting, 1899* [Chicago: University of Chicago Press, 1900], 72, 71, accessed March, 31, 2016, Google Books). Instead, invoking Kipling's notion of a "white man's burden," he argues that it is a "duty" to "hold conquered nations for their own benefit. . . . We must seek to give them civilization in the highest sense that we can conceive it" (77, 72).

70. Harris also argued in this 1875 essay on "German-English Instruction" that though German immigrants do not wish "to be and remain a German in America," they do wish to "keep" their "patrimony," including their language and customs. Positing the "public school" as the "instrumentality designed for the conservation of true democratic principles," Harris hoped to "eradicate caste distinctions" by educating people in both German and English, so that "illiteracy" is eliminated within both language communities. See the *Twenty-First Annual Report of the Board of Directors of the St. Louis Public Schools for the Year Ending August 1, 1875* (St. Louis: Globe-Democrat Job Printing Company, 1876), 111–13, accessed March 25, 2016, Google Books.

71. Erlin, "Absolute Speculation," 98.

72. Tatlock and Erlin, *German Culture in Nineteenth-Century America*, xii–xiii.

Chapter Two

1. Jean Toomer, *The Wayward and the Seeking: A Collection of Writings by Jean Toomer*, ed. Darwin T. Turner (Washington, DC: Howard University Press, 1980), 121.

220 | Notes to Chapter Two

2. Toomer, *The Wayward and the Seeking*, 121. Toomer includes "The First American" in an April 4, 1922, letter to Waldo Frank, noting that it was written almost two years ago (*Brother Mine: The Correspondence of Jean Toomer and Waldo Frank*, ed. Kathleen Pfeiffer [Urbana: University of Illinois Press, 2010], 31). Robert Jones and Margery Toomer Latimer note that there are no extant copies of "The First American" (Jean Toomer, *The Collected Poems of Jean Toomer*, ed. Robert Jones and Margery Toomer Latimer [Chapel Hill: University of North Carolina Press, 1988], 108).

3. Toomer, *The Wayward and the Seeking*, 121. George Hutchinson argues that this friend was part of the group of "New Negro" intellectuals who met at Georgia Douglas Johnson's home ("Jean Toomer and the 'New Negroes' of Washington," *American Literature* 63, no. 4 [1991]: 689). If so, the anecdote portends Toomer's fraught relationship with cultural pluralists like Alain Locke, who also was a member of the group.

4. Toomer, *The Wayward and the Seeking*, 121. The relative privilege that shaped Toomer's upbringing might explain the trace of condescension in his address to the "colored fellow of more than ordinary mental grasp." For more on Toomer's class status, see Charles Scruggs and Lee VanDemarr (*Jean Toomer and the Terrors of American History* [Philadelphia: University of Pennsylvania Press, 1998], 208–16).

5. Toomer, *The Wayward and the Seeking*, 112–13.

6. Jean Toomer, "Americans and Mary Austin," in "'My Chosen World': Jean Toomer's Articles in *The New York Call*," ed. Charles Scruggs, *Arizona Quarterly* 51, no. 2 (1995): 122, 126. What did Toomer mean when he said "what is true of this writer"? In a 1922 letter to *The Liberator*, Toomer explained that "racially, I seem to have (who knows for sure) seven blood mixtures: French, Dutch, Welsh, Negro, German, Jewish, and Indian. Because of these, my position in America has been a curious one. I have lived equally amid the two race groups. Now white, now colored. From my own point of view I am naturally and inevitably an American. I have striven for a spiritual fusion analogous to the fact of racial intermingling" (*A Jean Toomer Reader: Selected Unpublished Writings*, ed. Frederik L. Rusch, [New York: Oxford University Press, 1993], 15–16).

7. Toomer, *The Wayward and the Seeking*, 121.

8. See note 43 in chapter 1 for hints that Whitman endured shaming as a young adult on account of his sexuality.

9. Though Toomer had published *Cane* in 1923, after a brief period when his "growing need for artistic expression ha[d] pulled . . . [him] deeper and deeper into the Negro group," even then he insisted that he had "no desire to subdue, one to the other" any "single element in me" (*A Jean Toomer Reader*, 16). White and black colleagues and friends pressured him to foreground a "Negro" identity. Writing in a 1923 letter to Waldo Frank, Toomer states his concern about Sherwood Anderson "limit[ing] me to Negro" rather than understanding

that ethnicity as "part of the larger whole" of his identity (*Brother Mine*, 92). In another 1923 letter, Toomer tells his publisher, Horace Liveright, "[F]eature Negro if you wish, but do not expect me to feature it in advertisements for you." Instead, he affirms a "synthetic human and art point of view" paralleling his multiple ethnic backgrounds (*A Jean Toomer Reader*, 94). African American writers either sought to reprint (e.g., James Weldon Johnson) or reprinted without receiving permission (e.g., Alain Locke) portions of *Cane* in their anthologies of African American literature, a topic considered later in this chapter. These and other awkward interactions signaled the beginning of Toomer's separation from the literary world and gradual immersion into the teachings of Georges Gurdjieff, a mystic of Greek and Armenian heritage who attracted a broader following after traveling to Western Europe and the United States in the early twenties. See Jean Toomer, "Why I Entered the Gurdjieff Work," in *Jean Toomer: Selected Essays and Literary Criticism*, ed. Robert B. Jones (Knoxville: University of Tennessee Press, 1996), 106–9.

10. Thoughtful assessments of how Toomer variously presented his racial identity can be found in Barbara Foley (*Jean Toomer: Race, Repression, and Revolution* [Urbana: University of Illinois Press, 2014], 75–80) and in the introduction to *Cane* by Rudolph P. Byrd and Henry Louis Gates, Jr. (in *Cane*, by Jean Toomer, ed. Rudolph P. Byrd and Henry Louis Gates, Jr. [New York: Norton, 2011], xix–lxx). Other commentators specifically addressing Toomer's turning-away from being affiliated with an African American identity include Charles Larson (*Invisible Darkness: Jean Toomer and Nella Larsen* [Iowa City: University of Iowa Press, 1993], 202–3), Nellie McKay (*Jean Toomer—Artist: A Study of His Literary Life and Work, 1894–1936* [Chapel Hill: University of North Carolina Press, 1984], 240–41), and Alice Walker ("The Divided Life of Jean Toomer," in *In Search of Our Mothers' Gardens* [New York: Harcourt, Brace, and Jovanovich, 1982], 64–65).

11. George Hutchinson emphasizes Toomer's interest in forwarding a biracial identity as "a new difference" that is "the only (and the inevitable) route out of America's continuing racial nightmare" ("Jean Toomer and American Racial Discourse," *Texas Studies in Language and Literature* 35, no. 2 [1993]: 244). Emily Lutenski argues that Toomer sought "to theorize a kind of modern American mixed-race identity" ("'A Small Man in Big Spaces': The New Negro, the Mestizo, and Jean Toomer's Southwestern Writing," *MELUS: Multiethnic Literature of the United States* 33, no. 1 [2008]: 22). Stephanie Hawkins, somewhat similarly, finds Toomer "grop[ing] toward the development of a more racially inclusive language to express transracial difference" ("Building the 'Blue' Race: Miscegenation, Mysticism, and the Language of Cognitive Evolution in Jean Toomer's 'Blue Meridian,'" *Texas Studies in Language and Literature* 46, no. 2 [2004]: 170). Some scholars struggle to determine whether Toomer advocates for a multiethnic identity or hopes to transcend racial categories altogether. Ross Posnock describes Toomer's "new mixed and higher race consciousness" as well

222 | Notes to Chapter Two

as a perhaps somewhat different "paradoxical commitment to a raceless race of Americans" (*Color and Culture: Black Writers and the Making of the Modern Intellectual* [Cambridge: Harvard University Press, 1998], 30, 218). Kathleen Pfeiffer similarly argues that "Toomer consistently and vehemently denounced racial categorization," before contending somewhat differently that "Toomer understood the biracial or multiracial person to exist outside the black-white divide" (*Race Passing and American Individualism* [Amherst: University of Massachusetts Press, 2002], 91–92). Barbara Foley suggests that, "in Toomer's writings," there are "multiple slippages" between several identity categories, "'Negro,' 'New Negro,' and 'American race' . . . depending on whether he is stressing the political, economic, biological, or cultural features of their presumed referents" (*Jean Toomer: Race, Repression, and Revolution*, 11).

12. See Diana Williams, "Building the New Race: Jean Toomer's Eugenic Aesthetic" (in *Jean Toomer and the Harlem Renaissance*, ed. Geneviève Fabre and Michel Feith [New Brunswick, NJ: Rutgers University Press, 2001], 191) and Henry Louis Gates, Jr., "The Same Difference: Reading Jean Toomer, 1923–1982" (in *Figures in Black: Words, Signs, and the "Racial" Self* [New York: Oxford University Press, 1987], 208).

13. Obsession with determining Toomer's identity persists. Rudolph P. Byrd and Henry Louis Gates, Jr., conclude their introduction to the newest critical edition of *Cane* by offering extensive archival evidence that Toomer, at times, "decided to pass for white" (lxx). However, Toomer himself straightforwardly states, in at least two texts not published in Toomer's lifetime but now widely available, that "I have passed." "The Crock of Problems" anticipates endless debates about whether he "passed" and to what degree his life paralleled that of James Weldon Johnson's *Autobiography of an Ex-colored Man* by noting, "I have passed," before interrogating the concept of "passing" and rejecting similarities with Johnson's self-hating character (*Selected Essays and Literary Criticism*, 56–58). "Not Typically American" explains, "I have passed from one American group to another American group" before claiming, "while I lived in it, each group became mine." Here, once again, Toomer queries the ethics of "passing" and even what the term means (*A Jean Toomer Reader*, 99, 95–101, passim).

14. Woodrow Wilson, *The Papers of Woodrow Wilson*, vol. 12, *1900–1902*, ed. Arthur Link (Princeton, NJ: Princeton University Press, 1972), 183. Also see Priscilla Wald, *Constituting Americans: Cultural Anxiety and Narrative Form* (Durham, NC: Duke University Press, 1995), 201.

15. Charles W. Chesnutt, "The Future American: What the Race Is Likely to Become in the Process of Time," in *Essays and Speeches*, ed. Joseph R. McElrath, Jr., Robert C. Leitz III, and Jesse S. Crisler (Stanford, CA: Stanford University Press, 1999), 123.

16. W. E. B. DuBois, "The Conservation of Races," in *W. E. B. DuBois: A Reader*, ed. David Levering Lewis (New York: Holt, 1995), 20–21, 23. David

Levering Lewis notes that DuBois "would later consider" the essay "a youthful effusion that was something of an embarrassment as he strode through the new century as slayer of racial doctrines" (*W. E. B. DuBois, 1868–1919: Biography of a Race* [New York: Henry Holt, 1993], 174). Still earlier is Frederick Douglass's Reconstruction-era envisioning of a "composite nationality" including, on the one hand, "all who seek their shelter whether from Asia, Africa, or the Isles of the Sea" and promising that "we shall mold them all, each after his kind into Americans," while, on the other hand, acknowledging that this composite identity would "defy all the ethnological and logical classifications . . . rang[ing] all the way from black to white, with intermediate shades . . . no man can name or number" (*The Speeches of Frederick Douglass: A Critical Edition*, ed. John R. McKivigan, Julie Husband, and Heather L. Kaufman [New Haven, CT: Yale University Press, 2018], 302–3, 285).

17. W. E. B. DuBois, "The Conservation of Races," 24.

18. Horace M. Kallen, "Democracy versus the Melting-Pot: A Study of American Nationality—Part I," *Nation* 100, no. 2590 (February 18, 1915): 194, 193.

19. Horace M. Kallen, "Democracy versus the Melting-Pot: A Study of American Nationality—Part II," *Nation* 100, no. 2591 (February 25, 1915): 219.

20. Kallen, "Democracy versus the Melting-Pot—Part II," 217.

21. Kallen, "Democracy versus the Melting-Pot—Part II," 219.

22. Kallen, "Democracy versus the Melting-Pot—Part II," 220. See also Kallen, "Democracy versus the Melting-Pot—Part I," 194.

23. Kallen, "Democracy versus the Melting-Pot—Part II," 219–20.

24. Horace Kallen, *Culture and Democracy in the United States* (New York: Boni and Liveright, 1924), 43.

25. Waldo Frank, *The Re-discovery of America: An Introduction to a Philosophy of American Life* (New York: Charles Scribner's Sons, 1929), 279, 258, 257.

26. Walter Benn Michaels, *Our America: Nativism, Modernism, and Pluralism* (Durham, NC: Duke University Press, 1995), 64–65. Interest in preserving the distinction between and separation of races, at times, generated unexpected lines of affiliation. On one occasion, Marcus Garvey, the Jamaican-born founder of the Universal Negro Improvement Association who advised people of African descent to return to Africa, "met with Ku Klux Klan leaders, who agreed with his ideas of racial separation" (Greg Carter, *The United States of the United Races: A Utopian History of Racial Mixing* [New York: New York University Press, 2013], 130).

27. Walter Benn Michaels, *Our America*, 140.

28. See, for example, William James, *A Pluralistic Universe* (Lincoln: University of Nebraska Press, 1996). For scholarly commentary on this aspect of James's work, see Harvey Cormier, "William James on Nation and Race," in *Pragmatism, Nation, and Race: Community in the Age of Empire*, ed. Chad Kautzer and Eduardo Mendieta (Bloomington: Indiana University Press, 2009), 142–62; also see Posnock, *Color and Culture*, 23–24, 57–58, 192–93. Posnock, for example,

224 | Notes to Chapter Two

notes that Horace Kallen was a "less than careful student" of James's thought, incorrectly "link[ing] James to a notion of cultural pluralism as an array of irreducible differences" and thus missing how "Jamesian pluralism protested the deforming effect of segregation" (23–24). Stephanie Hawkins has seen affinities between James's anti-essentialist tendencies and Toomer's thought ("Building the Blue Race," 171–72).

29. Randolph Bourne, "Trans-National America," *Atlantic Monthly* 118, no. 1 (1916): 88, 93, 94. Bourne, for example, forwards a "cosmopolitan" ideal for American democracy founded on communication across ethnic and linguistic boundaries: "Let us cease to think of ideals like democracy as magical qualities inherent in certain peoples. Let us speak, not of inferior races, but of inferior civilizations. We are all to educate and to be educated" (87–88).

30. Barbara Foley, *Jean Toomer: Race, Repression, and Revolution*, 90, 84.

31. Ross Posnock has stated that "one of [Alain] Locke's enduring legacies is as a trenchant theorist and practitioner of what is now known as strategic essentialism" (*Color and Culture*, 197).

32. Virginia Jackson, "Specters of the Ballad," *Nineteenth-Century Literature* 71, no. 2 (2016): 193.

33. Jackson, "Specters of the Ballad," 191–92.

34. Jackson, "Specters of the Ballad," 192, 195.

35. Jackson, "Specters of the Ballad," 191.

36. Gavin Jones, *Strange Talk: The Politics of Dialect in Gilded Age America* (Berkeley: University of California Press, 1999), 181, 184.

37. Jones, *Strange Talk*, 186.

38. See, for example, Sonya Posmentier, "Lyric Reading in the Black Ethnographic Archive," *American Literary History* 30, no. 1 (2018): 55–84.

39. Virginia Jackson, *Before Modernism: Inventing American Lyric* (Princeton, NJ: Princeton University Press, 2023), 39. Here, Jackson credits Posmentier for "right[ly]" complicating "my theory of lyricization."

40. Virginia Jackson, "American Romanticism, Again," *Studies in Romanticism* 55, no. 3 (2016): 323.

41. Toomer and Frank, *Brother Mine*, 94. Frank, likely as a result of discussions with Toomer, would later accept that Toomer "did not only write as a Negro" but "of consciousness of Life itself," and he promised that his introduction to *Cane* would reflect this stance (99). Toomer eventually had an affair with Frank's wife, Margaret Naumberg, an act that, along with possible misunderstandings about the eventual introduction to *Cane* as well as Toomer's rejection of cultural pluralism, frayed their friendship.

42. Hutchinson, "The 'New Negroes' of Washington," 683. In 1921, Toomer had sought Locke's participation in a reading group that was seeking to conceptualize "a sound and just criticism of the actual place and condition of the mixed-blood group in this country." Locke had facilitated some of Toomer's

first significant publications (Leonard Harris and Charles Molesworth, *Alain L. Locke: The Biography of a Philosopher* [Chicago: University of Chicago Press, 2008], 171–72).

43. Alain Locke, "Enter the New Negro," *Survey Graphic* 53, no. 11 (1925): 631–34. Locke had wrestled with the implications of cultural pluralism well before Toomer came to know him in the early twenties. As an undergraduate student at Harvard in the first decade of the twentieth century, Locke got to know Horace Kallen, who was then a graduate student. Their conversations about political challenges posed by racial and ethnic difference continued a few years later at Oxford University, where Kallen was on fellowship and where Locke was studying as the first African American Rhodes Scholar. Kallen insisted, in Ross Posnock's words, with a "bullying paternalism," that Locke ground his thinking on the fact of racial difference (Posnock, *Color and Culture*, 192).

44. Locke, "Enter the New Negro," 631.

45. Locke, "Enter the New Negro," 632.

46. Locke, "Enter the New Negro," 632–33, 631, 632.

47. Locke, "Enter the New Negro," 632.

48. Henry Louis Gates, Jr. argues that Alain Locke took the already well-established trope of the "New Negro" and "transformed the militancy associated with the trope and translated this into an apolitical movement of the arts" ("The Trope of a New Negro and the Reconstruction of the Image of the Black," *Representations* 24 [Autumn 1988]: 147). Locke's envisioning of the New Negro may not be militant, but he does foreground some politicized (if not necessarily radically so) poetry in his introductory essay and in the selections published in that issue of *Survey Graphic* (e.g., Langston Hughes and Claude McKay).

49. Locke, "Enter the New Negro," 634, 633.

50. Locke, "Enter the New Negro," 633.

51. Locke, "Enter the New Negro," 633.

52. For more on this topic, see, for example, William Maxwell, *New Negro, Old Left: African-American Writing and Communism between the Wars* (New York: Columbia University Press, 1999).

53. Jean Toomer, "The Negro Emergent," in *Selected Essays and Literary Criticism*, ed. Robert B. Jones, 51, 54, 51, 54. Barbara Foley has argued that Robert Jones's dating of "The Negro Emergent" is incorrect. She offers evidence that it was written in 1925, after Toomer read Locke's introductory essay, rather than in 1924 as Jones alleges. Foley also helpfully discusses the details of Toomer's quarrel with Locke about anthologizing material from *Cane* (Foley, *Jean Toomer: Race, Repression, and Revolution*, 70–74).

54. Jean Toomer, "The Negro Emergent," 49, 51–52. Karen Ford observes that Toomer's occasional "deploy[ing of] essentialist formulations does not preclude" a parallel, "simultaneous interest in more fluid and complicated notions of identity" (*Split-Gut Song: Jean Toomer and the Poetics of Modernity* [Tuscaloosa: University

226 | Notes to Chapter Two

of Alabama Press, 2005], 16). Toomer's deep engagement with Locke's strategic essentialism may help to explain what otherwise might appear to be an almost paradoxical stance. Of course, it can be difficult, at times, to determine whether essentialist gestures are being mobilized as principles believed or as temporary, politically strategic concessions.

55. Alain Locke, "The Negro Poets of the United States," in *Anthology of Magazine Verse for 1926*, ed. William Stanley Braithwaite (Boston: B. J. Brimmer, 1926), 143, 144, 145.

56. Locke, "The Negro Poets of the United States," 144.

57. Locke, "The Negro Poets of the United States," 146–47.

58. Locke, "The Negro Poets of the United States," 146–47.

59. Locke, "The Negro Poets of the United States," 147, 150, 149.

60. Locke, "The Negro Poets of the United States," 147–48.

61. Locke, "The Negro Poets of the United States," 150.

62. Paul Laurence Dunbar, "Negro in Literature," in *The New Negro: Readings on Race, Representation, and African American Culture, 1892–1938*, ed. Henry Louis Gates, Jr. and Gene Andrew Jarrett (Princeton, NJ: Princeton University Press, 2007), 172–73.

63. Dunbar, "Negro in Literature," 172.

64. Dunbar, "Negro in Literature," 172–73.

65. For another early expression of anxiety about linking African Americans with lyricism, see James Weldon Johnson's 1922 preface to *The Book of American Negro Poetry*, especially his concern that "Negro dialect is at present a medium that is not capable of giving expression to the varied conditions of Negro life in America" (*James Weldon Johnson: Writings*, ed. William L. Andrews [New York: The Library of America, 2004], 714). Occasionally, in an effort to thwart associations between dialect and racist stereotypes, critics contextualized African American poets in relation to Scottish and Irish poets who also used dialect and folk idioms. William Stanley Braithwaite identifies William Dean Howells as the originator of this practice, while also pointing to Dunbar as "our first lyric utterance" and affirming that it will be "by his dialect work he will survive" ("The Negro in Literature," *The Crisis* 28, no. 5 [1924]: 207–8). Alain Locke hoped that the current generation of poets would be less "handicapped" by the "dilemma of dialect" ("The Negro Poets of the United States," 147). Charlotte Taussig somewhat similarly worries in 1927 that "it is quite useless to try to understand these men and women who are selves in art, literature and music if we continue making a place for them to conjure visions of 'Aunties' and 'Uncles' and 'Mammies,'" before affirming "a new generation" of African American writers challenging these stereotypes ("The New Negro as Revealed in His Poetry," *Opportunity* 5 [1927]: 108). James Weldon Johnson, in a 1928 essay titled "Race Prejudice and the Negro Artist," affirms how "folk-art contributions" of African Americans, including poetry, "have been exerting an ameliorating effect," albeit

a "slight" one, on race relations (*James Weldon Johnson: Writings*, 754). In another essay from the same year, "The Dilemma of the Negro Author," Johnson expresses concern about how certain "conventions . . . have become binding . . . hard-set stereotypes which are not easily broken up" (*James Weldon Johnson: Writings*, 746).

66. W. E. B. DuBois, "Criteria of Negro Art," in *W. E. B. DuBois: A Reader*, ed. David Levering Lewis (Holt: New York, 1995), 512.

67. DuBois, "Criteria of Negro Art," 514–15. For a helpful discussion of DuBois's relationship to Hegelian thinking (including St. Louis Hegelian thinking), see Shamoon Zamir, *Dark Voices: W. E. B. DuBois and American Thought, 1888–1903* (Chicago: The University of Chicago Press, 1995), 113–68.

68. Michael North, *The Dialect of Modernism: Race, Language, and Twentieth-Century Literature* (Oxford: Oxford University Press, 1994), 150.

69. Sterling Brown, "Our Literary Audience," *Opportunity* 8 (1930): 42.

70. Claude McKay, "A Negro Writer to his Critics," in *The Passion of Claude McKay: Selected Poetry and Prose 1912–1948*, ed. Wayne F. Cooper (New York: Schocken, 1973), 138.

71. Alain Locke, "Sterling Brown: The New Negro Folk-Poet," in *Negro: Anthology Made by Nancy Cunard, 1931–1933* (New York: Negro Universities Press, 1969), 111.

72. Only a couple sentences later, Locke goes on to emphasize his opposition to "poetry conceived in doctrinaire Marxist formulae" (Alain Locke, "Propaganda—or Poetry?," in *The Works of Alain Locke*, ed. Charles Molesworth [Oxford: Oxford University Press, 2012], 239).

73. Jean Toomer, "Race Problems and Modern Society," in *Jean Toomer: Selected Essays and Literary Criticism*, ed. Robert Jones (Knoxville: University of Tennessee Press, 1996), 60–76. In *Jean Toomer: Race, Repression, and Revolution*, Barbara Foley argues that Toomer was a committed economic progressive early in his career (prior to *Cane*). "Race Problems and Modern Society," she notes, shows how Toomer "deepened his involvement with the Gurdjieff movement" while "remain[ing] drawn to a class analysis of the roots of racism" (48). For more on Toomer's relationship to Gurdjieff, see the first chapter of Jon Woodson, *To Make a New Race: Gurdjieff, Toomer, and the Harlem Renaissance* (Jackson: University Press of Mississippi, 1999), 29–46.

74. Toomer, "Race Problems and Modern Society," 61–62, 67.

75. Toomer, "Race Problems and Modern Society," 71, 70.

76. Toomer, "Race Problems and Modern Society," 71.

77. Toomer, "Race Problems and Modern Society," 69.

78. Toomer, "Race Problems and Modern Society," 72–73.

79. Toomer, "Race Problems and Modern Society," 71. Earlier in the essay, Toomer asserts that biological essentialism was being demolished by scholars like "Roland Dixon, Franz Boas, A. L. Kroeber, Ellsworth Huntington, and Flinders Petrie," who agreed that "the whole subject of race [as a biological category]

228 | Notes to Chapter Two

is uncertain and somewhat confused" at best (63). Toomer agrees and insists that "if we were never taught and never acquired ideas, opinions, beliefs, and superstitions about race[,] . . . we would never have any responses or behavior in terms of race" (64–65).

80. Toomer, "Race Problems and Modern Society," 73–74.

81. Toomer, "Race Problems and Modern Society," 70.

82. Toomer, "Race Problems and Modern Society," 72.

83. Robert Jones and Margery Toomer Latimer offer the following helpful note about the composition of "The Blue Meridian": "A variation of the first 125 lines of 'The Blue Meridian' was first published as 'Brown River, Smile' in *Pagany* 3 (Winter 1932): 29–33. ('The First American,' the germinal text for 'Brown River, Smile,' is not among Toomer's unpublished manuscripts and is apparently nonextant.) Several years later, a revised and expanded version of this text appeared in *New Caravan*, ed. Alfred Kreymborg, Lewis Mumford, and Paul Rosenfeld (New York: W. W. Norton and Company, 1936): 633–53 as 'Blue Meridian' (no definite article). A revised version of the 1936 text appeared in *The Poetry of the Negro*, 1746–1970, ed. Langston Hughes and Arna Bontemps (Garden City, N.Y.: Doubleday, 1970): 107–33. Darwin Turner adopts the 1970 text for inclusion in *The Wayward and The Seeking*, asserting that this latest draft constitutes Toomer's final version of the poem. I agree with Turner's assertion and have similarly adopted the 1970 text for inclusion in this volume" (*The Collected Poems of Jean Toomer*, ed. Robert B. Jones and Margery Toomer Latimer [Chapel Hill: University of North Carolina Press, 1988], 108). This chapter follows that rendering of the text. Due to the poem's length, quotes from "The Blue Meridian" will be cited in the main text according to page number.

84. George Hutchinson, *The Harlem Renaissance in Black and White* (Cambridge, MA: Harvard University Press, 1995), 418.

85. Claude McKay, "The Mulatto," in *Complete Poems*, ed. William J. Maxwell (Urbana: University of Illinois Press, 2004), 210.

86. Langston Hughes, "Mulatto," in *The Collected Poems of Langston Hughes*, ed. Arnold Rampersad (New York: Vintage Classics, 1994), 100–101.

87. Georgia Douglas Johnson, "The Riddle," in *The New Negro: An Interpretation*, ed. Alain Locke (New York: Albert and Charles Boni, 1925), 147. George Hutchinson speculates that the person described in "'The Riddle' . . . may owe something to Jean Toomer" (*The Harlem Renaissance in Black and White*, 418).

88. Langston Hughes, "Daybreak in Alabama," in *The Collected Poems of Langston Hughes*, 220–21.

89. Hughes's "Let America Be America Again" offers an intriguing (and Whitmanian, with its cataloguing of peoples, seeming reference to "Pioneers! O Pioneers!," and impulse toward self-querying) if only partial analogy (*The Collected Poems of Langston Hughes*, 189–91). First published in 1936, decidedly after the highpoint of cultural pluralism and amid a Depression-era upsurge of economic

Notes to Chapter Two | 229

leftism, the poem is written so that its "I" becomes associated with a range of identities, including, among others, the "poor white" (19) or "Negro" (20) or "red man" (21) or "immigrant" (22) or "farmer" (31) or "worker" (32). The poem, however, does not address multiethnic identities, and its recognizing impulse reinforces established identity categories while suggesting that the political and economic interests of vulnerable members of various groups may, at least partially, align.

90. Writing about "The Blue Meridian," Karen Jackson Ford argues that Toomer's "poems [after *Cane*] became antipoetical tracts" (*Split-Gut Song*, 161). Rudolph Byrd similarly hears only "a voice shouting a thesis" (*Jean Toomer's Years with Gurdjieff: Portrait of an Artist, 1923–1936* [Athens, GA: University of Georgia Press, 1990], 181). Byrd also finds Toomer drawing from and sometimes reacting against a cultural context including Walt Whitman, Hart Crane, T. S. Eliot, Carl Sandburg, Sterling Brown, and Robert Frost (157–58). Charles Larson finds an almost embarrassing amount of "indebtedness to Walt Whitman, Carl Sandburg, T. S. Eliot, Hart Crane, and even Robinson Jeffers[, making the poem] a hodgepodge of borrowed ideas and images from Toomer's contemporaries" (*Invisible Darkness*, 147).

91. Ford, *Split-Gut Song*, 144. For another reading of Toomer's poetry in *Cane* and, in particular, how these poems reflect Toomer's "quest for generic innovation" while being "tormented by the racialized logic of lyric," see Ben Glaser, *Modernism's Metronome: Meter and Twentieth-Century Poetics* (Baltimore: Johns Hopkins University Press, 2020), 136.

92. Ford, *Split-Gut Song*, 156.

93. Ford, *Split-Gut Song*, 157.

94. Karen Ford associates Toomer's desire to "speak for the one and the all because the one is the all" with Whitman's "Song of Myself" (*Split-Gut Song*, 151).

95. Hawkins, "Building the 'Blue' Race," 164.

96. See Scruggs and VanDemarr, *Jean Toomer and the Terrors of American History*, 216–17.

97. Jon Woodson describes "The Blue Meridian" as "a Whitmanian paraphrase of the major themes and ideas found in [H. P.] Blavatsky's *The Secret Doctrine*. Toomer meant by 'Blue Meridian' (a term he compounded from Blavatsky's 'Meridian of Races' . . . and 'azure seats' . . .) that mankind was crossing the balance point between spirit and matter in the direction of spiritual ascent" (*To Make a New Race*, 44).

98. See also Rudolph Byrd, *Jean Toomer's Years with Gurdjieff*, 163–65; Ford, *Split-Gut Song*, 152–55; Charles Larson, *Invisible Darkness*, 148. It is additionally clear that Toomer is building on a line of thinking that goes back at least as far as Charles Chesnutt's turn-of-the-century idea that these same three races would amalgamate. As I note earlier in this chapter, Chesnutt thought that this "future American race," though it is multiethnic in origin, nevertheless "will be predominantly white" ("The Future American," 123). However, while Toomer centers his

230 | Notes to Chapter Two

poem on the same three races, he ends it by describing the new race in terms that defy racial categorization as "the man of blue or purple / Beyond the little tags and small marks" (72). In a passage from his unpublished prose, Toomer is more blunt in words that amplify and go beyond the poem: "In America, the white race, the black race, the red race, the brown race must die before there can be a new race. They are dying. America is eating them. . . . There is a new race here. . . . This new race is neither white nor black nor red nor brown" (*A Jean Toomer Reader*, 107).

99. Waldo Frank, *Our America* (New York: Boni and Liveright, 1919), 97, 115.

100. Ford, *Split-Gut Song*, 156.

101. See Frederik Rusch, "The Blue Man: Jean Toomer's Solution to His Problems of Identity," *Obsidian* 6 (1980): 48.

102. Cynthia Earl Kerman and Richard Eldridge, *The Lives of Jean Toomer: A Hunger for Wholeness* (Baton Rouge: Louisiana State University Press, 1987), 226.

103. Jean Toomer, "Race Problems and Modern Society," 74. For more on Toomer's eugenic rhetoric, see Diana Williams, "Building the New Race." Stephanie Hawkins argues that Toomer's references to eugenics show him "grop[ing] toward the development of a more racially inclusive language to express transracial difference" ("Building the 'Blue' Race," 170). Toomer was not alone among writers associated with the Harlem Renaissance in using eugenic rhetoric that, at the time, had not been thoroughly interrogated in the way it would be after the fall of the Third Reich. For more on Harlem Renaissance writers and eugenics, see Daylanne K. English, *Unnatural Selections: Eugenics in American Modernism and the Harlem Renaissance* (Chapel Hill: University of North Carolina Press, 2004).

104. See also Justin Parks, "Race and National Identity in Modernist Anthropology and Jean Toomer's 'The Blue Meridian,'" *Texas Studies in Literature and Language* 62, no. 3 (2020): 356.

105. Toomer, "Race Problems and Modern Society," 73.

106. James Weldon Johnson, "Preface to the Book of American Negro Poetry," in *Writings*, ed. William L. Andrews (New York: Literary Classics of the United States, 2004), 688.

107. Johnson, "Preface to the Book of American Negro Poetry," 712.

108. Johnson, "Preface to the Book of American Negro Poetry," 713–14.

109. Correspondence between James Weldon Johnson and Jean Toomer, in *Letters from Black America*, ed. Pamela Newkirk (New York: Farrar, Straus and Giroux, 2009), 281–82.

110. Correspondence between James Weldon Johnson and Jean Toomer, *Letters from Black America*, 282–83.

111. Correspondence between James Weldon Johnson and Jean Toomer, *Letters from Black America*, 282.

112. James Weldon Johnson, "Preface to the Book of American Negro Poetry," 712.

Chapter Three

1. *Laws of New York, 1923*, ch. 642, pp. 960–61. The amended law went into effect on May 22, 1923. Also see George Chauncey, *Gay New York: Gender, Urban Culture, and the Making of the Gay Male World, 1890–1940* (New York: Basic Books, 1994), 172.

2. George Chauncey, "The Forgotten History of Gay Entrapment," *theatlantic.com*, June 25, 2019, https://www.theatlantic.com/ideas/archive/2019/06/before-stonewall-biggest-threat-was-entrapment/590536/.

3. Crane, for example, wondered in a May 29, 1927, letter to Yvor Winters whether prejudice against "homosexuals" (and their "missing sensibilities") informed Winters's estimation of artists like Leonardo Da Vinci. Three years later, in a June 4, 1930, letter, Crane would express the same worry (in slightly coded language) about whether "prejudices toward a biological (or is it autobiographical) approach to [analyzing] poetry" shaped Winters's negative estimation of *The Bridge* (Hart Crane, *Complete Poems and Selected Letters*, ed. Langdon Hammer [New York: Literary Classics of the United States, 2006], 544, 641).

4. Hart Crane, *Complete Poems and Selected Letters*, 329.

5. See Michael Snediker, *Queer Optimism: Lyric Personhood and Other Felicitous Persuasions* (Minneapolis: University of Minnesota Press, 2009); John Vincent, *Queer Lyrics: Difficulty and Closure in American Poetry* (New York: Palgrave Macmillan, 2002); Brian Reed, *Hart Crane: After His Lights* (Tuscaloosa: University of Alabama Press, 2006), especially ch. 4, "How to Write a Lyric," 97–125.

6. By the mid-twentieth century, criminalization, along with psychological and psychiatric pathologizing and other forms of social exclusion, led many people impacted by "prejudices . . . *of that nature*" (to use Crane's phrase) toward an understanding of sexuality as a political identity needing social recognition. But Crane, as Christopher Nealon observes, could not write "an 'ethnic' literature," a "designation" best used for "queer literature that has been published since Stonewall, by which time a national lesbian and gay culture provides a pool of character types (the queen, the ingenue, the bartender) and narrative tropes (coming out, first love, breaking up, homophobic violence) to draw on" while relying "on a complicity with queer audiences." Yet it is also important to keep in mind that the "pathology to politics" narrative, as Nealon notes, can be too neatly drawn (*Foundlings: Lesbian and Gay Historical Emotion before Stonewall* [Durham, NC: Duke University Press, 2001], 10, 9).

7. Hart Crane, *Complete Poems and Selected Letters*, 199, 759.

232 | Notes to Chapter Three

8. See, for example, letters to William Wright (in Hart Crane, *Complete Poems and Selected Letters*, 256, 654) and a March 31, 1932, letter to Caresse Crosby (in Hart Crane, *The Letters of Hart Crane*, ed. Brom Weber [Berkeley: University of California Press, 1965], 405; this letter is not in the other editions of Crane's letters).

9. These numbers are based on keyword searches of the edition of *The Letters of Hart Crane* edited by Brom Weber. Though this edition, in certain ways, has been superseded by those of Langdon Hammer, *O My Land, My Friends: The Selected Letters of Hart Crane* (New York: Four Walls Eight Windows, 1997), which Hammer coedited with Brom Weber, and the letters included in the Library of America's *Complete Poems and Selected Letters*, I could find no searchable version of these later editions.

10. Virginia Jackson and Yopie Prins, eds., *The Lyric Theory Reader* (Baltimore: Johns Hopkins University Press, 2014), 4–5.

11. See Ezra Pound, *Des Imagistes: An Anthology* (New York: Frank Shay, 1917). Stanton Coblentz explains that, in both of his volumes, *Modern American Lyrics* (New York: Minton, Balch, and Company, 1924) and *Modern British Lyrics* (New York: Minton, Balch, and Company, 1925), he chose only "poems with a lyrical element; and, as in 'Modern American Lyrics,' I have confined myself to verse in traditional forms and meters, making the quality of music the primary technical test of the poetic" (vi). Introducing L. D'O. Walters's *The Year's at the Spring: An Anthology of Recent Poetry* [(New York: Brentano, 1920), Project Gutenberg], Harold Monro interchangeably describes "lyrical poetry," "English lyrical poetry," and "English poetry" and advises that "this anthology as a whole is romantic." The Georgian poet, J. C. Squire introduces his *Selections from Modern Poets* (London: Martin Secker, 1921) by noting "a very large number of poets who write only or mainly in lyrical forms" (v), before asking, "[W]here is the ambitious work on a large scale?" (vi) and then asserting that "I do not think that the age, even if admitted to be purely lyrical, stands in need of defence" (vi), and "Should our literary age be remembered by posterity solely as an age during which fifty men had written lyrics of some durability for their truth and beauty, it would not be remembered with contempt" (vi–vii)

12. Bruce Weirick's *From Whitman to Sandburg in American Poetry: A Critical Survey* (New York: Macmillan, 1924) weighs the merits of both "lyricists" and "the *new* poetry" (167ff). Harriet Monroe and Alice Henderson's *The New Poetry: An Anthology of Twentieth-Century Verse in English* (New York: Macmillan, 1923) critiques clichéd, "'poetic' shifts of language" and "rhetorical excesses" associated with "Victorian poetry" while emphasizing that modern poets "follow the great tradition when they seek a vehicle suited to their own epoch" (xxxv–xxxvi). In finding this balance, Monroe and Henderson's introductory materials only use the word lyric a few times, perhaps because it does not seem to reflect

Notes to Chapter Three | 233

sufficiently the expansiveness of the "modern" or "new" poetry they anthologize. Babette Deutsch, in her critical study *This Modern Poetry* (London: Faber and Faber, 1935) would seem to agree, structuring her book according to "isms" (e.g., chapters entitled "Returning to Realism," "The Imagists and their Bequest," "Heirs of the Symbolists," "Filiations with the Metaphysicals," and so on) with only a smattering of references to lyrics or more specific genres. And Louis Untermeyer's introduction to his *Modern American Poetry: A Critical Anthology* 3rd rev. ed. (New York: Harcourt, Brace, 1925) describes a moment with "lyric significance which no other period can equal" (26) but also emphasizes an unprecedented "catholicity. . . . All forms are being used—new ones even are being invented. Both in the conventional and in the experimental modes, America has become a literary melting pot in every sense" (27). The resulting text is indeed quite wide-ranging and reflects this range by toggling between a more generalized use of "lyric" and more specific references to genres. Sharon Brown's *Poetry of Our Times* (Chicago: Scott, Foresman, 1928) and *Twentieth-Century Poetry*, eds. John Drinkwater, Henry Seidel Canby, and William Rose Benet (New York: Houghton Mifflin, 1929) also largely follow this model with fairly expansive inclusion of a variety of idioms.

13. Only, briefly, in Deutsch, *This Modern Poetry*, where Crane is noted for an "eclecticism" characteristic of the modern poet who "moves from the style of one period or of one predecessor to that of another with unexampled freedom" (23) and in Drinkwater, Canby, and Benet, *Twentieth-Century Poetry*, where he is represented by one poem, "The Tunnel" (573ff).

14. Alan Golding's *From Outlaw to Classic: Canons in American Poetry* (Madison: University of Wisconsin Press, 1995) contains an overview of American poetry anthologies that remains useful as a starting point (3–40).

15. Crane, *Complete Poems and Selected Letters*, 646.

16. At the time of the 1923 drafts, Crane imagined "The Bridge" as a long poem that would conclude his first collection rather than being a book-length poem itself (see *Complete Poems and Selected Letters*, 322). Discussion of the early drafts, thus, will reference "The Bridge," whereas discussion of the later, book-length conceptualization of the project will reference *The Bridge*.

17. According to Edward Brunner, these poems "evince such strong connections to Crane's original idea of his epic that they are best considered as extensions of it" (*Splendid Failure: Hart Crane and the Making of The Bridge* [Urbana: University of Illinois Press, 1985], 29).

18. Crane, *Complete Poems and Selected Letters*, 163, 18–19.

19. Hart Crane and Jean Toomer, "Bright Stones: An Exchange of Letters," ed. Langdon Hammer, *Yale Review* 84, no. 2 (1996): 22.

20. Crane, *Complete Poems and Selected Letters*, 321.

21. Crane, *Complete Poems and Selected Letters*, 347.

234 | Notes to Chapter Three

22. Crane, *Complete Poems and Selected Letters*, 359.

23. This is the draft of the poem Crane sent to Toomer that can be found in Hart Crane and Jean Toomer, "Bright Stones: An Exchange of Letters," 26–27.

24. Robert Martin has declared "Possessions" to be "the first poem of the modern urban homosexual in search of sex. . . . He desires and yet he fears; he will go and yet he hesitates" (*The Homosexual Tradition in American Poetry* [Iowa City: University of Iowa Press, 1998], 128). According to Michael Snediker, the poem "suggests the stratagems of a cruise in its capacity to cover its own tracks." In this way, it "cannot guarantee its being understood . . . so much as guarantee its ever potentially occluded availability" (*Queer Optimism*, 64).

25. Crane, *Complete Poems and Selected Letters*, 13.

26. Crane, *Complete Poems and Selected Letters*, 349. Hammer makes it clear that "the poem" Crane mentions in this letter was indeed "Possessions" (Crane and Toomer, "Bright Stones: An Exchange of Letters," 25).

27. Crane and Toomer, "Bright Stones: An Exchange of Letters," 27–28.

28. Crane, *Complete Poems and Selected Letters*, 350.

29. Crane, *Complete Poems and Selected Letters*, 164.

30. John Irwin associates this imagery with the return of Christ described in Revelation (*Hart Crane's Poetry: "Appollinaire Lived in Paris, I live in Cleveland, Ohio"* [Baltimore: Johns Hopkins University Press, 2011], 288–89). But Crane equally might have in mind the conflation of the "cloud" and "pillar of fire" by which God led the people of Israel (Exodus 13:21) along with (given the poem's initial imperative to "[w]itness") St. Paul's "cloud of witnesses" who watch "us run the race marked out for us" (Hebrews 12:1).

31. Corresponding with Joseph Stella on January 24, 1929, Crane explains that he "ha[s] been busy" with writing *The Bridge* "for the last three years," which would date the inception of *The Bridge* to early 1926, when he returned to the project, not when he first began conceptualizing it in 1923 (*Complete Poems and Selected Letters*, 606). Similarly, in a June 1930 letter to Yvor Winters, Crane describes the "over five years of sustained something-or-other" involved in "compos[ing] *The Bridge*," placing the commencement of the project slightly earlier, around mid-1925, but still long after early 1923 (*Complete Poems and Selected Letters*, 644).

32. Thomas E. Yingling, *Hart Crane and the Homosexual Text: New Thresholds, New Anatomies* (Chicago: University of Chicago Press, 1990), 143, 251.

33. Langdon Hammer, *Hart Crane and Allen Tate: Janus-Faced Modernism* (Princeton, NJ: Princeton University Press, 1993), 172.

34. Reed, *Hart Crane: After His Lights*, 5, 40.

35. One thinks of how Pound wrote his more intensely historically engaged Malatesta Cantos in 1922–1923, immediately after *The Waste Land* was published. In 1923, William Carlos Williams published *Spring and All* and Marianne Moore wrote "Marriage" and "An Octopus." Crane explained to Louis

Untermeyer on January 19, 1923 that "For the Marriage of Faustus and Helen" was "designed to erect an almost antithetical spiritual attitude to the pessimism of *The Waste Land*, although the poem was well finished before *The Wasteland* [*sic*] appeared," an affirmation "that ecstacy [*sic*] and beauty are as possible to the active imagination now as ever" (*Complete Poems and Selected Letters*, 310). But shortly thereafter, Crane begins to feel as if "Faustus and Helen" was not a sufficient reply to Eliot. On February 6, 1923, Crane informs Gorham Munson that he is "ruminating on a new longish [at this point, single] poem under the title of *The Bridge*, which carries on further the tendencies manifest in 'F and H,'" but he says little more than that "it will be extremely difficult to accomplish it as I see it now," sentiments echoed in a letter on the same day to Allen Tate (*Complete Poems and Selected Letters*, 314–15).

36. In late 1922 and early 1923, Crane and Frank exchange letters, leading to a meeting a few months later. Shortly thereafter, Frank positioned himself as a mentor, advocating for Crane's work in much the same way he did for Toomer by praising it in print and making initial contacts with publishers (Hart Crane and Waldo Frank, *The Correspondence between Hart Crane and Waldo Frank*, ed. Steve H. Cook [Troy, NY: Whitson, 1998], 45–51). Writing to Gorham Munson on February 18, 1923, only a matter of weeks after he began conceptualizing "the least outline" of what would become *The Bridge*, he describes the project in terms somewhat affiliated with Frank's work: "Very roughly, it concerns a mystical synthesis of 'America.' History and fact, location, etc. all have to be transfigured into abstract form that would almost function independently of its subject matter. The initial impulses of 'our people' will have to be gathered up toward the climax of the bridge, symbol of our constructive future, our unique identity, in which is included also our scientific hopes and achievements of the future" (Crane, *Complete Poems and Selected Letters*, 321).

References to a "mystical synthesis of 'America'" and "our people" raise the possibility that Crane has in mind Waldo Frank's *Our America*, a work from 1919 that deems "America" a "mystic word" whose meaning is still being disclosed. Frank hopes that his book will be "a gesture of self-knowledge" about an "America we are discovering for ourselves" or, put more precisely in cultural pluralist terms, the "discovery of adumbrating groups," an "adventure" in which "the quality of our search shall be the nature of the America we create" (Waldo Frank, *Our America* [New York: Boni and Liveright, 1919], 10, 5, 9–10). In a February 20, 1923, letter to Wilbur Underwood, Crane describes "a synthesis of America and its structural identity now, called *The Bridge*," a phrase that further echoes Waldo Frank (*Complete Poems and Selected Letters*, 325). The early drafts themselves, however, do not allude to Frank or his larger national agenda. As we shall see, Crane begins by writing the climax of the poem. Perhaps he intended that the beginning of the poem would eventually arrive at this conclusion by way of Frank's thought, only to find that this was not possible within his 1923

236 | Notes to Chapter Three

conception of the poem. It is also possible that Crane described *The Bridge* to his friends with phrases associated with Frank's work as a kind of shorthand expression of his ambition within politically understandable terms that served as a veneer over (or point of entry into) a project that he intended, at least initially, to be stranger, more radically democratic than Frank's. In any case, Crane's early drafts of *The Bridge* show a wariness toward or even disinterest in Frank and his cultural pluralist ideology that disappears when he recommences the project in 1925–1926.

37. In a November 20, 1922, letter to Gorham Munson, Crane deems *The Waste Land* "good, of course, but so damned dead" (*Complete Poems and Selected Letters*, 298). Crane's January 19, 1923, letter to Louis Untermeyer expresses his hope to create "a kind of bridge that is . . . a more creative and stimulating thing than the settled formula of Mr. Eliot, superior technician that he is!" (*Complete Poems and Selected Letters*, 310–11).

38. Crane, *Complete Poems and Selected Letters*, 308.

39. Crane, *Complete Poems and Selected Letters*, 219, 290.

40. Both Eliot and Frank would influence the post-1925/1926 version of *The Bridge* more explicitly. For example, "The Tunnel," a poem Eliot himself published in the *Criterion*, features a Prufrock-esque speaker, while "The Dance," as we shall see, owes much to Waldo Frank's work.

41. Crane often noted that he began composing *The Bridge* by writing its conclusion (*Complete Poems and Selected Letters*, 325, 348), explaining that he knew where he wanted to go but struggled to get there (314, 321–22, 348). Some scholars have suggested that this writing strategy portended a work that could never be completed successfully. Margaret Dickie argued that, from a formal perspective alone, Crane set himself a project that inevitably resulted in such a rupture: "By starting his poem with the ending and then writing an opening section that essentially repeats the ending, Crane made the intervening sections, the bridge between first and last, not only unnecessary but impossible to write" ("The Backward Flight of *The Bridge*" *American Literature* 57, no. 1 [1985]: 83). See also Lee Edelman, *Transmemberment of Song: Hart Crane's Anatomies of Rhetoric and Desire* (Palo Alto, CA: Stanford University Press, 1987), 192–93.

42. Though it hardly counts as a draft, about a week earlier, on February 12, 1923, Crane sent Allen Tate a single quatrain that later would be used, after some editing, in the "Van Winkle" section: "Macadam, gun grey as the tunny's pelt, / Leaps from Far Rockaway to Golden Gate, / For first it was the road, the road only / We heeded in joint piracy and pushed" (*Complete Poems and Selected Letters*, 320).

43. Crane, *Complete Poems and Selected Letters*, 324.

44. Crane, *Complete Poems and Selected Letters*, 325.

45. Langdon Hammer notes that Crane's phrasing nevertheless draws attention to the suicidal potential even as his poem's narrative swerves away from it (*Hart Crane and Allen Tate: Janus-Faced Modernism,* 187–88).

Notes to Chapter Three | 237

46. Hammer, *Janus-Faced Modernism*, 187.

47. This draft was not part of Crane's correspondence and is available in the appendix labeled "The Development of 'Atlantis'" in Brom Weber, *Hart Crane: A Biographical and Critical Study* (New York: Bodley Press, 1948), 425–26.

48. Crane, *Complete Poems and Selected Letters*, 321.

49. All of the quotes in this paragraph are drawn from Crane, *Complete Poems and Selected Letters*, 340–42.

50. For the former, see Ezra Pound's "A Retrospect" (in *Ezra Pound's Early Writings: Poems and Prose*, ed. Ira Nadel [New York: Penguin, 2005], 252–65). For the latter, see Gillian White's discussion of a strand of poets influenced by William Carlos Williams, who became wary, even ashamed, of metaphor, insofar as it can become associated with a kind of subjective expression that does not "respect alterity" (*Lyric Shame: The "Lyric" Subject of Contemporary American Poetry* [Cambridge, MA: Harvard University Press, 2014], 56). Other modernist peers like Marianne Moore sought to use metaphor to do just that: to respect alterity rather than attempt to possess it. For example, the scene depicted in "A Grave," a poem critiquing the tendency in "human nature to stand in the middle of a thing," features "firs . . . with an emerald turkey-foot at the top" and "birds swim[ming] through the air at top speed, emitting cat-calls" (*Complete Poems* [New York: Macmillan/Penguin, 1994], 49). Respecting alterity, in this poem, requires jumbling readers' taxonomies of the world in a way that challenges anthropocentrism.

51. Hart Crane and Harriet Monroe, "A Discussion with Hart Crane," *Poetry* 29, no. 1 (1926): 35.

52. Crane and Monroe, "A Discussion with Hart Crane," 36.

53. Leonard Diepeveen, *The Difficulties of Modernism* (New York: Routledge, 2003), 35, xv.

54. Crane and Monroe, "A Discussion with Hart Crane," 36.

55. Crane and Monroe, "A Discussion with Hart Crane," 36; Crane, *Complete Poems and Selected Letters*, 341.

56. Crane and Monroe, "A Discussion with Hart Crane," 36.

57. Crane and Monroe, "A Discussion with Hart Crane," 38.

58. Contemporary scholarship on the "logic of metaphor" has been more sympathetic to Crane's interrogation of norms. But assessment of the alternate social formations potentially generated by this aspect of Crane's lyricism has been curtailed by a tendency to confine Crane within quasi-psychoanalytic readings often prompted by Crane's reference, in his short essay "General Aims and Theories," to "associational meanings" (*Complete Poems and Selected Letters*, 163). In a valuable essay, John Irwin notes the potential to develop a "counterworld of the poem" that is "not . . . a denial of objective reality" but instead "a questioning of the status of objective reality as the sole criterion of value." But Irwin does not explore this counterworld as a space for a different kind of sociality that might generate the "higher quality of life" Crane yearns for ("Hart Crane's 'Logic of

238 | Notes to Chapter Three

Metaphor,' in *Critical Essays on Hart Crane*, ed. David R. Clark [Boston: G. K. Hall, 1982], 218). Irwin reads the "logic of metaphor" psychoanalytically in terms of a "shattering of the surface-form relationships of normal lexicon and syntax" that generates a reading experience akin to "the controlled free association used by psychoanalysts to reach the universals of the unconscious" (219). Tim Dean analogizes Crane's "metaphoric logic . . . to rational logic as poetic language is to ordinary language—and, we might add, as the unconscious is to consciousness." But Dean explains (in terms that perhaps merge Irwin with Leo Bersani) that "metaphoric logic produces . . . images of intensity that involve forms of shattering and destruction," such that even Crane's conceptualization of "transmemberment" becomes a "shattering of the self" akin to a kind of dismemberment ("Hart Crane's Poetics of Privacy," *American Literary History* 8, no. 1 [1996]: 86, 88, 95). Lee Edelman describes a similarly disjunctive dynamic, foregrounding the language of rhetoric and arguing that the "logic of metaphor" might best be understood as a "logic of catechresis" driven by an "ideology of rupture, of violent transvaluation" (*Transmemberment of Song*, 42, 13). More recently Angela Beckett has asked whether this "emphasis on self-shattering discounts the importance of feeling and the role of emotional connectives in the recuperation of semantic excess." Beckett instead looks to Paul Ricoeur's conceptualization of metaphor in terms of "rapprochement," which maintains acknowledgment of the "disjunctive pressure between dissimilar terms" while "abolish[ing] the distance between terms," as a means of understanding how "Crane's poetry encrypts and transfigures ambivalent forms of sexual desire" ("The [Il]logic of Metaphor in Crane's *The Bridge*," *Textual Practice* 25, no. 1 [2011]: 160, 163, 159).

59. Crane, *Complete Poems and Selected Letters*, 163 (Crane's emphasis).

60. Irwin, "Hart Crane's 'Logic of Metaphor,' " 216.

61. Crane explains to Yvor Winters: "[I]t [a 'poem'] must convey and even accentuate the reality of it's subject [*sic*]. That's the service of metaphor. And it must not only convey but locate and focus the *value* of the material in our complete consciousness" (*Complete Poems and Selected Letters*, 532; Crane's emphasis).

62. Crane, *Complete Poems and Selected Letters*, 342.

63. Langdon Hammer includes this letter in *Complete Poems and Selected Letters* but does not include the enclosed draft of what would become "Atlantis." This draft can be found in Brom Weber, *Hart Crane: A Biographical and Critical Study*, 426–28.

64. A year later, in an April 21, 1924, letter to Waldo Frank, Crane describes his intense new relationship with Emil Opffer in strikingly similar imagery: "It's true, Waldo, that so much more than my frustrations and multitude of humiliations has been answered in this reality and promise that I feel that whatever event the future holds is justified beforehand. And I have been able to give freedom and life which was acknowledged in the ecstacy [*sic*] of walking hand in hand across the most beautiful bridge in the world, the cables enclosing us and pulling us

Notes to Chapter Three | 239

upward in such a dance as I have never walked and never can walk with another" (*Complete Poems and Selected Letters*, 384). For more on the relationship between Crane and Opffer, see Clive Fisher, *Hart Crane: A Life* (New Haven, CT: Yale University Press, 2002), 218–26.

65. The ellipsis at the end of line 2 is Crane's. The remainder of the draft continues, incorporating most of the text sent to Steiglitz. Like the draft sent to Steiglitz, this draft sent to the Rychtariks can be found in Weber, *Hart Crane: A Biographical and Critical Study*, 428–29.

66. Crane, *Complete Poems and Selected Letters*, 348.

67. In a 1919 interview in the *Akron Sunday Times*, Crane explained how, in earning a living in the business world, the artist would learn his "relation to . . . an age of the most violent commercialism the world has ever known." Crane also stated that the artist had to take care to keep the "art and business" sides of his life "entirely separate," resulting in (to use Unterecker's words) "a deliberately split personality" (John Unterecker, *Voyager: A Life of Hart Crane* [New York: Farrar, Straus and Giroux, 1969], 156–57). Sustaining this balance proved to be impossible (Crane, *Complete Poems and Selected Letters*, 344, 346, 355).

68. In the letter to Gorham Munson on February 6, 1923, that offers the first description of "The Bridge," Crane fears that "it will be extremely difficult to accomplish" (*Complete Poems and Selected Letters*, 314). Crane's June 10, 1923, letter to his mother reveals that Waldo Frank wanted him to complete "The Bridge" so that he could begin to pitch a collection of poems to publishers (338). Little more than a month later, in a July 21, 1923, letter to the Rychterics, Crane anticipates that the poem will need to be "four or five times as long as" the draft he included (and that is discussed above), though he still hopes that it will be in his first book (344).

69. After quarreling with Harriet Monroe's "rationalistic" expectations for poetry, Crane did the same in a virtually contemporaneous letter to Gorham Munson who, like Monroe, had asserted that "rationality" must govern poetic "recognition[s]" and had held against Crane, a high school dropout, a general lack of "knowledge" of philosophy and other academic disciplines. Crane dryly concedes his "wholesale lack of knowledge," before then accusing Munson of losing sight of his own presumptions about the particular shape rationality must take (*Complete Poems and Selected Letters*, 166, 437, 436). Allen Tate mused in a tart critique written very shortly after Crane's suicide that his "fundamental mistake lay in . . . an irrational surrender of the intellect to the will," a mistake that enables one to deem "morally appropriate" the "courage with which he brought his work to its logical conclusion in personal violence" ("Hart Crane and the American Mind," *Poetry* 40, no. 4 [July 1932]: 216). Crane had disagreed with Tate about an earlier iteration of this argument after Tate had published a 1929 review stating that Crane's "chief defect is the lack of a system of disciplined values which would clarify and control the most prodigal poetic gift in America. . . . [H]is literary

240 | Notes to Chapter Three

talent exceeds at the moment what he has coherently to say" ("American Poetry Since 1920," *Bookman: A Review of Books and Life* 68, no. 5 [1929]: 507). Yvor Winters, hitting similar notes much more emphatically, deems Crane's "misuse of metaphor . . . irresponsible almost to madness" and indeed "confused in a manner which is suicidal" ("The Significance of *The Bridge*, By Hart Crane, or, What Are We to Think of Professor X?," in *In Defense of Reason* [New York: The Swallow Press, 1947], 593). Though this essay by Winters was written after Crane's death, they too had argued about such matters in the late twenties and thirties. See, for example, *Complete Poems and Selected Letters*, 641–44. Again and again, Crane's alleged irrationalism is linked to Walt Whitman, a connection that, as Langdon Hammer has shown, tacitly connected Crane's poetics with his sexuality (*Janus-Faced Modernism*, 176–77). Winters begins his negative review of *The Bridge* by stating that "[m]ost of Crane's thought, and this is especially true of *The Bridge*, was derived from Whitman" ("The Significance of *The Bridge*," 577). Winters and Crane earlier had quarreled about Whitman. A March 1927 letter is particularly telling when Crane defends Whitman precisely for not trying to be "logical" in his pursuit of "some universal law which he apprehends but which cannot be expressed in any one attitude or formula," a point that aligns the logic of metaphor with Whitman and that directly anticipates Winters's later critique of *The Bridge* (*Complete Poems and Selected Letters*, 531; see also 642–43). Allen Tate also quarreled with Crane about Whitman; see *Complete Poems and Selected Letters*, 647. And writing of Crane in 1935 (though collected later), R. P. Blackmur identifies Whitman as "an impediment to the *practice* . . . of poetry" due to "an accustomed disorder seem[ing] the order most to be cherished" (*The Double Agent: Essays in Craft and Elucidation* [Gloucester, MA: Peter Smith, 1962], 124, 126; Blackmur's emphasis).

70. Crane, *Complete Poems and Selected Letters*, 445.

71. Crane mentions Frank's presence in a number of letters (*Complete Poems and Selected Letters*, 455–59).

72. Crane, *Complete Poems and Selected Letters*, 479.

73. Horace Kallen, *Culture and Democracy in the United States* (New York: Boni and Liveright, 1924), 121, 124–25. Kallen introduced the concept of a symphonic America in the essay "Democracy versus the Melting-Pot: A Study of American Nationality," pts. 1 and 2, *Nation* 100, nos. 2590 and 2591 (1915).

74. Waldo Frank, *The Re-discovery of America* (New York: Scribner's, 1929), 255. Steve H. Cook explains that "Frank came to know Hegel (whose emphasis on dialectical movement toward wholeness had no small influence on other forms of idealistic personalism) through W. E. Hocking, one of Frank's undergraduate professors at Yale University." Hocking had been a student of a still more influential advocate for Hegel's thought, Josiah Royce (in Crane and Frank, *The Correspondence between Hart Crane and Waldo Frank*, 16). A footnote in Frank's

Notes to Chapter Three | 241

Re-discovery of America chides Kallen for not having a more explicitly synthetic (quasi-Hegelian) depiction of his vision of a "symphonic" America (260–61).

75. Waldo Frank, *The Re-discovery of America*, 255, 257.

76. Waldo Frank, *The Re-discovery of America*, 259, 258.

77. Waldo Frank, *The Re-discovery of America*, 259–260.

78. Frank's *Re-discovery of America* was published serially in the *New Republic* starting in late 1928. Letters between Frank and Crane indicate that the poet may not have been reading the book as it was being written, though their conversations likely concerned some of the ideas it contained. Frank, on the other hand, certainly had read a great many of Crane's works, including "Atlantis," as they were being drafted (Crane and Frank, *The Correspondence between Hart Crane and Waldo Frank*, 151, 155).

79. Waldo Frank, *Memoirs*, ed. Allen Trachtenberg (Amherst: University of Massachusetts Press, 1973), 243. Frank also notes Crane's debt to his book *Virgin Spain: Scenes from the Spiritual Drama of a Great People* (New York: Boni and Liveright, 1926), which included a chapter on Columbus that seems to have influenced the "Ave Maria" section of *The Bridge*.

80. Crane described the "pseudo-symphonic construction" and "symphonic rhythm" of "For the Marriage of Faustus and Helen" (*Complete Poems and Selected Letters*, 282, 309). In February 1923, Crane notes that "form [of "The Bridge"] will be symphonic" and that it will be a "mystical synthesis of America" in which "'our people' will have to be gathered up toward the climax of the bridge, symbol of our constructive future" (322, 321). Later, on January 18, 1926, Crane sends to Waldo Frank a thoroughly revised version of "the last part of *The Bridge*," now near its final form, and twice describes it as "symphonic," while referencing "Columbus, conquests of water, land, etc., Pokahantus," and notes that he's "busy on the *Nina, Santa Maria, Pinta* episode" (430–31). And appealing for cash from Otto Kahn on March 18, 1926, Crane notes the poem's "unusually symphonic form" (441).

81. Crane, *Complete Poems and Selected Letters*, 479.

82. D. H. Lawrence, for example, describes the dueling American "desire to extirpate the Indian. And the contradictory desire to glorify him. Both are rampant still, today." He then announces, "I doubt if there is possible any real reconciliation, in the flesh, between the white and the red. . . . There is no mystic conjunction between the spirit of the two races" (*Studies in Classic American Literature* [New York: Penguin, 1977], 41–42). Crane avidly read Lawrence throughout his career, so it is not unlikely that he used such pronouncements as a provocation in formulating his poetic identification with a Native American. Crane, however, draws most heavily from Frank's *Our America*, especially in "The Dance." *Our America* includes descriptions of Native American dances and depicted the "ravage of the white man" as an oncoming "[s]torm" (116). There is also a shared sense

242 | Notes to Chapter Three

of inevitability in their works. Frank explains that "the Indian is dying and is doomed" and "will be destroyed" (115–16). Steve Cook notes that Crane had marked the pages in *Our America* that concerned Native Americans (in Crane and Frank, *The Correspondence between Hart Crane and Waldo Frank*, 21). Crane claims in a November 21, 1926, letter to Frank that, sensing similarities between his project and Williams's, he intentionally "put off reading" *In the American Grain* "until I felt my own way cleared" (*Complete Poems and Selected Letters*, 498). Of course, the racist stereotype of the dying Indigenous person present in each of these works was established long before the twentieth century.

83. George W. Cronyn, ed., *The Path on the Rainbow: An Anthology of Songs and Chants from the Indians of North America* (New York: Boni and Liveright, 1918), vi.

84. Crane, *Complete Poems and Selected Letters*, 554.

85. Though he does not directly reference the challenge of Eliot, R. W. B. Lewis suggests that, "in the guise of bridging the distance between the modern American world and the old Indian world, Crane is in fact reuniting the modern consciousness (that is, *his* modern consciousness) with the mythic sensibility" (*The Poetry of Hart Crane: A Critical Study* [Princeton, NJ: Princeton University Press, 1967], 313).

86. Crane, *Complete Poems and Selected Letters*, 522.

87. See Jared Gardner, "'Our Native Clay': Racial and Sexual Identity and the Making of Americans in *The Bridge*," *American Quarterly* 44, no. 1 (1992): 35, 41. See also Niall Munro, *Hart Crane's Queer Modernist Aesthetic* (New York: Palgrave MacMillan, 2015), 102. Some have argued that the post-1925 transformation of *The Bridge* into a paean to cultural pluralism did not totally obscure the work's initial impetus. Angela Beckett claims that, while the "subject matter [of *The Bridge*] may require a compulsory heterosexuality, the poem's form allows for the creation of moments of recognition in spite of, and through, semantic and structural impertinence, creating a discordant concordance available to the reader through his/her experience of the poem." These highly localized "moments of recognition" (in brief phrases, like "gleaming mail," that contain gendered/sexual overtones) offer "metaphoric moments in individual poems [that] intend toward the recovery of a homosexual narrative" even amid a heterosexual superstructure and even show the "poet recogniz[ing] himself by way of the poem" ("The [Il] logic of Metaphor in Crane's *The Bridge*," 165–67). The suggestion that the "logic of metaphor" operates at a micro level in a way that is conceptually at odds with the poem's macro level, however, may bring Beckett's argument closer than she admits to the kinds of dissonance or nearly deconstructive catachresis seen by the scholars (like Lee Edelman, Tim Dean, etc.) she tends to critique.

88. Waldo Frank, *Our America*, 109, 107, 115.

89. Hart Crane, *Complete Poems and Selected Letters*, 556.

90. Hart Crane, *Complete Poems and Selected Letters*, 550.

Notes to Chapter Three | 243

91. Succeeding stanzas only underscore the narrator's imperious position. The death-bound Maquokeeta is next instructed to "dance."

> And every tendon scurries toward the twangs
> Of lightning deltaed down your saber hair.
> Now snaps the flint in every tooth; red fangs
> And splay tongues thinly busy the blue air . . .
>
> Dance, Maquokeeta! snake that lives before,
> That casts his pelt, and lives beyond! Sprout, horn!
> Spark, tooth! Medicine-man, relent, restore—
> Lie to us,—dance us back the tribal morn!
>   (53–60; Crane's ellipsis)

In an exchange following publication of *The Bridge*, Yvor Winters characteristically quarreled with Crane on moral grounds, claiming that to implore Maquokeeta to "dance us back the tribal morn" betrayed a dangerous "moral surrender" to the ethics (or alleged lack thereof) of a premodern era. Crane dryly replied that all he meant by the phrase was "Mimic the scene of yesterday; I want to see how it looked" (*Complete Poems and Selected Letters*, 643). One can sense Crane playing with Winters here, using a flatly literalistic interpretation to combat Winter's shrill moralizing. But Crane is also being deceptive. For even if one disagrees with Winters's argument, he does isolate a key moment in both "The Dance" and *The Bridge* as a whole. Crane's goal is not mere mimesis. He wants and needs, given his goals for "The Dance," to be capable of both recognizing and identifying with Maquokeeta.

92. The book's end, however, reflects lingering ambivalence about whether time and space will be overcome, which the poem's final lines present as an open-ended question: "The serpent with the eagle in the leaves . . . ?"

93. "[V]irgin to the last of men" mirrors the beginning of a poem by Juan Ramon Jimenez, a mystical Spanish poet who was a favorite of Waldo Frank. In the fall of 1924, Frank translated Jimenez's "Ante La Sombra Virjen" for Crane and included it in a letter. The poem begins (according to Frank's translation): "I forever piercing thee, / but thou forever virgin." The poem does not appear to have any American (or indigenous) context (Crane and Frank, *The Correspondence between Hart Crane and Waldo Frank*, 85).

94. Reed, *Hart Crane: After His Lights*, 230. Also see Edward Brunner, who suggests that fragments of early sketches for "Calgary Express" may have been incorporated into "The River" (*Splendid Failure*, 190–91).

95. Brunner, *Splendid Failure*, 30, 56. Crane tells Gorham Munson that he will have enough poems "for a collected publication" after "I get *The Bridge* done," which he then anticipated would "probably approximate the same length in lines"

244 | Notes to Chapter Three

as "For the Marriage of Faustus and Helen" (*Complete Poems and Selected Letters*, 322). Writing to his mother on June 10, 1923, Crane states that "I am all ready to start again on The Bridge. Waldo Frank is very anxious for me to have that finished, as he intends to take me up to his publisher, (Boni and Liveright) and have me published in volume form. But, of course, such things *can't* be rushed as he understands" (*Complete Poems and Selected Letters*, 338; Crane's emphasis). According to Steve Cook's account of Crane's correspondence with Waldo Frank, only in 1925 do Crane and Frank come to realize that *The Bridge* would require a volume of its own (93).

96. Crane, *The Letters of Hart Crane*, 161. (This letter was not included in the *Complete Poems and Selected Letters* edited by Langdon Hammer.) Here is the text of the poem as it was first published in the *Little Review* 10, no. 1 (1924): 19, immediately after the first published version of "Possessions":

> Regard the capture here, O Janus-faced—
> As double as the hands that crash this glass:
> Such eyes at search or rest you cannot see—
> Reciting pain and glee, you cannot bear!
>
> Twin shadowed halves: the second's glancing holds
> In each the skin alone, and so it is
> I crust a plate of vibrant mercury
> Borne cleft to you, and brother in the half.
>
> Resist this much-exacting fragment smile,
> Its drums and darkest blowing leaves deny
> In favor, only, of your listening tears
> Reserved to greet an ancient common sign.
>
> In alternating bells have you not heard
> All hours clapped dense into a single stride?
> Forgive me for an echo of these things,
> And walk through Time, yourselves, in equal pride.

97. Crane, *Complete Poems and Selected Letters*, 375–76.

98. Yingling, *Hart Crane and the Homosexual Text*, 46.

99. Precisely when the poem took its final form is unclear. Langdon Hammer only briefly notes an "early version" written in 1923 (in Crane, *Complete Poems and Selected Letters*, 747). Marc Simon's edition of Crane's poetry estimates that the poem was "composed October 1923—c. March 1924; first published Spring 1924," but it is not clear whether that chronology only takes into account the earlier, shorter version (Hart Crane, *The Complete Poems of Hart Crane*, ed. Marc

Simon [New York: Liveright, 1986], 232). Clive Fisher's biography of Crane simply states that the poem was "expanded from four to seven quatrains before its final completion in 1926," but it is not clear whether "completion" is simply a reference to the publication of *White Buildings* in that year (*Hart Crane: A Life*, 202). Edward Brunner estimates that it was "revised perhaps in early 1925" (*Splendid Failure*, 30).

100. Yingling reads the "twist[ing of] this glass" as a "transformation of the trope of narcissism" that "reject[s] the familiar charge of solipsism" characterizing the Freudian narrative of homosexuality (*Hart Crane and the Homosexual Text*, 49).

101. Crane, *Complete Poems and Selected Letters*, 323.

102. Crane, *Complete Poems and Selected Letters*, 525. Niall Munro notes that, in "Recitative," Crane "suggests ways in which both he and they [his reader] are oppressed within their shared world, through the mechanics of capitalism, and then offers a means of escape [with the bridge]" (*Hart Crane's Queer Modernist Aesthetic*, 58.)

103. See also Lewis, *The Poetry of Hart Crane*, 130–31.

104. Crane associated his halting progress on *The Bridge* to Absalom. In a June 20, 1926, letter to Waldo Frank, Crane expresses frustration about how the "little last section of my poem [i.e., "Atlantis"] . . . hangs suspended somewhere in ether like an Absalom by his hair" (*Complete Poems and Selected Letters*, 467).

105. Julie Taylor, "On Holding and Being Held: Hart Crane's Queer Intimacy," *Twentieth-Century Literature* 60, no. 3 (2014): 330. With reference to Jessica Benjamin's model of recognition, Taylor contends that "Recitative" "registers the difficulties of mutual recognition" in how its "mirroring and doubling . . . suggest a relationship variously governed by mutuality and domination," a sometimes difficult "unintegration that [nevertheless] can ultimately be tolerated" (327–28). Taylor explains that she favors Jessica Benjamin's model of recognition over Hegel's model, since a "fundamental paradox entailed in the need for recognition . . . that in order to affirm itself the self must acknowledge the other" is "a paradox ignored in classical psychoanlytic theory and Hegelian dialectics" (326). This is a somewhat strange claim because much of Hegel's elaboration of recognition engages precisely this paradox, which he understands as providing an impetus for the dialectical process he describes (see chapter 1 for further discussion of this topic).

Chapter Four

1. Helen Vendler, "Braving the Elements," *New York Times*, September 24, 1972, BR5.

2. Langdon Hammer, *James Merrill: Life and Art* (New York: Knopf, 2015), 514.

246 | Notes to Chapter Four

3. Louise Bogan, "Verse," *New Yorker* 27, no. 17 (June 9, 1951): 110; James Dickey, "The Human Power," *Sewannee Review* 67, no. 3 (1959): 504–5.

4. Use of free verse, of course, does not necessarily entail advocacy of progressive politics. Since most published poetry in the mid-to-late twentieth century was written in free verse, there was also conservative and reactionary free verse. This is how it has always been. As chapter one shows, Whitman's later poetry aligned his free verse with an imperialist vision of America. Ezra Pound's free verse, at times, forwarded a fascist sensibility. The point here is that Merrill's reliance on traditional forms, for many readers (as evidenced by some of the reviews cited in this essay), would have coded him implicitly as politically conservative.

5. Vendler, "Braving the Elements," BR5.

6. Hammer, *James Merrill: Life and Art*, 514.

7. Richard Pevear, "Poetry Chronicle," *Hudson Review* 26, no. 1 (1973): 201. By 1972, the *Hudson Review* had published Merrill eight times over more than two decades and would publish him only one more time, later in 1973. Whether Merrill stopped sending them submissions or the *Hudson Review* lost interest in publishing Merrill is not clear. Either way, Pevear's review occurred at an inflection point in the relationship between poet and periodical. James Merrill author page, *Hudson Review*, https://hudsonreview.com/authors/james-merrill/#.XQkvCI97mUk.

8. Pevear, "Poetry Chronicle," 201–3. In early collections, "Childlessness" is perhaps the closest Merrill came to naming homophobic norms, though it leaves his sexuality unclear. "To My Greek" moved closer to identifying Merrill's sexuality (though his addressee is wryly deemed a "siren" and "fishwife") but did not locate it as a locus of social prejudice. References to and quotations of Merrill's poetry follow the texts presented in *Collected Poems*, ed. J. D. McClatchy and Stephen Yenser (New York: Knopf, 2001).

9. Hammer, *James Merrill: Life and Art*, 532–33.

10. Hammer's biography also notes that Merrill's trusts yielded roughly $300,000 in 1995, the year that he died (*James Merrill: Life and Art*, xvii).

11. Hammer, *James Merrill: Life and Art*, 176.

12. Hammer, *James Merrill: Life and Art*, 290–92.

13. Steve Evans positions Merrill, an "elegant poet" who used his "inherited millions" to sustain "the clubby uptown world of old-style patronage," as the antithesis of an exceedingly broad range of poets (with an equally broad range of politics) he characterizes as "barbarians . . . at the gate[, including]—L=A=N=G=U=A=G=E poets, HipHop poets, Neo-Formalists, Surrealists, Nuyorican slam poets" ("Free (Market) Verse," *Baffler*, no. 17 [2006]: https://thebaffler.com/salvos/free-market-verse). While Evans's characterization might be understood in relation to Pevear's critiques, many other scholars, including Mutlu Konuk Blasing ("Rethinking Models of Literary Change: The Case of

Notes to Chapter Four | 247

James Merrill," *American Literary History* 2, no. 2 [1990]: 299–317), Frederick Dolan (*Allegories of America: Narratives, Metaphysics, Politics* [Ithaca, NY: Cornell University Press, 1994], 137–99), Walter Kalaidjian (*Languages of Liberation: The Social Text in Contemporary American Poetry* [New York: Columbia University Press, 1989], 93–119), and Brian McHale (*The Obligation toward the Difficult Whole: Postmodernist Long Poems* [Tuscaloosa: University of Alabama Press, 2004], 18–54) during the past several decades have associated Merrill with various postmodern trends in order to make a case for his cultural relevance. Several other critics identify a Merillean politics that draws from what appear to be competing streams of thought. Reena Sastri has described Merrill in terms of a "knowing innocence" that rejects the judgment of "poststructuralist thinkers . . . [who] have put the self-determining human subject on trial and pronounced its death sentence" and, in doing so, retains an "active responsibility" that is not "apolitical" and is "on the contrary crucially engaged" (*James Merrill: Knowing Innocence* [New York: Routledge, 2007], 2–3). And Timothy Materer notes how Merrill has been characterized simultaneously as "both a conventional formalist and an anti-traditional postmodernist" before going on to suggest that his "fascination with apocalyptic themes" helps to clarify this seeming paradox (*James Merrill's Apocalypse* [Ithaca, NY: Cornell University Press, 2000], 2). Far fewer scholars, as this chapter will show, bring Merrill deeply into conversation with the political poetry of his period, something that Hammer's recent biography makes more possible.

14. Piotr K. Gwiazda, *James Merrill and W. H. Auden: Homosexuality and Poetic Influence* (New York: Palgrave MacMillan, 2007), 3–4.

15. Hammer, *James Merrill: Life and Art*, 515, 514.

16. Members of the Gay Liberation Front, a movement that emerged first in New York only a few months after the Stonewall riots, announced their agenda in the first issue (November 14, 1969) of their newspaper *Come Out!* Elements of their program reassert, albeit more emphatically, the hopes of their predecessors in the Mattachine Society. They encourage gay people to come out, to tell their stories, to make visible how "every homosexual and lesbian in this country survives solely by sufferance, not by law or even that cold state of grace known as tolerance. Our humanity is questioned, our choice of housing is circumscribed, our employment is tenuous" (*Come Out!* 1, no. 1 [1969]: 1). But there is no discussion of assimilation to the mainstream. They assert that "we will not be gay bourgeoisie, searching for the sterile 'American dream'" (1). Instead, they reach out to other "militant oppressed groups" and promise to use their "economic power" in order to make it "political suicide to speak of further repression of the homosexual" (1).

17. See David Schneer and Caryn Aviv, eds., *American Queer, Now and Then* (Boulder, CO: Paradigm, 2006), 223–25. Edward Carpenter's *Iolaus: An Anthology of Friendship* (New York: Mitchell Kenerley, 1917) offers a kind of genealogy,

248 | Notes to Chapter Four

drawing from historical accounts, political speech, and artistic writing, that keeps blurry boundaries between nonerotic and erotic feelings of affiliation between people of the same gender from ancient Greece up to Walt Whitman. See also Carpenter's chapter on the "Intermediate Sex" in his collection of essays, *Love's Coming of Age* (New York: Vanguard, 1927), 112–30.

18. Robert Duncan, "The Homosexual in Society," *Politics* 1, no. 7 (1944): 210–11.

19. Harry Hay, *Radically Gay: Gay Liberation in the Words of Its Founder*, ed. Will Roscoe (Boston: Beacon, 1996), 65–66. Hay continued to provoke throughout his long life, sometimes with very problematic judgment, as when he began to affiliate with an organization that advocated reductions in the legal age of consent in order to support relationships between men and underage boys (see John Weir, "Mad about the Boys," *Advocate*, no. 661/662 [1994]: 37).

20. Hay, *Radically Gay*, 65, 63.

21. Hay, *Radically Gay*, 65.

22. Hay, *Radically Gay*, 70, 66, 131.

23. Hay, *Radically Gay*, 69, 65, 66.

24. *Ladder* 1, no. 1 (1956): 5.

25. Frank Kameny, letter to John F. Kennedy, May 15, 1961, https://web.archive.org/web/20160524153258/http://www.jfklibrary.org/Asset-Viewer/Archives/JFKWHCNF-1418-002.aspx.

26. Locke, "Enter the New Negro," *Survey Graphic* 53, no. 11 (1925): 633, 634.

27. W. E. B. DuBois, "A Negro Nation within a Nation," *Current History* 42, no. 3 (1935): 270.

28. Huey Newton and Bobby Seale, "October 1966 Black Panther Party Platform and Program," in *Call and Response: Key Debates in African American Studies*, ed. Henry Louis Gates, Jr., and Jennifer Burton (New York: Norton, 2011), 584–85. Principally the product of the poet/activist Alurista, *El Plan Espiritual de Aztlán* was further developed with the help of the leaders and attendees of the first National Chicano Liberation Conference in Denver, Colorado, which was organized by Rodolfo "Corky" Gonzales in 1969. A copy of the manifesto can be found in *Aztlán: Essays on the Chicano Homeland*, ed. Rudolfo Anaya and Francesco Lomelí (Albuquerque: University of New Mexico Press, 1989), 1–5. Larry Kubota, "Necessary but Not Sufficient: Yellow Power!," *Gidra* 1, no. 1 (1969): 3–4, http://www.discovernikkei.org/en/nikkeialbum/albums/492/slide/?page=1. Amiri Baraka, "State/meant," in *The LeRoi Jones / Amiri Baraka Reader*, ed. William J. Harris in collaboration with Amiri Baraka (New York: Basic Books, 2009), 169–70.

29. For example, Carl Wittman, who was a member of the Red Butterfly, a Marxist faction within the Gay Liberation Front, wrote *The Gay Manifesto* encouraging the gay liberation movement, whenever possible, to align itself with other liberation movements on socialist grounds (Carl Wittman, *The Gay Manifesto* [New York: Red Butterfly, n.d.]). For more on the Red Butterfly cell and for

copies of several of its documents, including Carl Wittman's manifesto, see https://
paganpressbooks.com/jpl/TRB-WITT.PDF. Intra- and intergroup negotiations
between black and white women in the feminist movement and black women and
black men in the Black Arts and Black Power movements dominate *The Black
Woman: An Anthology*, ed. Toni Cade (New York: New American Library, 1970).

30. Melissa S. Williams, "Introduction: On the Use and Abuse of Recog-
nition in Politics," in *Recognition vs. Self-Determination: Dilemmas of Emancipatory
Politics*, ed. Avigail Eisenberg, Jeremy Webber, Glen Coulthard, and Andrée
Boiselle (Vancouver: University of British Columbia Press, 2014), 5.

31. Melissa S. Williams, "Introduction," 6. All of the essays in *Recognition
vs. Self-Determination* address facets of this dynamic, including Jakeet Singh's
"Recognition and Self-determination: Approaches from Above and Below"
(47–74). "From below" also has been used to describe transnational activist efforts
that often attempt to blend the goals of different groups. See Jeremy Brecher,
Tim Costello, and Brendan Smith, eds., *Globalization from Below: The Power
of Solidarity* (Cambridge, MA: South End Press, 2000); Donatella della Porta,
Massimiliano Andretta, Lorenzo Mosca, and Herbert Reiter, *Globalization from
Below: Transnational Activists and Protest Networks* (Minneapolis: University of
Minnesota Press, 2006).

32. Christopher Nealon, *Foundlings: Lesbian and Gay Historical Emotion
before Stonewall* (Durham, NC: Duke University Press, 2001), 9.

33. James Smethurst, *The Black Arts Movement: Literary Nationalism in the
1960s and 1970s* (Chapel Hill: University of North Carolina Press, 2005), 94.

34. Keith D. Leonard, "'Which Me Will Survive': Rethinking Identity,
Reclaiming Audre Lorde," *Callaloo* 35, no. 3 (2012): 759.

35. Amiri Baraka, "Black Art," in *The LeRoi Jones / Amiri Baraka Reader*,
edited by William J. Harris in collaboration with Amiri Baraka (New York: Basic
Books, 2009), 219–20.

36. Gloria Anzaldúa, *Borderlands/La Frontera: The New Mestiza* (San Francisco: Aunt Lute Books, 2012), 85.

37. The inaugural issue featured both a series of original lyrics and an
essay identifying Christopher Marlowe's "Hero and Leander" to be "sensuously
gay" despite being "ostensibly . . . a description of straight love" (*Come Out!* 1,
no. 1 [1969]: 6, 13). The third issue explicitly identifies the importance of gay
lyricism within the movement in an essay, "Erotic Poets of the Liberation Front
Unite?," that emphasizes how nonheteronormative erotic lyrics "create, in our lives
and art, the models of love, including genital love, which transcends [*sic*] gender,
possession and domination." Liberation from heterosexism and patriarchalism, the
essay goes on to say, will come when "erotic poets . . . bring out the erotic poet
which is in every human being" (*Come Out* 1, no. 3 [1970], 11).

38. Winston Leyland, "Introduction," in *The Gay Sunshine Interviews*, vol.
1, ed. Winston Leyland (San Francisco: Gay Sunshine, 1978), 8, 7.

250 | Notes to Chapter Four

39. Winston Leyland, ed., *Angels of the Lyre: A Gay Poetry Anthology* (San Francisco: Panjandrum/Gay Sunshine, 1975). Shortly thereafter, Leyland published *Now the Volcano: An Anthology of Latin American Gay Literature* (San Francisco: Gay Sunshine, 1979), a volume intended to bear "signification of real sexual liberation" and "my belief that the Gay Cultural Renaissance is a world-wide phenomenon" (6). One of the first anthologies of LGBT+ literature distributed by a mainstream publisher is *The Penguin Book of Homosexual Verse*, ed. Stephen Coote (New York: Viking Penguin, 1983).

40. Leyland, *Angels of the Lyre*, 10.

41. Judy Grahn, *The Highest Apple: Sappho and the Lesbian Poetic Tradition* (San Francisco: Spinsters, Ink, 1985), 61, 11.

42. Hammer, *James Merrill: Life and Art*, 237. Merrill and Ginsberg eventually came to a measure of qualified respect for each other's very different aesthetics. See James Merrill, *Collected Prose*, ed. J. D. McClatchy and Stephen Yenser (New York: Knopf, 2004), 58. Also see Hammer, *James Merrill: Life and Art*, 635.

43. Merrill, *Collected Prose*, 72.

44. Hammer, *James Merrill: Life and Art*, 274.

45. Hammer, *James Merrill: Life and Art*, 277.

46. Merrill, *Collected Prose*, 143.

47. Merrill, *Collected Prose*, 123.

48. Unless otherwise specified, all quotes from James Merrill's poems will come from *Collected Poems*, ed. J. D. McClatchy and Stephen Yenser (New York: Knopf, 2001).

49. Hammer, *James Merrill: Life and Art*, 531.

50. Hammer, *James Merrill: Life and Art*, 533.

51. David Kalstone, *Five Temperaments* (New York: Oxford University Press, 1977), 88–89.

52. In one of the few critical commentaries on this poem, Timothy Materer does not address the way that the poem reflects the speaker's confrontation with his wealth (a thread that has become clearer due to Hammer's biography revealing the links between Pevear's review and the poem's first draft) and reads this first sonnet as a "dream" (*James Merrill's Apocalypse*, 75). But neither the text nor the context suggest this to be the case, and it begins a narrative that straightforwardly continues in the third sonnet. Merrill indicates with parentheses the sonnets extensively drawn from dreams (the second and the twelfth, with the latter being a sonnet interpolated within a sonnet).

53. Since "The Will" and "Clearing the Title" are both relatively long (and *The Changing Light at Sandover* very long) and are not indexed with line numbers, I will cite the page numbers from *Collected Poems* and *The Changing Light at Sandover* (New York: Knopf, 1996).

54. Materer, *James Merrill's Apocalypse*, 75.

Notes to Chapter Four | 251

55. Nikki Skillman, *The Lyric in the Age of the Brain* (Cambridge, MA: Harvard University Press, 2016), 130.

56. Merrill, in fact, did lose his manuscripts, more or less in the way that he describes in the poem (*Collected Prose*, 108).

57. Merrill acknowledges his interest in spiritualism at least twice previously in his career—in his poem "Voices from the Other World" (*Collected Poems*, 112–13) and in his novel *The Seraglio* (New York: Knopf, 1957), which includes a spirit named (with Plato, it seems, in mind) Meno.

58. There is an extensive literature on this debate. A useful exchange between two leading scholars can be found in Nancy Fraser and Axel Honneth, *Redistribution or Recognition? A Political-Philosophical Exchange* (New York: Verso, 2003).

59. Gwiazda, *James Merrill and W. H. Auden: Homosexuality and Poetic Influence*, 54–55.

60. Merrill explained to J. D. McClatchy that the Ouija board was "not something to start me *writing*. In other ways, evidently, it did start us 'going'—thinking, puzzling, resisting, testing the messages against everything we knew or thought possible" (*Collected Prose*, 109).

61. Blasing, "Rethinking Models of Literary Change," 312, 302. Merrill himself stated that he got the idea for interrupting a form in this way from Mozart's twenty-seventh piano concerto, where "you get a minuet somehow encapsulated in the rondo" (*Collected Prose*, 131).

62. Stephen Yenser, *The Consuming Myth: The Work of James Merrill* (Cambridge, MA: Harvard University Press, 1987), 14.

63. Thom Gunn, "A Heroic Enterprise," in *A Reader's Guide to James Merrill's "The Changing Light at Sandover*," ed. Robert Polito (Ann Arbor: University of Michigan Press, 1994), 157.

64. Merrill, *Collected Prose,* 40–41.

65. A similar ambivalence informs his response to Helen Vendler, when she asked "what would you especially like a reader to be caught up by in your trilogy." Merrill replies that "for me the talk and the tone—along with the elements of plot—are the candy coating. The pill itself is another matter. The reader who can't swallow it has my full sympathy. I've choked on it again and again" (*Collected Prose*, 86). All the same, Merrill was not embarrassed about using a Ouija board to facilitate his writing. Speaking with J. D. McClatchy, he bluntly states that "the mechanics of the board—this absurd, flimsy contraption, creaking along—serves wonderfully as a hedge against inflation. I think it does embarrass the sort of reader who can't bear to face the random or trivial elements that coalesce, among others, to produce an 'elevated' thought. That doesn't bother me *at all*" (*Collected Prose*, 110; Merrill's emphasis).

66. Langdon Hammer explains that Merrill's experiences reflect how users of a Ouija board may experience an "automatism," wherein something is done

252 | Notes to Chapter Four

without a sense of having done it: "[T]he thought that a letter might turn out to be the first part of a specific word is gradually realized by the spelling out of that same word, the lapse of time, combined with the sense of 'not doing' that comes with the force of another person's hand on the planchette, makes the initial thought feel more like an intuition than an intention. When it works, the Ouija board produces a pleasingly double sensation of surprise and inevitability, like an effective rhyme or witty remark" (*James Merrill: Life and Art*, 202).

67. Another example: "THE JAP MIND," for example, partly contains "PLANT-SOUL DENSITIES," which, in an unfortunate pun to "PHOTO-SYNTHESIS," explains "THEIR PASSION FOR THE CAMERA" (Merrill, *Sandover*, 151–52).

68. For further examples, see "Mirabell's Books of Number," sections 2:5, 2:6, 2:7, 3:2, 4:9, 5:4, 7:4.

69. James Merrill, *Collected Prose*, 159; J. D. McClatchy, "DJ: A Conversation with David Jackson," *Shenandoah* 30, no. 4 (1979): 34.

70. Washington University in St. Louis houses the Merrill archive. Evidence of Merrill's editing of the Ouija manuscripts gradually is becoming available to the public on the archive's website (http://digital.wustl.edu/jamesmerrillarchive/).

71. Materer, *James Merrill's Apocalypse*, 100. Some scholars tend to dodge the elitist content. One might partially agree, for example, with Christopher Yu, who finds in *Sandover* the "liberal laughter of the satirist" providing "an irreverent defense of our personal eccentricities" as a means of "offer[ing] us a saving hope of freedom and a chastening awareness of our reciprocal obligations" (*Nothing to Admire: The Politics of Poetic Satire from Dryden to Merrill* [Oxford: Oxford University Press, 2003)], 192, 194). But Yu does not fully grapple with the decidedly illiberal eugenicism *Sandover* consistently features.

72. Hammer, *James Merrill: Life and Art*, 596.

73. Lynn Keller helpfully notes that "Auden's largest legacies to Merrill concern the theory and practice of poetry as theater. . . . [Merrill] too has come to insist on poetry as play, as tall-tale, and as performance, and in this he too stands apart from the dominant poetic fashions of his time" (*Re-making It New: Contemporary American Poetry in the Modernist Tradition* [Cambridge: Cambridge University Press, 1987], 207).

74. One might wonder why Merrill allows his characteristic domestic imagery to evolve into explicitly theatrical imagery but chooses to continue writing poetry rather than plays. Part of the answer may lie in the fact that, after having already tried writing novels and plays early in his career, Merrill simply felt most comfortable writing poetry. He did make one notable exception, a one-act play, *The Image Maker*, his last drama, a work collected in *The Inner Room* (*Collected Poems*, 513–26).

75. "Clearing the Title" is not quite a farewell to *Sandover*. "From the Cutting-Room Floor," a series of excerpts from Ouija transcripts not collected

Notes to Chapter Five | 253

in *Sandover* appears in *Late Settings* (*Collected Poems*, 463–67). And "Nine Lives," which appears in Merrill's final book, *A Scattering of Salts*, serves as a wistful coda to JM and DJ's spiritualist practice (*Collected Poems*, 591–601).

76. Hammer, *James Merrill: Life and Art*, 626.

77. In *Sandover*, Merrill defines "Art" as "The tale that all but shapes itself—survives / By feeding on its personages' lives. / The stripping process, sort of. What to say? / Our lives led *to* this. It's the price we pay" (218; Merrill's emphasis).

78. "A Room at the Heart of Things" is another late poem featuring theater imagery. In the final stanza (the poem is a sonnet sequence like "The Will"), lovers are left "ma[king] room for" each other and other others on stage. Merrill does not deny that each self "ma[de] room for" on stage brings their own agenda. But he depicts them not attempting to recognize and thus stabilize an other's identity. Instead, as befits a fluid model of self in which the "out there" and "here" are not wholly distinguishable, they engage each other in an improvisational fashion. They "meet" each other as a "bare hypothesis" that "approach[es] nonsense," as not fully understood and never fully understandable, not requiring containment through recognition but, instead, inventive engagement by "swordplay or soliloquy or kiss" (*Collected Poems*, 511).

79. Luke Carson's reading of Merrill's late tribute to Elizabeth Bishop, "Overdue Pilgrimage to Nova Scotia," notes how the poem acknowledges that the speaker's "fail[ure]" in manners exposes "the limits of a social circle constituted by class and upbringing" ("James Merrill's Manners and Elizabeth Bishop's Dismay," *Twentieth-Century Literature* 50, no. 2 [2004]: 185). "Clearing the Title" makes a similar acknowledgment while trying to imagine how the speaker might become morally prepared to join a community.

Chapter Five

1. This manuscript, which was being compiled and edited by Thomas Sayers Ellis in the early 2000s, does not appear to have been published, perhaps in part as a result of sexual harassment and abuse allegations that came to light in 2016. For more on those accusations, as well as some broader context, see Maggie Doherty, "Unfinished Work: How Sexism and Machismo Shaped a Prestigious Writing Program," *newrepublic.com*, April 24, 2019, https://newre-public.com/article/153487/sexism-machismo-iowa-writers-workshop. Pieces of the projected volume, including Moss's paragraph, appeared in Thomas Sayers Ellis, ed., "An Excerpt from *Quotes Community: Notes for Black Poets*," *Callaloo* 27, no. 3 (2004): 631–45.

2. Thylias Moss, untitled (labeled no. 4), in Ellis, "An Excerpt from *Quotes Community: Notes for Black Poets*," 631–32.

254 | Notes to Chapter Five

3. Gillian White, *Lyric Shame: The "Lyric" Subject of Contemporary American Poetry* (Cambridge, MA: Harvard University Press, 2014), 48.

4. Thylias Moss, "Fork Addiction," *Columbia: A Journal of Literature and Art* 42 (2005): 84; "A Generalized Mapping of Limited Fork Poetics" (2006), 11, http://www-personal.umich.edu/~thyliasm/limitedfork/TMossLFPessay(5_06).pdf.

5. Moss, "Fork Addiction," 85.

6. Moss, "Fork Addiction," 84–85.

7. Moss, "A Generalized Mapping," 6.

8. Karen Ford argues that "while Black Arts movement excesses had established a public aesthetic program that enabled a community of voices to express themselves, its fundamental misogyny ultimately disabled most black women writers" by drawing them first toward an identification with "hypermasculinity" and then toward a no less confining "hyperfemininity." But Ford points to Gwendolyn Brooks, who was already an established poet by the time of the Black Arts movement, as well as Lucille Clifton and Audre Lorde as crucial counterexamples (*Gender and the Poetics of Excess: Moments of Brocade* [Jackson: University Press of Mississippi, 1997], 215–16). Aldon Nielsen highlights how Jayne Cortez refuted the sometimes patriarchal discourse of the movement with a "sweeping redefinition of the place of woman's voice" (*Black Chant: Languages of African-American Postmodernism* [Cambridge: Cambridge University Press, 1997], 227). Meta Jones describes how a number of poets navigated "assumptions about codes of masculinity, femininity, and heteronormativity . . . [sometimes present] in representations of sexuality in jazz performance and its accordant literature" (*The Muse Is Music: Jazz Poetry from the Harlem Renaissance to Spoken Word* [Urbana: University of Illinois Press, 2011], 137). James Smethurst explains that "the Black Arts and Black Power movements," in fact, "were among the few intellectual spaces in the United States in the 1960s where it was comparatively easy to raise the issue of male supremacy as opposed to, say, the institutions of mainstream academia" (*The Black Arts Movement: Literary Nationalism in the 1960s and 1970s* [Chapel Hill: University of North Carolina Press, 2005], 86).

9. Ajuan Maria Mance, *Inventing Black Women: African American Women Poets and Self-representation, 1877–2000* (Knoxville: University of Tennessee Press, 2007), 95–96.

10. Moss in Malin Pereira, ed., *Into a Light Both Brilliant and Unseen: Conversations with Contemporary Black Poets* (Athens: University of Georgia Press, 2010), 137. See also Thylias Moss, "The Extraordinary Hoof," *Boston Review* 23, no. 3 (1998): 26; *Last Chance for the Tarzan Holler* (New York: Persea, 1998); *Tale of a Sky-Blue Dress* (New York: Avon, 1998).

11. Moss in Pereira, *Into a Light Both Brilliant and Unseen*, 133. Moss describes her poetic idiom as "a complex adaptive or dynamic system" in her introduction to limited fork poetics entitled "The Available Coastline of the Veil," 3, http://www-personal.umich.edu/~thyliasm/TMossLFPbook_of_coastlines.pdf.

Notes to Chapter Five | 255

12. Moss in Pereira, *Into a Light Both Brilliant and Unseen*, 149, 137.

13. Moss in Pereira, *Into a Light Both Brilliant and Unseen*, 149.

14. Moss, *Tale of a Sky-Blue Dress*, 227.

15. Moss, *Tale of a Sky-Blue Dress*, 227–28 (Moss's emphasis).

16. Moss in Pereira, *Into a Light Both Brilliant and Unseen*, 146–47.

17. Moss in Pereira, *Into a Light Both Brilliant and Unseen*, 147, 149.

18. Moss in Pereira, *Into a Light Both Brilliant and Unseen*, 147–48, 148–49.

19. Moss in Pereira, *Into a Light Both Brilliant and Unseen*, 149.

20. Moss in Pereira, *Into a Light Both Brilliant and Unseen*, 149.

21. Carolyn Rodgers, for example, itemized ten genres in 1969, including, with a definite nod toward Amiri Baraka, the "shoutin" poem featuring "word bullets," which "for a while, . . . seemed to be the only kind of poem being written," as well as "signifying . . . teachin/rappin . . . coversoff . . . [and] spaced (spiritual)" poems (among others) while preserving space for poems that combine categories as well as poems presenting "forms which are yet to be acknowledged" ("Black Poetry—Where It's At," in *SOS—Calling All Black People: A Black Arts Movement Reader*, ed. John H. Bracey, Sonia Sanchez, and James Smethurst [Amherst: University of Massachusetts Press, 2014], 193, 188–89). Looking back on the movement in 1989, Sonia Sanchez, after also invoking Baraka's "Black Art," rehistoricizes poetry itself, starting from Africa and the Middle East, before foregrounding a persistently anti-imperialist edge in African American poetry from Phyllis Wheatley to the present. Out of such a lineage "Black pride emerged as a social value on the lips of [contemporary] poets" ("The Poetry of the BAM: Meditation, Critique, Praise," in *SOS—Calling All Black People: A Black Arts Movement Reader*, 248).

22. Many contributors to Toni Cade (Bambara)'s groundbreaking 1970 anthology *The Black Woman* foreground these concerns. With the emergent "feminist movement . . . almost totally composed of white females. . . . the Black woman," Kay Lindsey argues, "finds herself on the outside of both political entities ['the liberation of Blacks' and 'women's liberation'], in spite of the fact that she is the object of both forms of oppression" ("The Black Woman as a Woman," in *The Black Woman: An Anthology*, ed. Toni Cade [New York: New American Library, 1970], 85). Lindsey, Jean Carey Bond and Patricia Peery, and Gwen Patton all query some of the conclusions their male peers derived from an understanding of white supremacism as emasculation. They agree that racism manifested itself in figurative and literal acts of castration, but they worried that such a narrative, at times, obscured the suffering of black women, making it possible for documents like Daniel Moynihan's report *The Negro Family* to project the blame for this emasculation not upon white men but upon black women who held positions of leadership in their families and communities (Toni Cade, ed., *The Black Woman: An Anthology*, 89, 114–15, 146). The challenge, as Lindsey argues, is not only for black women to perceive that "the qualities ascribed to us are not in our interests"

256 | Notes to Chapter Five

but to find ways to "determine our own destiny" by "project[ing] ourselves into the revolution" ("The Black Woman as a Woman," 89).

23. Lindsey, "The Black Woman as a Woman," 85.

24. Toni Cade, "On the Issue of Roles," in *The Black Woman: An Anthology*, ed. Toni Cade (New York: New American Library, 1970), 101, 103. Black lesbian thinkers further extended this line of thought concerning the powers and limits of social recognizability. Audre Lorde insists that "I cannot be simply a Black person and not be a woman too, nor can I be a woman without being a lesbian . . . for all change and progress from within comes about from the recognition and use of differences between ourselves" ("My Words Will Be There," in *Black Women Writers (1950–1980): A Critical Evaluation*, ed. Mari Evans [New York: Anchor, 1984], 262–63). But she also notes the paradox that inevitably results. For recognition is both required and doomed to failure: "[I]t's easier to deal with a poet, certainly with a Black woman poet, when you categorize her, narrow her so that she can fulfill your expectations. But I have always felt that I cannot be categorized" (261).

25. See Thylias Moss, *Hosiery Seams on a Bowlegged Woman* (Cleveland: Cleveland State University Press, 1983); *Pyramid of Bone* (Charlottesville: University Press of Virginia, 1989); *At Redbones* (Cleveland: Cleveland State University Press, 1990); *Rainbow Remnants in Rock Bottom Ghetto Sky* (New York: Persea Books, 1991); *Small Congregations: New and Selected Poems* (Hopewell, NJ: Ecco, 1993).

26. Howard Rambsy II, "Catching Holy Ghosts: The Diverse Manifestations of Black Persona Poetry," *African American Review* 42, nos. 3–4 (2008): 549–50.

27. See, for example, consideration of Anthony Reed's concept of the "postlyric" later in this chapter. See also Gillian White's *Lyric Shame* on how avant-garde anti-lyricism participates in lyricization by oversimplifying the poetics of writers like Elizabeth Bishop and Anne Sexton. White asks, "What productive possibilities come by reframing the antilyric aims of the avant-garde not as a formal accomplishment, or aesthetic-political progress out of the shame of 'the lyric,' but as an ashamed mode of lyric reading—the uneasy twin to the New Critical lyric reading it meant to cast aside?" (26).

28. Moss, *Pyramid of Bone*, 3.

29. Moss, *Pyramid of Bone*, 2.

30. See Moss in Pereira, *Into a Light Both Brilliant and Unseen*, 134; Moss, *Tale of a Sky-Blue Dress*, 247.

31. Moss in Pereira, *Into a Light Both Brilliant and Unseen*, 137.

32. Moss, "The Extraordinary Hoof," 26.

33. Harold Bloom, "They Have the Numbers; We, the Heights," *Boston Review* 23, no. 2 (1998): 24–29. The essay also was featured as the introduction to *The Best of the Best American Poetry, 1988–1997*, which Harold Bloom also edited (New York: Scribner, 1998), 15–25.

34. For example, critics positioned Moss's poetry written in the eighties and early nineties as "startling[ly] new" (Tim Martin, review of *Rainbow Remnants in Rock Bottom Ghetto Sky, Prairie Schooner* 68, no. 2 [1994]: 157) and emphasized how Moss "flays the sacred and profane assumptions about a black woman's life" (Joyce Peseroff, review of *At Redbones*, by Thylias Moss, *Ploughshares* 17, no. 1 [1991]: 231) and "asks wide ranging questions about contemporary society and world history" (Marilyn Nelson Waniek, "A Multitude of Dreams," *Kenyon Review* 13, no. 4 [1991]: 221). Yet they also argued that her "anger, self-loathing, and defiance" (review of *Pyramid of Bone*, by Thylias Moss, *Virginia Quarterly Review* 65, no. 3 [1989]: 100), "fine rage" (Waniek, "Multitude," 221), and "anguish and anger" (Martin, review, 157) were "distinctly Black" (Waniek, "Multitude," 221) and what "one usually expects . . . in poems on the African-American experience" (Martin, review, 156). Moss has summarized her opinion about being categorized as an African American woman poet by stating, "I don't mind adding to the African American female aesthetic—whatever that is. I hope it is not easy to define" (Eve Silberman, "Thylias Moss: A Poet of Many Voices and a Spellbinding Delivery," *Michigan Today* 27, no. 3 [1995]: 9). Harryette Mullen and Reginald Shepherd, Moss's peers in the post–Black Arts movement generation, have expressed varying degrees of discomfort at the ways their racial identity too often determined how their poetry is categorized. See Harryette Mullen, "Poetry and Identity," in *Telling It Slant: Avant-Garde Poetics of the 1990s*, ed. Mark Wallace and Steven Marks (Tuscaloosa: University of Alabama Press, 2001), 27–31; Reginald Shepherd, "The Other's Other: Against Identity Poetry," *Michigan Quarterly Review* 42, no. 4 (2003): 648–60.

35. Anthony Reed, *Freedom Time: The Poetics and Politics of Black Experimental Writing* (Baltimore: Johns Hopkins University Press, 2014), 6–7.

36. Reed, *Freedom Time*, 7, 98. Elements of Reed's work can be placed in conversation with Evie Shockley's *Renegade Poetics: Black Aesthetics and Formal Innovation in African American Poetry* (Iowa City: University of Iowa Press, 2011), which argues, in part, that "the expanded, descriptive conception of black aesthetics" that her book considers "might be understood . . . as referring to a mode of writing adopted by African American poets in their efforts to work within, around, or against the constraint of being read and heard as being 'black'" (12).

37. Reed, *Freedom Time*, 105.

38. Reed, *Freedom Time*, 99, 98.

39. Moss in Pereira, *Into a Light Both Brilliant and Unseen*, 137.

40. Moss in Pereira, *Into a Light Both Brilliant and Unseen*, 135, 136, 139.

41. Since "Advice" is a dense, five-page poem, I will cite quotations by page number rather than line number. I will do the same in the subsequent readings of similarly expansive poems from *Last Chance for the Tarzan Holler* and *Tokyo Butter: A Search for Forms of Deirdre* (New York: Persea, 2006).

258 | Notes to Chapter Five

42. In an essay about Moss's "position as a[n] . . . African American woman with a cross-racial, affiliative postmemory of Holocaust survivors," John Claborn describes "Advice" as a "long autobiographical poem" featuring "a dialogue between the poet and her professor" ("Postmemory and Race: Thylias Moss and the African Americanization of the Holocaust," *Studies in American Jewish Literature* 40, no. 1 [2021]: 7). It is debatable whether one should deem the poem "autobiographical," even if it is possible that some elements may parallel Moss's life. See the comments earlier in the chapter referencing Howard Rambsy II's description of a persona poem tradition in African American poetry. Claborn's essay briefly cites Michael Rothberg's work on collective memory but not in relation to "Advice," as this reading does.

43. Michael Rothberg, *Multidirectional Memory: Remembering the Holocaust in the Age of Decolonization* (Palo Alto, CA: Stanford University Press, 2009), 5.

44. Rothberg, *Multidirectional Memory*, 4.

45. Rothberg, *Multidirectional Memory*, 4, 16.

46. Rothberg, *Multidirectional Memory*, 5.

47. Rothberg, *Multidirectional Memory*, 17, 20–21.

48. Rothberg, *Multidirectional Memory*, 5, 18.

49. Moss, "A Generalized Mapping," 4.

50. Michael Rothberg additionally warns about the risks of constructing what Freud called "screen memories" that "stand in for and distract from something disturbing" (*Multidirectional Memory*, 16).

51. Sylvia Plath, "Lady Lazarus," in *The Collected Poems*, ed. Ted Hughes (New York: Harper Perennial, 1981), 244–46.

52. The poet asks, "What sparkle / in me makes him choose me to come to him / as if my virginity were an ignorance / I would appreciate his exposing / so that I might be ashamed" (101)? Then the poet narrates, "He has an office . . . // . . . I am invited / each Tuesday so that he may know exactly why / he feels so much like repenting / in me, but I can't absorb his wrong; it trickles / down my legs" (102).

53. Phillis Wheatley, "On Being Brought from Africa to America," in *The Collected Works of Phillis Wheatley*, ed. John Shields (New York: Oxford University Press, 1988), 18.

54. As Henry Louis Gates, Jr., has shown in *The Trials of Phillis Wheatley: America's First Black Poet and Her Encounters with the Founding Fathers* (New York: Basic Civitas Books, 2003), Wheatley endured intense and insulting scrutinizing of her talents by white men.

55. Tyrone S. Palmer, "'What Feels More than Feeling?': Theorizing the Unthinkability of Black Affect," *Critical Ethnic Studies* 3, no. 2 (2017): 36.

56. Palmer, "'What Feels More than Feeling?,'" 38, 47.

57. Moss, "The Available Coastline of the Veil," 3.

58. Moss, "The Available Coastline of the Veil," 3.

59. Moss, "A Generalized Mapping," 5.

60. Moss, "The Available Coastline of the Veil," 51.

61. Moss in Pereira, *Into a Light Both Brilliant and Unseen*, 156.

62. Moss, "The Available Coastline of the Veil," 5.

63. Moss's YouTube channel (https://www.youtube.com/channel/UCZCah7_KHs2eMp4ePGub_RQ/featured) offers several videos featuring her alter-ego, Forkergirl.

64. Moss in Pereira, *Into a Light Both Brilliant and Unseen*, 162, 161, 158.

65. Moss in Pereira, *Into a Light Both Brilliant and Unseen*, 158.

66. Moss in Pereira, *Into a Light Both Brilliant and Unseen*, 162.

67. Moss in Pereira, *Into a Light Both Brilliant and Unseen*, 149–50.

68. Anonymous review of *Tokyo Butter*, by Thylias Moss, *The Great American Pinup* (blog), https://greatamericanpinup.wordpress.com/2011/11/21/thylias-moss-tokyo-butter/.

69. Moss in Pereira, *Into a Light Both Brilliant and Unseen*, 155.

70. Moss, "A Generalized Mapping," 11.

71. For more information about the Ronald Cotton case, see the Innocence Project website (https://innocenceproject.org/cases/ronald-cotton/).

72. "The Subculture of the Wrongfully Accused" features unusual spacing that has been approximated here and in the other quoted passages.

73. One wonders whether Moss also might have had in mind another poem by Dickinson, "There's a certain Slant of light," which describes the source of "internal difference – / Where the Meanings, are."

74. Moss, untitled, in Ellis, "An Excerpt from *Quotes Community: Notes for Black Poets*," 632.

Coda

1. Mei-mei Berssenbrugge, *Empathy*, rev. ed. (New York: New Directions, 2020), 67.

2. For a nuanced study of how "Berssenbrugge's poems, as 'avant-garde' as they are, are poems that have everything to do with her formation as a racialized American, an Asian American," see Dorothy Wang, *Thinking Its Presence: Form, Race, and Subjectivity in Asian American Poetry* (Palo Alto, CA: Stanford University Press, 2014), 268.

3. Berssenbrugge, *Empathy*, 67.

4. Berssenbrugge, *Empathy*, 43.

5. For the biographical background, see Mei-mei Berssenbrugge, "Three Conversations with Mei-mei Berssenbrugge," interview by Laura Hinton, *Jacket*, no. 27 (2005), http://jacketmagazine.com/27/hint-bers.html.

6. Berssenbrugge, *Empathy*, 69.

260 | Notes to Coda

7. Berssenbrugge, *Empathy*, 57.

8. Berssenbrugge, *Empathy*, 57.

9. Berssenbrugge, *Empathy*, 57. The poem confronts a particularly fraught form of representation, the "doll," an emblem that carries gendered and racialized overtones, given Berssenbrugge's ethnic heritage: "He / has a doll in his mind, on which he can predict what she will be feeling." That this "predict[ion]" may be wrong does not necessarily register to "him." And the "doll" remains the representation through which he engages with "her" insofar as he expects "her actual feeling" to "make contact with the object of his thought [the doll]" (*Empathy*, 59). But the "doll . . . seems rags to her," a clearly inadequate representation of her, albeit one that she has been pressured by him to internalize. The only escape is in learning that "[n]ot recognizing the doll would have to be something you both study," a task especially burdensome to "her," given how she was the one subjected to and interpellated within this fantasy (61).

10. Berssenbrugge, *Empathy*, 59, 58.

11. Berssenbrugge, *Empathy*, 59.

12. Berssenbrugge, *Empathy*, 62.

13. Charles Altieri, "Intimacy and Experiment in Mei-mei Berssenbrugge's *Empathy*," in *We Who Love to Be Astonished: Experimental Women's Writing and Performance Poetics*, ed. Laura Hinton and Cynthia Hogue (Tuscaloosa: University of Alabama Press, 2002), 63.

14. Berssenbrugge, *Empathy*, 44.

15. Herrera, *Half of the World in Light: New and Selected Poems* (Tucson: University of Arizona Press, 2008), 267.

16. Herrera, *Half of the World in Light*, 263.

17. Herrera, *Half of the World in Light*, 263.

18. Herrera, *Half of the World in Light*, 267.

19. Herrera, *Half of the World in Light*, 289.

20. Herrera, *Half of the World in Light*, 267.

21. Herrera, *Half of the World in Light*, 267.

22. Herrera, *Half of the World in Light*, 266, 301.

23. Rankine, *Citizen: An American Lyric* (Minneapolis: Graywolf, 2014), 73.

24. Rankine, *Citizen*, 71.

25. Rankine, *Citizen*, 69, 70.

26. Rankine, *Citizen*, 71.

27. Rankine, *Citizen*, 71–72. Kamran Javadizadeh notes how Claudia Rankine borrows a number of words and phrases from Robert Lowell's "Skunk Hour" in the sentence "Your ill-spirited, cooked, hell on Main Street, nobody's here, broken-down, first person could be one of many definitions of being to pass on" ("The Atlantic Ocean Breaking on Our Heads: Claudia Rankine, Robert Lowell, and the Whiteness of the Lyric Subject," *PMLA* 134, no. 3 [2019]: 483). In a brief interview with Sandra Lim, Rankine explains that "Robert Lowell's *Life Studies*

was in the back of my mind, with its poems and prose and portraits." She also notes that "[i]t's difficult to find critical work on the construction of whiteness in Lowell, but that is what I am reading in there—a struggle with that" (Claudia Rankine, "An Interview with Claudia Rankine," interview by Sandra Lim, n.d., https://krauseessayprize.org/winners-2/claudia-rankine/interview/).

28. Rankine, *Citizen*, 72–73.

29. Robert Lowell, "Skunk Hour," in *Collected Poems*, ed. Frank Bidart and David Gewanter (New York: Farrar, Straus and Giroux, 2003), 192.

30. Javadizadeh, "The Atlantic Ocean Breaking on Our Heads," 480.

31. Rankine, *Citizen*, 160–61.

32. Fred Moten, *Black and Blur* (Durham, NC: Duke University Press, 2017), 243–44.

33. The small archive of case studies offered in this book points to how, if space permitted, a range of other modes of lyric sociality also might be highlighted, including, for example, those that foreground economic class or ecological concerns.

34. This largely holds true for Rankine's *Just Us: An American Conversation* (Minneapolis: Graywolf, 2020), even if the change in subtitle (from lyric to conversation) perhaps suggests a response to the impasse. I do not have the space here to unpack the premises for and models of conversation Rankine traces throughout the book, which include, for example, meditations on whether it is possible to build "reciprocation[s] of understanding" or an "entangled empathy" or "a love of close readings of who we each are" (251, 335). Even so, the final page of the book emphasizes "[t]here is no beyond of citizenship" (335).

35. Relatively few Americans report that they read poetry. One exception is Rankine's *Citizen*. Casey O'Neil, the sales director of Graywolf Press, stated that the "number [of copies sold] is above 400,000 now" (personal email July 19, 2021). Sunil Iyengar, National Endowment for the Arts director of research and analysis, reports that the most recent NEA poll concerning poetry readership indicates that 9.2 percent of adults "read poetry in the last year," a percentage that increases to 11.5 percent when one includes "web streaming and social media" ("New Survey Reports Size of Poetry's Audience—Streaming Included," National Endowment for the Arts, April 6, 2023, https://www.arts.gov/stories/blog/2023/new-survey-reports-size-poetrys-audience-streaming-included). Iyengar previously reported that the 2017 poll revealed 11.7 percent of adult Americans reading at least one poem in the past year. Earlier polls have shown some variability, while reflecting consistently low readership levels, with 12.1 percent reading at least one poem in 2002, 8.3 percent in 2008, and an all-time low of 6.7 percent in 2012 (Sunil Iyengar, "Taking Note: Poetry Reading Is Up—Federal Survey Results," National Endowment for the Arts, June 7, 2018, www.arts.gov/stories/blog/2018/taking-note-poetry-reading-federal-survey-results). As a point of comparison, in 1992, 17 percent of Americans reported reading poetry in the past year (National Endowment for the Arts, *How Do We Read? Let's Count the Ways* [Washington,

262 | Notes to Coda

DC: National Endowment for the Arts, 2020], www.arts.gov/sites/default/files/How%20Do%20We%20Read%20report%202020.pdf).

36. Anahid Nersessian, *The Calamity Form: On Poetry and Social Life* (Chicago: University of Chicago Press, 2020), 8. Nersessian warns her fellow scholars against the self-congratulatory assumption that the study of literature can serve "as an effective contribution to the global struggle against social and ecological catastrophe" (7).

Bibliography

Alcoff, Linda Martín, Michael Hames-Garcia, Satya Mohanty, and Paula M. L. Moya, eds. *Identity Politics Reconsidered*. New York: Palgrave MacMillan, 2006.

Allen, Gay Wilson. *The Solitary Singer: A Critical Biography of Walt Whitman*. New York: Macmillan, 1955.

Altieri, Charles. "Intimacy and Experiment in Mei-Mei Berssenbrugge's *Empathy*." In *We Who Love to Be Astonished: Experimental Women's Writing and Performance Poetics*, edited by Laura Hinton and Cynthia Hogue, 54–68. Tuscaloosa: University of Alabama Press, 2002.

———. "Spectacular Antispectacle: Ecstasy and Nationality in Whitman and His Heirs." *American Literary History* 11, no. 1 (1999): 34–62.

Anderson, Quentin. *The Imperial Self: An Essay in American Literary and Cultural History*. New York: Vintage, 1971.

Anzaldúa, Gloria. *Borderlands/La Frontera: The New Mestiza*. San Francisco: Aunt Lute Books, 2012.

Barad, Karen. *Meeting the Universe Halfway: Quantum Physics and the Entanglement of Matter and Meaning*. Durham, NC: Duke University Press, 2007.

Baraka, Amiri. *The LeRoi Jones / Amiri Baraka Reader*, edited by William J. Harris in collaboration with Amiri Baraka. New York: Basic Books, 2009.

Bauerlein, Mark. *Whitman and the American Idiom*. Baton Rouge: Louisiana State University Press, 1991.

Beach, Christopher. *The Politics of Distinction: Whitman and the Discourses of Nineteenth-Century America*. Athens: University of Georgia Press, 1996.

Beckett, Angela. "The (Il)logic of Metaphor in Crane's *The Bridge*." *Textual Practice* 25, no. 1 (2011): 157–80.

Berssenbrugge, Mei-mei. *Empathy*. Rev. ed. New York: New Directions, 2020.

———. "Three Conversations with Mei-mei Berssenbrugge." Interview by Laura Hinton. *Jacket* 27 (2005). http://jacketmagazine.com/27/hint-bers.html.

Bhambra, Gurminder, and Victoria Margree. "Identity Politics and the Need for a 'Tomorrow.'" *Economic and Political Weekly* 45, no. 15 (2010): 59–66.

264 | Bibliography

Blackmur, R. P. *The Double Agent: Essays in Craft and Elucidation.* Gloucester, MA: Peter Smith, 1962.

Blasing, Mutlu Konuk. *Lyric Poetry: The Pain and the Pleasure of Words.* Princeton, NJ: Princeton University Press, 2007.

———. "Rethinking Models of Literary Change: The Case of James Merrill." *American Literary History* 2, no. 2 (1990): 299–317.

Bloom, Harold, ed. *The Best of the Best American Poetry, 1988–1997.* New York: Scribner, 1998.

———. "They Have the Numbers; We, the Heights." *Boston Review* 23, no. 2 (1998): 24–29.

Bogan, Louise. "Verse." *New Yorker* 27, no. 17 (1951): 109–13.

Bourne, Randolph. "Trans-national America." *Atlantic Monthly* 118, no. 1 (1916): 86–97.

Braithwaite, William Stanley. "The Negro in Literature." *Crisis* 28, no. 5 (1924): 204–10.

Brecher, Jeremy, Tim Costello, and Brendan Smith, eds. *Globalization from Below: The Power of Solidarity.* Cambridge, MA: South End Press, 2000.

Brown, Sharon, ed. *Poetry of Our Times.* Chicago: Scott, Foresman, 1928.

Brown, Sterling. "Our Literary Audience." *Opportunity* 8, no. 2 (1930): 42–46, 61.

Brunner, Edward. *Splendid Failure: Hart Crane and the Making of "The Bridge."* Urbana: University of Illinois Press, 1985.

Butler, Judith. *Frames of War: When Is Life Grievable.* New York: Verso, 2010.

———. *Giving an Account of Oneself.* New York: Fordham University Press, 2005.

———. *Notes toward a Performative Theory of Assembly.* Cambridge, MA: Harvard University Press, 2015.

———. *Subjects of Desire: Hegelian Reflections in Twentieth-Century France.* New York: Columbia University Press, 1987.

Byrd, Rudolph. *Jean Toomer's Years with Gurdjieff: Portrait of an Artist, 1923–1936.* Athens: University of Georgia Press, 1990.

Cacho, Lisa. *Social Death: Racialized Rightlessness and the Criminalization of the Unprotected.* New York: New York University Press, 2012.

Cade, Toni, ed. *The Black Woman: An Anthology.* New York: New American Library, 1970.

———. "On the Issue of Roles." In *The Black Woman: An Anthology*, edited by Toni Cade, 101–10. New York: New American Library, 1970.

Carpenter, Edward. *Iolaus: An Anthology of Friendship.* New York: Mitchell Kenerley, 1917.

———. *Love's Coming of Age.* New York: Vanguard, 1927.

Carson, Luke. "James Merrill's Manners and Elizabeth Bishop's Dismay." *Twentieth-Century Literature* 50, no. 2 (2004): 167–91.

Carter, Greg. *The United States of the United Races: A Utopian History of Racial Mixing.* New York: New York University Press, 2013.

Chauncey, George. "The Forgotten History of Gay Entrapment." *theatlantic.com*, June 25, 2019. https://www.theatlantic.com/ideas/archive/2019/06/before-stonewall-biggest-threat-was-entrapment/590536/.

———. *Gay New York: Gender, Urban Culture, and the Making of the Gay Male World, 1890–1940*. New York: Basic Books, 1994.

Chesnutt, Charles. W. *Essays and Speeches*. Edited by Joseph R. McElrath, Jr., Robert C. Leitz III, and Jesse S. Crisler. Stanford, CA: Stanford University Press, 1999.

Claborn, John. "Postmemory and Race: Thylias Moss and the African Americanization of the Holocaust." *Studies in American Jewish Literature* 40, no. 1 (2021): 1–17.

Coblentz, Stanton, ed. *Modern American Lyrics*. New York: Minton, Balch, 1924.

———. *Modern British Lyrics*. New York: Minton, Balch, 1925.

Cohen, Matt, Ed Folsom, and Kenneth Price, eds. *The Walt Whitman Archive*. https://whitmanarchive.org.

Cohen, Tom. "Only the Dead Know Brooklyn Ferry: The Inscription of the Reader in Whitman." *Arizona Quarterly* 49, no. 2 (1993): 23–51.

Come Out! Archive of the newspaper, 1969–1972. https://outhistory.org/exhibits/show/come-out-magazine-1969-1972/the-come-out-archive.

Coote, Stephen, ed. *The Penguin Book of Homosexual Verse*. New York: Viking Penguin, 1983.

Cormier, Harvey. "William James on Nation and Race." In *Pragmatism, Nation, and Race: Community in the Age of Empire*, edited by Chad Kautzer and Eduardo Mendieta, 142–62. Bloomington: Indiana University Press, 2009.

Coviello, Peter. "Intimate Nationality: Anonymity and Attachment in Whitman." *American Literature* 73, no. 1 (2001): 85–119.

Crane, Hart. *Complete Poems and Selected Letters*. Edited by Langdon Hammer. New York: Literary Classics of the United States, 2006.

———. *The Complete Poems of Hart Crane*. Edited by Marc Simon. New York: Liveright, 1986.

———. *The Letters of Hart Crane*. Edited by Brom Weber. Berkeley: University of California Press, 1965.

———. *O My Lands, My Friends: The Selected Letters of Hart Crane*. Edited by Langdon Hammer and Brom Weber. New York: Four Walls Eight Windows, 1997.

———. "Recitative." *Little Review* 10, no. 1 (1924): 19.

Crane, Hart, and Waldo Frank. *The Correspondence between Hart Crane and Waldo Frank*. Edited by Steve H. Cook. Troy, NY: Whitson, 1998.

Crane, Hart, and Harriet Monroe. "A Discussion with Hart Crane." *Poetry Magazine* 29, no. 1 (1926): 34–41.

Crane, Hart, and Jean Toomer. "Bright Stones: An Exchange of Letters." Edited by Langdon Hammer. *Yale Review* 84, no. 2 (1996): 22–38.

266 | Bibliography

Cronyn, George W., ed. *The Path on the Rainbow: An Anthology of Songs and Chants from the Indians of North America.* New York: Boni and Liveright, 1918.

Culler, Jonathan. "Apostrophe." *Diacritics* 7, no. 4 (1977): 59–69.

———. *Theory of the Lyric.* Cambridge, MA: Harvard University Press, 2015.

Dean, Tim. "Hart Crane's Poetics of Privacy." *American Literary History* 8, no. 1 (1996): 83–109.

della Porta, Donatella, Massimiliano Andretta, Lorenzo Mosca, and Herbert Reiter. *Globalization from Below: Transnational Activists and Protest Networks.* Minneapolis: University of Minnesota Press, 2006.

Deutsch, Babette. *This Modern Poetry.* London: Faber and Faber, 1935.

Dickey, James. "The Human Power." *Sewanee Review* 67, no. 3 (1959): 497–519.

Dickie, Margaret. "The Backward Flight of *The Bridge.*" *American Literature* 57, no. 1 (1985): 79–97.

Dickinson, Emily. *The Poems of Emily Dickinson.* Edited by R. W. Franklin. Cambridge, MA: Belknap Press of Harvard University Press, 1998.

Diepeveen, Leonard. *The Difficulties of Modernism.* New York: Routledge, 2003.

Dimock, Wai Chee. *Residues of Justice: Literature, Law, Philosophy.* Berkeley: University of California Press, 1996.

Doherty, Maggie. "Unfinished Work: How Sexism and Machismo Shaped a Prestigious Writing Program." *newrepublic.com*, April 24, 2019. https://newrepublic.com/article/153487/sexism-machismo-iowa-writers-workshop.

Dolan, Frederick. *Allegories of America: Narratives, Metaphysics, Politics.* Ithaca, NY: Cornell University Press, 1994.

Dougherty, James. "Crossing Brooklyn Ferry." In *A Companion to Walt Whitman*, edited by Donald Kummings, 484–95. Malden, MA: Blackwell, 2006.

Douglass, Frederick. *The Speeches of Frederick Douglass: A Critical Edition.* Edited by John R. McKivigan, Julie Husband, and Heather L. Kaufman. New Haven, CT: Yale University Press, 2018.

Dowling, Sarah. *Translingual Poetics: Writing Personhood under Settler Colonialism.* Iowa City: University of Iowa Press, 2018.

Drinkwater, John, Henry Seidel Canby, and William Rose Benet, eds. *Twentieth-Century Poetry.* New York: Houghton Mifflin, 1929.

DuBois, W. E. B. "A Negro Nation within a Nation." *Current History* 42, no. 3 (1935): 265–70.

———. *W. E. B. DuBois: A Reader.* Edited by David Levering Lewis. New York: Henry Holt, 1995.

Dunbar, Paul Laurence. "Negro in Literature." In *The New Negro: Readings on Race, Representation, and African American Culture, 1892–1938*, edited by Henry Louis Gates, Jr., and Gene Andrew Jarrett, 172–73. Princeton, NJ: Princeton University Press, 2007.

Duncan, Robert. "The Homosexual in Society." *Politics* 1, no. 7 (1944): 209–11.

Edelman, Lee. *Transmemberment of Song: Hart Crane's Anatomies of Rhetoric and Desire.* Palo Alto, CA: Stanford University Press, 1987.

Eisenberg, Avigail, Jeremy Webber, Glen Coulthard, and Andrée Boisselle, eds. *Recognition versus Self-Determination: Dilemmas of Emancipatory Politics.* Vancouver: University of British Columbia Press, 2014.

Ellis, Thomas Sayers, ed. "An Excerpt from *Quotes Community: Notes for Black Poets.*" *Callaloo* 27, no. 3 (2004): 631–45.

El Plan Espiritual de Aztlán. In *Aztlán: Essays on the Chicano Homeland,* edited by Rudolfo Anaya and Francesco Lomelí, 1–5. Albuquerque: University of New Mexico Press, 1989.

English, Daylanne K. *Unnatural Selections: Eugenics in American Modernism and the Harlem Renaissance.* Chapel Hill: University of North Carolina Press, 2004.

Erlin, Matt. "Absolute Speculation: The St. Louis Hegelians and the Question of American National Identity." In *German Culture in Nineteenth-Century America: Reception, Adaptation, Transformation,* edited by Lynne Tatlock and Matt Erlin, 89–106. Rochester, NY: Camden House, 2005.

Espiritu, Yen Le. *Home Bound: Filipino American Lives across Cultures, Communities, and Countries.* Berkeley: University of California Press, 2003.

Evans, Steve. "Free (Market) Verse." *Baffler,* no. 17 (2006). https://thebaffler.com/salvos/free-market-verse.

Fanon, Frantz. *Black Skin, White Masks.* Translated by Charles Lam Markmann. London: Pluto, 1986.

Farred, Grant. "Citizen, a Lyric Event." *Diacritics* 45, no. 4 (2017): 94–113.

Fisher, Clive. *Hart Crane: A Life.* New Haven, CT: Yale University Press, 2002.

Foley, Barbara. *Jean Toomer: Race, Repression, and Revolution.* Urbana: University of Illinois Press, 2014.

———. *Spectres of 1919: Class and Nation in the Making of the New Negro.* Urbana: University of Illinois Press, 2003.

Foner, Eric. *The Fiery Trial: Abraham Lincoln and American Slavery.* New York: Norton, 2010.

Ford, Karen. *Gender and the Poetics of Excess: Moments of Brocade.* Jackson: University Press of Mississippi, 1997.

———. *Split-Gut Song: Jean Toomer and the Poetics of Modernity.* Tuscaloosa: University of Alabama Press, 2005.

Frank, Waldo. *Memoirs.* Edited by Allen Trachtenberg. Amherst: University of Massachusetts Press, 1973.

———. *Our America.* New York: Boni and Liveright, 1919.

———. *The Re-discovery of America: An Introduction to a Philosophy of American Life.* New York: Scribner's, 1929.

Fraser, Nancy, and Axel Honneth. *Redistribution or Recognition? A Political-Philosophical Exchange.* New York: Verso, 2003.

268 | Bibliography

Freehling, William W. *The Road to Disunion*. Vol. 2, *Secessionists Triumphant 1854–1861*. New York: Oxford University Press, 2007.

Frisina, Kyle. "From Performativity to Performance: Claudia Rankine's *Citizen* and Autotheory." *Arizona Quarterly* 76, no. 1 (2020): 141–66.

Gardner, Jared. "'Our Native Clay': Racial and Sexual Identity and the Making of Americans in *The Bridge*." *American Quarterly* 44, no. 1 (1992): 24–52.

Gates, Henry Louis, Jr. "The Same Difference: Reading Jean Toomer, 1923–1982." In *Figures in Black: Words, Signs, and the "Racial" Self*, 196–224. New York: Oxford University Press, 1987.

——. *The Trials of Phillis Wheatley: America's First Black Poet and Her Encounters with the Founding Fathers*. New York: Basic Civitas Books, 2003.

——. "The Trope of a New Negro and the Reconstruction of the Image of the Black." *Representations*, no. 24 (1988): 129–55.

Gilbert, Roger. "From Anxiety to Power: Grammar and Crisis in 'Crossing Brooklyn Ferry.'" *Nineteenth-Century Literature* 42, no. 3 (1987): 339–61.

Gitelman, Lisa. *Paper Knowledge: Toward a Media History of Documents*. Durham, NC: Duke University Press, 2014.

Glaser, Ben. *Modernism's Metronome: Meter and Twentieth-Century Poetics*. Baltimore: Johns Hopkins University Press, 2020.

Glissant, Édouard. *Poetics of Relation*. Translated by Betsy Wing. Ann Arbor: University of Michigan Press, 1997.

Golding, Alan. *From Outlaw to Classic: Canons in American Poetry*. Madison: University of Wisconsin Press, 1995.

Gorin, Andrew. "Lyric Noise: Lisa Robertson, Claudia Rankine, and the Phatic Subject of Poetry in the Mass Public Sphere." *Criticism* 61, no. 1 (2019): 97–131.

Gostwick, Joseph. *German Literature*. Edinburgh: William and Robert Chambers, 1849.

Grahn, Judy. *The Highest Apple: Sappho and the Lesbian Poetic Tradition*. San Francisco: Spinsters, Ink, 1985.

Grossman, Allen. *The Long Schoolroom: Lessons in the Bitter Logic of the Poetic Principle*. Ann Arbor: University of Michigan Press, 1997.

Grossman, Allen, with Mark Halliday. *The Sighted Singer: Two Works on Poetry for Readers and Writers*. Baltimore: Johns Hopkins University Press, 1992.

Gunn, Thom. "A Heroic Enterprise." In *A Reader's Guide to James Merrill's "The Changing Light at Sandover,"* edited by Robert Polito, 153–57. Ann Arbor: University of Michigan Press, 1994.

Gwiazda, Piotr K. *James Merrill and W. H. Auden: Homosexuality and Poetic Influence*. New York: Palgrave MacMillan, 2007.

Haider, Asad. *Mistaken Identity: Race and Class in the Age of Trump*. New York: Verso, 2018.

Haines, Christian. *A Desire Called America: Biopolitics, Utopia, and the Literary Commons*. New York: Fordham University Press, 2019.

Hammer, Langdon. *Hart Crane and Allen Tate: Janus-Faced Modernism*. Princeton, NJ: Princeton University Press, 1993.

———. *James Merrill: Life and Art*. New York: Knopf, 2015.

Harris, Leonard, and Charles Molesworth. *Alain Locke: Biography of a Philosopher*. Chicago: University of Chicago Press, 2008.

Harris, William Torrey. "An Educational Policy for Our New Possessions." In *National Education Association: Journal of Proceedings and Addresses of the Thirty-Eighth Annual Meeting 1899*, 69–79. Chicago: University of Chicago Press, 1900.

———. "German-English Instruction." In *Twenty-First Annual Report of the Board of Directors of the St. Louis Public Schools for the Year Ending August 1, 1875*, 111–30. St Louis: Globe-Democrat Job Printing Company, 1876.

Hawkins, Stephanie. "Building the 'Blue' Race: Miscegenation, Mysticism, and the Language of Cognitive Evolution in Jean Toomer's 'Blue Meridian.'" *Texas Studies in Language and Literature* 46, no. 2 (2004): 149–80.

Hay, Harry. *Radically Gay: Gay Liberation in the Words of Its Founder*. Edited by Will Roscoe. Boston: Beacon, 1996.

Hedge, Frederick Henry. *Prose Writers of Germany*. 2nd ed. Philadelphia: A. Hart, 1852.

Hegel, G. W. F. *Aesthetics: Lectures on Fine Art*. Vol. 2. Translated by T. M. Knox. Oxford: Clarendon Press, 1975.

———. *Phenomenology of Mind*. Translated by J. B. Baillie. New York: Macmillan, 1910.

———. *Phenomenology of Spirit*. Translated by A. V. Miller. Oxford: Oxford University Press, 1977.

Herrera, Juan Felipe. *Half of the World in Light: New and Selected Poems*. Tucson: University of Arizona Press, 2008.

Hollis, Carroll. *Language and Style in "Leaves of Grass."* Baton Rouge: Louisiana State University Press, 1983.

Hughes, Langston. *The Collected Poems of Langston Hughes*. Edited by Arnold Rampersad. New York: Vintage, 1994.

Hutchinson, George. *The Harlem Renaissance in Black and White*. Cambridge, MA: Harvard University Press, 1996.

———. "Jean Toomer and American Racial Discourse." *Texas Studies in Language and Literature* 35, no. 2 (1993): 226–50.

———. "Jean Toomer and the New Negroes of Washington." *American Literature* 63, no. 4 (1991): 683–92.

Irwin, John. *Hart Crane's Poetry: "Apollinaire Lived in Paris; I live in Cleveland, Ohio."* Baltimore: Johns Hopkins University Press, 2011.

270 | Bibliography

———. "Hart Crane's 'Logic of Metaphor.'" In *Critical Essays on Hart Crane*, edited by David R. Clark, 207–20. Boston: G. K. Hall, 1982.

Iyengar, Sunil. "New Survey Reports Size of Poetry's Audience—Streaming Included." National Endowment for the Arts, April 6, 2023. https://www.arts.gov/stories/blog/2023/new-survey-reports-size-poetrys-audience-streaming-included.

———. "Taking Note: Poetry Reading Is Up—Federal Survey Results." National Endowment for the Arts, June 7, 2018. www.arts.gov/stories/blog/2018/taking-note-poetry-reading-federal-survey-results.

Izenberg, Oren. *Being Numerous: Poetry and the Ground of Social Life*. Princeton, NJ: Princeton University Press, 2011.

Jackson, Virginia. "American Romanticism, Again." *Studies in Romanticism* 55, no. 3 (2016): 319–46.

———. *Before Modernism: Inventing American Lyric*. Princeton, NJ: Princeton University Press, 2023.

———. *Dickinson's Misery: A Theory of Lyric Reading*. Princeton, NJ: Princeton University Press, 2005.

———. "The Function of Criticism at the Present Time." *Los Angeles Review of Books*, April 12, 2015. https://lareviewofbooks.org/article/function-criticism-present-time/.

———. "Lyric." In *The Princeton Encyclopedia of Poetry and Poetics*, edited by Roland Greene and Stephen Cushman, 826–34. Princeton, NJ: Princeton University Press, 2012.

———. "Poe's Common Meter." In *The Oxford Handbook of Edgar Allan Poe*, edited by J. Gerald Kennedy and Scott Peeples, 121–38. New York: Oxford University Press, 2019.

———. "Specters of the Ballad." *Nineteenth-Century Literature* 71, no. 2 (2016): 176–96.

———. "Thinking Dickinson Thinking Poetry." In *A Companion to Emily Dickinson*, edited by Martha Nell Smith and Mary Loeffelholz, 205–21. Malden, MA: Wiley, 2014.

Jackson, Virginia, and Yopie Prins, eds. *The Lyric Theory Reader*. Baltimore: Johns Hopkins University Press, 2014.

James, William. *A Pluralistic Universe*. Lincoln: University of Nebraska Press, 1995.

Javadizadeh, Kamran. "The Atlantic Ocean Breaking on Our Heads: Claudia Rankine, Robert Lowell, and the Whiteness of the Lyric Subject." *PMLA* 134, no. 3 (2019): 475–90.

Johnson, Barbara. "Apostrophe, Animation, and Abortion." *Diacritics* 16, no. 1 (1986): 29–47.

Johnson, Georgia Douglas. "The Riddle." In *The New Negro: An Interpretation*, edited by Alain Locke, 147. New York: Albert and Charles Boni, 1925.

Johnson, James Weldon. *James Weldon Johnson: Writings*. Edited by William L. Andrews. New York: Library of America, 2004.

Jones, Gavin. *Strange Talk: The Politics of Dialect Literature in Gilded Age America.* Berkeley: University of California Press, 1999.

Jones, Meta. *The Muse Is Music: Jazz Poetry from the Harlem Renaissance to Spoken Word.* Urbana: University of Illinois Press, 2011.

Kalaidjian, Walter. *Languages of Liberation: The Social Text in Contemporary American Poetry.* New York: Columbia University Press, 1989.

Kallen, Horace M. *Culture and Democracy in the United States.* New York: Boni and Liveright, 1924.

———. "Democracy versus the Melting-Pot: A Study of American Nationality—Part I." *Nation* 100, no. 2590 (1915): 190–94.

———. "Democracy versus the Melting-Pot: A Study of American Nationality—Part II." *Nation* 100, no. 2591 (1915): 217–20.

Kalstone, David. *Five Temperaments.* New York: Oxford University Press, 1977.

Kameny, Frank. Letter to John F. Kennedy, May 15, 1961. https://web.archive.org/web/20160524153258/http://www.jfklibrary.org/Asset-Viewer/Archives/JFKWHCNF-1418-002.aspx.

Kaplan, Justin. *Walt Whitman: A Life.* New York: Simon and Schuster, 1980.

Keats, John. *The Letters of John Keats, 1814–1821.* Vol. 1. Edited by Hyder Edward Rollins. Cambridge, MA: Harvard University Press, 1958.

Keenaghan, Eric. *Queering Cold War Poetry: Ethics of Vulnerability in Cuba and the United States.* Columbus: Ohio State University Press, 2009.

Keller, Lynn. *Re-making It New: Contemporary Poetry in the Modernist Tradition.* Cambridge: Cambridge University Press, 1987.

Keniston, Ann. *Overheard Voices: Address and Subjectivity in Postmodern American Poetry.* New York: Routledge, 2006.

Kerman, Cynthia Earl, and Richard Eldridge. *The Lives of Jean Toomer: A Hunger for Wholeness.* Baton Rouge: Louisiana State University Press, 1987.

Kinnahan, Linda. *Lyric Interventions: Feminism, Experimental Poetry, and Contemporary Discourse.* Iowa City: University of Iowa Press, 2004.

Kubota, Larry. "Necessary but Not Sufficient: Yellow Power!" *Gidra* 1, no. 1 (1969): 3–4. http://www.discovernikkei.org/en/nikkeialbum/albums/492/slide/?page=1.

Ladder 1, no. 1 (1956). https://archive.org/details/the-ladder-1956-1972-lesbian-periodical.

Lai, Fernanda. "Publication without the Publicity of the Self: The lyric 'I' in Emily Dickinson and Claudia Rankine." *Oxford Research in English*, no. 8 (2019): 77–96.

Larson, Charles. *Invisible Darkness: Jean Toomer and Nella Larson.* Iowa City: University of Iowa Press, 1993.

Larson, Kerry. *Whitman's Drama of Consensus.* Chicago: University of Chicago Press, 1988.

Lawrence, D. H. *Studies in Classic American Literature.* New York: Penguin, 1977.

272 | Bibliography

Laws of the State of New York: One Hundred and Forty-Sixth Session of the Legislature Begun January 3, 1923 and Ended May 4, 1923. "Disorderly Conduct." Chapter 642, article 70, p. 961.

Leidecker, Kurt F. *Yankee Teacher: The Life of William Torrey Harris.* New York: Philosophical Library, 1946.

Leonard, Keith D. "'Which Me Will Survive': Rethinking Identity, Reclaiming Audre Lorde." *Callaloo* 35, no. 3 (2012): 758–77.

Lewis, David Levering. *W. E. B. DuBois, 1868–1919: Biography of a Race.* New York: Holt, 1993.

Lewis, R. W. B. *The Poetry of Hart Crane: A Critical Study.* Princeton, NJ: Princeton University Press, 1967.

Leyland, Winston, ed. *Angels of the Lyre: A Gay Poetry Anthology.* San Francisco: Panjandrum Press—Gay Sunshine Press, 1975.

———. *The Gay Sunshine Interviews.* Vol. 1. San Francisco: Gay Sunshine, 1978.

———. *Now the Volcano: An Anthology of Latin American Gay Literature.* San Francisco: Gay Sunshine, 1979.

Lincoln, Abraham. *The Collected Works of Abraham Lincoln.* Vol. 2. Edited by Roy Basler. New Brunswick, NJ: Rutgers University Press, 1953.

Lindsey, Kay. "The Black Woman as a Woman." In *The Black Woman: An Anthology,* edited by Toni Cade, 85–89. New York: New American Library, 1970.

Locke, Alain. "Enter the New Negro." *Survey Graphic* 53, no. 11 (1925): 631–34.

———. "The Negro Poets of the United States." In *Anthology of Magazine Verse for 1926,* edited by William Stanley Braithwaite, 143–51. Boston: B. J. Brimmer, 1926.

———. "Propaganda—or Poetry?" In *The Works of Alain Locke,* edited by Charles Molesworth, 228–39. Oxford: Oxford University Press, 2012.

———. "Sterling Brown: The New Negro Folk-Poet." In *Negro: Anthology Made by Nancy Cunard, 1931–1933,* 111–15. New York: Negro Universities Press, 1969.

Lorde, Audre. "My Words Will Be There." In *Black Women Writers, 1950–1980: A Critical Evaluation,* edited by Mari Evans, 261–68. New York: Anchor, 1984.

Lowell, Robert. *Life Studies.* In *Collected Poems,* edited by Frank Bidart and David Gewanter, 109–92. New York: Farrar, Straus and Giroux, 2003.

———. "Man and Wife." In *Collected Poems,* edited by Frank Bidart and David Gewanter, 189–90. New York: Farrar, Straus and Giroux, 2003.

———. "Skunk Hour." In *Collected Poems,* edited by Frank Bidart and David Gewanter, 191–92. New York: Farrar, Straus and Giroux, 2003.

Lutenski, Emily. "'A Small Man in Big Spaces': The New Negro, the Mestizo, and Jean Toomer's Southwestern Writing." *MELUS: Multiethnic Literature of the United States* 33, no. 1 (2008): 11–32.

Mance, Ajuan Maria. *Inventing Black Women: African American Women Poets and Self-representation, 1877–2000.* Knoxville: University of Tennessee Press, 2007.

Markell, Patchen. *Bound by Recognition*. Princeton, NJ: Princeton University Press, 2003.

Marrs, Cody. "Whitman's Latencies: Hegel and the Politics of Time in *Leaves of Grass*." *Arizona Quarterly* 67, no. 1 (2011): 47–72.

Martin, Robert. *The Homosexual Tradition in American Poetry*. Iowa City: University of Iowa Press, 1998.

Martin, Tim. Review of *Rainbow Remnants in Rock Bottom Ghetto Sky*, by Thylias Moss. *Prairie Schooner* 68, no. 2 (1994): 156–58.

Materer, Timothy. *James Merrill's Apocalypse*. Ithaca, NY: Cornell University Press, 2000.

Maxwell, William. *New Negro, Old Left: African-American Writing and Communism between the Wars*. New York: Columbia University Press, 1999.

McClatchy, J. D. "DJ: A Conversation with David Jackson." *Shenandoah* 30, no. 4 (1979): 23–44.

McHale, Brian. *The Obligation toward the Difficult Whole: Postmodernist Long Poems*. Tuscaloosa: University of Alabama Press, 2004.

McKay, Claude. *Complete Poems*. Edited by William J. Maxwell. Urbana: University of Illinois Press, 2004.

———. "A Negro Writer to His Critics." In *The Passion of Claude McKay: Selected Poetry and Prose, 1912–1948*, edited by Wayne F. Cooper, 132–39. New York: Schocken, 1973.

McKay, Nellie. *Jean Toomer—Artist: A Study of His Literary Life and Work, 1894–1936*. Chapel Hill: University of North Carolina Press, 1984.

Merrill, James. *The Changing Light at Sandover*. New York: Knopf, 1996.

———. *Collected Poems*. Edited by J. D. McClatchy and Stephen Yenser. New York: Knopf, 2001.

———. *Collected Prose*. Edited by J. D. McClatchy and Stephen Yenser. New York: Knopf, 2004.

———. *The Seraglio*. New York: Knopf, 1957.

Michaels, Walter Benn. *Our America: Nativism, Modernism, and Pluralism*. Durham, NC: Duke University Press, 1995.

Mill, John Stuart. "Thoughts on Poetry and Its Varieties." *Crayon* 7, no. 4 (1860): 93–97.

Miller, Cristanne. *Reading in Time: Emily Dickinson in the Nineteenth Century*. Amherst: University of Massachusetts Press, 2012.

Mills, Charles. "Multiculturalism as/and/or Anti-racism?" In *Multiculturalism and Political Theory*, edited by Anthony S. Laden and David Owen, 89–114. New York: Cambridge University Press, 2007.

Mohanty, Satya. *Literary Theory and the Claims of History: Postmodernism, Objectivity, and Multicultural Politics*. Ithaca, NY: Cornell University Press, 1997.

Monroe, Harriet, and Alice Henderson, eds. *The New Poetry: An Anthology of Twentieth-Century Verse in English*. New York: Macmillan, 1923.

274 | Bibliography

Moore, Marianne. "A Grave." In *Complete Poems*, 49–50. New York: Macmillan/ Penguin, 1994.

Moss, Thylias. *At Redbones*. Cleveland: Cleveland State University Press, 1990.

———. "The Available Coastline of the Veil." http://www-personal.umich. edu/~thyliasm/TMossLFPbook_of_coastlines.pdf.

———. "The Extraordinary Hoof." *Boston Review* 23, no. 3 (1998): 26.

———. "Fork Addiction." *Columbia: A Journal of Literature and Art* 42 (2005): 84–89.

———. "A Generalized Mapping of Limited Fork Poetics." 2006. http:// www-personal.umich.edu/~thyliasm/limitedfork/TMossLFPessay(5_06).pdf.

———. *Hosiery Seams on a Bowlegged Woman*. Cleveland: Cleveland State University Press, 1983.

———. *Last Chance for the Tarzan Holler*. New York: Persea, 1998.

———. *Pyramid of Bone*. Charlottesville: University Press of Virginia, 1989.

———. *Rainbow Remnants in Rock Bottom Ghetto Sky*. New York: Persea, 1991.

———. *Small Congregations: New and Selected Poems*. Hopewell, NJ: Ecco, 1993.

———. *Tale of a Sky-Blue Dress*. New York: Avon, 1998.

———. *Tokyo Butter: A Search for Forms of Deirdre*. New York: Persea, 2006.

Moten, Fred. *Black and Blur*. Durham, NC: Duke University Press, 2017.

———. *The Universal Machine*. Durham, NC: Duke University Press, 2018.

Moten, Fred, and Stefano Harney. *The Undercommons: Fugitive Planning and Black Study*. New York: Minor Compositions, 2013.

Mullen, Harryette. "Poetry and Identity." In *Telling It Slant: Avant-Garde Poetics of the 1990s*, edited by Mark Wallace and Steven Marks, 27–31. Tuscaloosa: University of Alabama Press, 2001.

Muñoz, José Esteban. *Disidentifications: Queers of Color and the Performance of Politics*. Minneapolis: University of Minnesota Press, 1999.

Munro, Niall. *Hart Crane's Queer Modernist Aesthetic*. New York: Palgrave MacMillan, 2015.

Nathanson, Tenney. *Whitman's Presence: Body, Voice, and Writing in Leaves of Grass*. New York: New York University Press, 1992.

National Endowment for the Arts. *How Do We Read? Let's Count the Ways*. Washington, DC: National Endowment for the Arts, 2020. www.arts. gov/sites/default/files/How%20Do%20We%20Read%20report%202020.pdf.

Nealon, Christopher. *Foundlings: Lesbian and Gay Historical Emotion before Stonewall*. Durham, NC: Duke University Press, 2001.

Nelson, Cary. *Repression and Recovery: Modern American Poetry and the Politics of Cultural Memory, 1910–1945*. Madison: University of Wisconsin Press, 1989.

———. *Revolutionary Memory: Recovering the Poetry of the American Left*. New York: Routledge, 2001.

Nersessian, Anahid. *The Calamity Form: On Poetry and Social Life*. Chicago: University of Chicago Press, 2020.

Neruda, Pablo. "We Live in a Whitmanesque Age." In *Walt Whitman: The Measure of His Song*, edited by Jim Perlman, Ed Folsom, and Dan Campion, 139–41. Minneapolis: Holy Cow! Press, 1981.

Newkirk, Pamela, ed. Correspondence between James Weldon Johnson and Jean Toomer. In *Letters from Black America*, 281–83. New York: Farrar, Straus and Giroux, 2009.

Newton, Huey, and Bobby Seale. "October 1966 Black Panther Party Platform and Program." In *Call and Response: Key Debates in African American Studies*, edited by Henry Louis Gates, Jr., and Jennifer Burton, 584–85. New York: Norton, 2011.

Nielsen, Aldon. *Black Chant: Languages of African-American Postmodernism*. Cambridge: Cambridge University Press, 1997.

Noel, Urayoán. *In Visible Movement: Nuyorican Poetry from the Sixties to Slam*. Iowa City: University of Iowa Press, 2014.

North, Michael. *The Dialect of Modernism: Race, Language, and Twentieth-Century Literature*. Oxford: Oxford University Press, 1994.

Oliver, Kelly. *Witnessing: Beyond Recognition*. Minneapolis: University of Minnesota Press, 2001.

Palmer, Tyrone S. "'What Feels More than Feeling?': Theorizing the Unthinkability of Black Affect." *Critical Ethnic Studies* 3, no. 2 (2017): 31–56.

Parks, Justin. "Race and National Identity in Modernist Anthropology and Jean Toomer's 'The Blue Meridian.'" *Texas Studies in Literature and Language* 62, no. 3 (2020): 344–67.

Patterson, Orlando. *Slavery and Social Death*. Cambridge, MA: Harvard University Press, 1982.

Pereira, Malin, ed. *Into a Light Both Brilliant and Unseen: Conversations with Contemporary Black Poets*. Athens: University of Georgia Press, 2010.

Perlow, Seth. *The Poem Electric: Technology and the American Lyric*. Minneapolis: University of Minnesota Press, 2018.

Peseroff, Joyce. Review of *At Redbones*, by Thylias Moss. *Ploughshares* 17, no. 1 (1991): 231.

Pevear, Richard. "Poetry Chronicle." *Hudson Review* 26, no. 1 (1973): 192–218.

Pfeiffer, Kathleen. *Race Passing and American Individualism*. Amherst: University of Massachusetts Press, 2002.

Plath, Sylvia. "Lady Lazarus." In *The Collected Poems of Sylvia Plath*, edited by Ted Hughes, 244–46. New York: Harper Perennial, 1981.

Pochmann, Henry. *German Culture in America: Philosophical and Literary Influences, 1600–1900*. Madison: University of Wisconsin Press, 1957.

Posmentier, Sonya. "Lyric Reading in the Black Ethnographic Archive." *American Literary History* 30, no. 1 (2018): 55–84.

Posnock, Ross. *Color and Culture: Black Writers and the Making of the Modern Intellectual*. Cambridge, MA: Harvard University Press, 1998.

276 | Bibliography

Pound, Ezra, ed. *Des Imagistes: An Anthology*. New York: Frank Shay, 1917.

———. "A Retrospect." In *Ezra Pound's Early Writings: Poems and Prose*, edited by Ira Nadel, 252–65. New York: Penguin, 2005.

Railton, Stephen. "'As If I Were with You'—the Performance of Whitman's Poetry." In *The Cambridge Companion to Walt Whitman*, edited by Ezra Greenspan, 7–26. Cambridge: Cambridge University Press, 1995.

Rambsy, Howard, II. "Catching Holy Ghosts: The Diverse Manifestations of Black Persona Poetry." *African American Review* 42, nos. 3–4 (2008): 549–64.

Rankine, Claudia. *Citizen: An American Lyric*. Minneapolis: Graywolf, 2014.

———. "Claudia Rankine on Confronting Whiteness Head-On through Language." Interview by Spencer Bailey. *Time Sensitive* (podcast), episode 60 (2022). https://timesensitive.fm/episode/claudia-rankine-on-confronting-whiteness-head-on-through-language/.

———. *Don't Let Me Be Lonely: An American Lyric*. Minneapolis: Graywolf, 2004.

———. "Interview: Claudia Rankine." Interview by Jenny Buschner, Braulio Fonseca, Kristen Paz, and Josalyn Knapic. *South Loop Review* 14 (2012): 63–67. https://www.yumpu.com/en/document/read/35429709/an-interview-with-claudia-rankine.

———. "An Interview with Claudia Rankine." Interview by Claire Schwartz. *TriQuarterly* 150 (2016). https://www.triquarterly.org/issues/issue-150/interview-claudia-rankine.

———. "An Interview with Claudia Rankine." Interview by Sandra Lim. n.d. https://krauseessayprize.org/winners-2/claudia-rankine/interview/.

———. *Just Us: An American Conversation*. Minneapolis: Graywolf, 2020.

———. "Visionaries Series: Claudia Rankine in Conversation with Judith Butler." Interview by Judith Butler. New Museum, October 29, 2020. https://vimeo.com/473984783.

Reed, Anthony. *Freedom Time: The Poetics and Politics of Black Experimental Writing*. Baltimore: Johns Hopkins University Press, 2016.

Reed, Brian M. *Hart Crane: After His Lights*. Tuscaloosa: University of Alabama Press, 2006.

Review of *Pyramid of Bone*, by Thylias Moss. *Virginia Quarterly Review* 65, no. 3 (1989): 100.

Review of *Tokyo Butter*, by Thylias Moss. *The Great American Pinup* (blog). Accessed October 4, 2021. https://greatamericanpinup.wordpress.com/2011/11/21/thylias-moss-tokyo-butter/.

Reynolds, David S. *Walt Whitman's America: A Cultural Biography*. New York: Knopf, 1995.

Rodgers, Carolyn. "Black Poetry—Where It's At." In *SOS—Calling All Black People: A Black Arts Movement Reader*, edited by John H. Bracey, Sonia Sanchez, and James Smethurst, 188–97. Amherst: University of Massachusetts Press, 2014.

Rodriguez, Ralph. *Latinx Literature Unbound: Undoing Ethnic Expectation.* New York: Fordham University Press, 2018.

Rothberg, Michael. *Multidirectional Memory: Remembering the Holocaust in the Age of Decolonization.* Palo Alto, CA: Stanford University Press, 2009.

Rusch, Frederik. "The Blue Man: Jean Toomer's Solution to His Problems of Identity." *Obsidian* 6 (1980): 38–54.

Samito, Christian. *Becoming American under Fire: Irish Americans, African Americans, and the Politics of Citizenship during the Civil War Era.* Ithaca, NY: Cornell University Press, 2009.

Sanchez, Sonia. "The Poetry of the BAM: Meditation, Critique, Praise." In *SOS—Calling All Black People: A Black Arts Movement Reader*, edited by John H. Bracey, Sonia Sanchez, and James Smethurst, 243–53. Amherst: University of Massachusetts Press, 2014.

Sastri, Reena. *James Merrill: Knowing Innocence.* New York: Routledge, 2007.

Schneer, David, and Caryn Aviv, eds. *American Queer, Now and Then.* Boulder, CO: Paradigm, 2006.

Scruggs, Charles, and Lee Van Demarr. *Jean Toomer and the Terrors of American History.* Philadelphia: University of Pennsylvania Press, 1998.

Shepherd, Reginald. "The Other's Other: Against Identity Poetry." *Michigan Quarterly Review* 42, no. 4 (2003): 648–60.

Shockley, Evie. "Race, Reception, and Claudia Rankine's 'American Lyric.'" *Los Angeles Review of Books*, January 6, 2016. https://lareviewofbooks.org/article/reconsidering-claudia-rankines-citizen-an-american-lyric-a-symposium-part-i/.

———. *Renegade Poetics: Black Aesthetics and Formal Innovation in African American Poetry.* Iowa City: University of Iowa Press, 2011.

Silberman, Eve. "Thylias Moss: A Poet of Many Voices and a Spellbinding Delivery." *Michigan Today* 27, no. 3 (1995): 8–9.

Singh, Jakeet. "Recognition and Self-determination: Approaches from Above and Below." In *Recognition vs. Self-determination: Dilemmas of Emancipatory Politics*, edited by Avigail Eisenberg, Jeremy Webber, Glen Coulthard, and Andrée Boiselle, 47–74. Vancouver: University of British Columbia Press, 2014.

Skillman, Nikki. *The Lyric in the Age of the Brain.* Cambridge, MA: Harvard University Press, 2016.

———. "Lyric Reading Revisited: Passion, Address, and Form in *Citizen*." *American Literary History* 31, no. 3 (2019): 419–57.

Smethurst, James. *The Black Arts Movement: Literary Nationalism in the 1960s and 1970s.* Chapel Hill: University of North Carolina Press, 2005.

Snediker, Michael. *Queer Optimism: Lyric Personhood and Other Felicitous Persuasions.* Minneapolis: University of Minnesota Press, 2009.

Spivak, Gayatri. "Can the Subaltern Speak?" In *Marxism and the Interpretation of Culture*, edited by Cary Nelson and Lawrence Grossberg, 271–313. Urbana: University of Illinois Press, 1988.

278 | Bibliography

Squire, J. C. *Selections from Modern Poets*. London: Martin Secker, 1921.

St. Armand, Barton Levi. "Transcendence through Technique: Whitman's 'Crossing Brooklyn Ferry' and Impressionist Painting." *Bucknell Review* 24, no. 2 (1978): 56–74.

Stewart, Susan. *Poetry and the Fate of the Senses*. Chicago: University of Chicago Press, 2002.

Stovall, Floyd. *The Foreground of "Leaves of Grass."* Charlottesville: University Press of Virginia, 1974.

Tate, Allen. "American Poetry Since 1920." *Bookman* 68, no. 5 (1929): 503–8.

———. "Hart Crane and the American Mind." *Poetry* 40, no. 4 (1932): 210–16.

Tatlock, Lynne, and Matt Erlin, eds. *German Culture in Nineteenth-Century America: Reception, Adaptation, Transformation*. Rochester, NY: Camden House, 2005.

Taussig, Charlotte. "The New Negro as Revealed in His Poetry." *Opportunity* 5 (1927): 108–11.

Taylor, Charles. "The Politics of Recognition." In *Multiculturalism: Examining the Politics of Recognition*, edited by Amy Gutmann, 25–73. Princeton, NJ: Princeton University Press, 1994.

Taylor, Julie. "On Holding and Being Held: Hart Crane's Queer Intimacy." *Twentieth-Century Literature* 60, no. 3 (2014): 305–35.

Thomas, Wynn. *The Lunar Light of Whitman's Poetry*. Cambridge, MA: Harvard University Press, 1987.

Toomer, Jean. "Americans and Mary Austin." In "My Chosen World: Jean Toomer's Articles in *The New York Call*," edited by Charles Scruggs. *Arizona Quarterly* 51, no. 2 (1995): 103–26.

———. *Cane*. Edited by Rudolph P. Byrd and Henry Louis Gates, Jr. New York: Norton, 2011.

———. *The Collected Poems of Jean Toomer*. Edited by Robert Jones and Margery Toomer Latimer. Chapel Hill: University of North Carolina Press, 1988.

———. *A Jean Toomer Reader: Selected Unpublished Writings*. Edited by Frederik L. Rusch. New York: Oxford University Press, 1993.

———. "Race Problems and Modern Society." In *Jean Toomer: Selected Essays and Literary Criticism*, edited by Robert Jones, 60–76. Knoxville: University of Tennessee Press, 1996.

———. *Selected Essays and Literary Criticism*. Edited by Robert B. Jones. Knoxville: University of Tennessee Press, 1996.

———. *The Wayward and the Seeking: A Collection of Writings by Jean Toomer*. Edited by Darwin T. Turner. Washington, DC: Howard University Press, 1980.

Toomer, Jean, and Waldo Frank. *Brother Mine: The Correspondence of Jean Toomer and Waldo Frank*. Edited by Kathleen Pfeiffer. Urbana: University of Illinois Press, 2010.

Unterecker, John. *Voyager: A Life of Hart Crane*. New York: Farrar, Straus and Giroux, 1969.

Untermeyer, Louis, ed. *Modern American Poetry: A Critical Anthology*. 3rd rev. ed. New York: Harcourt, Brace, 1925.

Vendler, Helen. "Braving the Elements." *New York Times*, September 24, 1972, BR5.

Vincent, John. *Queer Lyrics: Difficulty and Closure in American Poetry*. New York: Palgrave Macmillan, 2002.

von Hallberg, Robert. *Lyric Powers*. Chicago: University of Chicago, 2008.

Wald, Priscilla. *Constituting Americans: Cultural Anxiety and Narrative Form*. Durham, NC: Duke University Press, 1995.

Walker, Alice. *In Search of Our Mother's Gardens*. New York: Harcourt, Brace, and Jovanovich, 1982.

Walters, L. D'Oyly, ed. *The Year's at the Spring: An Anthology of Recent Poetry*. New York: Brentano, 1920.

Wang, Dorothy. *Thinking Its Presence: Form, Race, and Subjectivity in Asian American Poetry*. Palo Alto, CA: Stanford University Press, 2014.

Waniek, Marilyn Nelson. "A Multitude of Dreams." *Kenyon Review* 13, no. 4 (1991): 214–26.

Warner, Michael. "The Pleasures and Dangers of Shame." In *Gay Shame*, edited by David Halperin and Valerie Traub, 283–96. Chicago: University of Chicago Press, 2009.

———. *Publics and Counterpublics*. New York: Zone Books, 2002.

Waters, William. *Poetry's Touch: On Lyric Address*. Ithaca, NY: Cornell University Press, 2003.

Weber, Brom. *Hart Crane: A Biographical and Critical Study*. New York: Bodley, 1948.

Weir, John. "Mad about the Boys." *Advocate*, no. 661/662 (1994): 32–37.

Weirick, Bruce. *From Whitman to Sandburg in American Poetry: A Critical Survey*. New York: Macmillan, 1924.

Wheatley, Phillis. "On Being Brought from Africa to America." In *The Collected Works of Phillis Wheatley*, edited by John Shields, 18. New York: Oxford University Press, 1988.

White, Gillian. *Lyric Shame: The "Lyric" Subject of Contemporary American Poetry*. Cambridge, MA: Harvard University Press, 2014.

Whitman, Walt. *The Correspondence*. Vol. 3, *1876–1885*. Edited by Edwin Haviland Miller. New York: New York University Press, 2007.

———. *Daybooks and Notebooks*. Vol. 1, *Daybooks 1876–November 1881*. Edited by William White. New York: New York University Press, 1978.

———. *Leaves of Grass and Other Writings*. Edited by Michael Moon. New York: Norton, 2002.

———. *Leaves of Grass: A Textual Variorum of the Printed Poems*. Vols. 1–3. Edited by Sculley Bradley, Harold W. Blodgett, Arthur Golden, and William White. New York: New York University Press, 1980.

280 | Bibliography

———. *Notebooks and Unpublished Prose Manuscripts.* Vol. 1, *Family Notes and Autobiography.* Edited by Edward F. Grier. New York: New York University Press, 1984.

———. *Notebooks and Unpublished Prose Manuscripts.* Vol. 6, *Notes and Index.* Edited by Edward F. Grier. New York: New York University Press, 1984.

———. *Poetry and Prose.* Edited by Justin Kaplan. New York: Library of America, 1996.

———. *Prose Works, 1892.* Vol. 1. Edited by Floyd Stovall. New York: New York University Press, 1963.

———. *The Uncollected Poetry and Prose of Walt Whitman.* Vol. 1. Edited by Emory Holloway. Garden City, NY: Doubleday, Page, 1921.

Wilderson, Frank. *"We're Trying to Destroy the World": Anti-Blackness and Police Violence after Ferguson.* Ill Will Editions, 2014. https://illwill.com/print/were-trying-to-destroy-the-world.

Williams, Diana. "Building the Race: Jean Toomer's Eugenic Aesthetic." In *Jean Toomer and the Harlem Renaissance*, edited by Geneviève Fabre and Michael Feith, 188–201. New Brunswick, NJ: Rutgers University Press, 2001.

Williams, Melissa S. "Introduction: On the Use and Abuse of Recognition in Politics." In *Recognition vs. Self-determination: Dilemmas of Emancipatory Politics*, edited by Avigail Eisenberg, Jeremy Webber, Glen Coulthard, and Andrée Boiselle, 3–19. Vancouver: University of British Columbia Press, 2014.

Williams, Robert R. *Hegel's Ethics of Recognition.* Berkeley: University of California Press, 1997.

Williams, William Carlos. *In the American Grain.* New York: Albert and Charles Boni, 1925.

Wilson, Ivy. *Specters of Democracy: Blackness and the Aesthetics of Politics in the Antebellum U. S.* Oxford: Oxford University Press, 2011.

Wilson, Woodrow. *The Papers of Woodrow Wilson.* Vol. 12, *1900–1902.* Edited by Arthur Link. Princeton, NJ: Princeton University Press, 1972.

Windell, Maria. "Citizenship in Citizen." *Los Angeles Review of Books*, January 6, 2016. https://lareviewofbooks.org/article/reconsidering-claudia-rankines-citizen-an-american-lyric-a-symposium-part-i/.

Winters, Yvor. "The Significance of *The Bridge*, by Hart Crane, or, What Are We to Think of Professor X?" In *In Defense of Reason*, 577–603. New York: Swallow, 1947.

Wittman, Carl. *The Gay Manifesto.* New York: Red Butterfly, n.d. https://paganpressbooks.com/jpl/TRB-WITT.PDF.

Woodson, Jon. *To Make a New Race: Gurdjieff, Toomer, and the Harlem Renaissance.* Jackson: University Press of Mississippi, 1999.

Yenser, Stephen. *The Consuming Myth: The Work of James Merrill.* Cambridge, MA: Harvard University Press, 1987.

Yingling, Thomas E. *Hart Crane and the Homosexual Text: New Thresholds, New Anatomies.* Chicago: University of Chicago Press, 1990.

Young, Iris Marion. *Inclusion and Democracy.* Oxford: Oxford University Press, 2000.

Yu, Christopher. *Nothing to Admire: The Politics of Poetic Satire from Dryden to Merrill.* Oxford: Oxford University Press, 2003.

Zamir, Shamoon. *Dark Voices: W. E. B. DuBois and American Thought, 1888–1903.* Chicago: University of Chicago Press, 1995.

Index

abstraction, 9, 49, 85, 169, 187
  as lyric, 11–13, 37–38, 58, 69–70, 76, 178, 188–190
accountability, 2, 4, 142–143, 195–197
activist movements, 136–137, 141, 183, 248n29, 249n31. *See also* Black Arts movement; gay rights movement; Harlem Renaissance
address, 3–5, 9–11, 118–119, 197
  direct, 1–2, 29, 42–44, 54–55, 121, 187–188, 196, 199n5
  first-person, 137–138, 169, 192–195
  Toomer and, 69, 80–81, 86, 220n4
"Advice" (Moss), 162, 170–174, 258n42
affect, 14, 28, 56–57, 176, 182, 184
agency, 14, 40, 53, 176–178
Altieri, Charles, 189, 216n41
ambiguity, 45, 145, 149–151, 192
America
  1850s in, 34–42, 213n20
  Great Depression in, 84–86, 88
  Hegel and, 32, 58–59
  mysticism and, 89, 104, 116, 235n36, 241n80
  readers of poetry in, 2, 13, 26, 39, 43–44, 54, 76, 83, 96, 101, 109, 121–122, 126, 169, 192, 195–197, 261n35

American race, 25, 62–67, 70–71, 83, 86, 90–91, 152, 229n98
"Americans and Mary Austin" (Toomer), 62
anontic spaces, 7, 20–22, 29, 191, 195. *See also* Moten, Fred; paraontic spaces; undercommons
antipoetry, of Toomer, 80, 229n90
Anzaldúa, Gloria, 138
appropriation
  lyricization and, 137, 187
  metaphor and, 159, 162, 172
assimilation, 132, 247n16
  cultural pluralism and, 66–67, 131, 135
  individual and, 32–33
  liberation movements, 139, 148–149
  multiculturalism and, 65–66
"Atlantis" (Crane), 97, 102–103, 117, 119, 243n92
Austin, Mary, 62, 116

Barad, Karen, 209n93
Baraka, Amiri, 138, 255n21
Bauerlein, Mark, 39
Beach, Christopher, 36
Beckett, Angela, 238n58, 242n87
Before Modernism (Jackson, V.), 12–13, 15, 70, 206n56

283

284 | Index

Being Numerous (Izenberg), 202n32
being-with, 22, 185, 196
  in "Crossing Brooklyn Ferry,"
    41–42, 44–45
  knowing-who compared to, 5–7,
    18, 44, 190, 192
  sexuality and, 45–46, 52–53
Berlant, Lauren, 14, 205n52
Berssenbrugge, Mei-mei
  Empathy, 187–190
  "Honeymoon," 188–190, 260n9
  recognition and, 188
Bishop, Elizabeth, 133, 140, 160,
  253n79
Black Arts movement, 3, 27–28, 137–
  138, 249n29, 254n8, 255n21
  Moss and, 160–161, 163–168
Black radical tradition, 21–22, 135–
  136
Black Skin, White Masks (Fanon), 3,
  21, 200n12
The Black Woman (Cade), 249n29,
  255n22
Blasing, Mutlu Konuk, 148
  Lyric Poetry, 203n33
Bloom, Harold, 168–169
"The Blue Meridian" (Toomer), 6, 25,
  64–65, 70, 78–89, 120, 228n83
Bogan, Louise, 129
Bourne, Randolph, 28, 224n29
Braithwaite, William Stanley, 226n65
Braving the Elements (Merrill),
  129–130
The Bridge (Crane), 6, 25–26, 233n16,
  242n87, 245n104
  "Atlantis," 97, 102–103, 117, 119,
    243n92
  "Crossing Brooklyn Ferry" and,
    104–106, 112
  cultural pluralism and, 113–121,
    241n80
  "The Dance," 116–120, 236n40,
    241n82, 243n91

  drafts of, 96–97, 102–113, 121–127,
    233n16–17, 235n35–36, 236n40–
    42
  "Powhatan's Daughter," 116–120
  "Recitative" and, 120–121, 125–126,
    244n96, 244n99, 245n102
  "The Tunnel," 236n40
Brown, Sharon, 233n12
Brown, Sterling, 76
Brunner, Edward, 120, 233n17,
  243n94, 245n99
burlesque
  of recognition, 141–142, 149, 151,
    153–158
  of spiritualism, 132
Butler, Judith, 19, 200n12, 205n54,
  208n78
Byrd, Rudolph P., 222n13, 229n90

Cacho, Lisa, 209n78
Cade, Toni, 165
  The Black Woman (Cade), 249n29,
    255n22
Cane (Toomer), 63–64, 80, 220n9
capitalism, 85–86, 88, 97, 121,
  125–126
Carson, Luke, 253n79
The Changing Light at Sandover
  (Merrill), 27, 131–132, 149–156,
  252n71, 253n77
Chesnutt, Charles, 65–66, 229n98
Citizen (Rankine), 1, 261n35
  nowhere in, 29, 191, 193–196
  recognition in, 2–4, 192–197
citizenship, 2, 24, 261n34
  eligibility and, 34–42
  slavery and, 34–35
Claborn, John, 258n42
class consciousness, 76, 122
  community and, 253n79
  in poetry, 85, 125, 145–146, 196
  race and, 77, 91
  radicalism and, 130

social recognition and, 10, 147, 201n27
"Clearing the Title" (Merrill), 27, 153–158, 252n75
Coblentz, Stanton, 232n11
Cohen, Tom, 216n42
community, 15–16, 106, 135–136, 157–158, 162, 191–192
class consciousness and, 253n79
eligibility and, 24–25, 34, 52–53, 55–56
elitism and, 153–154
recognition and, 7
contradiction, 26, 160
Crane and, 120
Merrill and, 130–132, 141, 148
recognition and, 22–23, 25, 33–34, 89, 120, 132, 141
Toomer and, 76, 84, 86, 89
Whitman and, 33, 58
Cook, Steve H., 240n74, 242n82
Coviello, Peter, 44, 52, 218n58
Crane, Hart, 196, 233n13, 239n67
contradiction and, 120
criticism of, 237n58, 240n69
cultural pluralism and, 97, 113–121, 235n36, 241n80
drafts of, 96–97, 102–113, 121–127, 233n16–17, 235n35–36, 236n40–42
Eliot and, 95, 97, 103–104, 116–117, 234n35, 236n37, 242n85
Frank and, 98, 103–104, 113–116, 235n36, 238n64, 240n71, 241n78–80
Hammer on, 98, 103, 105–106, 234n26, 236n45, 244n99
letters of, 94–95, 112, 118, 234n3, 234n31, 239n68–69, 244n95–96
logic of metaphor and, 26–27, 101–102, 107–108, 121–123
looking without recognizing and, 96–99, 102, 106, 110, 117, 121–124, 127

lyric sociality of, 94, 97–98, 102, 115, 126
lyricization and, 6, 95–96
Merrill and, 152
on metaphors, 108–109, 238n61, 242n87
misrecognition and, 123–125
Munson letters of, 93–94, 113, 121–122, 235n35–36, 236n37, 239n68–69, 243n95
politics of recognition and, 96, 104, 113–116, 123
reader and, 26–27, 101, 109–110, 123–126
sexuality and, 94–96, 98–104, 112–113, 117–118, 121–127
Toomer and, 24–25, 98–102, 234n23
Whitman and, 96, 104, 110–111, 120, 240n69
Crane, Hart, works of. See also *The Bridge*
"Atlantis," 97, 102–103, 117, 119, 243n92
"The Dance," 97, 116–120, 236n40, 241n82, 243n91
"General Aims and Theories," 109–110
"Possessions," 96–102, 234n23–24, 234n26, 234n30
"Powhatan's Daughter," 116–120
"Recitative," 121–127, 244n96, 244n99, 245n102
"The Tunnel," 236n40
White Buildings, 113, 121–122, 125
"Criteria of Negro Art" (DuBois), 74–75
criticism
of Crane, 237n58, 240n69
of *Leaves of Grass*, 36–37, 212n16, 212n18, 213n20–22
of Merrill, 129–131, 246n13
of Moss, 169, 178–179, 257n34

286 | Index

criticism *(continued)*
  of poetry, 232n11–12
  of Toomer, 63–64, 221n11
  of Whitman, 38, 213n26
"Crossing Brooklyn Ferry"
    (Whitman), 5, 24–25, 39–40,
    47–48, 203n33, 215n37, 218n62
  being-with in, 41–42, 44–45
  The Bridge and, 104–106, 112
  democratic sociality and, 53–54
  direct address and, 42–44, 54–55
  eligibility and, 32–34, 41, 45–46,
    52–59
  intimacy and, 52–56
  misrecognition in, 49–52
  politics and, 56–58
  Rankine and, 29, 196
  sociality and, 43–44, 55–56
Culler, Jonathan, 204n37
  Theory of the Lyric, 11
cultural pluralism, 24, 26, 90–92
  assimilation and, 66–67, 131, 135
  The Bridge and, 113–121, 241n80
  Crane and, 97, 113–121, 235n36,
    241n80
  of Frank, 67–68, 114–115
  gay rights movement and, 131,
    134–135
  Harlem Renaissance and, 64,
    69–78, 138
  of Kallen, 66–68, 114
  "melting pot" compared to, 66–67
  race and, 65–78
  racism and, 63, 67, 69, 75, 77
  recognition and, 63, 68
  Toomer and, 63–64, 71–72, 77–78,
    84, 87–88
  Whitman and, 58–59

Dana, Charles Henry, 36
"The Dance" (Crane), 97, 116–120,
    236n40, 241n82, 243n91

Dean, Tim, 238n58
Deutsch, Babette, 233n12–13
dialects, 21, 35, 69–70, 73–74, 90,
    226n65
Dickey, James, 129
Dickie, Margaret, 236n41
Dickinson, Emily, 180
Dickinson's Misery (Jackson, V.), 13,
    204n49
Diepeveen, Leonard, 108
digressions, of Moss, 162, 170, 179
Dimock, Wai Chee, 44–45, 216n41
direct address
  "Crossing Brooklyn Ferry" and,
    42–44, 54–55
  reader and, 1–2, 29, 42–44, 54–55,
    121, 187–188, 196, 199n5
disidentification, 201n20
  recognition and, 6–7
distance, 43–44, 50–51
  intimacy and, 105–107, 188–190
Divine Comedies (Merrill), 141–150
domesticity, 132, 143–144, 153
Dougherty, James, 56
Douglass, Frederick, 223n16
Dowling, Sarah, 16
drafts
  of Crane, 96–97, 102–113, 121–
    127, 233n16–17, 235n35–36,
    236n40–42
  of Merrill, 142, 145–146
  of Whitman, 33, 38–42, 211n7,
    212n8, 215n37
DuBois, W. E. B., 66, 135–136,
    222n16
  "Criteria of Negro Art," 74–75
Dunbar, Paul Laurence, 69–70, 73,
    74
Duncan, Robert, 133–134

Edelman, Lee, 238n58
1850s in America, 34–42, 213n20

"The Eighteenth Presidency" (Whitman), 39, 214n30–31
eligibility, 5–6
  blackness and, 91–92, 187, 192
  citizenship and, 34–42
  community and, 24–25, 34, 52–53, 55–56
  "Crossing Brooklyn Ferry" and, 32–34, 41, 45–46, 52–59
  legibility and, 7, 29, 109–110, 196–197
  metaphor and, 180
  ontological proximity and, 43–45, 52–53, 55, 57–58, 96, 110, 120–122
  politics of, 54–57
  recognition and, 7, 22–23, 34, 191
  Whitman and, 32–34, 41, 63–64, 211n7, 215n37
Eliot, T. S., 82
  Crane and, 95, 97, 103–104, 116–117, 234n35, 236n37, 242n85
elitism, 87–88, 108
  of Merrill, 152–154, 252n71
Empathy (Berssenbrugge), 187–190
entanglement, 23, 28, 163, 209n93
  metaphor and, 183–184
Erlin, Matt, 32
eroticism, 34, 54–55, 104, 107, 122, 184
  gay poetry and, 129, 249n37
Espiritu, Yen Le, 208n70
ethnic nationalism, 26–27, 72, 129, 135–136, 139
  Moss and, 161–162, 169
eugenics, 25, 65, 87, 151–152, 159, 230n103
Evans, Steve, 246n13
exclusion, 4, 98, 169, 177–178, 231n6
  recognition and, 2, 21–22, 24, 68–69, 75–76, 163
  representation and, 10

"The Extraordinary Hoof" (Moss), 168–169

Fanon, Frantz, *Black Skin, White Masks*, 3, 21, 200n12
Farred, Grant, 3
feminisms, 161, 206n63, 249n29, 255n22
"The First American" (Toomer), 61–62, 83, 220n2
first-person address, 137–138, 169, 192–195
Fisher, Clive, 244n99
Foley, Barbara, 58, 69, 222n11, 225n53, 227n73
folk tradition, poetry and, 73–76, 82, 226n65
Foner, Eric, 35
Ford, Karen, 80, 84, 225n54, 229n90, 229n94, 254n8
formalism, 142–143, 149–150, 251n61
  free verse and, 131–132
  liberation movements and, 141
  normativity and, 144, 148
  politics and, 129, 140
Frank, Waldo
  Crane and, 98, 103–104, 113–116, 235n36, 238n64, 240n71, 241n78–80
  cultural pluralism of, 67–68, 114–115
  Hegel and, 67–68, 114, 240n74
  Our America, 84, 116, 118, 235n36, 241n82
  Re-discovery of America, 67–68, 114–115, 240n74, 241n78
  Toomer and, 71, 84, 224n41
Fraser, Nancy, 10, 201n27
free verse, 57, 95, 140–142
  formalism and, 131–132
  politics of, 129–130, 246n4

288 | Index

freedom, 126
  slavery and, 48–49
friendship, 93–94, 98, 113, 184
"from above" recognition, 137, 142, 147, 151, 166. *See also* cultural pluralism
"from below" recognition, 137, 142, 147, 161–162, 166, 249n31. *See also* ethnic nationalism; liberation movements

Garvey, Marcus, 72, 135, 223n26
Gates, Henry Louis, Jr., 222n13, 225n48, 258n54
gay culture, 134, 247n17
  Merrill and, 131–133, 139–141
Gay Liberation Front (GLF), 133, 138, 247n16, 248n29, 249n37
gay poetry, 103, 138–140
  eroticism and, 129, 249n37
gay rights movement, 133, 247n16
  cultural pluralism and, 131, 134–135
"General Aims and Theories" (Crane), 109–110
Genette, Gérard, 12
genre, 70, 197, 204n46, 255n21. *See also* lyric
  history and, 12
  identity and, 14–15, 205n52
  lyricization and, 4–5, 12, 38, 213n26
  misrecognition and, 14
  postlyric, 169
  recognition and, 15, 206n56
Gilbert, Roger, 44
Ginsberg, Allen, 139–140, 250n42
Gitelman, Lisa, 12–13, 204n46
GLF. *See* Gay Liberation Front
"Glory" (Moss), 175
"The Glue Under" (Herrera), 190–191
Grahn, Judy, 139

Great Depression, 84–86, 88
Grossman, Allen
  Hegel and, 11, 202n32, 203n33
  Jackson, V., and, 13–15
  The Long Schoolroom, 10–11
  poetry and, 10–11, 202n28
  The Sighted Singer, 9–10, 201n26
groups
  identity and, 65–68, 77–78, 88, 114–115, 133, 135–138, 165, 170–171, 207n65
  recognition and, 26–27, 139, 141, 165–166, 178
Gunn, Thom, 150
Gurdjieff, Georges, 63–64, 80, 87, 220n9, 227n73
Gwiazda, Piotr, 131

Haines, Christian, 53
Hammer, Langdon
  on Crane, 98, 103, 105–106, 234n26, 236n45, 244n99
  on Merrill, 130–131, 133, 140, 142, 152, 155
Harlem Renaissance, 3, 25, 59, 63, 116, 135, 164, 169, 230n103
  cultural pluralism and, 64, 69–78, 138
  debate about use of dialect in, 69–70, 73–74, 90, 226n65
Harney, Stefano, 21–22
Harris, William Torrey, 32, 58–59, 219n69–70
Hawkins, Stephanie, 221n11, 230n103
Hay, Harry, 134–135, 248n19
Hegel, G. W. F., 200n12
  Culler and, 11
  Fanon and, 3
  Frank and, 67–68, 114, 240n74
  Grossman and, 11, 202n32, 203n33

historicity and, 32, 49
Jackson, V., and, 12–15
Oliver and, 18–19
The Phenomenology of Spirit, 34, 45–60, 205n54
poetics and, 8–9, 201n26, 206n56
recognition and, 9–11, 13–16, 47–51, 137, 162, 171, 174–175, 182, 205n54, 245n105
St. Louis Hegelians, 32, 34, 58–59, 84, 114, 211n4–6, 219n69–70, 227n67
Whitman and, 5, 32–34, 46–47, 49–51, 217n46–47
Henderson, Alice, 232n12
Herrera, Juan Felipe, 187
"The Glue Under," 190–191
heteronormativity, 53, 144, 148–150, 249n37
hierarchies, 27, 29, 77–78, 141, 196
in poetics, 13, 179, 193–194
recognition and, 2, 15, 18–19, 22, 26, 41, 58–59, 65, 70, 75, 89, 115–116, 126, 152–153, 165, 184
historicity, 17, 47–49, 206n56
Hegel and, 32, 49
lyric and, 8, 64–65, 69–70, 94–95, 131–132, 137–139, 193–194, 208n69, 213n26
lyricization and, 6, 12–15, 23
history
democratic sociality and, 193
genre and, 12
solidarity and, 171–174
universalism and, 28–29
white supremacy and, 135–136, 196
homosexuality, 45–46, 62, 234n3, 244n100
Crane and, 93–94, 97, 100, 103, 107, 117–118, 242n87
cruising and, 100, 234n24

laws and, 93–94, 123–124, 231n1
Merrill and, 129–130, 132–133, 144, 149, 152
recognition and, 132–135, 138–139, 231n6
"Honeymoon" (Berssenbrugge), 188–190, 260n9
hospitality, 6, 23, 27, 132, 143, 153–158, 177
Hughes, Langston, 79–80
Whitman and, 228n89
Hutchinson, George, 79, 220n3, 221n11, 228n87

identity, 7, 34–35, 228n89
burlesque and, 141–142
disidentification and, 6–7, 201n20
genre and, 14–15, 205n52
groups and, 65–68, 77–78, 88, 114–115, 133, 135–138, 165, 170–171, 207n65
memory and, 51, 53, 145–147, 171–173, 182, 189
performance of, 52–53, 79–80, 139–140, 156–158, 163–164, 178, 205n52, 253n78
resistance to, 52–53, 61–65, 89–91, 101, 110, 133, 218n58
transcendence of, 3, 59, 63, 168–171, 221n11
immigration, 24, 34–35, 59, 65–69, 215n33, 219n70
imperialism, 24, 34, 57–58, 120, 246n4
intersectionality, 161
solidarity and, 162, 171–175
intimacy
"Crossing Brooklyn Ferry" and, 52–56
distance and, 105–107, 188–190
race and, 52–53, 79–80
Irwin, John, 109, 237n58

290 | Index

Iyengar, Sunil, 261n35
Izenberg, Oren, *Being Numerous*,
 202n32

Jackson, David, 152
Jackson, Virginia, 4, 11, 37–38, 95,
 205n52
 Before Modernism, 12–13, 15, 70,
 206n56
 Dickinson's Misery, 13, 204n49
 Grossman and, 13–15
 on lyricization, 12–15, 69–70,
 204n49, 224n39
James, William, 68, 224n28
Javadizadeh, Kamran, 3–4, 194–195,
 260n27
Jewishness, 133–135, 151–152, 162,
 171–174
Jimenez, Juan Ramon, 243n93
Johnson, Georgia Douglas, 79,
 228n87
Johnson, James Weldon, 226n65
 Toomer and, 90–92
Jones, Gavin, 69–70
Jones, Meta, 254n8
Just Us (Rankine), 261n34

Kallen, Horace, 224n28, 225n43,
 240n73
 cultural pluralism of, 66–68, 114
Kalstone, David, 143
Kameny, Frank, 135
Keats, John, 213n25
Keenaghan, Eric, 207n63
Keller, Lynn, 252n73
Kennedy, John F., 135
Kinnahan, Linda, 206n63
KKK. *See* Ku Klux Klan
knowing-who, being-with compared
 to, 5–7, 18, 44, 190, 192
Ku Klux Klan (KKK), 67–68, 223n26

lapse, of memory, 145, 251n56

Larson, Charles, 229n90
Last Chance for the Tarzan Holler
 (Moss), 28, 162, 170–176, 179
Lawrence, D. H., 216n42, 241n82
laws, homosexuality and, 93–94,
 123–124, 231n1
Leaves of Grass (Whitman), 35, 38–
 39, 211n7, 214n28
 criticism of, 36–37, 212n16,
 212n18, 213n20–22
legibility, 17–18, 36, 113, 134, 163,
 192
 eligibility and, 7, 29, 109–110,
 196–197
 recognition and, 7, 46, 117, 196
 the state and, 136–137
Leonard, Keith, 138
"Lessons from a Mirror" (Moss),
 166–167
letters
 of Crane, 94–95, 112, 118, 234n3,
 234n31, 239n68–69, 244n95–96
 between Crane and Munson, 93–
 94, 113, 121–122, 235n35–36,
 236n37, 239n68–69, 243n95
 between Crane and Toomer, 98–
 102, 234n23
 of Merrill, 133, 251n65
 of Whitman, 32, 211n6
Levinas, Emmanuel, 202n32
Lewis, David Levering, 223n16
Lewis, R. W. B., 242n85
Leyland, Winston, 138–139, 250n39
liberation movements
 assimilation and, 139, 148–149
 formalism and, 141
 gay liberation, 26–27, 136, 247n16,
 250n39, 255n22
 poets and, 131–132, 138–139
 self-recognition and, 136, 161
limited fork poetics, 28, 162–163,
 177–185, 254n11
 logic of metaphor and, 160–161

Index | 291

Lincoln, Abraham, 35
Lindsey, Kay, 165, 255n22
Locke, Alain, 225n43, 226n65
  Black poets and, 73–74, 76
  "The New Negro," 71–74, 76,
    220n3, 225n48
  radicalism and, 76, 135, 227n71
  Toomer and, 71–72, 224n42,
    225n53, 226n54
logic of metaphor, 111–112, 115,
  237n58
  Crane and, 26–27, 101–102, 107–
    108, 121–123
  limited fork poetics and, 160–161
  poetics and, 97, 109–110
  Whitman and, 240n69
The Long Schoolroom (Grossman),
  10–11
looking without recognizing, 96–99,
  102, 106, 110, 117, 121–124, 127
Lorde, Audre, 256n24
Lowell, Robert, 29, 194–195, 260n27
Lutenski, Emily, 221n11
Lyric Poetry (Blasing), 203n33
Lyric Powers (von Hallberg), 203n33
lyricization, 4–5
  appropriation and, 137, 187
  Crane and, 6, 95–96
  genre and, 12, 38, 213n26
  historicity and, 6, 12–15, 23
  Jackson, V., on, 12–15, 69–70,
    204n49, 224n39
  Merrill and, 6
  Moss and, 6, 160, 166, 177–178
  race and, 13, 15, 69, 204n49
  recognition and, 6, 12–15, 137–138
  resistance to, 37–38, 96, 213n25
  speaker and, 37
  Toomer and, 6, 69–71, 73, 76,
    83–84
  white supremacy and, 64–65, 70–
    71, 83, 160, 195
  Whitman and, 34, 37–38, 58

"A Man" (Moss), 175–176
Mance, Ajuan Maria, 161
manifestoes, 136, 211n7, 248n28
Markell, Patchen, 19–20
Marrs, Cody, 46
Martin, Robert, 234n24
Marx, Karl, 202n32
Marxism, 208n69
mastery, 19–20, 118, 195
  Merrill and, 141, 147–149, 152–
    153, 155
  Moss and, 159–161, 183
  slavery and, 48–49, 159, 183
  Whitman and, 43–44, 216
Materer, Timothy, 144–145, 152,
  247n14, 250n52
McKay, Claude, 76, 79
"melting pot," cultural pluralism
  compared to, 66–67
memory
  identity and, 51, 53, 145–147,
    171–173, 182, 189
  lapse of, 145, 251n56
  lyric and, 9
  lyricization and, 4–5, 12
  recognition and, 51, 174
Merrill, James, 26, 196
  Bishop and, 133, 140, 253n79
  burlesque of, 132, 141–142, 149,
    151, 153–158
  contradiction and, 130–132, 141, 148
  Crane and, 152
  criticism of, 129–131, 246n13
  drafts of, 142, 145–146
  elitism of, 152–154, 252n71
  formalism of, 129, 131–132, 140–
    144, 148–150, 251n61
  gay culture and, 131–133, 139–141
  gay rights movement and, 133
  generosity, privilege and, 130–131,
    246n13
  Hammer on, 130–131, 133, 140,
    142, 152, 155

292 | Index

Merrill, James *(continued)*
  homosexuality and, 129–130, 132–133, 144, 149, 152
  hospitality and, 6, 27, 132, 143, 153–158
  letters of, 133, 251n65
  lyricization and, 6
  mastery and, 141, 147–149, 152–153, 155
  mysticism and, 146–152
  Ouija board and, 146, 150–151, 251n60, 251n65–66
  politics of recognition in, 131–132, 137–138, 142, 149–150, 157–158
  sexuality and, 129–130, 133, 140–142, 144, 146–153, 246n8
  theater imagery and, 153, 155–156, 252nn73–74, 253n78
  Toomer and, 152
Merrill, James, works of
  Braving the Elements, 129–130
  The Changing Light at Sandover, 27, 131–132, 149–156, 252n71, 253n77
  "Clearing the Title," 27, 153–158, 252n75
  Divine Comedies, 141–150
  "A Room at the Heart of Things," 253n78
  "The Will," 132, 141–150, 250n52
metaphor, 26, 197, 237n50. *See also* logic of metaphor
  appropriation and, 159, 162, 172
  Crane on, 108–109, 238n61, 242n87
  eligibility and, 180
  entanglement and, 183–184
  Moss and, 159–160, 162, 172, 177, 185
  racism and, 182
  recognition and, 160–161
  slavery and, 159
  violence of, 181

Michaels, Walter Benn, 68
Middle Passage, 29
Mill, John Stuart, 2–3, 200n10
Miller, Cristanne, 36
Mills, Charles, 201n27
misrecognition, 2, 89, 115–116
  Crane and, 123–125
  in "Crossing Brooklyn Ferry," 49–52
  genre and, 14
  Moss and, 162, 165–167, 180–184
  oppression and, 10–11, 16, 42, 167, 180–184, 201n27
modernism, 25, 73, 75, 108, 232n11–12, 233n13, 237n50
Monro, Harold, 232n11
Monroe, Harriet, 108–109, 232n12, 239n69
Moore, Marianne, 237n50
morality, 10–11, 49, 91, 108–109, 113, 123–125, 172, 239n69, 243n91
Moss, Thylias, 26–27, 196, 253n1
  Black Arts movement and, 160–161, 163–168
  criticism of, 169, 178–179, 257n34
  digressions of, 162, 170, 179
  ethnic nationalism and, 161–162, 169
  limited fork poetics of, 162–163, 177–185, 254n11
  lyric politics of, 161–162, 176
  lyricization and, 6, 160, 166, 177–178
  mastery and, 159–161, 183
  metaphor and, 159–160, 162, 172, 177, 185
  misrecognition and, 162, 165–167, 180–184
  politics of recognition and, 161, 168–176
  recognition and, 161–162, 166–167, 170, 176, 184–185
  sexuality and, 166–167, 174

speed of invention of, 28, 161–162, 170, 179, 188

systems of meaning of, 160–163, 177–179, 184–185

Moss, Thylias, works of

"Advice," 162, 170–174, 258n42

"The Extraordinary Hoof," 168–169

"Glory," 175

Last Chance for the Tarzan Holler, 28, 162, 170–176, 179

"Lessons from a Mirror," 166–167

"A Man," 175–176

"Quotes Community," 159–160, 184, 253n1

"The Subculture of the Wrongfully Accused," 163, 179–185

Tokyo Butter, 177–185

"The Wreckage on the Wall of Eggs," 167–168

Moten, Fred, 20–22, 179, 195–196

movements

activist, 136–137, 141, 248n29, 249n31

Black Arts, 3, 27–28, 137–138, 160–161, 163–168, 249n29, 254n8, 255n21

gay rights, 131, 133–135, 247n16

Harlem Renaissance, 3, 25, 59, 63–64, 69–76, 90, 116, 135, 164, 169

multiculturalism, 65–66, 135, 169, 201n27, 207n65, 223n16

multiethnicity, 191–192

recognition and, 79–89

Toomer and, 6, 25, 62–67, 70, 78–81, 83, 86, 89, 91, 152, 221n11, 222n13, 229n98

white supremacy and, 78

Muñoz, José Esteban, 201n20

Munson, Gorham, 93–94, 113, 121–122, 235n35–36, 236n37, 239n68–69, 243n95

mutual recognition, 3, 9–11, 47–51, 124–125, 137, 162, 171, 174–175, 182

mysticism, 243n93, 251n65

America and, 98, 104, 116, 235n36, 241n80

poetry and, 31, 64, 76, 80, 146–152

Rankine and, 3–4

Toomer and, 64, 76, 80, 221n9

Whitman and, 31, 215n38

Nathanson, Tenney, 44, 53

nationalism, 36, 43, 213n20

ethnic, 26–27, 72, 129, 135–136, 139, 161–162, 169

Native American characters, in poetry, 116–120, 241n80, 241n82, 242n85, 243n91

Nealon, Christopher, 137, 231n6

Nersessian, Anahid, 197, 262n36

Neruda, Pablo, 216n42

"The New Negro" (Locke), 71–74, 76, 220n3, 225n48

Nielsen, Aldon, 254n8

Noel, Urayoán, 15–16

normativity, 45, 112–113, 141

formalism and, 144, 148

heteronormativity, 53, 144, 148–150, 249n37

identity and, 148

North, Michael, 75

notebooks, of Whitman, 33–34, 38–41, 212n8, 215n33–34, 215n37

nowhere, in *Citizen*, 29, 191, 193–196

Oliver, Kelly, 18–19

"On Being an American" (Toomer), 61–62

ontological equality, 6–7, 23, 35, 41, 110–111, 187, 190–192

recognizability compared to, 5, 18, 24, 26

294 | Index

ontological immanence, 23, 29, 43, 52, 106, 193, 195–196
ontological proximity, 5–7, 18, 28, 163, 190
  eligibility and, 43–45, 52–53, 55, 57–58, 96, 110, 120–122
Opffer, Emil, 126, 238n64
Ouija board, 146, 150–151, 251n60, 251n65–66
Our America (Frank), 84, 116, 118, 235n36, 241n82

Palmer, Tyrone, 176
paraontic spaces, 20–22, 24, 26, 53–54, 58, 62, 70, 91, 97, 104, 109, 115, 188, 191. *See also* anontic spaces; Moten, Fred; undercommons
passing, 61–62, 222n13
patriarchy, 79, 130, 165
  racism and, 255n22
  radicalism and, 161, 254n8
Patterson, Orlando, 208n78
performance, of identity, 52–53, 79–80, 139–140, 156–158, 163–164, 178, 205n52, 253n78
"persona poem," 165–166, 258n42
personhood, 9, 16, 162
  lyric and, 3–5, 10, 13, 15, 137
  recognition and, 4, 10, 18, 40, 57, 96, 170
  universalism and, 15
  whiteness as, 3, 5, 167–168
Pevear, Richard, 130–131, 246n7
Pfeiffer, Kathleen, 222n11
The Phenomenology of Spirit (Hegel), 34, 45–60, 205n54
"Poem of Many in One" (Whitman), 33
poetry, 115. *See also* gay poetry
  antipoetry, 80, 229n90
  class consciousness in, 85, 125, 145–146, 196

folk tradition and, 73–76, 82, 226n65
Grossman and, 10–11, 202n28
mysticism and, 31, 64, 76, 80, 146–152
Native American characters in, 116–120, 241n80, 241n82, 242n85, 243n91
slavery and, 29, 37, 74, 82, 159, 167–168, 195, 211n7
Poetry and the Fate of the Senses (Stewart), 11, 202n32
politics of recognition, 2, 18–23, 207n65
  Crane and, 96, 104, 113–116, 123
  lyric and, 3–17
  Merrill and, 131–132, 137–138, 142, 149–150, 157–158
  Moss and, 161, 168–176
  Toomer and, 62–65, 73–74, 76, 86, 88, 90–92
  Whitman and, 24, 40–42, 47–54, 57–60
Polk, James K., 57–58, 219n67
Posnock, Ross, 221n11, 224n28, 224n31, 225n43
"Possessions" (Crane), 96–102, 234n23–24, 234n26, 234n30
postlyric genre, 169
Pound, Ezra, 246n4
"Powhatan's Daughter" (Crane), 116–120
Prins, Yopie, 95
privilege, 126–127, 157
  generosity and, 130–131, 246n13
  poetics and, 95–96, 142
  Toomer and, 61, 220n4
  whiteness and, 166–167

queerness, 53, 58, 120, 231n6
  recognition and, 27, 137, 141, 147, 157

"Quotes Community" (Moss), 159–160, 184, 253n1

race, 227n79
American, 25, 62–67, 70–71, 83, 86, 152, 229n98
class consciousness and, 77, 91
cultural pluralism and, 65–78
hybridized, 62, 89, 220n6, 220n9
intimacy and, 52–53, 79–80
lyric and, 3, 80, 83–84
lyricization and, 13, 15, 69, 204n49
separation of, 66–68, 71, 77–78, 87, 223n26
sexuality and, 152, 256n24
social recognition and, 20–21, 25, 72, 76, 164
solidarity and, 64, 71, 171–172
stereotypes and, 118, 151–152, 164, 242n82, 252n67
"Race Problems and Modern Society" (Toomer), 64, 76–78, 85, 87–88, 227n73, 227n79
racism, 1, 4, 118, 152, 174, 195, 242n82
cultural pluralism and, 63, 67, 69, 75, 77
metaphor and, 182
patriarchy and, 255n22
recognition and, 2, 117, 163–164
radicalism, 72
Black radical tradition and, 21–22, 135–136
class consciousness and, 130
Locke and, 76, 135, 227n72
manifestoes and, 136, 211n7, 248n28
patriarchy and, 161, 254n8
self-recognition and, 131
Ramsby, Howard, II, 166
Rankine, Claudia, 260n27
Citizen, 1–4, 29, 191–197, 261n35
"Crossing Brooklyn Ferry" and, 29, 196

Just Us, 261n34
on lyric, 2–3, 200n10
mysticism and, 3–4
reader and, 1–2, 195, 199n5
recognition and, 1–4, 193
Whitman and, 29, 196
reader
Crane and, 26–27, 101, 109–110, 123–126
direct address and, 1–2, 29, 42–44, 54–55, 121, 187–188, 196, 199n5
Rankine and, 1–2, 195, 199n5
recognition and, 13, 34, 42–44, 57, 96, 106
speaker and, 5, 9
Whitman and, 41–45, 50–56, 216n42
"Recitative" (Crane), 121–127, 244n96, 244n99, 245n102
recognition. *See also* politics of recognition; social recognition
Berssenbrugge and, 188
burlesque of, 141–142, 149, 151, 153–158
in *Citizen*, 2–4, 192–197
community and, 7
contradiction and, 22–23, 25, 33–34, 89, 120, 132, 141
Crane and, 96, 116
cultural pluralism and, 63, 68
disidentification and, 6–7
eligibility and, 7, 22–23, 34, 191
equality compared to, 18
exclusion and, 2, 21–22, 24, 68–69, 75–76, 163
Fanon and, 200n12
"from above," 137, 142, 147, 151, 166
"from below," 137, 142, 147, 161–162, 166, 249n31
genre and, 15, 206n56
group, 26–27, 139, 141, 165–166, 178

296 | Index

recognition *(continued)*
  Hegel and, 9–11, 13–16, 47–51,
    137, 162, 171, 174–175, 182,
    205n54, 245n105
  hierarchies and, 2, 15, 18–19, 22,
    26, 41, 58–59, 65, 70, 75, 89,
    115–116, 126, 152–153, 165, 184
  historicity and, 8, 47–49
  homosexuality and, 132–135, 138–
    139, 231n6
  legibility and, 7, 46, 117, 196
  looking without, 96–99, 102, 106,
    110, 117, 121–124, 127
  lyric and, 2–5, 9, 11–12, 192–193,
    200n10, 202n32, 203n33
  lyric beyond, 17–23
  lyricization and, 6, 12–15, 137–138
  memory and, 51, 174
  Merrill and, 132, 149, 157–158
  metaphor and, 160–161
  Moss and, 161–162, 166–167, 170,
    176, 184–185
  multiethnicity and, 79–89
  mutual, 3, 9–11, 47–51, 124–125,
    137, 162, 171, 174–175, 182
  New Negroes and, 71–74
  personhood and, 4, 10, 18, 40, 57,
    96, 170
  queer, 27, 137, 141, 147, 157
  racism and, 2, 117, 163–164
  Rankine and, 1–4, 193
  reader and, 13, 34, 42–44, 57, 96,
    106
  of self, 6, 26–27, 94, 131, 136, 161
  Toomer and, 62–63, 86
  violence of, 87–88, 93, 118–119,
    122, 151–152, 175
  Whitman and, 34, 40–46, 50–54,
    56–60
recognizability, ontological equality
  compared to, 5, 18, 24, 26

recognizers, 4, 10, 14–15, 41, 58–59,
    65, 75, 87, 117–118, 120, 141,
    147, 152
  poets as, 22–23, 25–26
Re-discovery of America (Frank), 67–
    68, 114–115, 240n74, 241n78
Reed, Anthony, 16, 169
Reed, Brian, 120
religion, 50, 59, 82, 89, 111, 133–134,
    162
resistance
  identity and, 52–53, 61–65, 89–91,
    101, 110, 133, 218n58
  to lyricization, 37–38, 96, 213n25
  vulnerability and, 49, 171
responsibility, 63–64, 109
  sociopolitical, 146–147, 192
Reynolds, David S., 35, 217n47,
    219n67
Rodgers, Carolyn, 165, 255n21
Rodriguez, Ralph, 16
"A Room at the Heart of Things"
  (Merrill), 253n78
Rothberg, Michael, 171–172, 258n50
Różewicz, Tadeusz, 190–191

Samito, Christian, 34
Sastri, Reena, 247n14
"Says" (Whitman), 211n7
self, 123, 253n78
  meaning and, 145
  sociality and, 47–48
self-awareness, 9, 14–15, 144–145
  culture and, 134–135
self-recognition, 6, 26–27, 94
  liberation movements and, 136, 161
  radicalism and, 131
separation of races, 66–68, 71, 77–78,
    87, 223n26
sexuality
  being-with and, 45–46, 52–53

Crane and, 94–96, 98–104, 112–113, 117–118, 121–127
Merrill and, 129–130, 133, 140–142, 144, 146–153, 246n8
Moss and, 166–167, 174
poetry and, 94, 103, 105
race and, 152, 256n24
Toomer and, 81–82
Whitman and, 53, 55, 62, 133, 217n43–44, 248n17
Shockley, Evie, 257n36
The Sighted Singer (Grossman), 9–10, 201n26
Simon, Marc, 244n99
Singh, Jakeet, 249n31
Skillman, Nikki, 3–4, 145, 200n13
slavery, 29, 74, 82–83, 136, 167–168, 194–195, 208n78
citizenship and, 34–35
freedom and, 48–49
mastery and, 48–49, 159, 183
metaphor and, 159
Whitman on, 37, 40, 211n7, 214n30–31, 215n33–34
Smethurst, James, 137, 254n8
Snediker, Michael, 234n24
social death, 1–2, 20–21, 176, 193, 196, 208n78
social recognition, 3–5, 8, 17, 46, 89, 133, 161, 169, 200n12, 207n63
class consciousness and, 10, 147, 201n27
homosexuality and, 132, 134, 149, 231n6
Moss and, 170, 176
poetry and, 9, 14, 91, 98, 203n33
race and, 20–21, 25, 72, 76, 164
socialism, 84–86, 208n69, 248n29
solidarity, 124, 134–135, 184
class consciousness and, 125, 196
history and, 171–174

intersectionality and, 162, 171–175
race and, 64, 71, 171–172
socialism and, 84–86, 248n29
"Song of Myself" (Whitman), 86, 110–111, 229n94
"Song of the Universal" (Whitman), 31–33, 43, 58, 212n7
speaker. *See also* address
lyricization and, 37
reader and, 5, 9, 54–56
universalism and, 13, 15, 96
speed of invention, of Moss, 28, 161–162, 170, 179, 188
spiritualism, 156, 251n57
burlesque of, 132
Ouija board and, 146, 150–151, 251n60, 251n65–66
spirituality, 81, 85, 147. *See also* mysticism
Squire, J. C., 232n11
St. Louis Hegelians, 32, 34, 58–59, 84, 114, 211n4–6, 219nn69–70, 227n67
the state
legibility and, 136–137
violence and, 2, 93, 180–185, 192
Steiglitz, Alfred, 107–110, 112
Stella, Joseph, 234n31
stereotypes, race and, 71, 74, 76, 79, 81–83, 90, 118, 151–152, 157, 164, 226n65, 242n82, 252n67
Stewart, Susan, *Poetry and the Fate of the Senses*, 11, 202n32
Stonewall uprisings, 131
Stovall, Floyd, 47
"The Subculture of the Wrongfully Accused" (Moss), 163, 179–185
systems of meaning, of Moss, 160–163, 177–179, 184–185

Tate, Allen, 121, 239n69

298 | Index

Taussig, Charlotte, 226n65
Taylor, Charles, 207n65
Taylor, Julie, 126, 245n105
theater imagery, Merrill and, 153,
    155–156, 252nn73–74, 253n78
Theory of the Lyric (Culler), 11
Thomas, Wynn, 53, 218n57
Tokyo Butter (Moss), 177–185
Toomer, Jean, 196
    address and, 69, 80–81, 86, 220n4
    antipoetry of, 80, 229n90
    contradiction and, 76, 84, 86, 89
    Crane and, 24–25, 98–102, 234n23
    criticism of, 63–64, 221n11
    cultural pluralism and, 63–64,
        71–72, 77–78, 84, 87–88
    Frank and, 71, 84, 224n41
    identity and, 73–74, 225n54
    Johnson, J. W., and, 90–92
    Locke and, 71–72, 224n42, 225n53,
        226n54
    lyric and, 72–73
    lyricization and, 6, 69–71, 73, 76,
        83–84
    Merrill and, 152
    multiethnicity and, 6, 25, 62–67,
        70, 78–81, 83, 86, 89, 91, 152,
        221n11, 222n13, 229n98
    mysticism and, 64, 76, 80, 221n9
    politics of recognition and, 62–65,
        73–74, 76, 86, 88, 90–92
    privilege and, 61, 220n4
    sexuality and, 81–82
    Whitman and, 62–63, 80–82, 86–
        89, 229n90, 229n94, 229n97
Toomer, Jean, works of
    "Americans and Mary Austin," 62
    "The Blue Meridian," 6, 25, 64–65,
        70, 78–89, 120, 228n83
    Cane, 63–64, 80, 220n9
    "The First American," 61–62, 83,
        220n2

"On Being an American," 61–62
"Race Problems and Modern
    Society," 64, 76–78, 85, 87–88,
    227n73, 227n79
transcendence, 37, 117, 120
    of identity, 3, 59, 63, 168–171, 221n11
"The Tunnel" (Crane), 236n40
Turner, J. M. W., 195

undercommons, 21–22, 104, 190–191.
    See also anontic spaces; Harney,
    Stefano; Moten, Fred; paraontic
    spaces
universalism, 5–6, 28–29, 31–33, 45,
    73, 88–89, 133–134, 170, 196,
    202n32
    speaker and, 13, 15, 96
Untermeyer, Louis, 233n12, 234n35,
    236n37
utopias, 125–126

Vendler, Helen, 129–130, 251n65
violence, 123
    of metaphor, 181
    of misrecognition, 50–51, 89,
        180–184
    of recognition, 87–88, 93, 118–119,
        122, 151–152, 175
    the state and, 2, 93, 180–185, 192
visibility, 1–4, 10, 15–16, 63, 100, 188
von Hallberg, Robert, *Lyric Powers*,
    203n33
vulnerability, 1–2, 123–125, 165, 176
    resistance and, 49, 171

Wang, Dorothy, 207n64
Warner, Michael, 218n57
Watkins, Frances Ellen, 206n56
wealth, 142–143, 250n52
Weirick, Bruce, 232n12
Wheatley, Phyllis, 73, 174, 206n56,
    258n54

White, Gillian, 160, 208n77, 237n50, 256n27
White Buildings (Crane), 113, 121–122, 125
white supremacy, 69, 163, 255n22
  history and, 135–136, 196
  lyricization and, 64–65, 70–71, 83, 160, 195
  multiethnicity and, 78
whiteness
  blackness and, 66
  as personhood, 3, 5, 167–168
  privilege and, 166–167
Whitman, Walt
  America and, 31–33, 58
  contradiction and, 33, 58
  Crane and, 96, 104, 110–111, 120, 240n69
  criticism of, 38, 213n26
  cultural pluralism and, 58–59
  democracy and, 37, 58–60, 213n23
  democratic sociality of, 34, 47–54, 213n23
  drafts of, 33, 38–42, 211n7, 212n8, 215n37
  eligibility and, 32–34, 41, 63–64, 211n7, 215n37
  Hegel and, 5, 32–34, 46–47, 49–51, 217n46–47
  Hughes and, 228n89
  letters of, 32, 211n6
  logic of metaphor and, 240n69
  lyricization and, 34, 37–38, 58
  mastery and, 43–44, 216
  mysticism and, 31, 215n38
  notebooks of, 33–34, 38–41, 212n8, 215n33–34, 215n37
  politics and, 33–34, 36–37, 39–42, 57–60, 212n7, 216n42, 246n4
  politics of recognition in, 24, 40–42, 47–54, 57–60
  Rankine and, 29, 196

reader and, 41–45, 50–56, 216n42
  recognition and, 34, 40–46, 50–54, 56–60
  sexuality and, 53, 55, 62, 133, 217n43–44, 248n17
  on slavery, 37, 40, 211n7, 214n30–31, 215n33–34
  Toomer and, 62–63, 80–82, 86–89, 229n90, 229n94, 229n97
Whitman, Walt, works of. *See also* "Crossing Brooklyn Ferry"
  "The Eighteenth Presidency," 39, 214n30–31
  Leaves of Grass, 35–39, 211n7, 212n16, 212n18, 213n20–22, 214n28
  "Poem of Many in One," 33
  "Says," 211n7
  "Song of Myself," 86, 110–111, 229n94
  "Song of the Universal," 31–33, 43, 58, 212n7
Wilderson, Frank, 20, 209n80
"The Will" (Merrill), 132, 141–150, 250n52
Williams, Melissa, 136–137
Williams, Robert R., 48, 218n52
Williams, William Carlos, 116, 237m50, 242n82
Wilson, Ivy, 214n30
Wilson, Woodrow, 65–66, 68
Winters, Yvor, 125, 231n3, 234n31, 238n61, 240n69, 243n91
witness, 19, 69, 98–101, 172, 182, 234n30
Woodson, Jon, 229n97
"The Wreckage on the Wall of Eggs" (Moss), 167–168

Yenser, Stephen, 148–149
Yingling, Thomas, 103, 244n100
Young, Iris Marion, 201n27, 207n65
Yu, Christopher, 252n71